SELECTED WRITINGS ON OCCULTISM, ANGELS AND REINCARNATION

CHARLES W. LEADBEATER   ALFRED PERCY SINNETT
THÉOPHILE PASCAL

FV Editions

CONTENTS

THE OCCULT WORLD

PREFACE TO THE AMERICAN EDITION	3
INTRODUCTION	8
OCCULTISM AND THE ADEPTS	16
THE THEOSOPHICAL SOCIETY	24
FIRST OCCULT EXPERIENCES	32
TEACHINGS OF OCCULT PHILOSOPHY	93
LATER OCCULT PHENOMENA	104
APPENDIX	123

INVISIBLE HELPERS

1. The Universal Belief in Them	153
2. Some Modern Instances	156
3. A Personal Experience	161
4. The Helpers	165
5. The Reality of Superphysical Life	170
6. A Timely Intervention	173
7. The "Angel Story."	175
8. The Story of a Fire	179
9. Materialization and Repercussion	182
10. The Two Brothers	186
11. Wrecks and Catastrophes	191
12. Work Among the Dead	194
13. Other Branches of the Work	201
14. The Qualifications Required	204
15. The Probationary Path	209
16. The Path Proper	214
17. What Lies Beyond	219

REINCARNATION A STUDY IN HUMAN EVOLUTION

AUTHOR'S PREFACE	227
THE SOUL AND THE BODIES.	229
REINCARNATION AND THE MORAL LAW.	242

REINCARNATION AND SCIENCE.	268
REINCARNATION AND THE RELIGIOUS AND PHILOSOPHIC CONSENSUS OF THE AGES.	296
CONCLUSION.	362

THE OCCULT WORLD

By Alfred Percy Sinnett

Alfred Percy Sinnett (1840-1921) was an English author, journalist, and Theosophist. In 1879 he joined the Theosophical Society of London, of which he afterwards became president.

PREFACE TO THE AMERICAN EDITION

I VENTURE to think that this volume has acquired an importance that did not attach to it at first, now that subsequent experience has enabled me to follow it up with a more elaborate philosophical treatise. In the later work I have endeavored to set forth the general outlines of that knowledge concerning the higher mysteries of Nature which the following pages describe as possessed by the Indian "Mahatmas," or Adept Brothers. To that later work the reader whose attention may be arrested by the story told here must of course be referred; but meanwhile, the present introduction to the subject may be recommended to public notice now in a more confident tone than that which I was justified in taking up when it was first put forward. At that time the experiences I felt impelled to relate embodied no absolute promise of the systematic teaching accorded to me afterwards. Certainly those experiences in themselves appeared to me to claim telling. They seemed by far too remarkable to be left buried unfruitfully in the consciousness of the few persons concerned with them. It was true they elucidated no great principles of science; they merely suggested that for some of the abnormal phenomena which have arrested public attention during the last few years a more scientific explanation than those usually assigned might be possible. They afforded, if not absolute proof, at least an overwhelming assumption, that living men might actually develop faculties qualified to operate freely on that superior plane of Nature beyond the reach of the physical senses which, had been generally supposed accessible only to the spirits of the dead. But all was still shadowy and ill-defined. The story I had to tell revealed a magnificent possibility rather than a definite prospect. It would still, perhaps, have been an interesting story, even if the curtain had gone down upon the situation as I left it when these pages were first put together, but it would have been nothing then, compared to what it has since become.

Now the position in which the subject stands has altogether changed. The tentative communications addressed to me by my Mahatma correspondent in the first instance have paved the way for a long series of still more instructive and valuable letters. Assisted in other ways as well, my comprehension of occult philosophy advanced so far during the two years following the first appearance of this volume, that I was enabled to publish a more important statement, defining the outlines of that teaching, and exhibiting in a connected and intelligible shape the great esoteric theory of human evolution on this earth (and of the cosmogony on which it depends) with which the Adepts deal. The opening which presented itself to me in 1880 proved, in fact, no passing adventure, but the beginning of a new intellectual life. Attracted to it as I was at the time, I was certainly far then from divining the magnitude of the results destined to flow from it. But now that the proportions of the revelation I have thus been happily instrumental in procuring for the service of my readers have become apparent, I revert to the introductory episode of the undertaking with the certain assurance that I shall be engaging no one who will spare me his attention in any waste of time.

I am bold enough to say this because the Mahatmas, or great philosophical teachers of Asia, into some relations with whom I was enabled to come under the circumstances described in the following narrative, have now surrendered to the outer world so much of the spiritual science they have hitherto jealously guarded, that the whole framework of their stupendous doctrine has grown intelligible. Fragments of esoteric truth—of that science of superphysical nature which the Adepts explore—have been thrown out into the world at large from time to time before now, but in puzzling and unattractive disguises. The esoteric doctrine is no new system of belief, but, on the contrary, can be discerned now as lurking in a good deal of old Kabalistic and Oriental literature, that very few ordinary readers could have made sense of without the help of the keys now put in their hands. But now at last the subject has emerged into the clear daylight of modern thinking, and the central principle of the sublime esoteric doctrine stands plainly revealed as one which harmonizes in absolute perfection with the preparatory conceptions of Nature that have been derived by physical science from the observation and reflection of the current century. Biology is the latest, and, in some respects, the greatest of the physical sciences; and as the corollary, the complement, the crown of the science of Life, we are now furnished, by the teaching that has come to us from the East, with the science of spiritual evolution. Without this it may now be seen by those who appreciate the necessity of this doctrine, —

the manifest, inherent self-evidence of it when it is once fairly understood, —without it, the doctrine of physical evolution is a libel on Nature, a caricature of her grandest purposes. The great idea to which I am now referring exhibits the human soul as a continuous entity, subject to an individual evolution of vast duration, and developing on the spiritual plane of existence, as a result of its successive returns to Earth life. Mounting always upward, it has passed through the lower manifestations of the animal kingdom, and can never again revert to them; but as regards the future, it will not merely pass through a purposeless succession of human lives like those going on around us. It will advance and expand in its individual progress towards perfection, *pari passu* with that general improvement of physical types on Earth which is still going forward, though the short views of human nature afforded us by mere historic observation may not render this process of improvement as perceptible to uninitiated intelligence as it becomes to the psychic discernment of the Adept.

To comprehend the way the work goes on, we have to contemplate the operations of Nature on other planes besides those cognizable to the physical senses. And it soon becomes apparent that the physical life of the Earth is only one process of the long series over which the evolution of humanity extends. But—and this is one of the most admirably scientific and ethically beautiful of the ideas brought out by occult study—the physical life of the Earth is shown to be no incoherent episode in the experiences of a human soul, no futile incident in the course of a spiritual evolution, the major portion of which is accomplished in higher spheres of being. It is inseparably blended along its whole course with the spiritual growth of the soul. The Earth is shown to be no cosmic railway carriage which we enter for the purpose of accomplishing a more or less laborious journey, and the discomforts of which we may carelessly forget when we are able to jump out of it on reaching our destination. It is the home of our race for a long time to come, if not for eternity, and it is our interest, as well as our duty, to embellish and improve and ennoble it. "In my Father's house," says the old symbolical text, "are many mansions," and in this planetary house of humanity there are many more states of existence than the physical state. Some of these states may be far more enjoyable, for that matter, than the physical state as this is at present; and the esoteric doctrine shows us that the duration of the higher spiritual states, when each individual Ego passes each time into these, is enormously more prolonged than its physical states, but both kinds of existence are equally necessary in the whole scheme of things.

All these views, and the vast mass of explanatory detail which has since been furnished to the inquirers of the Theosophical Society, were still undeveloped for those of us who were pursuing the clue afforded by my experiences of 1880, when the present book was written. But I refer to them here because I want very briefly to indicate the direction which our later inquiries took when, our attention having been arrested by the strange and startling phenomena here described, it dawned upon us by degrees that the intellectual instruction the Mahatmas could give us, if they would, would be enormously more interesting than even the exhibition of their abnormal powers. The same considerations I hope will follow in due order, in the case of readers whom this volume may have the good fortune to attract. It has been sometimes argued in my hearing that it would have been better if the authors of this great new movement of spiritual thought—new for us, though so old in one sense—which theosophy embodies had furnished us with the results of their philosophical thinking without impairing the pure dignity of that exalted scheme by mingling it in the first instance with sensational displays of thaumaturgic skill. I am not inclined myself to quarrel with the order in which events were actually unfolded, Miracles, it is quite true, are illogical guarantees for theological dogma; but the manifest possession of great faculties and powers in other planes of Nature than those on which ordinary conclusions concerning her processes are formed, does certainly afford a presumption that persons so endowed may gather observations on those higher planes which it is well worth our while to correlate with our own. Meanwhile, I do not put forward the narrative of occult phenomena, of which this volume largely consists, as a statement which in itself constitutes a foundation for the very stupendous edifice of doctrines which later opportunities enabled me to construct. But I know that the experiences I record in this book were neither futile nor fruitless in their effects on my own development; and in anticipation of events that may contribute in no small degree, in a near future, to give a great impetus to theosophic speculation in America, I venture to recommend this book with special urgency to the American public, in the hope that a reflection on their minds of the influence produced on my own, by the incidents described, may serve to attract a good many fresh explorers into the paths of study and meditation, in which I believe myself to have gained such inestimable advantage.

I have not found much to alter in the original text of this book, though I am glad to, take advantage of this opportunity to append some notes here and there, and amplify some passages. But important additions to its contents have been made from time to time, and now especially I am anxious to call the attention of American readers to the latest of these, which will be found in an appendix. It is possible that in America some persons, to whom the existence of theosophy as a new school of thought is not altogether strange, may have heard of it especially in connection with a correspondence which has attracted a good deal of attention in the spiritualistic press. The discussion to which I refer has borne reference to a manifest identity of language traced between a certain passage in one of my Mahatma teacher's letters and a similar passage in an address delivered a few years ago by an American lecturer. The explanation I am now enabled to give of the curious circumstances under which this state of things arose, constitutes in itself, I venture to think, not merely a complete refutation of some unfriendly theories which were started to account for it, but also affords a very interesting contribution to our acquaintanceship with the ways and faculties of the Mahatmas.

INTRODUCTION

THERE is a school of Philosophy still in existence of which modern culture has lost sight. Glimpses of it are discernible in the ancient philosophies with which all educated men are familiar, but these are hardly more intelligible than fragments of forgotten sculpture,—less so, for we comprehend the human form, and can give imaginary limbs to a torso; but we can give no imaginary meaning to the truth coming down to us from Plato or Pythagoras, pointing, for those who hold the clue to their significance, to the secret knowledge of the ancient world. Side lights, nevertheless, may enable us to decipher such language, and a very rich intellectual reward offers itself to persons who are willing to attempt the investigation.

For, strange as the statement will appear at first sight, modern metaphysics, and to a large extent modern physical science, have been groping for centuries blindly after knowledge which occult philosophy has enjoyed in full measure all the while. Owing to a train of fortunate circumstances, I have come to *know* that this is the case; I have come into some contact with persons who are heirs of a greater knowledge concerning the mysteries of Nature and humanity than modern culture has yet evolved; and my present wish is to sketch the outlines of this knowledge, to record with exactitude the experimental proofs I have obtained that occult science invest its adepts with a control of natural forces superior to that enjoyed by physicists of the ordinary type, and the grounds there are for bestowing the most respectful consideration on the theories entertained by occult science concerning the constitution and destinies of the human soul. Of course people in the present day will be slow to believe that any knowledge worth considering can be found outside the bright focus of Western culture. Modern science has accomplished grand results by the open method of investigation, and is very impatient of the theory that persons who ever attained to real knowledge, either in sciences or metaphysics, could have been content to hide their light under a bushel. So the tendency has been to conceive that occult philosophers of old-Egyptian priests, Chaldean Magi, Essenes, Gnostics, theurgic Neo-Platonists, and the rest—who kept their knowledge secret, must have adopted that policy to conceal the fact that they knew very little. Mystery can only have been loved by charlatans who wished to mystify. The conclusion is pardonable from the modern point of view, but it has given rise to an impression in the popular mind that the ancient mystics have actually been turned inside out, and found to know very little. This impression is absolutely erroneous. Men of science in former ages worked in secret, and instead of publishing their discoveries, taught them in secret to carefully selected pupils. Their motives for adopting that policy are readily intelligible, even if the merits of the policy may seem still open to discussion. At all events, their teaching has not been forgotten; it has been transmitted by secret initiation to men of our own time, and while its methods and its practical achievements remain secrets in their hands, it is open to any patient and earnest student of the question to satisfy himself that these methods are of supreme efficacy, and these achievements far more admirable than any yet standing to the credit of modern science.

For the secrecy in which these operations have been shrouded has never disguised their existence, and it is only in our own time that this has been forgotten. Formerly at great public ceremonies, the initiates displayed the powers with which their knowledge of natural laws invested them. We carelessly assume that the narratives of such displays describe performances of magic: we have decided that there is no such thing as magic, therefore the narratives must have been false, the persons whom they refer to, impostors. But supposing that magic, of old, was simply the science of magi, of learned men, there is no magic, in the modern sense, left in the matter. And supposing that such science—even in ancient times already the product of long ages of study—had gone in some directions further than our much younger modern science has yet reached, it is reasonable to conclude that some displays in connection with ancient mysteries may have been strictly scientific experiments, though they sound like displays of magic, and would look like displays of magic for us now if they could be repeated.

On that hypothesis modem sagacity applying modem knowledge to the subject of ancient mysteries, may be merely modem folly evolving erroneous conclusions from modem ignorance.

But there is no need to construct hypotheses in the matter. The facts are accessible if they are sought for in the right way, and the facts are these: The wisdom of the ancient world—science and religion commingled, physics and metaphysics combined—was a reality, and it still survives. It is that which will be spoken of in these pages as Occult Philosophy. It was already a complete system of knowledge that had been cultivated in secret, and handed down to initiates for ages, before its professors performed experiments in public to impress the popular mind in Egypt and Greece. Adepts of occultism in the present day are capable of performing similar experiments, and of exhibiting results that prove them immeasurably further advanced than ordinary modern science in a comprehension of the forces of Nature. Furthermore, they inherit from their great predecessors a science which deals not merely with physics, but with the constitution and capacities of the human soul and spirit. Modern science has discovered the circulation of the blood; occult science understands the circulation of the life-principle. Modem physiology deals with the body only; occultism with the soul as well—not as the subject of vague, religious rhapsodies; but it is an actual entity, with properties that can be examined in combination with, or apart from, those of the body.

It is chiefly in the East that occultism is still kept up in India and in adjacent countries. It is in India that I have encountered it; and this little volume is written to describe the experiences I have enjoyed, and to retail the knowledge I have acquired.

II

My narrative of events must be preceded by some further general explanations, or it would be unintelligible. The identity of occultism as practised in all ages, must be kept in view, to account for the magnitude of its organization, and for the astounding discovery that secluded Orientals may understand more about electricity than Faraday, more about physics than Tyndall. The culture of Europe has been developed by Europeans for themselves within the last few hundred years. The culture of occultists is the growth of vast periods long anterior to these, when civilization inhabited the East. And during a career which has carried occultism in the domain of physical science far beyond the point we have reached, physical science has merely been an object for occultism of secondary importance. Its main strength has been devoted to metaphysical inquiry, and to the latent psychological faculties in man, faculties which, in their development, enable the occultist to obtain actual experimental knowledge concerning the soul's condition of extra-corporeal existence. There is thus something more than a mere archaeological interest in the identification of the occult system with the doctrines of the initiated organisations in all ages of the world's history, and we are presented by this identification with the key to the philosophy of religious development. Occultism is not merely an isolated discovery showing humanity to be possessed of certain powers over Nature, which the narrower study of Nature from the merely materialistic standpoint has failed to develop; it is an illumination cast over all previous spiritual speculation worth anything, of a kind which knits together some apparently divergent systems. It is to spiritual philosophy much what Sanskrit was found to be to comparative philology; it is a common stock of philosophical roots. Judaism, Christianity, Buddhism and the Egyptian theology are thus brought into one family of ideas. Occultism, as it is no now invention, is no specific sect, but the professors of no sect can afford to dispense with the sidelights it throws upon the conception of Nature and Man's destinies which they may have been induced by their own specific faith to form; occultism, in fact, must be recognised by anyone who will take the trouble to put before his mind clearly the problems with which it deals, as a study of the most sublime importance to every man who cares to live a life worthy of his human rank in creation, and who can realise the bearing on ethics of certain knowledge concerning his own survival after death. It is one thing to follow the lead of a hazy impression that a life beyond the grave, if there is one, may be somehow benefited by abstinence from wrongdoing on this side; it will clearly be another to realise if that can be shown to be the case, that the life beyond the grave must, with the certainty of a sum total built up of a series of plus and minus quantities, be the final expression of the use made of opportunities in this.

I have said that the startling importance of occult knowledge turns on the manner in which it affords exact and experimental knowledge concerning spiritual things which under all other systems must remain the subject of speculation or blind religious faith. It may be further asserted that occultism shows that the harmony and smooth continuity of Nature observable in physics extend to those operations of Nature that are concerned with the phenomena of metaphysical existence.

Before approaching an exposition of the conclusions concerning the nature of man that occult philosophy has reached, it may be worth while to meet an objection that may perhaps be raised by the reader on the threshold of the subject. How is it that conclusions of such great weight have been kept the secret property of a jealous body of initiates? Is it not a law of progress that truth asserts itself and courts the free air and light? Is it reasonable to suppose that the greatest of all truths—the fundamental basis of truth concerning man and Nature—should be afraid to show itself? With what object could the ancient professors of, or proficients in, occult philosophy keep the priceless treasures of their researches to themselves?

Now, it is no business of mine to defend the extreme tenacity with which the proficients in occultism have hitherto not only shut out the world from the knowledge of their knowledge, but have almost left it in ignorance that such knowledge exists. It is enough here to point out that it would be foolish to shut our eyes to a revelation that may now be partially conceded, merely because we are piqued at the behaviour of those who have been in a position to make it before, but have not chosen to do so. Nor would it be wiser to say that the reticence of the occultists so far discredits anything we may now be told about their acquirements. When the sun is actually shining it is no use to say that its light is discredited by the behaviour of the barometer yesterday. I have to deal, in discussing the acquirements of occultism, with facts that have actually taken place, and nothing can discredit what is known to be true. No doubt it will be worth while later on to examine the motives which have rendered the occultists of all ages so profoundly reserved. And there may be more to say in justification of the course that has been pursued than is visible at the first glance. Indeed, the reader will not go far in an examination of the nature of the powers which proficients in occultism actually possess, without seeing that it is supremely desirable to keep back the practical exercise of such powers from the world at large. But it is one thing to deny mankind generally the key which unlocks the mystery of occult power; it is another to withhold the fact that there is a mystery to unlock. However, the further discussion of that question here would be premature. Enough for the present to take note of the fact that secrecy after all is not complete if external students of the subject are enabled to learn as much about the mysteries as I shall have to tell. Manifestly, there is a great deal more behind, but, at all events, a great deal is to be learned by inquirers who will set to work in the right way.

And that which may now be learned is no new revelation at last capriciously extended to the outer world for the first time. In former periods of history, a great deal more has been known about the nature of occultism by the world at large than is known at this moment to the modern West. The bigotry of modem civilization, and not the jealousy of the occultist, is to blame if the European races are at this moment more generally ignorant of the extent to which psychological research has been carried, than the Egyptian populace in the past, or the people of India in the present day. As regards the latter, amongst whom the truth of the theory just suggested can easily be put to the test, you will find the great majority of Hindus perfectly convinced of the truth of the main statements which I am about to put forward. They do not generally or readily talk about such subjects with Europeans, because these are so prone to stupid derision of views they do not understand or believe in already. The Indian native is very timid in presence of such ridicule. But it does not affect in the slightest degree the beliefs which rest in his own mind on the fundamental teaching he will always have received, and in many cases on odds and ends of experiences he may himself have had. The Hindus are thus well aware, as a body, of the fact that there are persons who by entire devotion to certain modes of life acquire unusual powers in the nature of such as Europeans would very erroneously call supernatural. They are quite familiar with the notion that such persons live secluded lives, and are inaccessible to ordinary curiosity, and that they are nonetheless approachable by fit and determined candidates for admission to occult training. Ask any cultivated Hindu if he has ever heard of Mahatmas and Yog Vidya or occult science, and it is a hundred to one that you will find he has—and, unless he happens to be one of the hybrid products of Anglo-Indian Universities, that he fully believes in the reality of the powers ascribed to Yoga. It does not follow that he will at once say "Yes" to a European asking the question. He will probably say just the reverse from the apprehension I have spoken of above, but push your questions home and, you will discover the truth, as I did, for example, in the case of a very intelligent English-speaking native vakeel in an influential position and in constant relations with high European officials, last year. At first my new acquaintance met my inquiries as to whether he knew anything about these subjects with a wooden look of complete ignorance, and an explicit denial of any knowledge as to what I meant at all. It was not till the second time I saw him in private, at my own house, that by degrees it grew upon him that I was in earnest, and knew something about Yoga myself, and then he quietly opened out his real thoughts on the subject, and showed me that he knew not only perfectly well what I meant all along, but was stocked with information concerning occurrences and phenomena of an occult or apparently supernatural order, many of which had been observed in his own family and some by himself.

The point of all this is that Europeans are not justified in attributing to the jealousy of the occultists the absolute and entire ignorance of all that concerns them which pervades the modern society of the West. The West has been occupied with the business of material progress to the exclusion of psychological development. Perhaps it has done best for the world in confining itself to its specially; but however this may be, it has only itself to blame if its concentration of purpose has led to something like retrogression in another branch of development.

Jacolliot, a French writer, who has dealt at great length with various phases of Spiritism in the East, was told by one who must have been an adept to judge by the language used: "You have studied physical Nature, and you have obtained through the laws of Nature marvellous results—steam, electricity, etc., etc. For twenty-thousand years or more we have studied the intellectual forces; we have discovered their laws, and we obtain, by making them act alone or in concert with matter, phenomena still more astonishing than your own." Jacolliot adds: "We have seen things such as one does not describe for fear of making his readers doubt his intelligence......... but still we have seen them."

III

Occult phenomena must not be confused with the phenomena of spiritualism. The latter, whatever they may be, are manifestations which mediums can neither control nor understand in a scientific sense. The former are achievements of a conscious, living operator comprehending the laws with which he works. If these achievements appear miraculous, that is the fault of the observer's ignorance. The spiritualist knows perfectly well, in spite of ignorant mockery on the part of outsiders content to laugh without knowing what they are laughing at, that all kinds of occurrences distinctly outside the range of physical causation do constantly take place for inquirers who hunt them with sufficient diligence. But he has never been able to do more than frame hypotheses in respect to the hidden laws of Nature by virtue of which they have been produced. He has taken up a certain hypothesis *faute de mieux* in the first instance, and working always on this idea, has constructed such an elaborate edifice of theory round the facts that he is very reluctant to tolerate the interposition of a new hypothesis which will oblige him to revise his conclusions in some very important particulars. There will be no way of avoiding this necessity, however, if he belongs to the order of inquirers who care rather to be sure they have laid hold of the truth than to fortify a doctrine they have espoused for better or for worse.

Broadly speaking, there is scarcely one of the phenomena of spiritualism that adepts in occultism cannot reproduce by the force of their own will, supplemented by a comprehension of the resources of Nature. As will be seen when I come to a direct narrative of my own experiences, I have seen some of the most familiar phenomena of spiritualism produced by purely human agency. The old original spirit—rap which introduced the mightier phenomena of spiritualism has been manifested for my edification in a countless variety of ways, and under conditions which render the hypothesis of any spiritual agency in the matter wholly preposterous. I have seen flowers fall from the blank ceiling of a room under circumstances that gave me a practical assurance that no spiritual agency was at work, though in a manner as absolutely "supernatural" in the sense of being produced without the aid of any material appliances, as any of the floral showers by which some spiritual mediums are attended. I have over and over again received "direct writing," produced on paper in sealed envelopes of my own, which was created or precipitated by a living human correspondent. I have information, which, though second-hand, is very trustworthy, of a great variety of other familiar spiritual phenomena produced in the same way by human adepts in occultism. But it is not my present task to make war on spiritualism. The announcements I have to make will, indeed, be probably received more readily among spiritualists than in the outer circles of the ordinary world, for the spiritualists are at all events aware, from their own experience, that the orthodox science of the day does not know the last word concerning mind and matter, while the orthodox outsider stupidly clings to a denial of facts when these are of a nature which he foresees himself unable to explain. As the facts of spiritualism, though accessible to any honest man who goes in search of them, are not of a kind which anyone can carry about and fling in the faces of pragmatic "sceptics," these latter are enabled to keep up their professions of incredulity without the foolishness of their position being obvious to each other, plain as it is to "the initiated." However, although in this way the ordinary scientific mind will be reluctant to admit either the trustworthiness of my testimony or the conceivability of my explanations, it may allay some hostile prejudices to make clear at the onset that occult science deals with no guesswork concerning the post-mortem intervention of human beings in the affairs of this world. Its methods are as precise, and its mental discipline as rigid, as those of the laboratory or the university lecture-room. Wedding with theosophic research, spiritualism itself might guard itself from all those hasty inferences which have done so much to turn large sections of the cultivated people against it, and if they will but take the trouble to approach the subject from the point of view of occult science, students of physical Nature will be enabled at last to handle the *phenomena* of spiritualism freely, to consider them apart from the theories to which they have prematurely given rise; and thus relieved of the repugnance they feel for them at present, to bring them within the area of that which they at last will willingly recognise as true scientific generalisations.

OCCULTISM AND THE ADEPTS

I

THE POWERS with which occultism invests its adepts include, to begin with, a control over various forces in Nature which ordinary science knows nothing about, and by means of which an adept can hold conversation with any other adept, whatever intervals on the earth's surface may lie between them. This psychological telegraphy is wholly independent of all mechanical conditions or appliances whatever. And the clairvoyant faculties of the adept are so perfect and complete that they amount to a species of omniscience as regards mundane affairs. The body is the prison of the soul for ordinary mortals. We can see merely what comes before its windows; we can take cognisance only of what is brought within its bars. But the adept has found the key of his prison and can emerge from it at pleasure. It is no longer a prison for him—merely a dwelling. In other words, the adept can project his soul out of his body to any place he pleases with the rapidity of thought.

The whole edifice of occultism from basement to roof is so utterly strange to ordinary conceptions that it is difficult to know how to begin an explanation of its contents. How could one describe a calculating machine to an audience unfamiliar with the simplest mechanical contrivances and knowing nothing of arithmetic. And the highly cultured classes of modern Europe, as regards the achievements of occultism, are, in spite of the perfection of their literary scholarship and the exquisite precision of their attainments in their own departments of science, in the position as regards occultism of knowing nothing about the A B C of the subject, nothing about the capacities of the soul at all as distinguished from the capacities of body and soul combined. The occultists for ages have devoted themselves to that study chiefly; they have accomplished results in connexion with it which are absolutely bewildering in their magnificence; but suddenly introduced to some of these, the prosaic intelligence is staggered and feels in a world of miracle and enchantment. On charts that show the stream of history, the nations all intermingle more or less, except the Chinese, and that is shown coming down in a single river without affluents and without branches from out of the clouds of time. Suppose that civilized Europe had not come into contact with the Chinese till lately, and suppose that the Chinamen, very much brighter in intelligence than they really are, had developed some branch of physical science to the point it actually has reached with us; suppose that particular branch had been entirely neglected with us, the surprise we should feel at taking up the Chinese discoveries in their refined development without having gradually grown familiar with their small beginnings would be very great. Now this is exactly the situation as regards occult science. The occultists have been a race apart from an earlier period than we can fathom—not a separate race physically, not a uniform race physically at all, nor a nation in any sense of the word, but a continuous association of men of the highest intelligence linked together by a bond stronger than any other tie of which mankind has experience, and carrying on with a perfect continuity of purpose the studies and traditions and mysteries of self-development handed down to them by their predecessors. All this time the stream of civilization, on the foremost waves of which the culture of modern Europe is floating, has been wholly and absolutely neglectful of the one study with which the occultists have been solely engaged. What wonder that the two lines of civilization have diverged so far apart that their forms are now entirely unlike each other. It remains to be seen whether this attempt to reintroduce the long—estranged cousins will be tolerated or treated as an impudent attempt to pass off an impostor as a relation.

I have said that the occultist can project his soul from his body. As an incidental discovery, it will be observed, he has thus ascertained beyond all shadow of doubt that he really has got a soul. A comparison of myths has sometimes been called the science of religion. If there can really be a science of religion it must necessarily be occultism. On the surface, perhaps, it may not be obvious that religious truth must necessarily open out more completely to the soul as temporarily loosened from the body, than to the soul as taking cognisance of ideas through the medium of the physical senses. But to ascend into a realm of immateriality, where cognition becomes a process of pure perception while the intellectual faculties are in full play and centred in the immaterial man, must manifestly be conducive to an enlarged comprehension of religious truth.

I have just spoken of the "immaterial man" as distinguished from the body of the physical senses; but, so complex is the statement I have to make, that I must no sooner induce the reader to tolerate the phrase than I must reject it for the future as inaccurate. Occult philosophy has ascertained that the inner ethereal self, which is the man as distinguished from his body, is itself the envelope of something more ethereal still—is itself, in a subtle sense of the term, material.

The majority of civilized people believe that man has a soul which will somehow survive the dissolution of the body; but they have to confess that they do not *know* very much about it. A good many of the most highly civilized, have grave doubts on the subject, and some think that researches in physics which have suggested the notion that even thought may be a mode of motion, tend to establish the strong probability of the hypothesis that when the life of the body is destroyed nothing else survives. Occult philosophy does not speculate about the matter at all; it knows the state of the facts.

St. Paul, who was an occultist, speaks of man as constituted of body, soul, and spirit. The distinction is one that hardly fits in with the theory, that when a man dies his soul is translated to heaven or hell for ever. What then becomes of the spirit, and what is the spirit as different from the soul, on the ordinary hypothesis. Orthodox thinkers work out each some theory on the subject for himself. Either that the soul is the seat of the emotions and the spirit of the intellectual faculties, or *vice versa*. No one can put such conjectures on a solid foundation, not even on the basis of an alleged revelation. But St. Paul was not indulging in vague fancies when he made use of the expression quoted. The spirit he was referring to may be described as the soul of the soul. With that for the moment we need not be concerned. The important point which occultism brings out is that the soul of man, while something enormously subtler and more ethereal and more lasting than the body, is itself a *material* reality. Not material as chemistry understands matter, but as physical science en *bloc* might understand it if the tentacle of each branch of science were to grow more sensitive and were to work more in harmony. It is no denial of the materiality of any hypothetical substance to say that one cannot determine its atomic weight and its affinities. The ether that transmits light is held to be material by anyone who holds it to exist at all, but there is a gulf of difference between it and the thinnest of the gases. You do not always approach a scientific truth from the same direction. You may perceive some directly; you have to infer others indirectly; but these latter may not on that account be the less certain. The materiality of ether is inferable from the behaviour of light: the materiality of the soul may be inferable from its subjection to forces. A mesmeric influence is a force emanating from certain physical characteristics of the mesmerist. It impinges on the soul of the subject at a distance and produces an effect perceptible to him, demonstrable to others. Of course this is an illustration and no proof. I must set forth as well as I am able—and that can but be very imperfectly—the discoveries of occultism without at first attempting the establishment by proof of each part of these discoveries. Further on, I shall be able to prove some parts at any rate, and others will then be recognised as indirectly established, too.

The soul is material, and inheres in the ordinarily more grossly material body; and it is this condition of things which enables the occultist to speak positively on the subject, for he can satisfy himself at one coup that there is such a thing as a soul, and that it is material in its nature, by dissociating it from the body under some conditions, and restoring it again. The occultist can even do this sometimes with other souls; his primary achievement, however, is to do so with his own. When I say that the occultist *knows* he has a soul I refer to this power. He knows it just as another man knows he has a great coat. He can put it from him, and render it manifest as something separate from himself. But remember that to him, when the separation is effected, he *is* the soul and the thing put off is the body. And this is to attain nothing less than absolute certainty about the great problem of survival after death. The adept does not rely on faith, or on metaphysical speculation, in regard to the possibilities of his existence apart from the body. He experiences such an existence whenever he pleases, and although it may be allowed that the more art of emancipating himself temporarily from the body would not necessarily inform him concerning his ultimate destinies after that emancipation should be final at death, it gives him, at all events, exact knowledge concerning the conditions under which he will start on his journey in the next world. While his body lives, his soul is, so to speak, a captive balloon (though with a very long, elastic and imponderable cable). Captive ascents will not necessarily tell him whether the balloon will float when at last the machinery below breaks up, and he finds himself altogether adrift; but it is something to be an aeronaut already, before the journey begins, and to know definitely, as I said before, that there are such things as balloons, for certain emergencies, to sail in.

There would be infinite grandeur in the faculty I have described alone, supposing that were the end of adeptship; but instead of being the end, it is more like the beginning. The seemingly magic feats which the adepts in occultism have the power to perform, are accomplished, I am given to understand, by means of familiarity with a force in nature which is referred to in Sanskrit writings as *akas*. Western science has done much in discovering some of the properties and powers of electricity. Occult science, ages before, had done much more in discovering the properties and powers of *akas*. In "The Coming Race," the late Lord Bulwer Lytton, whose connexion with occultism appears to have been closer than the world generally has yet realised, gives a fantastic and imaginative account of the wonders achieved in the world to which his hero penetrates, by means of Vril. In writing of Vril, Lord Lytton has clearly been poetising *akas*. "The Coming Race" is described as a people entirely unlike adepts in many essential particulars—as a complete nation, for one thing, of men and women all equally handling the powers, even from childhood, which—or some of which among others not described— the adepts have conquered. This is a mere fairy-tale, founded on the achievements of occultism. But no one who has made a study of the latter can fail to see, can fail to recognise with a conviction amounting to certainty, that the author of "The Coming Race" must have been familiar with the leading ideas of occultism, perhaps with a great deal more. The same evidence is afforded by Lord Lytton's other novels of mystery, "Zanoni," and "The Strange Story." In "Zanoni," the sublime personage in the background, Mejnour, is intended plainly to be a great adept of Eastern occultism, exactly like those of whom I have to speak. It is difficult to know why in this case, where Lord Lytton has manifestly intended to adhere much more closely to the real facts of occultism than in "The Coming Race," he should have represented Mejnour as a solitary survivor of the Rosicrucian fraternity. The guardians of occult science are content to be a small body as compared with the tremendous importance of the knowledge which they save from perishing, but they have never allowed their numbers to diminish to the extent of being in any danger of ceasing to exist as an organised body on earth. It is difficult again to understand why Lord Lytton, having learned so much as he certainly did, should have been content to use up his information merely as an ornament of fiction, instead of giving it to the world in a form which should claim more serious consideration. At all events, prosaic people will argue to that effect; but it is not impossible that Lord Lytton himself had become, through long study of the subject, so permeated with the love of mystery which inheres in the occult mind apparently, that he preferred to throw out his information in a veiled and mystic shape, so that it would be intelligible to readers in sympathy with himself, and would blow unnoticed past the commonplace understanding without awakening the angry rejection which these pages, for example, if they are destined to attract any notice at all, will assuredly encounter at the hands of bigots in science, religion, and the great philosophy of the commonplace.

Akas, be it then understood, is a force for which we have no name, and in reference to which we have no experience to guide us to a conception of its nature. One can only grasp at the idea required by conceiving that it is as much more potent, subtle, and extraordinary an agent than electricity, as electricity is superior in subtlety and variegated efficiency to steam. It is through his acquaintance with the properties of this force, that the adept can accomplish the physical phenomena, which I shall presently be able to show are within his reach, besides others of far greater magnificence.

II

Who are the adepts who handle the tremendous forces of which I speak? There is reason to believe that such adepts have existed in all historic ages, and there are such adepts in India at this moment, or in adjacent countries. The identity of the knowledge they have inherited, with that of ancient initiates in occultism, follows irresistibly from an examination of the views they hold and the faculties they exercise. The conclusion has to be worked out from a mass of literary evidence, and it will be enough to state it for the moment, pointing out the proper channels of research in the matter afterwards. For the present let us consider the position of the adepts as they now exist, or, to use the designation more generally employed in India, of "the Mahatmas." [1]

They constitute a Brotherhood, or Secret Association, which ramifies all over the East, but the principal seat of which for the present I gather to be in Tibet. But India has not yet been deserted by the adepts, and from that country they still receive many recruits. For the great fraternity is at once the least and the most exclusive organization in the world, and fresh recruits from any race or country are welcome, provided they possess the needed qualifications. The door, as I have been told by one who is himself an adept, is always open to the right man who knocks, but the road that has to be travelled before the door is reached is one which none but very determined travellers can hope to pass. It is manifestly impossible that I can describe its perils in any but very general terms, but it is not necessary to have learned any secrets of initiation to understand the character of the training through which a neophyte must pass before he attains the dignity of a proficient in occultism. The adept is not made: he becomes, as I have been constantly assured, and the process of becoming is mainly in his own hands.

Never, I believe, in less than seven years from the time at which a candidate for initiation is accepted as a probationer, is he ever admitted to the very first of the ordeals, whatever they may be, which bar the way to the earliest decrees of occultism, and there is no security for him that the seven years may not be extended *ad libitum*. He has no security that he will ever be admitted to any initiation whatever. Nor is this appalling uncertainty, which would alone deter most Europeans, however keen upon the subject intellectually, from attempting to advance, themselves, into the domain of occultism, maintained from the mere caprice of a despotic society, coquetting, so to speak, with the eagerness of its wooers. The trials through which the neophyte has to pass are no fantastic mockeries, or mimicries of awful peril. Nor, do I take it, are they artificial barriers set up by the masters of occultism, to try the nerve of their pupils, as a riding—master might put up fences in his school. It is inherent in the nature of the science that has to be explored, that its revelations shall stagger the reason and try the most resolute courage. It is in his own interest that the candidate's character and fixity of purpose, and perhaps his physical and mental attributes, are tested and watched with infinite care and patience in the first instance, before he is allowed to take the final plunge into the sea of strange experiences through which he must swim with the strength of his own right arm, or perish.

As to what may be the nature of the trials that await him during the period of his development, it will be obvious that I can have no accurate knowledge, and conjectures based on fragmentary revelations pictured up here and there are not worth recording, but as for the nature of the life led by the mere candidate for admission as a neophyte it will be equally plain that no secret is involved. The ultimate development of the adept requires amongst other things a life of absolute physical purity, and the candidate must, from the beginning, give practical evidence of his willingness to adopt this. He must, that is to say, for all the years of his probation, be perfectly chaste, perfectly abstemious, and indifferent to physical luxury of every sort. This regimen does not involve any fantastic discipline or obtrusive asceticism, nor withdrawal from the world. There would be nothing to prevent a gentleman in ordinary society from being in some of the preliminary stages of training for occult candidature without anybody about him being the wiser. For true occultism, the sublime achievement of the real adept, is not attained through the loathsome asceticism of the ordinary Indian fakir, the *yogi* of the woods and wilds, whose dirt accumulates with his sanctity—of the fanatic who fastens iron hooks into his flesh, or holds up an arm until it is withered. An imperfect knowledge of some of the external facts of Indian occultism will often lead to a misunderstanding on this point. *Yog Vidya* is the Indian name for occult science, and it is easy to learn a good deal more than is worth learning about the practices of some misguided enthusiasts who cultivate some of its inferior branches by means of mere physical exercises. Properly speaking, this physical development is called *Hatti Yog*, while the loftier sort, which is approached by the discipline of the mind, and which leads to the high altitudes of occultism, is called *Ragi yog*. No person whom a real occultist would ever think of as an adept, has acquired his powers by means of the laborious and puerile exercises of the *Hatti yog*. I do not mean to say that these inferior exercises are altogether futile. They do invest the person who pursues them with some abnormal faculties and powers. Many treatises have been written to describe them, and many people who have lived in India will be able to relate curious experiences they have had with proficients in this extraordinary craft. I do not wish to fill these pages with tales of wonder that I have had no means of sifting, or it would be easy to collect examples; but the point to insist on here is that no story anyone can have heard or read which seems to put an ignoble, or petty, or low-minded aspect on Indian *yogeeism* can have any application to the ethereal *yogeeism* which is called *Ragi yog*, and which leads to the awful heights of true adeptship.

---

1. Mahatma—Great Soul, or Great Spirit, derived from *Maha* and *Atma*.

THE THEOSOPHICAL SOCIETY

SECRET as the occult organization has always remained, there is a good deal more to be learned concerning the philosophical views which it has preserved or acquired, than might be supposed at the first glance. As my own experience when fully described will show, the great adepts of occultism themselves have no repugnance to the dissemination of their religions philosophy So far as a world untrained as ours is in pure psychological investigation can profit by such teaching. Nor even are they unconquerably averse to the occasional manifestation of those superior powers over the forces of Nature to which their extraordinary researches have led them. The many apparently miraculous phenomena which I have witnessed through occult agency could never have been exhibited if the general rule which precludes the Brothers from the exhibition of their powers to uninitiated persons were absolute. As a general rule, indeed, the display of any occult phenomenon for the purpose of exciting the wonder and admiration of beholders is strictly forbidden. And indeed I should imagine that such prohibition is absolute if there is no higher purpose involved. But it is plain that with a purely philanthropic desire to spread the credit of a philosophical system which is ennobling in its character, the Brothers may sometimes wisely permit the display of abnormal phenomena when the minds to which such an appeal t is made may be likely to rise from the appreciation of the wonder to a befitting respect for the philosophy in which it accredits. And the history of the Theosophical Society has been an expansion of this idea. That history has been a chequered one, because the phenomena that have been displayed have often failed of their effect, have sometimes become the subject of a premature publicity, and have brought down on the study of occult philosophy as regarded from the point of view of the outer world, and on the devoted persons who have been chiefly identified with its encouragement by means of the Theosophical Society, a great deal of stupid ridicule and some malevolent persecution. It may be asked why the Brothers, if they are really the great and all-powerful persons I represent them, have permitted indiscretions of the kind referred to, but the inquiry is not so embarrassing as it may seem at the first glance. If the picture of the Brothers that I have endeavoured to present to the reader has been appreciated rightly, it will show them less accurately qualified, in spite of their powers, than persons of lesser occult development, to carry on any undertaking which involves direct relations with a multiplicity of ordinary people in the commonplace world. I gather the primary purpose of the Brotherhood to be something very unlike the task I am engaged in, for example, at this moment—the endeavour to convince the public generally that there really are faculties latent in humanity capable of such extraordinary development, that they carry us at a bound to an immense distance beyond the dreams of physical science in reference to the comprehension of Nature, and at the same time afford us positive testimony concerning the constitution and destinies of the human soul. That is a task on which it is reasonable to suppose the Brothers would cast a sympathetic glance, but it will be obvious on a moment's reflection, that their primary duty must be to keep alive the actuality of that knowledge, and of those powers concerning which I am merely giving some shadowy account. If the Brothers were to employ themselves on the large, rough business of hacking away at the incredulity of a stolid multitude, at the acrimonious incredulity of the materialistic phalanx, at the terrified and indignant incredulity of the orthodox religious world, it is conceivable that they might—*propter vitam vivendi perdere causas*—suffer the occult science itself to decay for the sake of persuading mankind that it did really exist. Of course it might be suggested that division of labour might be possible in occultism as in everything else, and that some adepts qualified for the work might be told off for the purpose of breaking down the incredulity of modern science, while the others would carry on the primary duties of their career in their own beloved seclusion. But a suggestion of this kind, however practical it may sound to a practical world, would probably present itself as eminently unpractical to the true mystic. To begin with, an aspirant for occult honours does not go through the tremendous and prolonged effort required to win him success, in order at the end of all things to embrace a life in the midst of the ordinary world, which on the hypothesis of his success in occultism must necessarily be repugnant to him in the extreme.

Probably there is not one real adept who does not look with greater aversion and repugnance on any life *except* a life of seclusion, than we of the outer world would look on the notion of being buried alive in a remote mountain fastness where no foot or voice from the outer world could penetrate. I shall very soon be able to show that the love of seclusion, inherent in adeptship, does not imply a mind vacant of the knowledge of European culture and manners. It is, on the contrary, compatible with an amount of European culture and experience that people acquainted merely with the commonplace aspects of Eastern life will be surprised to find possible in the case of a man of Oriental birth. Now, the imaginary adept told off of the suggestion I am examining, to show the scientific world that there are realms of knowledge it has not yet explored and faculties attainable to man that it has not yet dreamed of possessing, would have to be either appointed to discharge that duty, or to volunteer for it. In the one case we have to assume that the occult fraternity is despotic in its treatment of its members in a manner which all my observation leads me to believe it certainly is not; in the other, we have to suppose some adept making a voluntary sacrifice of what he regards as not only the most agreeable but also the higher life—for what? for the sake of accomplishing a task which he does not regard as of very great importance—relatively, at any rate, to that other task in which he may take a part—the perpetuation and perhaps the development of the great science itself. But I do not care to follow the argument any further, because it will come on for special treatment in a different way presently. Enough for the moment to indicate that there are considerations against the adoption of that method of persuasion which, as far as the judgment of ordinary people would go, would seem the best suited to the introduction of occult truths to modern intelligence.

And these considerations appear to have prompted the acceptance by the Brothers, of the Theosophical Society as a more or less imperfect, but still the best available agency for the performance of a piece of work, in which, without being actually prepared to enter on it themselves, they nevertheless take a cordial interest.

And what are the peculiar conditions which render the Theosophical Society, the organization and management of which have been faulty in many ways, the best agency hitherto available for the propagation of occult truths? The zeal and qualifications of its founder, Madame Blavatsky, give the explanation required. It is obvious that to give any countenance or support at all to a society concerned with the promulgation of occult philosophy, it was necessary for the Brothers to be in occult communication with it in some way or other. For it must be remembered that though it may seem to us a very amazing and impossible thing to sit still at home and impress our thoughts upon the mind of a distant friend by an effort of will, a Brother living in an unknown Himalayan retreat is not only able to converse as freely as he likes with any of his friends who are initiates like himself, in whatever part of the world they may happen to be, but would find any other modes of communication, such as those with which the crawling faculties of the outer world have to be content, simply intolerable in their tedium and inefficacy. Besides, he must be able to afford assistance to any society having its sphere of operations among people in the world, be able to hear from it with the same facility that he can send communications to it. So there must be an initiate at the other end of the line Finally, the occult rules evidently require this last-named condition, or what amounts to the same thing, forbid arrangements which can only be avoided on this condition.

Now, Madame Blavatsky is an initiate—is an adept to the extent of possessing this magnificent power of psychological telegraphy with her occult friends. That she has stopped short of that further development in adeptship that would have tided her right over the boundary between this and the occult world altogether, is the circumstance which has rendered her assumption of the task with which the Theosophical Society is concerned compatible with the considerations pointed out above as operating to prevent the assumption of such a duty by a full adept. As regards the supremely essential characteristic, she has, in fact, been exactly suited to the emergency. How it came to pass that her occult training carried her as far as it did and no further, is a question into which it is fruitless to inquire, because the answer would manifestly entail explanations which would impinge too closely on the secrets of initiation which are never disclosed under any circumstances whatever. After all she is a woman—though her powerful mind, widely if erratically cultivated, and perfectly dauntless courage proved among other ways on the battlefield, but more than by any bravery with bullets, by her occult initiation, renders the name, connoting what I it ordinarily does, rather absurd in application to her—and this has, perhaps, barred her from the highest degrees in occultism that she might otherwise have attained. At all events, after a course of occult study carried on for seven years in a Himalayan retreat, and crowning a devotion to occult pursuits extending over five-and-thirty or forty years, Madame Blavatsky reappeared in the world, dazed, as she met ordinary people going about in commonplace, benighted ignorance concerning the wonders of occult science, at the mere thought of the stupendous gulf of experience that separated her from them. She could hardly at first bear to associate with them, for thinking of all she knew that they did not know and that she was bound not to reveal. Any one can understand the burden of a great secret, but the burden of such a secret as occultism, and the burden of great powers only conferred on condition that their exercise should be very strictly circumscribed by rule, must have been trying indeed.

Circumstances—or to put the matter more plainly, the guidance of friends from whom, though she had left them behind in the Himalayas on her return to Europe, she was no longer in danger of separation, as we understand the term, induced her to visit America, and there, assisted by some other persons whose interest in the subject was kindled by occasional manifestations of her extraordinary powers, and notably by Colonel Olcott, its life-devoted President, she founded the Theosophical Society, the objects of which, as originally defined, were to explore the latent psychological powers of man, and the ancient Oriental literature in which the clue to these may be hidden, and in which the philosophy of occult science may be partly discovered.

The Society took root readily in America, while branches were also formed in England and elsewhere; but, leaving these to take care of themselves, Madame Blavatsky ultimately returned to India, to establish the Society there among the natives, from whose natural hereditary sympathies with mysticism it was reasonable to expect an ardent sympathy with a psychological enterprise which not only appealed to their intuitive belief in the reality of *yog vidya*, but also to their best patriotism, by exhibiting India as the fountainhead of the highest if the least known and the most secluded culture in the world.

Here, however, began the practical blunders in the management of the Theosophical Society which led to the incidents referred to above, as having given it, so far, a chequered career. Madame Blavatsky, to begin with, was wholly unfamiliar with the everyday side of Indian life, her previous visits having brought her only into contact with groups of people utterly unconnected with the current social system and characteristics of the country Nor could she have undertaken a worse preparation for Indian life than that supplied by a residence of some years in the United States. This sent her out to India unfurnished with the recommendations which she could readily have obtained, if she had spent the time just referred to in England, and left her unprovided with information it was highly important for her to possess concerning the true character of the British ruling classes of India and their relations with the people.

The consequence was that Mme. Blavatsky, on her first arrival in India, adopted an attitude of obtrusive sympathy with the natives of the soil as compared with the Europeans, seeking their society in a manner which, coupled with the fact that she made none of the usual advances to European society, and with her manifestly Russian name, had the effect not unnaturally of rendering her *suspecte* to the rather clumsy organization which in India attempts to combine with sundry others, the functions of a political police. These suspicions, it is true, were allayed almost as soon as they were conceived, but not before Madame Blavatsky had been made for a short time the object of an *espionage* so awkward that it became grossly obvious to herself and roused her indignation to fever heat. To a more phlegmatic nature the incident would have been little more than amusing, but all accidents combined to develop trouble. A Russian by birth, though naturalised in the United States, Madame Blavatsky is probably more sensitive than an English woman, less experienced in political espionage would be to the insult involved in being taken for a spy. Then the inner consciousness of having, for enthusiasm in the purely intellectual or spiritual enterprise to which she had devoted her life, renounced the place in society to which her distinguished birth and family naturally entitled her, probably intensified the bitterness of her indignation, at finding the sacrifice not only unappreciated, but turned against her, and regarded as justifying a foul suspicion. At all events, the circumstances acting on an excitable temperament led her to make public protests which caused it to be widely known by natives as well as by Europeans, that she had been looked at askance by Government authorities. And this idea for a time impeded the success of her work. Nothing can be done in India without a European impulse in the beginning; at all events, it handicaps any enterprise frightfully to be without such an impulse if native co-operation is required. Not that the Theosophical Society failed to get members. The natives were flattered at the attitude towards them taken up by their new "European" friends, as Madame Blavatsky and Colonel Olcott were no doubt generally regarded in spite of their American nationality, and showed a shallow eagerness to become Theosophists. But their ardour did not always prove durable, and in some few cases they showed a lamentable want of earnestness by breaking away from the Society altogether.

Meanwhile, Madame Blavatsky began to make friends amongst the Europeans, and in 1880 visited Simla, where she began late in the day to approach her work from the right direction. Again, however, some mistakes were made which have retarded the establishment of the Theosophical Society, as far as India is concerned, on the dignified footing that it ought to occupy. A great many wonderful phenomena were manifested in the presence at various times of a great many people; but proper safeguards were not taken to avert the great danger that must always attend such a method of recommending occult science to public notice. It is beyond dispute that phenomena, exhibited under thoroughly satisfactory conditions to persons intelligent enough to comprehend their significance, create an effect in awakening a thirst for the study of occult philosophy that no other appeal can produce. But it is equally true, though at the first glance this may not be so apparent, that to minds, quite unprepared by previous training to grasp the operation of occult forces, the most perfectly unimpeachable phenomenon will be received rather as an insult to the understanding than as a proof of the operation of occult power. This is especially the case with persons of merely average intelligence, of whose faculties cannot stand the shock of a sudden appeal to an entirely new set of ideas. The strain is too great; the new chain of reasoning breaks, and the commonplace observer of abnormal occurrences reverts to his original frame of stolid incredulity, perfectly unaware of the fact that a revelation of priceless intellectual importance has been offered to him and has been misunderstood. Nothing is commoner than to hear people say: "I can't believe in the reality of a phenomenal occurrence unless I see it for myself. Show it me and I shall believe in it, but not till then." Many people who say this are quite mistaken as to what they would believe if the occurrence were shown to them. I have over and over again seen phenomena of an absolutely genuine nature pass before the eyes of people unused to investigating occurrences of the kind, and leave no impression behind beyond an irritated conviction that they were somehow being taken in. Just this happened in some conspicuous instances at Simla, and it is needless to say that many as were the phenomena that Madame Blavatsky produced, or was instrumental in producing, during the visit to which I am referring, the number of people in the place who had no opportunity of seeing them was considerably greater than that of the witnesses. And for these, as a rule, the whole series of incidents presented itself simply as an imposition. It was nothing to the purpose for the holders of this theory that there was a glaring absence from the whole business of any motive for imposture, that a considerable group of persons whose testimony and capacity would never have been impugned had any other matter been under discussion, were emphatic in their declarations as to the complete reality of the phenomena that had been displayed. The commonplace mind could not assimilate the idea that it was face to face with a new revelation in Nature, and any hypothesis, no matter how absurd and illogical in its details, was preferable for the majority to the simple grandeur of the truth.

On the whole, therefore, as Madame Blavatsky became a celebrity in India, her relations with European society were intensified. She made many friends, and secured some ardent converts to a belief in the reality of occult powers; but she became the innocent object of bitter animosity on the part of some other acquaintances, who, unable to assimilate what they saw in her presence, took up all attitude of disbelief, which deepened into positive enmity as the whole subject became enveloped in a cloud of more or less excited controversy.

And it is needless to say that many of the newspapers made great capital out of the whole situation ridiculing Madame Blavatsky's dupes, and twisting every bit of information that came out about her phenomena into the most ludicrous shape it could be made to assume. Mockery of that sort was naturally expected by English friends who avowed their belief in the reality of Madame Blavatsky's powers, and probably never gave one of them a moment's serious annoyance. But for the oversensitive and excitable person chiefly concerned they were indescribably tormenting, and eventually it grew doubtful whether her patience would stand the strain put upon it; whether she would not relinquish altogether the ungrateful task of inducing the world at large to accept the good gifts, which she had devoted her life to offering them. Happily, so far, no catastrophe has ensued; but no history of Columbus in chains for discovering a new world, or Galileo in prison for announcing the true principles of astronomy, is more remarkable for those who know all the bearings of the situation in India, as regards the Theosophical Society, than the sight of Madam Blavatsky, slandered and ridiculed by most of the Anglo-Indian papers, and spoken of as a charlatan by the commonplace crowd, in return for having freely offered them some of the wonderful fruits—as much as the rules of the great occult association permit her to offer—of the life-long struggle in which she has conquered her extraordinary knowledge.

In spite of all this, meanwhile, the Theosophical Society remains the one organization which supplies to inquirers who thirst for occult knowledge a link of communication, however slight, with the great fraternity in the background which takes an interest in its progress, and is accessible to its founder.

FIRST OCCULT EXPERIENCES

IT HAS BEEN through my connection with the Theosophical Society and my acquaintance with Madame Blavatsky that I have obtained experiences in connection with occultism, which have prompted me to undertake my present task. The first problem I had to solve was whether Madame Blavatsky really did, as I heard, possess the power of producing abnormal phenomena. And it may be imagined that, on the assumption of the reality of her phenomena, nothing would have been simpler than to obtain such satisfaction when once I had formed her acquaintance. It is, however, an illustration of the embarrassments which surround all inquiries of this nature—embarrassments with which so many people grow impatient, to the end that they cast inquiry altogether aside and remain wholly ignorant of the truth for the rest of their lives— that although on the first occasion of my making. Madame Blavatsky's acquaintance she became a guest at my house at Allahabad and remained there for six weeks, the harvest of satisfaction I was enabled to obtain during this time was exceedingly small. Of course I heard a great deal from her during the time mentioned about occultism and the Brothers, but while she was most anxious that I should understand the situation thoroughly, and I was most anxious to get at the truth, the difficulties to be overcome were almost insuperable. For the Brothers, as already described, have an unconquerable objection to showing off. That the person who wishes them to show off is an earnest seeker of truth, and not governed by mere idle curiosity, is nothing to the purpose. They do not want to attract candidates for initiation by an exhibition of wonders. Wonders have a very spirit-stirring effect on the history of every religion founded on miracles, but occultism is not a pursuit which people can safely take up in obedience to the impulse of enthusiasm created by witnessing a display of extraordinary power. There is no absolute rule to forbid the exhibition of powers in presence of the outsider; but it is clearly disapproved of by the higher authorities of occultism on principle, and it is practically impossible for less exalted proficients to go against this disapproval. It was only the very slightest of all imaginable phenomena that, during her first visit to my house, Madame Blavatsky was thus permitted to exhibit freely. She was allowed to show that "raps" like those which spiritualists attribute to spirit agency, could be produced at will. This was something, and *faute de mieux* we paid great attention to raps.

Spiritualists are aware that when groups of people sit round a table and put their hands upon it, they will, if a "medium" be present, generally hear little knocks which respond to questions and spell out messages. The large outer circle of persons who do not believe in spiritualism are fain to imagine that all the millions who do, are duped as regards this impression. It must sometimes be troublesome for them to account for the wide development of the delusion, but any theory, they think, is preferable to admitting the possibility that the spirits of deceased persons can communicate in this way; or, if they take the scientific view of the matter, that a physical effect, however slight, can be produced without a physical cause. Such persons ought to welcome the explanations I am now giving, tending as these do to show that the theory of universal self-deception as regards spirit-rapping, which must be rather an awkward theory for anyone but a ludicrously conceited objector to hold, is not the only one by means of which the asserted facts of spiritualism—those with which we are now dealing at all events—can be reconciled with a reluctance to accept the spiritual hypothesis as the explanation.

Now, I soon found out not only that raps would always come at a table at which Madame Blavatsky sat with the view of obtaining such results, but that all conceivable hypotheses of fraud in the matter were rapidly disposed of by a comparison of the various experiments we were able to make. To begin with, there was no necessity for other people to sit at the table at all. We could work with any table under any circumstances, or without a table at all. A windowpane would do equally well, or the wall, or any door, or anything whatever which could give out a sound if hit. A half glass door put ajar was at once seen to be a very good instrument to choose, because it was easy to stand opposite Madame Blavatsky in this case, to see her bare hands or hand (without any rings) resting motionless on the pane, and to hear the little ticks come plainly, as if made with the point of a pencil or, with the sound of electric sparks passing from one knob of an electrical apparatus to another. Another very satisfactory way of obtaining the raps—one frequently employed in the evening—was to set down a large glass clock-shade on the hearthrug, and get Madame Blavatsky, after removing all rings from her hands, and sitting well clear of the shade so that no part of her dress touched it, to lay her hands on it. Putting a lamp on the ground opposite, and sitting down on the hearthrug, one could see the under surfaces of the hands resting on the glass, and still under these perfectly satisfactory conditions the raps would come, clear and distinct, on the sonorous surface of the shade.

It was out of Madame Blavatsky's power to give an exact explanation as to how these raps were produced. Every effort of occult power is connected with some secret or other, and slight, regarded in the light of phenomena, as the raps were, they were physical effects produced by an effort of will, and the manner in which the will can be trained to produce physical effects may be too uniform, as regards great and small phenomena, to be made in accordance with the rules of occultism the subject of exact explanations to uninitiated persons. But the fact that the raps were obedient to the will was readily put beyond dispute, in this way amongst others: working with the windowpane or the clock-shade, I would ask to have a name spelled out, mentioning one at random. Then I would call over the alphabet, and at the right letters the raps would come. Or I would ask for a definite number of raps, and they would come. Or for series of raps in some defined rhythmical progression, and they would come. Nor was this all. Madame Blavatsky would sometimes put her hands, or one only, on someone else's head, and make the raps come, audibly to an attentive listener and perceptibly to the person touched, who would feel each little shock exactly as if he were taking sparks off the conductor of an electrical machine.

At a later stage of my inquiries I obtained raps under better circumstances again than these—namely, without contact between the object on which they were produced and Madame Blavatsky's hands at all. This was at Simla in the summer of last year (1880), but I may as well anticipate a little as far as the raps are concerned. At Simla Madame Blavatsky used to produce the raps on a little table set in the midst of an attentive group, with no one touching it at all. After starting it, or of charging it with some influence by resting her hands on it for a few moments, she would hold one about a foot above it and make mesmeric passes at it, at each of which the table would yield the familiar sound. Nor was this done only at our own house with our own tables. The same thing would be done at friends houses, to which Madame Blavatsky accompanied us. And a further development of the head experiment was this: It was found to be possible for several persons to feel the same rap simultaneously. Four or five persons used sometimes to put their hands in a pile, one on another on a table; then Madame Blavatsky would put hers on the top of the pile and cause a current, of whatever it is which produces the sound, to pass through the whole series of hands, felt by each simultaneously, and record itself in a rap on the table beneath. Anyone who has ever taken part in forming such a pile of hands must feel as to some of the hypotheses concerning the raps that have been put forward in the Indian papers by determined sceptics—hard-headed persons not to be taken in—to the effect that the raps are produced by Madame Blavatsky's thumbnails or by the cracking of some joint—that such hypotheses are rather idiotic.

Summing up the argument in language which I used in a letter written at the time, it stands as follows; "Madame Blavatsky puts her hands on a table and raps are heard on it. Some wiseacre suggests she does it with her thumbnails; she puts only one hand on the table; the raps comes still. Does she conceal any artifice under her hand? She lifts her hand from the table altogether, and merely holding it in the air above, the raps still come. Has she done anything to the table? She puts her hand on a windowpane, on a picture frame, on a dozen different places about the room in succession, and from each in turn come the mysterious raps. Is the house where she stays with her own particular friends about her prepared all over? She goes to half a dozen other houses at Simla and produces raps at them all. Do the raps really come from somewhere else than where they seem to come from—are they perhaps ventriloquism? She puts her hand on your head, and from the motionless fingers you feel something which resembles a minute series of electric shocks, and an attentive listener beside you will hear them producing little raps on your skull. Are you telling a lie when you say you feel the shocks? Half a dozen people put their hands one on top of the other in a pile on the table; Madame Blavatsky puts hers on the top of all, and each person feels the little throbs pass through, and hears them record themselves in faint raps on the table on which the pile of hands is resting. When a person has seen all these experiments many times, as I have, what impression do you think is made on his mind by a person who says. There is nothing in raps but conjuring—Maskelyne and Cooke can do them for £10 a night. Maskelyne and Cooke cannot do them for £10 a night nor for ten lakhs a night under the circumstances I describe."

The raps even as I heard them during the first visit that Madame Blavatsky paid us at Allahabad, gave me a complete assurance that she was in possession of some faculties of an abnormal character. And this assurance lent a credibility, that would not otherwise have belonged to them, to one or two phenomena of a different kind which also occurred at that time, the conditions of which wore not complete enough to make them worth recording here. But it was mortifying to approach no nearer to absolute certitude concerning the questions in which we were really interested—namely, whether there did indeed exist men with the wonderful powers ascribed to the adepts, and whether in this way it was possible for human creatures to obtain positive knowledge concerning the characteristics of their own spiritual nature. It must be remembered that Madame Blavatsky was preaching no specific doctrine on this subject. What she told us about the adepts and her own initiation was elicited by questions. Theosophy, in which she did seek to interest all her friends, did not proclaim any specific belief on the subject. It simply recommended the theory that humanity should be regarded as a Universal Brotherhood in which each person should study the truth as regards spiritual things, freed from the prepossessions of any specific religious dogma. But although her attitude, as regards the whole subject, put her under no moral obligation to prove the reality of occultism, her conversation and her book, "Isis Unveiled," disclosed a view of things which one naturally desired to explore further; and it was tantalising to feel that she could, and yet could not give us the final proofs we so much desired to have, that her occult training really had invested her with powers over material things of a kind which, if one could but feel sure they were actually in her possession, would utterly shatter the primary foundations of materialistic philosophy.

One conviction we felt had been fully attained. This was the conviction of her own good faith. It is disagreeable merely to recognise that this can be impugned; but this has been done in Indiana so recklessly and cruelly by people who take up an attitude of hostility to the views with which she is identified, that it would be affectation to pass the question by. On the other hand, it would be too great a concession to an ignoble attack to go minutely over the evidence of her honesty of character with which my intimacy with Madame Blavatsky has gradually supplied me. At various times she has been a guest of ours for periods now amounting in all to more than three months out of nearly two years. To any impartial intelligence it will be manifest that, under these circumstances, I must have been able to form a better opinion concerning her real character than can possibly be derived from the crude observations of persons who have perhaps met her once or twice. I am not, of course, attributing any scientific value to this sort of testimony as accrediting the abnormal character of phenomena she may be concerned in producing. With such a mighty problem at stake as the trustworthiness of the fundamental theories of modern physical science, it is impossible to proceed by any other but scientific modes of investigation. In any experiments I have tried I have always been careful to exclude, not merely the probability, but the possibility of trickery; and where it has been impossible to secure the proper conditions, I have not allowed the results of the experiment to enter into the sum total of my conclusions. But, in its place, it seems only right—only a slight attempt to redress the scandalous wrong which, as far as mere insult and slander can do a wrong, has been done to a very high-minded and perfectly honourable woman—to record the certainty at which in progress of time both my wife and myself arrived, that Madame Blavatsky is a lady of absolutely upright nature, who has sacrificed, not merely rank and fortune, but all thought of personal welfare or comfort in any shape, from enthusiasm for occult studies in the first instance, and latterly for the special task she has taken in hand as an initiate in, if relatively a humble member of, the great occult fraternity—the direction of the Theosophical Society.

Besides the production of the raps one other phenomenon had been conceded to us during Madame Blavatsky's first visit. We had gone with her to Benares for a few days, and were studying at a house lent to us by the Maharajah of Vizianagram—a big, bare, comfortless abode as judged by European standards—in the central hall of which we were sitting one evening after dinner. Suddenly three or four flowers—cut roses—fell in the midst of us—just as such things sometimes fall in the dark at spiritual seances. But in this case there were several lamps and candles in the room. The ceiling of the hall consisted simply of the solid, bare, painted rafters and boards that supported the flat cement roof of the building. The phenomenon was so wholly unexpected—as unexpected, I am given to understand, by Madame Blavatsky, sitting in an armchair reading at the time, as by the rest of us—that it lost some of the effect it would otherwise have had on our minds. If one could have been told a moment beforehand "now some flowers are going to fall", so that we could have looked up and seen them suddenly appear in the air above our heads, then the impressive effect of an incident so violently out of the common order of things would have been very great. Even as it was, the incident has always remained for those who witnessed it one of the stages on their road to a conviction of the reality of occult powers. Persons to whom it is merely related cannot be expected to rely upon it to any great extent. They will naturally ask various questions as to the construction of the room, who inhabited the house, etc., and even when all these questions had been answered, as they truthfully could be in a manner which would shut out any hypothesis by means of which the fall of the flowers could be explainable by any conjuring trick, there would still be an uncomfortable suspicion left in the questioner's mind as to the completeness of the explanation given. It might hardly have been worth while to bring the incident on to the present record at all, but for the opportunity it affords me of pointing out that the phenomena produced in Madame Blavatsky's presence need not necessarily be of her producing.

Corning now to details in connection with some of the larger mysteries of occultism, I am oppressed by the difficulty of leading up to a statement of what I know now to be facts—as absolute facts as Charing Cross—which shall, nevertheless, be gradual enough not to shock the understanding of people absolutely unused to any but the ordinary grooves of thought as regards physical phenomena. None the less is it true that any "Brother," as the adepts in occultism are familiarly referred to, who may have been seized with the impulse to bestow on our party at Benares the little surprise described above, may have been in Tibet or in the South of India, or anywhere else in the world at the time, and yet just as able to make the roses fall as if he had been in the room with us. I have spoken already of the adept's power of being present "in spirit" as we should say, "in astral body" as an occultist would say, at any distant place in the flash of a moment at will. So present, he can exercise in that distant place some of the psychological powers which he possesses, as completely as he can exercise them in physical body wherever he may actually be, as we understand the expression. I am not pretending to give an explanation of how he produces this or that result, nor for a moment hinting that I know. I am recording merely the certain fact that various occult results have been accomplished in my presence, and explaining as much about them as I have been able to find out. But at all events it has long since become quite plain to me, that wherever Madame Blavatsky is, there the Brothers, wherever they may be, can and constantly do produce phenomena of the most overwhelming sort, with the production of which she herself has little or nothing to do. In reference, indeed, to any phenomenon occurring in her presence, it must be remembered that one can never have any exact knowledge as to how far her own powers may have been employed, or how far she may have been "helped," or whether she has not been quite uninfluential in the production of the result. Precise explanations of this kind are quite contrary to the rules of occultism—which, it must always be remembered, is not trying to convince the world of its existence. In this volume I am trying to convince the world of its existence, but that is another matter altogether. Anyone who wishes to know how the truth really stands can only take up the position of a seeker of truth. He is not a judge before whom occultism comes to plead for credibility. It is useless, therefore, to quarrel with the observations we are enabled to make on the ground that they are not of the kind one would best like to make. The question is whether they yield data on which conclusions may safely rest.

And another consideration claims treatment in connexion with the character of the observations which, so far, I have been enabled to make—that is to say, in connexion with any search for proof of occult power as regards physical phenomena which but for such agency would be miraculous. I can foresee that, in spite of the abject stupidity of the remark, many people will urge that the force of the experiments with which I have had to deal is vitiated because they relate to phenomena which have a certain superficial resemblance to conjuring tricks. Of course this ensues from the fact that conjuring tricks all aim at achieving a certain superficial resemblance to occult phenomena. Let any reader, whatever his present frame of mind on the subject may be, assume for a moment that he has seen reason to conceive that there may be an occult fraternity in existence wielding strange powers over natural forces as yet unknown to ordinary humanity; that this fraternity is bound by rules which cramp the manifestation of these powers, but do not absolutely prohibit it; and then let him propose some comparatively small but scientifically convincing tests which he could ask to have conceded to him as a proof of the reality of some part, at all events, of these powers: it will be found that it is impossible to propose any such test that does not bear a certain superficial resemblance to a conjuring trick. But this will not necessarily impair the value of the test for people capable of dealing with those characteristics of experiments that are not superficial.

The gulf of difference which is really to be observed lying between any of the occult phenomena I shall have to describe presently and a conjuring trick which might imitate it, is due to the fact that the conditions would be utterly unlike. The conjuror would work in his own stage, or in a prepared room. The most remarkable of the phenomena I have had in the presence of Madame Blavatsky have taken place away out of doors in fortuitously chosen places in the woods and on the hills. The conjuror is assisted by any required number of confederates behind his scenes. Madame Blavatsky comes a stranger to Simla, and is a guest in my own house, under my own observation, during the whole of her visit. The conjuror is paid to incur the expenses of accomplishing this or that deception of the senses. Madame Blavatsky is, what I have already explained, a lady of honourable character, instrumental in helping her friends—at their earnest desire wherever phenomena are produced at all—to see some manifestation of the powers in the acquisition of which (instead of earning money by them as the conjuror does with his) she has sacrificed everything the world generally holds dear-station, and so forth, immeasurably above that to which any conjuror or any impostor could aspire. Pursuing Madame Blavatsky with injurious suspicions, persons who resent the occult hypothesis will constantly forget the dictates of common sense in overlooking these considerations.

About the beginning of September 1880, Madame Blavatsky came to Simla as our guest, and in the course of the following six weeks various phenomena occurred, which became the talk of all Anglo-India for a time, and gave rise to some excited feeling on the part of persons who warmly espoused the theory that they must be the result of imposture. It soon became apparent to us that whatever might have been the nature of the restrictions which operated the previous winter at Allahabad to prevent our guest from displaying more than the very least of her powers, these restrictions were now less operative than before. We were soon introduced to a phenomenon we had not been treated to previously. By some modification of the force employed to produce the sound of raps on any object, Madame Blavatsky can produce in the air, without the intermediation of any solid object whatever, the sound of a silvery bell—sometimes a chime or little run of three or four bells on different notes. We had often heard about these bells, but had never heard them produced before. They were produced for us for the first time one evening after dinner while we were still sitting round the table, several times in, succession in the air over our heads, and in one instance instead of the single bell-sound there came one of the chimes of which I speak. Later on I heard them on scores of occasions and in all sorts of different places—in the open air and at different houses where Madame Blavatsky went from time to time. As before with the raps, there is no hypothesis in the case of the bells which can be framed by an adherent of the imposture theory which does not break down on a comparison of the different occasions and conditions under which I have heard them produced. Indeed, the theory of imposture is one which in the matter of the bells has only one narrow conjecture to rest on. Unlike the sound of a rap, which in the ordinary way could be produced by many different methods—so that, to be sure any given example of such a sound is not produced by ordinary means, one has to procure its repetition under a great variety of conditions—the sound of a bell can only be made, physically, in a few ways. You must have a bell, or some sonorous object in the nature of a bell, to make it with. Now, when sitting in a well lighted room, and attentively watching, you get the sound of a bell up above your heads where there is no physical bell to yield it—what are the hypotheses which can attribute the result to trickery. Is the sound really produced outside the room altogether by some agent or apparatus in another. First of all no rational person who had heard this sound would advance that theory, because the sound itself is incompatible with the idea. It is never loud—at least I have never heard it very loud—but it is always clear and distinct to a remarkable extent. If you lightly strike the edge of a thin claret glass with a knife you may get a sound which it would be difficult to persuade anyone had come from another room; but the occult bell-sound is like that, only purer and clearer, with no sub-sound of jarring in it whatever. Independently of this, I have, as I say, heard the sound in the open air produced up in the sky in the stillness of evening. In rooms, it has not always been overhead, but sometimes down on the ground amongst the feet of a group of persons listening for it. Again, on one occasion, when it had been produced two or three times in the drawing-room of a friend's house where we had all been dining, one gentlemen of the party went back to the dining-room two rooms off, to get a finger glass with which to make a sound for the occult bells to repeat—a familiar form of the experiment. While by himself in the dining-room he heard one of the bell-sounds produced near him, though Madame Blavatsky had remained in the drawing-room. This example of the phenomenon satisfactorily disposed of the theory, absurd in itself for persons who frequently heard the bells in all manner of places, that Madame Blavatsky carried some apparatus about her with which to produce the sound. As for the notion of confederacy, that is disposed of by the fact that I have repeatedly heard the sounds when out walking beside Madame Blavatsky's jampan with no other person near us but the jampanees carrying it.

The bell-sounds are not mere sportive illustrations of the properties of the currents which—are set in action to produce them. They serve the direct, practical purpose among occultists of a telegraphic call-bell. It appears that when trained occultists are concerned, so that the mysterious magnetic connection, whatever it may be, which enables them to communicate ideas is once established, they can produce the bell-sounds at any distance in the neighbourhood of the fellow-initiate whose attention they wish to attract. I have repeatedly heard Madame Blavatsky called in this way, when our own little party being alone some evening, we have all been quietly reading. A little "ting" would suddenly sound, and Madame Blavatsky would get up and go to her room to attend to whatever occult business may have been the motive of her summons. A very pretty illustration of the sound, as thus produced by some brother-initiate at a distance, was afforded one evening under these circumstances. A lady, a guest at another house in Simla, had been dining with us, when about eleven o'clock I received a note from her host, enclosing a letter which he asked me to get Madame Blavatsky to send on by occult means to a certain member of the great fraternity to whom both he and I had been writing. I shall explain the circumstances of this correspondence more fully later on. We were all anxious to know at once—before the lady with us that evening returned up the hill, so that she could take back word to her host—whether the letter could be sent; but Madame Blavatsky declared that her own powers would not enable her to perform the feat. The question was whether a certain person, a half-developed brother then in the neighbourhood of Simla, would give the necessary help. Madame Blavatsky said she would see if she could "find him," and taking the letter in her hands, she went out into the veranda, where we all followed her. Leaning on the balustrade, and looking over the wide sweep of the Simla valley, she remained for a few minutes perfectly motionless and silent, as we all were; and the night was far enough advanced for all commonplace sounds to have settled down, so that the stillness was perfect. Suddenly, in the air before us, there sounded the clear note of an occult-bell. "All right," cried Madame, "he will take it." And duly taken the letter was shortly afterwards. But the phenomenon involved in its transmission will be better introduced to the reader in connection with other examples.

I come now to a series of incidents which exhibit occult power in a more striking light than any of those yet described. To a scientific mind, indeed, the production of sounds by means of a force unknown to ordinary science should be as clear a proof that the power in question is a power, as the more sensational phenomena which have to do with the transmission of solid objects by occult agency. The sound can only reach our ears by the vibration of air, and to set up the smallest undulation of air as the effect of a thought will appear to the ordinary understanding as no less outrageous an impossibility than the uprooting of a tree in a similar way. Still there are degrees in wonderfulness which the feelings recognise even if such distinctions are irrational.

The first incident of the kind which I now take up is not one which would in itself be a complete proof of anything for an outsider. I describe it rather for the benefit of readers who may be, either through spiritualistic experiences or in any other way, already alive to the possibility of phenomena as such, and interested rather in experiments which may throw light on their genesis than in mere texts. Managed a little better, the occurrence now to be dealt with would have been a beautiful test; but Madame Blavatsky, left to herself in such matters, is always the worst devisor of tests imaginable. Utterly out of sympathy with the positive and incredulous temperament; engaged all her life in the development amongst Asiatic mystics of the creative rather than the critical faculties, she never can follow the intricate suspicions with which the European observer approaches the consideration of the marvellous in its simplest forms. The marvellous, in forms so stupendously marvellous that they almost elude the grasp of ordinary conceptions, has been the daily food of her life for a great number of years, and it is easy to realise that, for her, the jealous distrust with which ordinary people hunt round the slightest manifestation of occult force to find any loophole through which a suspicion of fraud may creep, as no less tiresome and stupid, then the ordinary person conceives the too credulous spirit to be.

About the end of September my wife went one afternoon with Madame Blavatsky to the top of a neighbouring hill. They were only accompanied by one other friend. I was not present myself on this occasion. While there Madame Blavatsky asked my wife, in a joking way, what was her heart's desire. She said at random and on the spur or the moment, "to get a note from one of the Brothers." Madame Blavatsky took from her pocket a piece of blank pink paper that had been torn off a note received that day. Folding this up into a small compass she took it to the edge of the hill, held it up for a moment or two between her hands and returned saying that it was gone. She presently, after communicating mentally by her own occult methods with the distant Brother, said he asked where my wife would have the letter. At first, she said she should like it to come fluttering down into her lap, but some conversation ensued as to whether this would be the best way to get it, and ultimately it was decided that she should find it in a certain tree. Here, of course, a mistake was made which opens the door to the suspicions of resolutely disbelieving persons. It will be supposed that Madame Blavatsky had some reasons of her own for wishing the tree chosen. For readers who favour that conjecture after all that has gone before, it is only necessary to repeat that the present story is being told not as a proof, but as an incident.

At first, Madame Blavatsky seems to have made a mistake as to the description of the tree, which the distant Brother was indicating as that in which he was going to put the note, and with some trouble my wife scrambled on to the lower branch of a bare and leafless trunk on which nothing could be found. Madame then again got into communication with the Brother and ascertained her mistake. Into another tree at a little distance, which neither Madame nor the one other person present had approached, my wife now climbed a few feet and looked all round among the branches. At first, she saw nothing, but then, turning back her head without moving from the position she had taken up, she saw on a twig immediately before her face—where a moment previously there had been nothing but leaves—a little pink note. This was stuck on to the stalk of a leaf that had been quite freshly torn off, for the stalk was still green and moist—not withered as it would have been if the leaf had been torn off for any length of time. The note was found to contain these few words: "I have been asked to leave a note here for you. What can I do for you?", It was signed by some Tibetan characters. The pink paper on which it was written appeared to be the same which Madame Blavatsky had taken blank from her pocket shortly before.

How was it transmitted first to the Brother who wrote upon it and then back again to the top of our hill? not to speak of the mystery of its attachment to the tree in the way described. So far as I can frame conjectures on this subject, it would be premature to set them forth in detail till I have gone more fully into the facts observed. It is no use to discuss the way the wings of flying-fish are made for people who will not believe in the reality of flying fish at all, and refuse to accept phenomena less guaranteed by orthodoxy than Pharaoh's chariot wheels.

I come now to the incidents of a very remarkable day. The day before, I should explain, we started on a little expedition which turned out a *coup manqué*, though, but for some tiresome mishaps, it might have led, we afterwards had reason to think, to some very interesting results. We mistook our way to a place of which Madame Blavatsky had received an imperfect description—or a description she imperfectly understood—in an occult conversation with one of the Brothers then actually passing through Simla. Had we gone the right way that day we might have had the good fortune of meeting him, for he stayed one night at a certain old Tibetan temple, or rest-house, such as is often found about the Himalayas, and which the blind apathy of commonplace English people leads them to regard as of no particular interest or importance. Madame Blavatsky was wholly unacquainted with Simla, and the account she gave us of the place she wanted to go to led us to think she meant a different place. We started, and for a long time Madame declared that we must be going in the right direction because she felt certain currents. Afterwards it appeared that the road to the place we were making for, and to that for which we ought to have made, were coincident for a considerable distance; but a slight divergence at one point carried us into a wholly wrong system of hill-paths. Eventually Madame utterly lost her scent: we tried back; we who knew Simla discussed its topography and wondered where it could be she wanted to get to, but all to no purpose. We launched ourselves down a hillside where Madame declared she once more felt the missing current; but occult currents may flow where travellers cannot pass, and when we attempted this descent. I knew the case was desperate. After a while the expedition had to be abandoned, and we went home much disappointed.

Why, some one may ask, could not the omniscient Brother feel that Madame was going wrong, and direct us properly in time? I say this question will be asked, because I know from experience that people unused to the subject will not bear in mind the relations of the Brothers to such inquirers as ourselves. In this case, for example, the situation was not *one* in which the Brother in question was anxiously waiting to prove his existence to a jury of intelligent Englishmen. We can learn so little about the daily life of an adept in occultism, that we who are uninitiated can tell very little about the interests that really engage his attention; but we can find out this much—that his attention is constantly engaged on interests connected with his own work, and the gratification of the curiosity concerning occult matters of persons who are not regular students of occultism forms no part of that work at all. On the contrary, unless under very exceptional conditions, he is even forbidden to make any concessions whatever to such curiosity. In the case in point the course of events may probably have been something of this kind:— Madame Blavatsky perceived by her own occult tentacle that one of her illustrious friends was in the neighbourhood. She immediately—having a sincere desire to oblige us—may have asked him whether she might bring us to see him. Probably he would regard any such request very much as the astronomer royal might regard the request of a friend to bring a party of ladies to look through his telescopes; but nonetheless he might say, to please his half-fledged "brother" in occultism, Madame Blavatsky, "Very well, bring them, if you like: I am in such and such a place." And then he would go on with his work, remembering afterwards that the intended visit had never been paid, and perhaps turning an occult perception in the direction of the circumstances to ascertain what had happened.

However, this may have been, the expedition as first planned broke down. It was not with the hope of seeing the Brother, but on the general principle of hoping for something to turn up, that we arranged to go for a picnic the following day in another direction, which, as the first road had failed, we concluded to be probably the one we ought to have taken previously.

We set out at the appointed time next morning. We were originally to have been a party of six, but a seventh person joined us just before we started. After going down the hill for some hours a place was chosen in the wood near the upper waterfall for our breakfast: the baskets that had been brought with us were unpacked, and, as usual at an Indian picnic, the servants at a little distance lighted a fire and set to work to make tea and coffee. Concerning this some joking arose over the fact that we had one cup and saucer too few, on account of the seventh person who joined us at starting, and some one laughingly asked Madame Blavatsky to create another cup and saucer. There was no set purpose in the proposal at first, but when Madame Blavatsky said it would be very difficult, but that if we liked she would try, attention was of course at once arrested. Madame Blavatsky, as usual, held mental conversation with one of the Brothers, and then wandered a little about in the immediate neighbourhood of where we were sitting—that is to say, within a radius of half-a-dozen to a dozen yards from our picnic cloth—I'm closely following, waiting to see what would happen. Then she marked a spot on the ground, and called to one of the gentlemen of the party to bring a knife to dig with. The place chosen was the edge of a little slope covered with thick weeds and grass and shrubby undergrowth. The gentleman with the knife—let us call him X-------------- as I shall have to refer to him afterwards—tore up these in the first place with some difficulty, as the roots were tough and closely interlaced. Cutting then into the matted roots and earth with the knife, and pulling away the *débris* with his hands, he came at last, on the edge of something white, which turned out, as it was completely excavated, to be the required cup. A corresponding saucer was also found after a little more digging. Both objects were in among the roots which spread everywhere through the ground, so that it seemed as if the roots were growing round them. The cup and saucer both corresponded exactly, as regards their pattern, with those that had been brought to the picnic, and constituted a seventh cup and saucer when brought back to where we were to have breakfast. I may as well add at once that afterwards, when we got home, my wife questioned our principal khitmutgar as to how many cups and saucers of that particular kind we possessed. In the progress of years, as the set was an old set, some had been broken, but the man at once said that nine teacups were left. When collected and counted that number was found to be right, without reckoning the excavated cup. That made ten, and as regards the pattern—it was one of a somewhat peculiar kind, bought a good many years previously in London, and which assuredly could never have been matched in Simla.

Now, the notion that human beings can create material objects by the exercise of mere psychological power, will of course be revolting to the understandings of people to whom this whole subject is altogether strange. It is not making the idea much more acceptable to say that the cup and saucer appear in this case to have been "doubled" rather than created. The doubling of objects seems merely another kind of creation—creation according to a pattern. However, the facts, the occurrences of the morning I have described, were at all events exactly as I have related them. I have been careful as to the strict and minute truthfulness of every detail. If the phenomenon was not what it appeared to be—a most wonderful display of a power of which the modern scientific world has no comprehension whatever it was, of course, an elaborate fraud. That supposition, however, setting aside the moral impossibility from any point of view of assuming Madame Blavatsky capable of participation in such an imposture, will only bear to be talked of vaguely. As a way out of the dilemma it will not serve any person of ordinary intelligence who is aware of the facts, or who trusts my statement of them. The cup and saucer were assuredly dug up in the way I describe. If they were not deposited there by occult agency, they must have been buried there beforehand. Now, I have described the character of the ground from which they were dug up; assuredly that had been undisturbed for years by the character of the vegetation upon it. But it may be urged that from some other part of the sloping ground a sort of tunnel may have been excavated in the first instance through which the cup and saucer could have been thrust into the place where they were found. Now this theory is barely tenable as regards its physical possibility. If the tunnel had been big enough for the purpose it would have left traces which were not perceptible on the ground—which were not even discoverable when the ground was searched shortly afterwards with a view to that hypothesis. But the truth is that the theory of previous burial is morally untenable in view of the fact that the demand for the cup and saucer—of all the myriad things that might have been asked for—could never have been foreseen. It arose out of circumstances themselves the sport of the moment. If no extra person had joined us at the last moment the number of cups and saucers packed up by the servants would have been sufficient for our needs, and no attention would have been drawn to them. It was by the servants, without the knowledge of any guest, that the cups taken were chosen from others that might just as easily have been taken. Had the burial fraud been really perpetrated it would have been necessary to constrain us to choose the *exact* spot we did actually choose for the picnic with a view to the previous preparations, but the exact spot on which the ladies' jampans were deposited was chosen by myself in concert with the gentleman referred to above as X—, and it was within a few yards of this spot that the cup was found. Thus, leaving the other absurdities of the fraud hypothesis out of sight, who could be the agents employed to deposit the cup and saucer in the ground, and when did they perform the operation? Madame Blavatsky was under our roof the whole time from the previous evening when the picnic was determined on to the moment of starting. The one personal servant she had with her, a Bombay boy and a perfect stranger to Simla, was constantly about the house the previous evening, and from the first awakening of the household in the morning—and as it happened he spoke to my own bearer in the middle of the night, for I had been annoyed by a loft door which had been left unfastened, and was slamming in the wind, and called up servants to shut it. Madame Blavatsky it appears, thus awakened, had sent her servant, who always slept within call, to inquire what was the matter. Colonel Olcott, the President of the Theosophical Society, also a guest of ours at the time of which I am speaking, was certainly with us all the evening from the period of our return from the abortive expedition of the afternoon, and was also present at the start. To imagine that he spent the night in going four or five miles down a difficult *khud* through forest paths difficult to find, to bury a cup and saucer of a kind that we were not likely to take in a place we were not likely to go to, in order that in the exceedingly remote contingency of its being required for the perpetration of a hoax it might be there, would certainly be a somewhat extravagant conjecture. Another consideration—the destination for which we were making can be approached by two roads from opposite ends of the upper horseshoe of hills on which Simla stands. It was open to us to select either path, and certainly neither Madame Blavatsky nor Colonel Olcott had any share in the selection of that actually taken. Had we taken the other, we should never have come to the spot where we actually picnicked.

The hypothesis of fraud in this affair is, as I have said, a defiance of common sense when worked out in any imaginable way. The extravagance of this explanation will, moreover, be seen to heighten as my narrative proceeds, and as the incident just related is compared with others which took place later. But I have not yet done with the incidents of the cup-morning.

The gentleman called X --------------------------had been a good deal with us during the week or two that had already elapsed since Madame Blavatsky's arrival. Like many of our friends, he had been greatly impressed with much he had seen in her presence. He had especially come to the conclusion that the Theosophical Society, in which she was interested, was exerting a good influence with the natives, a view which he had expressed more than once in warm language in my presence. He had declared his intention of joining this Society as I had done myself. Now, when the cup and saucer were found most of us who were present, X among the number, were greatly impressed, and in the conversation that ensued the idea arose that X—might formally become a member of the Society then and there. I should not have taken part in this suggestion—I believe I originated it—if X ----------had not in cool blood decided, as I understood, to join the Society; in itself, moreover, a step which involved no responsibilities whatever, and simply indicated sympathy with the pursuit of occult knowledge and a general adhesion to broadly philanthropic doctrines of brotherly sentiments towards all humanity, irrespective of race and creed. This has to be explained in view of some little annoyances which followed.

The proposal that X ------------should then and there formally join the Society was one with which he was quite ready to fall in. But some documents were required-a formal diploma, the gift of which to a new member should follow his initiation into certain little Masonic forms of recognition adopted in the Society.

How could we get a diploma? Of course for the group then present a difficulty of this sort was merely another opportunity for the exercise of Madame's powers. Could she get a diploma brought to us by "magic?" After an occult conversation with the Brother who had then interested himself in our proceedings,Madame told us that the diploma would be forthcoming. She described the appearance it would present—a roll of paper wound round with an immense quantity of string, and then bound up in the leaves of a creeping plant. We should find it about in the woods where we were, and we could all look for it, but it would be X—, for whom it was intended, who would find it. Thus it fell out. We all searched about in the undergrowth or in the trees, wherever fancy prompted us to look, and it was X—who found the roll, done up as described.

We had had our breakfast by this time. X— was formally "initiated" a member of the society by Colonel Olcott, and after a time we shifted our quarters to a lower place in the wood where there was the little Tibetan temple, or rest-house, which the Brother who had been passing through Simla—according to what Madame Blavatsky told us—had passed the previous night. We amused ourselves by examining—the little building inside and out, "bathing in the "good magnetism," as Madame Blavatsky expressed it, and then, lying on the grass outside, it occurred to someone that we wanted more coffee. The servants were told to prepare some, but it appeared that they had used up all our water. The water to be found in the streams near Simla is not of a kind to be used for purposes of this sort, and for a picnic, clean filtered water is always taken out in bottles, It appears that all the bottles in our baskets had been exhausted. This report was promptly verified by the servants by the exhibition of the empty bottles. The only thing to be done was to send to a brewery, the nearest building, about a mile oft, and ask for water. I wrote a pencil note and a coolie went off with the empty bottles. Time passed, and the coolie returned, to our great disgust, without the water. There had been no European left at the brewery that day (It was Sunday) to receive the note, and the coolie had stupidly plodded back with the empty bottles under his arm, instead of asking about and finding someone able to supply the required water.

At this time our party was a little dispersed. X— and one of the other gentlemen had wandered off. No one of the remainder of the party was expecting fresh phenomena, when Madame suddenly got up, went over to the baskets, a dozen or twenty yards off, picked out a bottle-one of those, I believe, which had been brought back by the coolie empty—and came back to us holding it under the fold of her dress. Laughingly producing it, it was found to be full of water. Just like a conjuring trick, will some one say? Just like, except for the conditions. For such a conjuring trick, the conjurer defines the thing to be done. In our ease the want of water was as unforeseeable in the first instance as the want of the cup and saucer. The accident that left the brewery deserted by its Europeans, and the further accident that the coolie sent up for water should have been so abnormally stupid even for a coolie as to come back without, because there happened to be no European to take my note, were accidents but for which the opportunity for obtaining the water by occult agency could not have arisen. And those accidents supervened on the fundamental accident, improbable in itself, that our servants should have sent us out insufficiently supplied. That any bottle of water could have been left unnoticed at the bottom of the baskets is a suggestion that I can hardly imagine anyone present putting forward, for the servants had been found fault with for not bringing enough; they had just before had the baskets completely emptied out, and we had not submitted to the situation till we had been fully satisfied that there really was no more water left. Furthermore, I tasted the water in the bottle Madame Blavatsky produced, and it was not water of the same kind as that which came from our own filters. It was an earthy tasting water, unlike that of the modern Simla supply, but equally unlike, I may add, though in a different way, the offensive and discoloured water of the only stream flowing through those woods.

How was it brought? The how, of course, in all these cases is the great mystery which I am unable to explain except in general terms; but the impossibility of understanding the way adepts manipulate matter is one thing; the impossibility of denying that they do manipulate it in a manner which Western ignorance would describe as miraculous is another. The fact is there whether we can explain it or not. The rough, popular saying that you cannot argue the hind leg off a cow, embodies a sound reflection, which our prudent sceptics in matters of the kind with which I am now dealing are too apt to overlook. You cannot argue away a fact by contending that by the lights in your mind it ought to be something different from what it is. Still less can you argue away a mass of facts like those I am now recording by a series of extravagant and contradictory hypotheses about each in turn. What the determined disbeliever so often overlooks is that the scepticism which may show an acuteness of mind up to a certain point, reveals a deficient intelligence when adhered to in face of certain kinds of evidence.

I remember when the phonograph was first invented, a scientific officer in the service of the Indian Government sent me an article he had written on the earliest accounts received of the instrument—to prove that the story must be a hoax, because the instrument described was scientifically impossible. He had worked out the times of vibrations required to reproduce the sounds and so on, and very intelligently argued that the alleged result was unattainable. But when phonographs in due time were imported into India, he did not continue to say they were impossible, and that there must be a man shut up in each machine, even though there did not seem to be room. That last is the attitude of the self-complacent people who get over the difficulty about the causation of occult and spiritual phenomena by denying, in face of the palpable experience of thousands—in face of the testimony in shelves—full of books that they do not read—that any such phenomena take place at all.

X—, I should add here, afterwards changed his mind about the satisfactory character of the cup phenomena, and said he thought it vitiated as a scientific proof by the interposition of the theory that the cup and saucer might have been thrust up into their places by means of a tunnel cut from a lower part of the bank. I have discussed that hypothesis already, and mention the fact of X—'s change of opinion, which does not affect any of the circumstances I have narrated, merely to avoid the chance that readers, who may have heard or read about the Simla phenomenon in other pages, might think I was treating the change of opinion in question as something which it was worth while to disguise. And, indeed, the convictions which I ultimately attained were themselves the result of accumulated experiences I have yet to relate, so that I cannot tell how far my own certainty concerning the reality of occult power rests on anyone example that I have seen.

It was on the evening of the day of the cup phenomenon that there occurred an incident destined to become the subject of very wide discussion in all the Anglo-Indian papers. This was the celebrated "brooch incident." The facts were related at the time in a little statement drawn up for publication, and signed by the nine persons who witnessed it! This statement will be laid before the reader directly, but as the comments to which it gave rise showed that it was too meagre to convey a full and accurate idea of what occurred, I will describe the course of events a little more fully. In doing this, I may use names with a certain freedom, as these were all appended to the published document.

We, that is, my wife and myself with our guest, had gone up the hill to dine, in accordance with previous engagements, with Mr. and Mrs. Hume. We dined, a party of eleven, at a round table, and Madame Blavatsky, sitting next our host, tired and out of spirits as it happened, was unusually silent. During the beginning of dinner she scarcely said a word, Mr. Hume conversing chiefly with the lady on his other hand. It is a common trick at Indian dinner-tables to have little metal plate warmers with hot water before each guest, on which each plate served remains while in use. Such plate warmers were used on the evening I am describing, and over hers—in an interval during which plates had been removed—Madame Blavatsky was absently warming her hands. Now, the production of Madame Blavatsky's raps and bell-sounds we had noticed sometimes seemed easier and the effects better when her hands had been warmed in this way; so some one, seeing her engaged in warming them, asked her some question, hinting in an indirect way at phenomena. I was very far from expecting anything of the kind that evening, and Madame Blavatsky was equally far from intending to do anything herself or from expecting any display at the hands of one of the Brothers. So, merely in mockery, when asked why she was warming her hands, she enjoined us all to warm our hands too and see what would happen. Some of the people present actually did so, a few joking words passing among them. Then Mrs. Hume raised a little laugh by holding up her hands and saying, "But I have warmed my hands, what next". Now Madame Blavatsky, as I have said, was not in a mood for any occult performances at all, but it appears from what I learned afterwards that just at this moment, or immediately before, she suddenly perceived by those occult faculties of which mankind at large have no knowledge, that one of the Brothers was present "in astral body" invisible to the rest of us in the room. It was following his indications, therefore, that she acted in what followed; of course no one knew at the time that she had received any impulse in the matter external to herself. What took place as regards the surface of things was simply this: When Mrs. Hume said what I have set down above, and when the little laugh ensued, Madame Blavatsky put out her hand across the one person sitting between herself and Mrs. Hume and took one of that lady's hands, saying, "Well then, do you wish for anything in particular? or as the lawyers say," words to that effect." I cannot repeat the precise sentences spoken, nor can I say now exactly what Mrs. Hume first replied before she quite understood the situation; but this was made clear in a very few minutes. Some of the other people present catching this first, explained, "Think of something you would like to have brought to you; anything you like not wanted for any mere worldly motive; is there anything you can think of that will be very difficult to get?" Remarks of this sort were the only kind that were made in the short interval that elapsed between the remark by Mrs. Hume about having warmed her hands and the indication by her of the thing she had thought of. She said then that she had thought of something that would do. What was it? An old brooch that her mother had given her long ago and that she had lost.

Now, when this brooch, which was ultimately recovered by occult agency, as the rest of my story will show, came to be talked about, people said:— "Of course Madame Blavatsky led up the conversation to the particular thing she had arranged before-hand to produce." I have described *all* the conversation which took place on this subject, before the brooch was named. There was no conversation about the brooch or any other thing of the kind whatever. Five minutes before the brooch was named, there had been no idea in the mind of any person present that any phenomenon in the nature of finding any lost article, or of any other kind, indeed, was going to be performed. Nor while Mrs. Hume was going over in her mind the things she might ask for, did she speak any word indicating the direction her thoughts were taking.

From the point of the story now reached the narrative published at the time tells it almost as fully as it need be told, and, at all events, with a simplicity that will assist the reader in grasping all the facts—so I reprint it here in full—

> "On Sunday, the 3rd of October, at Mr. Hume's house at Simla, there were present at dinner Mr. and Mrs. Hume, Mr. and Mrs. Sinnett, Mrs. Gordon, Mr. F. Hogg, Captain P.J. Maitland, Mr. Beatson, Mr. Davidson, Colonel Olcott, and Madame Blavatsky. Most of the persons present having recently seen many remarkable occurrences In Madame Blavatsky's presence, conversation turned on occult phenomena, and in the course of this Madame Blavatsky asked Mrs. Hume if there was anything she particularly wished for. Mrs. Hume at first hesitated, but in a short time said there was something she would particularly like to have brought her, namely, a small article of jewellery that she formerly possessed, but had given away to a person who had allowed it to pass out of her possession. Madame Blavatsky then said if she would fix the image of the article in question very definitely on her mind, she, Madame Blavatsky, would endeavour to procure It. Mrs. Hume then said that she vividly remembered the article, and described it as an old-fashioned breast brooch set round with pearls, With glass at the front, and the back made to contain hair. She then, on being asked, drew a rough sketch of the brooch.

Madame Blavatsky then wrapped up a coin attached to her watch-chain In two cigarette papers, and put it in her dress, and said that she hoped the brooch might be obtained in the course of the evening. At the close of dinner she said to Mr. Hume that the paper in which the corn had been wrapped was gone. A little later, in the drawing room, she said that the brooch would not be brought into the house, but that it must be looked for in the garden, and then as the party went out accompanying her, she said she had clairvoyantly seen the brooch fall into a star-shaped bed of flowers. Mr. Hume led the way to such a bed in a distant part of the garden. A prolonged and careful search was made with lanterns, and eventually a small paper packet, consisting of two cigarette papers, was found amongst the leaves by Mrs. Sinnett. This being opened on the spot was found to contain a brooch exactly corresponding to the previous description, and which Mrs. Hume Identified as that which she had originally lost. None of the party, except Mr. and Mrs. Hume, had ever seen or heard of the brooch. Mr. Hume had not thought of it for years. Mrs. Hume had never spoken of it to anyone since she parted with it, nor had she, for long, even thought of it. She herself stated, after it was found, that it was only when Madame asked her whether there was anything she would like to have, that the remembrance of this brooch, the gift of her mother, flashed across her mind.

"Mrs. Hume is not a spiritualist, and up to the time of the occurrence described was no believer either in occult phenomena or in Madame Blavatsky's powers. The conviction of all present was, that the occurrence was of an absolutely unimpeachable character, as an evidence of the truth of the possibility of occult phenomena. The brooch is unquestionably the one which Mrs, Hume lost. Even supposing, which is practically impossible, that the article, lost months before Mrs. Hume ever heard of Madame Blavatsky, and bearing no letters or other indication of original ownership, could have passed in a natural way into Madame Blavatsky's possession, even then she could not possibly have foreseen that it would be asked for, and Mrs. Hume herself had not given it a thought for months

"This narrative, read over to the party, is signed by—

A. O. HUME,
ALICE GORDON,
M. A. HUME,
P. J.:MAITLAND, FRED. R. HOGG, WM. DAVIDSON,
A. P. SINNETT, STUART BEATSON. PATIENCE SINNETT.

It is needless to state that when this narrative was published the nine persons above mentioned were assailed with torrents of ridicule, the effect of which, however; has not been in any single case to modify, in the smallest degree, the conviction which their signatures attested at the time, that the incident related was a perfectly conclusive proof of the reality of occult power. Floods of more or less imbecile criticism have been directed to show that the whole performance must have been a trick; and for many persons in India it is now, no doubt, an established explanation that Mrs. Hume was adroitly led up to ask for the particular article produced, by a quantity of preliminary talk about a feat which Madame Blavatsky specially went to the house to perform. A further established opinion with a certain section of the Indian public is, that the brooch which it appears Mrs. Hume gave to her daughter, and which her daughter lost, must have been got from that young lady about a year previously, when she passed through Bombay, where Madame Blavatsky was living, on her way to England. The young lady's testimony to the effect that she lost the brooch before she went to Bombay, or ever saw Madame Blavatsky, is a little feature of this hypothesis which its contented framers do not care to enquire into. Nor do persons who think the fact that the brooch once belonged to Mrs. Hume's daughter, and that this young lady once saw Madame Blavatsky at Bombay, sufficiently "suspicious" to wipe out the effect of the whole incident as described above-ever attempt, as far as I have discerned, to trace out a coherent chain of events as illuminated by their suspicions, or to compare these with the circumstances of the brooch's actual recovery. No care, however, to arrange the circumstances of an occult demonstration so that the possibility of fraud and delusion may really be excluded, is sufficient to exclude the imputation of this afterwards by people for whom any argument, however illogical really, is good enough to attack a strange idea with.

As regards the witnesses of the brooch phenomenon the conditions were so perfect that when they were speculating as to the objections which might be raised by the public when the story should come to be told, they did not foresee either of the objections actually raised afterwards—the leading up in conversation theory, and the theory about Miss Hume having—put Madame Blavatsky in possession of the brooch. They knew that there had been no previous conversation at all about the brooch or any other proposed feat, that the idea about getting something Mrs. Hume should ask for, arose all in a moment, and that almost immediately afterwards, the brooch was named. As for Miss Hume having unconsciously contributed to the production of the phenomenon, it did not occur to the witnesses that this would be suggested, because they did not foresee that anyone could be so foolish as to shut their eyes to the important circumstances, to concentrate their attention entirely on one of quite minor importance. As the statement itself says, even supposing, which is practically impossible, that the brooch could have passed into Madame Blavatsky's possession in a natural way, she could not possibly have foreseen that it would have been asked for.

The only conjectures the witnesses could frame to explain beforehand the tolerably certain result that the public at large would refuse to be convinced by the brooch incident, were that they might be regarded as misstating the facts and omitting some which the superior intelligence of their critics—as their critics would regard the matter—would see to upset the significance of the rest, or that Mrs. Hume must be a confederate. Now, this last conjecture, which will no doubt occur to readers in England, had only to be stated, to be, for the other persons concerned in the incident, one of the most amusing results to which it could give rise. We all knew Mrs. Hume to be as little predisposed towards any such a conspiracy as she was morally incapable of the wrongdoing it would involve.

At one stage of the proceedings, moreover, we had considered the question as to the extent to which the conditions of the phenomenon were satisfactory. It had often happened that faults had eventually been found with Madame Blavatsky's phenomena by reason of some oversight in the conditions that had not been thought of at first. One of our friends, therefore, on the occasion I am describing, had suggested, after we rose from the dinner-table, that before going any further the company generally should be asked whether, if the brooch could be produced, that would under the circumstances be a satisfactory proof of occult agency in the matter. We carefully reviewed the matter in which the situation had been developed and we all came to the conclusion that the test, would be absolutely complete, and that on this occasion there was no weak place in the chain of the argument. Then it was that Madame Blavatsky said the brooch would be brought to the garden, and that we could go out and search for it.

An interesting circumstance for those who had already watched some of the other phenomena I have described was this: The brooch, as stated above, was found wrapped up in two cigarette papers, and these, when examined in a full light in the house, were found still to bear the mark of the coin attached to Madame Blavatsky's watch chain, which had been wrapped up in them before they departed on their mysterious errand. They were thus identified for people who had got over the first stupendous difficulty of believing in the possibility of transporting material objects by occult agency as the same papers that had been seen by us at the dinner-table.

The occult transmission of objects to a distance not being, "magic", as Western readers understand the word, is susceptible of some partial explanation even for ordinary readers, for whom the means by which the forces employed are manipulated must remain entirely mysterious. It is not contended that the currents which are made use of, convey the bodies transmitted in a solid mass just as they exist for the senses. The body, to be transmitted, is supposed first to be disintegrated, conveyed on the currents in infinitely minute particles, and then reintegrated at its destination. In the case of the brooch, the first thing to be done must have been to find it. This, however, would simply be a feat of clairvoyance—the scent of the object, so to speak, being taken up from the person who spoke of it and had once possessed it—and there is no clairvoyance of which the western world has any knowledge, comparable in its vivid intensity to the clairvoyance of an adept in occultism. Its resting-place thus discovered, the disintegration process would come into play, and the object desired would be conveyed to the place where the adept engaged with it would choose to have it deposited. The part played in the phenomenon by the cigarette papers would be this: In order that we might be able to find the brooch, it was necessary to connect it by an occult scent with Madame Blavatsky. The cigarette papers, which she always carried about with her, were thus impregnated with her magnetism, and taken from her by the Brother, left an occult trail behind them. Wrapped round the brooch, they conducted this trail to the required spot.

The magnetisation of the cigarette papers always with her, enabled Madame Blavatsky to perform a little feat with them which was found by everyone for whom it was done an exceedingly complete bit of evidence; though here again the superficial resemblance of the experiment to a conjuring trick misled the intelligence of ordinary persons who read about the incidents referred to in the newspapers. The feat itself may be most conveniently discussed by the quotation of three letters, which appeared in the *Pioneer* of the 23rd of October, and were as follows;—

"SIR,

—The account of the discovery of Mrs. Hume's brooch has called forth several letters, and many questions have been asked, some of which I may answer on a future occasion, but I think it only right to first contribute further testimony to the occult powers possessed by Madame Blavatsky. In thus coming before the public, one must be prepared for ridicule, but it is a weapon which we who know something of these matters can well afford to despise. On Thursday last, at about half-past ten o'clock, I was sitting in Madame Blavatsky's room conversing with her, and in a casual way asked her if she would be able to send me anything by occult means when I returned to my home. She said "No", and explained to me some of the laws under which she acts, one being that she must know the place and have been there—the more recently the better—in order to establish a magnetic current: She then recollected that she had been somewhere that morning, and after a moment's reflection remembered whose house it was she had visited.[1] She said she could send a cigarette there, if I would go *at once* to verify the fact. I of course, consented. I must here mention that I had seen her do this kind of thing once before; and the reason she gives for sending *cigarettes* is, that the paper and tobacco being always about her person, are highly magnetised, and therefore more amenable to her power, which she most emphatically declares is not super-natural, but merely the manifestation of laws unknown to us. To continue my story. She took out a cigarette paper and slowly tore oft a corner as zigzag as possible, I never taking my eyes off her hands. She gave me the corner, which I at once put into an envelope, and it never left my possession I can declare. She made the cigarette with the remainder of the paper, She then said she would try an experiment which might not succeed, but the failure would be of no consequence with me. She then most certainly put that cigarette into the fire, and I saw it burn, and I started at once to the gentleman's house, scarcely able to believe that I should find in the place indicated by her the counterpart of the cigarette paper I had with me; but sure enough there it was, and, in the presence of the gentleman and his wife, I opened out the cigarette and found my corner piece fitted exactly. It would be useless to try and explain any theory in connection with these phenomena, and it would be unreasonable to expect anyone to believe in them, unless their own experience had proved the possibility of such wonders. All one asks or expects is, that a few of the more intelligent members of the community may be led to look into the vast amount of evidence now accumulated of the phenomena taking place all over Europe and America. It seems a pity that the majority should be in such utter ignorance of these facts; it is within the power of anyone visiting England to convince himself of their truth.

ALICE GORDON

"Sir,

—I have been asked to give an account of a circumstance which took place in my presence on the 13th instant. On the evening of that day I was sitting alone with Madame Blavatsky and Colonel Olcott in the drawing-room of Mr. Sinnett's house in Simla. After some conversation on various matters, Madame Blavatsky said she would like to try an experiment in a manner which had been suggested to her by Mr. Sinnett. She, therefore, took two cigarette papers from her pocket and marked on each of them a number of parallel lines in pencil. She then tore a piece off the end of each paper across the lines, and gave them to me. At that time Madame Blavatsky was sitting close to me, and I intently watched her proceedings, my eyes being not more than two feet from her hands. She declined to let me mark or tear the papers alleging that if handled by others they would become imbued with their personal magnetism, which would counterset her own. However, the torn pieces were handed directly to me, and I could not observe any opportunity for the substitution of other papers by sleight of hand. The genuineness or otherwise of the phenomena afterwards presented appears to rest on this point. The torn off pieces of the paper remained in my closed left hand until the conclusion of the experiment. Of the larger pieces Madame Blavatsky made two cigarettes, giving the first to me to hold while the other was being made up. I scrutinised this cigarette very attentively, in order to be able to recognise it afterwards. The cigarettes being finished, Madame Blavatsky stood up, and took them between her hands, which she rubbed together. After about twenty or thirty seconds, the grating noise of the paper, at first distinctly audible, ceased. She then said the current[2] is passing round this end of the room, and I can only send them somewhere near here. A moment afterwards she said one had fallen on the piano, the other near that bracket. As I sat on a sofa with my back to the wall, the piano was opposite, and the bracket, supporting a few pieces of china, was to the right, between it and the door. Both were in full view across the rather narrow room. The top of the piano was covered with piles of music books, and it was among these Madame Blavatsky thought a cigarette would be found; The books were removed, one by one, by myself, but without seeing anything. I then opened the piano, and found a cigarette on a narrow shelf inside it. This cigarette I took out and recognised as the one I had held in my hand. The other was found in a covered cup on the bracket. Both cigarettes were still damp where—they had been moistened at the edges in the process of manufacture. I took the cigarettes to a table, without permitting them to be touched or even seen by Madame Blavatsky and Colonel Olcott. On being unrolled and smoothed out, the torn, jagged edges were found to fit exactly to the pieces that I had all this time retained in my hand. The pencil marks also corresponded. It would therefore appear that the papers were actually the same as those I had seen torn. Both the papers are still in my possession. It may be added that Colonel Olcott sat near me with his back to Madame Blavatsky during the experiment, and did not move till it was concluded.

"P. J. MAITLAND, *Captain*."

"SIR,

—With reference to the correspondence now filling your columns, on the subject of Madame Blavatsky's recent manifestations, it may interest your readers if I record a striking incident which took place last week in my presence. I had occasion to call on Madame, and in the course of our interview she tore off a corner from a cigarette paper, asking me to hold the same, which I did. With the remainder of the paper she prepared a cigarette in the ordinary manner, and in a few moments caused this cigarette to disappear from her hands. We were sitting at the time in the drawing-room.

I inquired if it were likely to find this cigarette again, and after a short pause Madame requested me to accompany her into the dining-room, where the cigarette would be found on the top of a curtain hanging over the window. By means of a table and a chair placed thereon, I was enabled with some difficulty to reach and take down a cigarette from the place indicated. This cigarette I opened, and found the paper to correspond exactly with that I had seen a few minutes before in the drawing-room. That is to say, the corner-piece, which I had retained in my possession, fitted exactly into the jagged edges of the torn paper in which the tobacco had been rolled. To the best of my belief, the test was as complete and satisfactory as any test can be. I refrain from giving my opinion as to the causes which produced the effect, feeling sure that your readers who take an interest in these phenomena will prefer exercising their own judgement in the matter. I merely give you an unvarnished statement of what I saw. I may be permitted to add I am not a member of the Theosophist Society, nor, so far as I know, am I biassed in favour of occult science, although a warm sympathiser with the proclaimed objects of the Society over which Colonel Olcott presides.

"CHARLES FRANCIS MASSY."

Of course, anyone familiar with conjuring will be aware that an imitation of this "trick" can be arranged by a person gifted with a little sleight of hand. You take two pieces of paper, and tear off a corner of both together, so that the jags of both are the same. You make a cigarette with one piece, and put it in the place where you mean to have it ultimately found. You then hold the other piece underneath the one you tear in presence of the spectator, slip in one of the already torn corners into his hand instead of that he sees you tear, make your cigarette with the other part of the original piece, dispose of that anyhow you please, and allow the prepared cigarette to be found. Other variations of the system may be readily imagined, and for persons who have not actually seen Madame Blavatsky do one of her cigarette feats it may be useless to point out that she does not do them as a conjuror would, and that the spectator, if he is gifted with ordinary common sense, can never have the faintest shadow of a doubt about the corner given to him being the corner torn off—a certainty which the pencil—marks upon it, drawn before his eyes, would enhance, if that were necessary. However, as I say, though experience shows me that the outsider is prone to regard the little cigarette phenomenon as "suspicious," it has never failed to be regarded as convincing by the most acute people among those who have witnessed it. With all phenomena, however, stupidity on the part of the observer will defeat any attempt to reach his understanding, no matter how perfect the tests supplied.

I realise this more fully now than at the time of which I am writing. Then I was chiefly anxious to get experiments arranged, which should be really complete in their details and leave no opening for the suggestion even of imposture. It was "an uphill struggle first, because Madame Blavatsky was intractable and excitable as an experimentalist, and herself no more than the recipient of favours from the Brothers in reference to the greater phenomena. And it seemed to me conceivable that the Brothers might themselves not always realise precisely the frame of mind in which persons of European training approached the consideration of such miracles as these with which we were dealing, so that they did not always make sufficient allowance for the necessity of rendering their test phenomena quite perfect and unassailable in all minor details. I knew, of course, that they were not primarily anxious to convince the commonplace world of anything whatever; but still they frequently did assist Madame Blavatsky to produce phenomena that had no other motive except the production of an effect on the minds of people belonging to the outer world; and it seemed to me that under these circumstances they might just as well do something that would leave no room for the imputation even of any trickery.

One day, therefore, I asked Madame Blavatsky whether if I wrote a letter to one of the Brothers explaining my views, she could get it delivered for me. I hardly thought this was probable, as I knew how very unapproachable the Brothers generally are; but as she said that at any rate she would try, I wrote a letter, addressing it "to the Unknown Brother," and gave it to her to see if any result would ensue. It was a happy inspiration that induced me to do this, for out of that small beginning has arisen the most interesting correspondence in which I have ever been privileged to engage—a correspondence which, I am happy to say, still promises to continue, and the existence of which, more than any experiences of phenomena which I have had, though the most wonderful of these are yet to be described, is the *raison d'être* of this little book.

The idea I had specially in my mind when I wrote the letter above referred to, was that of all test phenomena one could wish for, the best would be the production in our presence in India of a copy of the London *Times* of that day's date. With such a piece of evidence in my hand, I argued, I would undertake to convert everybody in Simla who was capable of linking two ideas together, to a belief in the possibility of obtaining by occult agency physical results which were beyond the control of ordinary science. I am sorry that I have not kept copies of the letter itself nor of my own subsequent letters, as they would have helped to elucidate the replies in a convenient way; but I did not at the time foresee the developments to which they would give rise and, after all, the interest of the correspondence turns almost entirely on the letters I received: only in a very small degree on those I sent.

A day or two elapsed before I heard anything of the fate of my letter, but Madame Blavatsky then informed me that I was to have an answer. I afterwards learned that she had not been able at first to find a Brother willing to receive the communication. Those whom she first applied to declined to be troubled with the matter. At last her psychological telegraph brought her a favourable answer from one of the Brothers with whom she had not for some time been in communication. He would take the letter and reply to it.

Hearing this, I at once regretted that I had not written at greater length, arguing my view of the required concession more fully. I wrote again, therefore, without waiting for the actual receipt of the expected letter.

A day or two after I found one evening on my writing-table the first letter sent me by my new correspondent. I may here explain, what I learned afterwards, that he was a native of the Punjab who was attracted to occult studies from his earliest boyhood. He was sent to Europe while still a youth at the intervention of a relative—himself an occultist—to be educated in Western knowledge, and since then has been fully initiated in the greater knowledge of the East. From the self complacent point of view of the ordinary European this will seem a strange reversal of the proper order of things, but I need not stop to examine that consideration now.

My correspondent is known to me as the Mahatma Koot Hoomi. This is his "Tibetan Mystic name "—occultists, it would seem, taking new names on initiation—a practice which has no doubt given rise to similar customs which we find perpetuated here and there in ceremonies of the Roman Catholic church.

The letter I received began, *in medias res*, about the phenomenon I had professed. "Precisely," the Mahatma wrote, "because the test of the London newspaper would close the mouths of the sceptics, "it was inadmissible." See it in what light you will, the world is yet in its first stage of disenthralment.... hence unprepared. Very true we work by natural, not supernatural, means and laws. But as on the one hand science would find itself unable, in its present state, to account for the wonders given in its name, and on the other the ignorant masses would still be left to view the phenomenon in the light of a miracle, everyone who would thus be made a witness to the occurrence would be thrown off his balance, and the result would be deplorable. Believe me it would be so especially for yourself, who originated the idea, and for the devoted woman who so foolishly rushes into the wide, open door leading to notoriety. This door, though opened by so friendly a hand as yours, would prove very soon a trap—and a fatal one, indeed, for her. And such is not surely your object...Were we to accede to your desires know you really what consequences would follow in the trail of success? The inexorable shadow which follows all human innovations moves on, yet few are they who are ever conscious of its approach and dangers. What are, then, they to expect who would offer the world an innovation which, owing to human ignorance, if believed in, will surely be attribute to those dark agencies the two-thirds of humanity believe in and dread as yet?.... The success of an attempt of such a kind as the one you propose must be calculated and based upon a thorough knowledge of the people around you. It depends entirely upon the social and moral conditions of the people in their bearing on these deepest and most mysterious questions which can stir the human mind—the deific powers in man and the possibilities contained in Nature. How many even of your best friends, of those who surround you, are more than superficially interested in these abstruse problems? You could count them upon the fingers of your right hand. Your race boasts of having liberated in their century the genius so long imprisoned in the narrow vase of dogmatism and intolerance—the genius of knowledge, wisdom, and free thought. It says that, in their turn, ignorant prejudice and religious bigotry, bottled up like the wicked *djin* of old, and sealed by the Solomons of science, rest at the bottom of the sea, and can never, escaping to the surface again, reign over the world as in the days of old: that the public mind is quite free, in short, and ready to accept any demonstrated truth. Ay, but is it verily so, my respected friend? Experimental knowledge does not quite date from 1662, when Bacon, Robert Boyle, and the. Bishop of Chester transformed under the royal charter their 'invisible college' into a society for the promotion of experimental science. Ages before the Royal Society found itself becoming a reality upon the plan of the 'Prophetic Scheme,' an innate longing for the hidden, a passionate love for, and the study of, Nature, had led men in every generation to try and fathom her secrets deeper than their neighbours did. *Roma ante Romulum fuit* is an axiom taught us in your English schools. The *Vril* of the *Coming Race* was the common property of races now extinct. And as the very existence of those gigantic ancestors of ours is now questioned-though in the Himavats, on the very territory belonging to you, we have a cave full of the skeletons of these giants—and their huge frames, when found, are invariably regarded as isolated freaks of Nature—so the *Vril*, or *akas* as we call it, is looked upon as an impossibility—a myth. And without a thorough knowledge of akas—its combinations and properties, how can science hope to account for such phenomena? We doubt not but the men of your science are open to conviction; yet facts must be first demonstrated to them; they must first have become their own property, have proved amenable to their modes of investigation, before you find them ready to admit them as facts. If you but look into the preface to the *Micrographia*, you will find, in Hookes' suggestions, that the intimate relations of object were of less account in his eyes than their external operation on the senses, and Newton's fine discoveries found in him their greatest opponent. The modern Hookeses are many. Like this learned but ignorant man of old, your modern men of science are less anxious to suggest a physical connection of facts which might unlock for them many an occult force in Nature, as to provide a convenient classification of scientific experiments, so that the most essential quality of a hypothesis is, not that it should be *true*, but only *plausible*, in their opinion.

"So far for science—as much as we know of it. As for human nature in general it is the same now as it was a million of years ago. Prejudice, based upon selfishness, a general unwillingness to give up an established order of things for new modes of life and thought—and occult study requires all that and much more—pride and stubborn resistance to truth, if it but upsets their previous notions of things—such are the characteristics of your age......

What, then, would be the results of the most astounding phenomena supposing we consented to have them produced? However successful, danger would be growing proportionately with success. No choice would soon remain but to go on, ever *crescendo*, or to fall in this endless struggle with prejudice and ignorance, killed by your own weapons. Test after test would be required, and would have to be furnished; every subsequent phenomenon expected to be more marvellous than the preceding one. Your daily remark is, that one cannot be expected to believe unless he becomes an eyewitness. Would the lifetime of a man suffice to satisfy the whole world of sceptics? It may an easy matter to increase the original number of believers at Simla to hundreds and thousands. But what of the hundreds of millions of those who could not be made eyewitnesses? The ignorant, unable to grapple with the invisible operators, might some day vent their rage on the visible agents at work; the higher and educated classes would go on disbelieving, as ever, tearing you to shreds as before. In common with many, you blame us for our great secrecy. Yet we know something of human nature, for the experience of long centuries—ay, ages, has taught us. And we know that so long as science has anything to learn, and a shadow of religious dogmatism lingers in the hearts of the multitude, the world's prejudices have to be conquered step by step, not at a rush. As hoary antiquity had more than one Socrates, so the dim future will give birth to more than one martyr. Enfranchised Science contemptuously turned away her face from the Copernican opinion renewing the theories of Aristarchus Samius, who 'affirmeth that the earth moveth circularly about her own centre', years before the Church sought to sacrifice Galileo as a *holocaust* to the Bible. The ablest mathematician at the Court of Edward VI., Robert Recorde, was left to starve in jail by his colleagues, who laughed at his *Castle of Knowledge*, declaring his discoveries vain fantasies All this is old history, you will think. Verily so, but the chronicles of our modern days do not differ very essentially from their predecessors. And we have but to bear in mind the recent persecutions of mediums in England, the burning of supposed witches and sorcerers in South America, Russia, and the frontiers of Spain, to assure ourselves that the only salvation of the genuine proficient in occult sciences lies in the scepticism of the public: the charlatans and the jugglers are the natural shields of the adepts. The public safety is only ensured by our keeping secret the terrible weapons which might otherwise be used against it, and which, as you have been told, become deadly in the hands of the wicked and selfish."

The remainder of the letter is concerned chiefly with personal matters, and need not be here reproduced. I shall, of course, throughout my quotations from letters, leave out passages which, specially addressed to myself, have no immediate bearing on the public argument. The reader must be fearful to remember, however, as I now most unequivocally affirm, that I shall in no case *alter* one syllable of the passages actually quoted. It is important to make this declaration very emphatically, because the more my readers may be acquainted with India, the less they will be willing to believe, except on the most positive testimony, that the letters from the Mahatma, as I now publish them, have been written by a native of India. That such is the fact, however, is beyond dispute.

I replied to the letter above quoted at some length, arguing, if I remember rightly, that the European mind was less hopelessly intractable than Koot Hoomi represented it. His second letter was as follows:—

"We will be at cross purposes in our correspondence until it has been made entirely plain that occult science has its own methods of research, as fixed and arbitrary as the methods of its antithesis, physical science, are in their way. If the latter has its dicta, so also have the former; and he who would cross the boundary of the unseen world can no more prescribe how he will proceed, than the traveller who tries to penetrate to the inner subterranean recesses of L'Hassa the Blessed could show the way to his guide. The mysteries never were, never can be, put within the reach of the general public, not, at least, until that longed—for day when our religious philosophy becomes universal. At no time have more than a scarcely appreciable minority of men possessed Nature's secret, though multitudes have witnessed the practical evidences of the possibility of their possession. The adept is the rare efflorescence of a generation of inquirers; and to become one, he must obey the inward impulse of his soul, irrespective of the prudential considerations of worldly science or sagacity. Your desire is to be brought to communicate with one of us directly, without the agency of either Madame Blavatsky or any medium. Your idea would be, as I understand it, to obtain such communications, either by letter, as the present one, or by audible words, so as to be guided by one of us in the management, and principally in the instruction of the Society. You seek all this, and yet, as you say yourself, hitherto you have not found sufficient reasons to even give up your modes of life, directly hostile to such modes of communication. This is hardly reasonable. He who would lift up high the banner of mysticism and proclaim its reign near at hand must give the example to others. He must be the first to change his modes of life, and, regarding the study of the occult mysteries as the upper step in the ladder of knowledge, must loudly proclaim it such, despite exact science and the opposition of society. The 'kingdom of Heaven is obtained by force', say the Christian mystics. It is but with armed hand, and ready to either conquer or perish, that the modern mystic can hope to achieve his object.

"My first answer covered, I believe, most of the questions contained in your second and even third letter. Having, then, expressed therein my opinion that the world in general was unripe for any too staggering proof of occult power, there but remains to deal with the isolated individuals who seek, like yourself, to penetrate behind the veil of matter into the "world of primal causes ---- *i.e.*, we need only consider now the cases of yourself and Mr. -----."

I should here explain that one of my friends at Simla, deeply interested with me in the progress of this investigation, had, on reading Koot Hoomi's first letter to me, addressed my correspondent himself. More favourably circumstanced than I, for such an enterprise, he had even proposed to make a complete sacrifice of his other pursuits, to pass away into any distant seclusion, which might he appointed for the purpose, where he might, if accepted as a pupil in occultism, learn enough to return to the world armed with powers which would enable him to demonstrate the realities of spiritual development and the errors of modern materialism, and then devote his life to the task of combating modern incredulity and leading men to a practical comprehension of a better life. I resume the letter:—

"This gentleman also has done me the great honour to address me by name, offering to me a few questions, and stating the conditions upon which he would be willing to work for us seriously. But your motives and aspirations being of diametrically opposite character, and hence leading to different results, I must reply to each of you separately."

"The first and chief consideration in determining us to accept or reject your offer lies in the inner motive which propels you to seek our instruction and, in a certain sense, our guidance; the latter in all cases under reserve, as I understand it, and therefore remaining a question independent of aught else. Now, what are your motives? I may try to define them in their general aspects, leaving details for further consideration. They are —(1) The desire to see positive and unimpeachable proofs that there really are forces in Nature of which science knows nothing; (2) The hope to appropriate them some day—the sooner the better, for you do not like to wait—so as to enable yourself; (*a*) to demonstrate their existence to a few chosen Western minds; (*b*) to contemplate future life as an objective reality built upon the rock of knowledge, not of faith; and (*c*) to finally learn—most important this, among all your motives, perhaps, though the most occult and the best guarded—the whole truth about our lodges and ourselves; to get, in short, the positive assurance that the 'Brothers,' of whom everyone hears so much and sees so little, are rare entities, not fictions of a disordered, hallucinated brain. Such, viewed in their best light, appear to us your motives for addressing me. And in the same spirit do I answer them, hoping that my sincerity will not be interpreted in a wrong way, or attributed to anything like an unfriendly spirit.

"To our minds, then, these motives, sincere and worthy of every serious consideration from the worldly standpoint, appear *selfish*. (You have to pardon me what you might view as crudeness of language, if your desire is that which you really profess—to learn truth and get instruction from us who belong to quite a different world from the one you move in.) They are selfish, because you must be aware that the chief object of the Theosophical Society is not so much to gratify individual aspirations as to serve our fellowmen, and the real value of this term 'selfish,' which may jar upon your ear, has a peculiar significance with us which it cannot have with you; therefore, to begin with, you must not accept it otherwise than in the former sense. Perhaps you will better appreciate our meaning when told that in our view the highest aspirations for the welfare of humanity become tainted with selfishness, if, in the mind of the philanthropist, there lurks the shadow of a desire for self-benefit, or a tendency to do injustice, even where these exist unconsciously to himself. Yet you have ever discussed but to put down, the idea of a Universal Brotherhood, questioned its usefulness, and advised to remodel the Theosophical Society on the principle of a college for the special study of occultism...

"Having disposed of personal motives, let us analyse your terms for helping us to do public good. Broadly stated, these terms are—first, that an independent Anglo-Indian Theosophical Society shall be founded through your kind services, in the management of which neither of our present representatives shall have any voice;[3] And second, that one of us shall take the new body 'under his patronage,' be 'in free and direct communication with its leaders,' and afford them 'direct proof that he really possessed that superior knowledge of the forces of Nature and the attributes of the human soul which would inspire them with proper confidence in his leadership.' I have copied your own words so as to avoid inaccuracy in defining the position.

"From your point of view, therefore, those terms may seem so very reasonable as to provoke no dissent, and, indeed, a majority of your countrymen—if not of Europeans—might share that opinion. What, will you say, can be more reasonable than to ask that that teacher anxious to disseminate his knowledge, and pupil offering him to do so, should be brought face to face, and the one give the experimental proof to the other that his instructions were correct? Man of the world, living in, and in full sympathy with it, you are undoubtedly right. But the men of this other world of ours, untutored in your modes of thought, and, who find it very hard at times to follow and appreciate the latter, can hardly be blamed for not responding as heartily to your suggestions as in your opinion they deserve. The first and most important of our objections is to be found in our *rules*. True, we have our schools and teachers, our neophytes and 'shaberons' (superior adepts) and the door is always opened to the right man who knocks. And we invariably welcome the new comer; only, instead of going over to him, he has to come to us. More than that, unless he has reached that point in the path of occultism from which return is impossible by his having irrevocably pledged himself to our Association, we never except in cases of utmost moment visit him or even cross the threshold of his door in visible appearance.

"Is any of you so eager for knowledge and the beneficent powers it confers, as to be ready to leave your world and come into ours? Then let him come, but he must not think to return until the seal of the mysteries has locked his lips even against the chances of his own weakness or indiscretion. Let him come by all means as the pupil to the master, and without conditions, or let him wait, as so many others have, and be satisfied with such crumbs of knowledge as may fall in his way.

"And supposing you were thus to come, as two of your own countrymen have already—as Madame B. did and Mr. O. wil—supposing you were to abandon all for the truth; to toil wearily for years up the hard, steep road, not daunted by obstacles, firm under every temptation; were to faithfully keep within your heart the secrets entrusted to you as a trial; had worked with all your energies and unselfishly to spread the truth and provoke men to correct thinking and a correct life—would you consider it just, if, after all your efforts, we were to grant to Madame B., or Mr. O. as 'outsiders' the terms you now ask for yourselves. Of these two persons, one has already given three-fourths of a life, the other six years of manhood's prime to us, and both will so labour to the close of their days; though ever working for their merited reward, yet never demanding it, nor murmuring when disappointed. Even though they respectively could accomplish far less then they do, would it not be a palpable injustice to ignore them in an important field of Theosophical effort? Ingratitude is not among our vices, nor do we imagine you would wish to advise it.

"Neither of them has the least inclination to interfere with the management of the contemplated Anglo-Indian Branch, nor dictate its officers. But the new Society, if formed at all, must, though bearing a distinctive title of its own, be, in fact, a branch of the parent body, as is the British Theosophical Society at London, and contribute to its vitality and usefulness by promoting its leading idea of a Universal Brotherhood, and in other practicable ways.

"Badly as the phenomena may have been shown, there have still been, as yourself admit, certain ones that are unimpeachable. The 'raps on the table when no one touches it', and the 'bell sounds in the air,' have, you say, always been regarded as satisfactory, etc. etc. From this, you reason that good test phenomena 'may easily be multiplied *ad infinitum*.' So they can—in any place where our magnetic and other conditions are constantly offered, and where we do not have to act with and through an enfeebled female body, in which, as we might say, a vital cyclone is raging much of the time. But imperfect as may be our visible agent, yet she is the best available at present, and her phenomena have for about half a century astonished and baffled some of the cleverest minds of the age...."

"Two or three little notes which I next received from the Mahatma had reference to an incident I must now describe, the perfection of which as a test phenomenon appears to me more complete than that of any other I have yet described. It is worth notice, by-the-bye, that although the circumstances of this incident were related in the Indian papers at the time, the happy company of scoffers who flooded the Press with their simple comments on the brooch phenomenon, never cared to discuss "the pillow incident."

Accompanied by our guests, we went to have lunch one day on the top of a neighbouring hill, The night before, I had had reason to think that my correspondent, Koot Hoomi, had been in what, for the purpose of the present explanation, I may call subjective communication with me. I do not go into any details, because it is unnecessary to trouble the general reader with impressions of that sort, After discussing the subject in the morning, I found on the hall-table a note from Koot Hoomi, in which he promised to give me something on the hill which should be a token of his (astral) presence near me the previous night.

We went to our destination, camped down on the top of the hill, and were engaged on our lunch, when Madame Blavatsky said Koot Hoomi was asking where we would like to find the object he was going to send me. Let it be understood that up to this moment there had been no conversation in regard to the phenomenon I was expecting. The usual suggestion will, perhaps, be made that Madame Blavatsky "led up" to the choice I actually made. The fact of the matter was simply that in the midst of altogether other talk Madame Blavatsky pricked up her ears on hearing her occult voice—at once told me what was the question asked, and did not contribute to the selection made by one single remark on the subject, In fact, there was no general discussion, and it was by an absolutely spontaneous choice of my own that I said, after a little reflection, "inside that cushion," pointing to one against which one of the ladies present was leaning. I had no sooner uttered the words than my wife cried out, "Oh no, let it be inside mine," or words to that effect. I said, "very well, inside my wife's cushion;" Madame Blavatsky asked the Mahatma by her own methods if that would do, and received an affirmative reply. My liberty of choice as regards the place where the object should be found was thus absolute and unfettered by conditions. The most natural choice for me to have made under the circumstances, and having regard to our previous experiences, would have been up some particular tree, or buried in a particular spot of the ground; but the inside of a sewn-up cushion, fortuitously chosen on the spur of a moment, struck me, as my eye happened to fall upon the cushion I mentioned first, as a particularly good place; and when I had started the idea of a cushion, my wife's amendment to the original proposal was really an improvement, for the particular cushion then selected had never been for a moment out of her own possession all the morning. It was her usual jampan cushion; she had been leaning against it all the way from home, and was leaning against it still, as her jampan had been carried right up to the top of the hill, and she had continued to occupy it. The cushion itself was very firmly made of worsted work and velvet, and had been in our possession for years. It always remained, when we were at home, in the drawing-room, in a conspicuous corner of a certain sofa whence, when my wife went out, it would be taken to her jampan and again brought in on her return.

When the cushion was agreed to, my wife was told to put it under her rug, and she did this with her own hands, inside her jampan. It may have been there about a minute, when Madame Blavatsky said we could set to work to cut it open. I did this with a penknife, and it was a work of some time, as the cushion was very securely sewn all round, and very strongly, so that it had to be cut open almost stitch by stitch, and no tearing was possible. When one side of the cover was completely ripped up, we found that the feathers of the cushion were enclosed in a separate inner case, also sewn round all the edges. There was nothing to be found between the inner cushion and the outer case; so we proceeded to rip up the inner cushion; and this done, my wife searched among the feathers.

The first thing she found was a little three-cornered note, addressed to me in the now familiar handwriting of my occult correspondent. It ran as follows:

"MY DEAR BROTHER,

—This brooch, N°. 2, is placed in this very strange place, simply to show you how very easily a real phenomenon is produced, and how still easier it is to suspect its genuineness. Make of it what you like, even to classing me with confederates.

"The difficulty you spoke of last night with respect to the interchange of our letters, I will try to remove. One of our pupils will shortly visit Lahore and the N. W. P.; and an address will be sent to you which you can always use; unless, indeed, you really would prefer corresponding through -----pillows! Please to remark that the present is not dated from a Lodge, but from a Kashmere valley."

While I was reading this note, my wife discovered, by further search among the feathers, the brooch referred to, one of her own, it very old and very familiar brooch which she generally left on her dressing-table when it was not in use. It would have been impossible to invent or imagine a proof of occult power, in the nature of mechanical proofs, more irresistible and convincing than this incident was for us who had personal knowledge of the various circumstances described. The whole force and significance to us of the brooch thus returned, hinged on to my subjective impressions of the previous night. The reason for selecting the brooch as a thing to give us, dated no earlier than then. On the hypothesis, therefore, idiotic hypothesis as it would be on all grounds, that the cushion must have been got at by Madame Blavatsky, it must have been got at since I spoke of my impressions that morning, shortly after breakfast; but from the time of getting up that morning, Madame Blavatsky had hardly been out of our sight, and had been sitting with my wife in the drawing-room. She had been doing this, by-the-by, against the grain, for she had writing which she wanted to do in her own room, but she had been told by her voices to go and sit in the drawing-room with my wife that morning, and had done so, grumbling at the interruption of her work, and wholly unable to discern any motive for the order. The motive was afterwards clear enough, and had reference to the intended phenomenon. It was desirable that we should have no *arrière pensée* in our minds as to what Madame Blavatsky might possibly have been doing during the morning, in the event of the incident taking such a turn as to make that a factor in determining its genuineness. Of course, if the selection of the pillow could have been foreseen, it would have been unnecessary to victimise our "old Lady," as we generally called her. The presence of the famous pillow itself, with my wife all the morning in the drawing-room, would have been enough. But perfect liberty of choice was to be left to me in selecting a *cache* for the brooch; and the pillow can have been in nobody's mind, any more than in my own, beforehand.

The language of the note given above embodied many little points which had a meaning for us. All through, it bore indirect reference to the conversation that had taken place at our dinner-table the previous evening. I had been talking of the little traces here and there which the long letters from Koot Hoomi bore, showing in spite of their splendid mastery over the language and the vigour of their style, a turn or two of expression that an Englishman would not have made use of; for example, in the form of address, which in the two letters already quoted had been tinged with Orientalism. "But what should he have written?" somebody asked, and I had said, "under similar circumstances an Englishman would probably have written simply: "My dear Brother." Then the allusion to the Kashmir Valley as the place from which the letter was written, instead of from a Lodge, was au allusion to the same conversation; and the underlining of the "k" was another, as Madame Blavatsky had been saying that Koot Hoomi's spelling of "Scepticism" with a "k" was not an Americanism in his case, but due to a philological whim of his.

The incidents of the day were not quite over, even when the brooch was found; for that evening, after we had gone home, there fell from my napkin, after I had unfolded it at dinner, a little note, too private and personal to be reprinted fully, but part of which I am impelled to quote, for the sake of the allusion it contains, to occult *modus operandi*. I must explain that, before starting for the hill, I had penned a few lines of thanks for the promise contained in the note then received as described. This note I gave to Madame Blavatsky, to despatch by occult methods if she had an opportunity. And she carried it in her hand as she and my wife went on in advance, in jampans, along the Simla Mall, not finding an opportunity until about halfway to our destination. Then she got rid of the note, occultism only knows how. This circumstance had been spoken of at the picnic; and as I was opening the note found in the pillow, someone suggested that it would, perhaps, be found to contain an answer to my note just sent. It did not contain any allusion to this, as the reader will be already aware.

The note I received at dinnertime said:—"A few words more. Why should you have felt disappointed at not receiving a direct reply to your last note. It was received in my room about half a minute after the currents for the production of the pillow *dak*, had been set ready, and in full play. And there was no necessity for an answer..."

It seemed to bring one in imagination one step nearer a realisation of the state of the facts to hear "the currents" employed to accomplish what would have been a miracle for all the science of Europe, spoken of thus familiarly.

A miracle for all the science of Europe, and as hard a fact for us, nevertheless, as the room in which we sat. We knew that the phenomenon we had seen was a wonderful reality; that the thought-power of a man in Kashmir had picked up a material object from a table in Simla, and, disintegrating it by some process of which Western science does not yet dream, had passed it through other matter, and had there restored it to its original solidarity, the dispersed particles resuming their precise places as before, and reconstituting the object down to every line or scratch upon its surface. (By-the-by, it bore some scratches when it emerged from the pillow which it never bore before—the initials of our friend.) And we knew that written notes on tangible paper had been flashing backwards and forwards that day between our friend and ourselves, though hundreds of miles of Himalayan mountains intervened between us, and had been flashing backwards and forwards with the speed of electricity, And yet we knew that an impenetrable wall, built up of its own prejudice and obstinacy, of its learned ignorance and polished dulness, was established round the minds of scientific men in the West, as a body, across which we should never be able to carry our facts and our experience. And it is with a greater sense of oppression than people who have never been in a similar position will realise, that I now tell the story I have to tell, and know all the while that the solemn accuracy of its minutest detail, the utter truthfulness of every syllable in this record, is little better than incense to my own conscience—that the scientific minds of the West with which of all cultivated minds my own has hitherto been most in sympathy, will be closed to my testimony most hopelessly. "Though one should rise from the dead," etc.. It is the old story. It is the old story, at all events as regards the crashing results on opinion which such evidence as that I have been giving, ought to have. The smile of incredulity which thinks itself so wise and is so foolish, the suspicions which flatter themselves they are so cunning, and are really the fruit of so much dulness, will gleam over these pages, and wither all their meaning—for the readers who smile. But I suppose that Koot Hoomi is not only right in declaring the world unripe as yet for too staggering a proof of occult power, but also in taking a friendly interest, as it will be seen presently that he does, in the little book I am writing, as one of the influences which bit by bit may sap the foundations of dogmatism and stupidity, on which science, which thinks itself so liberal, has latterly become so firmly rooted.

The next letter—the third long one—that I received from the Mahatma, reached me shortly after my return for the cold weather to Allahabad. But I received one communication from him—a telegram—before its arrival, on the day of my own return to Allahabad. This telegram, of no great importance as regards its contents, which were little more than an expression of thanks for some letters I had written in the papers, was, nevertheless, of great interest indirectly, affording me, as it ultimately did, evidence of a kind which could appeal to other minds besides my own, that Koot Hoomi's letters were not, as some ingenious persons may have been inclined to imagine—in spite of various mechanical difficulties in the way of the theory—the work of Madame Blavatsky. For me, knowing her as intimately as I did, the inherent evidence of the style was enough to make the suggestion that she might have written them, a mere absurdity. And, if it is urged that the authoress of "Isis Unveiled" has certainly a command of language which renders it difficult to say what she could not write, the answer is simple. In the production of this book she was so largely helped by the Brothers, that great portions of it are not really her work at all. She never makes any disguise of this fact, though it is one of a kind which it is useless for her to proclaim to the world at large, as it would be perfectly unintelligible, except to persons who knew something of the external facts, at all events, of occultism. Koot Hoomi's letters, as I say, are perfectly unlike her own style. But, in reference to some of them, receiving them as I did while she was in the house with me, it was not mechanically possible that she might have been the writer. Now, the telegram I received at Allahabad, which was wired to me from Jhelum, was in reply specially to a letter I addressed to Koot Hoomi just before leaving Simla, and enclosed to Madame Blavatsky, who had started some days previously, and was then at Amritsur. She received the letter, with its enclosure, at Amritsur on the 27th of October, as I came to know, not merely from knowing when I sent it, but positively by means of the envelope which she returned to me at Allahabad by direction of Koot Hoomi, not in the least knowing why he wished it sent to me. I did not at first see what on earth was the use of the old envelope to me, but I put it away and afterwards obtained the clue to the idea in Koot Hoomi's mind when Madame Blavatsky wrote me word that he wanted me to obtain the original of the Jhelum telegram. Through the agency of a friend connected with the administration of the telegraph department, I was enabled eventually to obtain a sight of the original of the telegram—a message of about twenty words; and then I saw the meaning of the envelope. The message was in Koot Hoomi's own handwriting, and it was an answer from Jhelum to a letter which the delivery postmark on the envelope showed to have been delivered at Amritsur on the same day the message was sent. Madame Blavatsky assuredly was herself at Amritsur on that date, seeing large numbers of people there in connection with the work of the Theosophical Society, and the handwriting of Koot Hoomi's letters, nevertheless, appears on a telegram undeniably handed in at the Jhelum office on that date. So although some of Koot Hoomi's letters passed through her hands to me, she is proved not to be their writer, as she is certainly not the producer of their handwriting.

Koot Hoomi was probably himself actually at or near Jhelum at the time, as he came down into the midst of the world for a few days, under peculiar circumstances, to see Madame Blavatsky: the letter I received at Allahabad shortly after my return explained this.

Madame Blavatsky had been deeply hurt by the behaviour of some incredulous persons at Simla whom she had met at our house and elsewhere, who, being unable to assimilate the experience they had had of her phenomena, got by degrees into that hostile frame of mind which is one of the phases of feeling I am now used to seeing developed. Perfectly unable to show how the phenomena can be the result of fraud, but thinking that, because they do not understand them, they must be fraudulent, people of a certain temperament become possessed with the spirit which animated persecution by religious authorities in the infancy of physical science. And, by a piece of bad luck, a gentleman who was thus affected was annoyed at a trifling indiscretion on the part of Colonel Olcott, who, in a letter to one of the Bombay papers, quoted some expressions he had made use of in praise of the Theosophical Society and its good influence on the natives. All the irritation thus set up, worked on Madame Blavatsky's excitable temperament to an extent which only those who know her will be able to imagine. The allusions in Koot Hoomi's letter will now be understood. After some reference to important business with which he had been concerned since writing to me last, Koot Hoomi went on:—

"You see, then, that we have weightier matters than small societies to think about; yet the Theosophical Society must not be neglected. The affair has taken an impulse which, if not well guided, might beget very evil issues. Recall to mind the avalanches of your admired Alps, and remember that at first their mass is small, and their momentum little. A trite comparison, you may say, but I cannot think of a better illustration when viewing the gradual aggregation of trifling events growing into a menacing destiny for the Theosophical Society. It came quite forcibly upon me the other day as I was coming down the defiles of Konenlun—Karakorum you call them —and saw an avalanche tumble. I had gone personally to our chief... and was crossing over to Lhadak on my way home. What other speculations might have followed I cannot say. But just as I was taking advantage of the awful stillness which usually follows such cataclysms, to get a clearer view of the present situation, and the disposition of the 'mystics' at Simla, I was rudely recalled to my senses. A familiar voice, as shrill as the one attributed to Saraswati's peacock—which, if we may credit tradition, frightened off the King of the Nagas—shouted along the currents—"Koot Hoomi,........ come quicker and help me!" and, in her excitement, forgot she was speaking English. I must say that the "old Lady's" telegrams do strike one like stones from a catapult.

"What could I do but come. Argument through space with one who was in cold despair and in a state of moral chaos, was useless. So I determined to emerge from a seclusion of many years, and spend some time with her to comfort her as well as I could. But our friend is not one to cause her mind to reflect the philosophical resignation of Marcus Aurelius. The Fates never wrote, that she could say:—'It is a royal thing when one is doing good to hear evil spoken of himself.' I had come for a few days, but now find that I myself cannot endure for any length of time the stifling magnetism even of my own countrymen. I have seen some of our proud old Sikhs drunk and staggering over the marble pavement of their sacred temple. I have heard an English-speaking Vakil declaim against *Yog Vidya* and Theosophy as a delusion and a lie, declaring that English science had emancipated them from such degrading superstitions, and saying that it was an insult to India to maintain that the dirty Yogees and Sunuyasis knew anything about the mysteries of Nature, or that any living man can, or ever could, perform any phenomena. I turn my face homeward tomorrow.

".........I have telegraphed you my thanks for your obliging compliance with my wishes in the matter you allude to in your letter of the 24th..... Received at Amritsur, on the 27th, at 2 P.M. I got your letter about thirty miles beyond Rawul Pinder, five minutes later, and had an acknowledgement wired to you from Jhelum at 4 P. M. on the same afternoon. Our modes of accelerated delivery and quick communications[4] are not, then, as you will see, to be despised by the Western world, or even the Aryan English-speaking and sceptical Vakils.

"I could not ask a more judicial frame of mind in an ally than that in which you are beginning to find yourself. My brother, you have already changed your attitude toward us in a distinct degree. What is to prevent a perfect mutual understanding one day?...... It is not possible that there should be much more at best than a. benevolent neutrality shown by your people towards ours. There is so very minute a point of contact between the two civilisations they respectively represent, that one might almost say they could not touch at all. Nor would they, but for the few—shall I say eccentrics?—who, like you, dream better and bolder dreams than the rest, and, provoking thought, bring the two together by their own admirable audacity."

The letter before me at present is occupied so much with matters personal to myself, that I can only make quotations here and there; but these are specially interesting, as investing with an air of reality subjects which are generally treated in "vague and pompous language. Koot Hoomi was anxious to guard me from idealising the Brothers too much on the strength of my admiration for their marvellous powers.

"Are you certain," he writes, "that the pleasant impression you now may have from our correspondence would not instantly be destroyed upon seeing me. And which of our holy *shaberons* has had the benefit of even the little university education and inkling of European manners that has fallen to my share. An instance: I desired Madame Blavatsky to select, among the two or three Aryian Punjabees who study Yog Vidya and are natural mystics, one whom, without disclosing myself to him too much, I could designate as an agent between yourself and us, and whom I was anxious to despatch to you with a letter of introduction, and have him to speak to you of Yoga and its practical effects. This young gentleman, who is as pure as purity itself, whose aspirations and thoughts are of the most spiritual, ennobling kind, and who, merely through self-exertion, is able to penetrate into the regions of the formless world—this young man is not fit for a drawing-room. Having explained to him that the greatest good might result for his country if he helped you to organise a branch of English mystics, by proving to them practically to what wonderful results led the study of Yog, Madame Blavatsky asked him, in guarded and very delicate terms, to change his dress and turban before starting for Allahabad; for—though she did not give him this reason—they were very dirty and slovenly. You are to tell Mr. Sinnett, she said, that you bring him a letter from the Brother, with whom he corresponds; but if he asks you anything either of him or the other Brothers, answer him simply and truthfully that you are not allowed to expatiate upon the subject. Speak of Yog, and prove to him what powers you have attained. 'This young man who had consented, wrote later on the following curious letter:—'Madame,' he said, 'you who preach the highest standard of morality, of truthfulness, etc., you would have me play the part of an impostor. You ask me to change, my clothes at the risk of giving a false idea of my personality and mystifying the gentleman you send me to. Here is an illustration of the difficulties under which we have to labour. Powerless to send you a neophyte before you have pledged yourself to us, we have to either keep back or despatch to you one who, at best, would shock, if not inspire, you at once with disgust."

The present letter yields only little more that it seems desirable to quote. In a guarded way, Koot Hoomi said that as often as it was practicable to communicate with me, "whether ....by letters (in or out of pillows) or personal visits in astral form, it will be done. But remember," he added, "that Simla is 7,000 feet higher than Allahabad, and the difficulties to be surmounted at the latter are tremendous." To the ordinary mind, feats of " magic " are hardly distinguishable by degrees of difficulty, and the little hint contained in the last sentence may thus help to show that, magical as the phenomena of the Brothers appear (as soon as the dull-witted hypothesis of fraud is abandoned), they are magic of a kind which is amenable to its own laws. Most of the bodies in Nature were elements, in the infancy of chemistry; but in turn the number is reduced by deeper and deeper researches into the law of combinations—and so with magic. To ride the clouds in a basket, or send messages under the sea, would have been magic in one age of the world, but becomes the commonplace of the next. The Simla phenomena are magic for the majority of this generation, but psychological telegraphy itself may become, if not the property of mankind a few generations hence, a fact of science as undeniable as the differential calculus, and known to be attainable by its own appropriate students. That it is easier to accomplish it and cognate achievements, in certain strata of the atmosphere rather than in others, is already a practical suggestion which tends to drag it down from the realms of magic; or, as the same idea might be differently expressed, to lift it towards the region of exact science.

I am here enabled to insert the greater part of a letter addressed by Koot Hoomi to the friend referred to in a former passage, as having opened up a correspondence with him in reference to the idea which he contemplated under certain conditions, of devoting himself entirely to the pursuit of occultism. This letter throws a great deal of light upon some of the metaphysical conceptions of the occultists, and their metaphysics, be it remembered, are a great deal more than abstract speculation.

"DEAR SIR

—Availing of the first moments of leisure to formally answer your letter of the 17th ultimo, I will now report the result of my conference with our chiefs upon the proposition therein contained, trying at the same time to answer all your questions.

"I am first to thank you on behalf of the whole section of our fraternity that is especially interested in the welfare of India for an offer of help whose importance and sincerity no one can doubt. Tracing our lineage through the vicissitudes of Indian civilization from a remote past, we have a love for our motherland no deep and passionate that it has survived even the broadening and cosmopolitanizing (pardon me if that is not an English word) effect of our studies in the laws of Nature. And so I, and every other Indian patriot, feel the strongest gratitude for every kind word or deed that is given in her behalf.

"Imagine, then, that since we are all convinced that the degradation of India is largely due to the suffocation of her ancient spirituality, and that whatever helps to restore that higher standard of thought and morals, must be regenerating in national force, everyone of us would naturally and without urging, be disposed to push forward a society whose proposed formation is under debate, especially if it really is meant to become a society untainted by selfish motive, and whose object is the revival of ancient science, and tendency, to rehabilitate our country in the world's estimation. Take this for granted without further asseverations. But you know, as any man who has read history, that patriots may burst their hearts in vain if circumstances are against them. Sometimes it has happened that no human power, not even the fury and force of the loftiest patriotism, has been able to bend an iron destiny aside from its fixed course, and nations have gone out like torches dropped into the water in the engulfing blackness of ruin. Thus, we who have the sense of our country's fall, though not the power to lift her up at once, cannot do as we would either as to general affairs or this particular one. And with the readiness, but not the right to meet your advances more than half way, we are forced to say that the idea entertained by Mr. Sinnett and yourself is impracticable in part. It is, in a word, impossible for myself or any Brother, or even an advanced neophyte, to be specially assigned and set apart as the guiding spirit or chief of the Anglo-Indian branch. We know it would be a good thing to have you and a few of your colleagues regularly instructed and shown the phenomena and their rationale. For though none but you few would be convinced, still it would be a decided gain to have even a few Englishmen, of first-class ability, enlisted as students of Asiatic Psychology. We are aware of all this, and much more; hence we do not refuse to correspond with, and otherwise help you in various ways. But what we do refuse is, to take any other responsibility upon ourselves than this periodical correspondence and assistance with our advice, and, as occasion favours, such tangible, possibly visible, proofs, as would satisfy you of our presence and interest. To "guide" you we will not consent. However much we may be able to do, yet we can promise only to give you the full measure of your deserts. Deserve much, and we will prove honest debtors; little, and you need only expect a compensating return. This is not a mere text taken from a schoolboy's copybook, though it sounds so, but only the clumsy statement of the law of our order, and we cannot transcend it. Utterly unacquainted with Western, especially English, modes of thought and action, were we to meddle in an organization of such a kind, you would find all your fixed habits and traditions incessantly clashing, if not with the new aspirations themselves, at least with their modes of realisation as suggested by us. You could not get unanimous consent to go even the length you might yourself. I have asked Mr. Sinnett to draft a plan embodying your joint ides for submission to our chiefs, this seeming the shortest way to a mutual agreement. Under our 'guidance' your branch could not live, you not being men to be guided at all in that sense.—Hence the society would be a premature birth and a failure, looking as incongruous as a Paris Daumont drawn by a team of Indian yaks or camels. You ask us to teach you true science—the occult aspect of the known side of Nature; and this you think can be as easily done as asked. You do not seem to realise the tremendous difficulties in the way of imparting even the rudiments of *our* science to those who have been trained in the familiar methods of yours. You do not see that the more you have of the one the less capable you are of instinctively comprehending the other, for a man can only think in his worn grooves, and unless he has the courage to fill up these, and make new ones for himself, he must perforce travel on the old lines. Allow me a few instances. In conformity with exact science you would define but one cosmic energy, and see no difference between the energy expended by the traveller who pushes aside the bush that obstructs his path, and the scientific experimenter who expends an equal amount of energy in setting a pendulum in motion. We do; for we know there is a world of difference between the two. The one uselessly dissipates and scatters force, the other concentrates and stores it. And here please understand that I do not refer to the relative utility of the two, as one might imagine, but only to the fact that in the one case there is but brute force flung out without any transmutation of that brute energy into the higher potential form of spiritual dynamics, and in the other there is just that. Please do not consider me vaguely metaphysical. The idea I wish to convey is that the result of the highest intellection in the scientifically occupied brain is the evolution of a sublimated form of spiritual energy, which, in the cosmic action, is productive of illimitable results; while the automatically acting brain holds, or stores up in itself, only a certain quantum of brute force that is unfruitful of benefit for the individual or humanity. The human brain is an exhaustless generator of the most refined quality of cosmic force out of the low, brute energy of Nature; and the complete adept has made himself a centre from which irradiate potentialities that beget correlations upon correlations through Aeons of time to come. This is the key to the mystery of his being able to project into and materialise in the visible world the forms that his imagination has constructed out of inert cosmic matter in the invisible world. The adept does not create anything new, but only utilizes and manipulates materials which Nature has in store around him, and material which, throughout eternities, has passed through all the forms. He has but to choose the one he wants, and recall it into objective existence. Would not this sound to one of your 'learned' biologists like a madman's dream?

"You say there are few branches of science with which you do not possess more or less acquaintance, and that you believe you are doing a certain amount of good having acquired the position to do this by long years of study. Doubtless you do; but will you permit me to sketch for you still more clearly the difference between the modes of physical (called exact out of mere compliment) and metaphysical sciences. The latter, as you know, being incapable of verification before mixed audiences, is classed by Mr. Tyndall with the fictions of poetry. The realistic science of fact on the other hand is utterly prosaic. Now, for us, poor unknown philanthropists, no fact of either of these sciences is interesting except in the degree of its potentiality of moral results, and in the ratio of its usefulness to mankind. And what, in its proud isolation, can be more utterly indifferent to everyone and everything, or more bound to nothing but the selfish requisites for its advancement, then, this materialistic science of fact? May I ask then, what have the laws of Faraday, Tyndall, or others to do with philanthropy in their abstract relations with humanity, viewed as an intelligent whole? What care they for *Man* as an isolated atom of this great and harmonious whole, even though they may be sometimes of practical use to him? Cosmic energy is something eternal and incessant; matter is indestructible and there stand the scientific facts. Doubt them, and you are an ignoramus; deny them, a dangerous lunatic, a bigot; pretend to improve upon the theories—an impertinent charlatan. And yet even these scientific facts never suggested any proof to the word of experimenters that Nature consciously prefers that matter should be indestructible under organic rather than inorganic forms, and that she works slowly but incessantly towards the realisation of this object—the evolution of conscious life out of inert material. Hence, their ignorance about the scattering and concretion of cosmic energy in its metaphysical aspects, their division about Darwin's theories, their uncertainty about the degree of conscious life in separate elements, and, as a necessity, the scornful rejection of every phenomenon outside their own stated conditions, and the very idea of worlds of semi-intelligent if not intellectual forces at work in hidden corners of Nature. To give you another practical illustration—we see a vast difference between the two qualities of two equal amounts of energy expended by two men, of whom one, let us suppose, is on his way to his daily quiet work, and another on his way to denounce a fellow creature at the police-station, while the men of science see none; and we—not they—see a specific difference between the energy in the motion of the wind and that of a revolving wheel. And why? Because every thought of man upon being evolved passes into the inner world, and becomes an active entity by associating itself, coalescing we might term it, with an elemental—that is to say, with one of the semi-intelligent forces of the kingdoms. It survives as an active intelligence—a creature of the mind's begetting—for a longer or shorter period proportionate with the original intensity of the cerebral action which generated it. Thus, a good thought is perpetuated as an active, beneficent power, an evil one as a maleficent demon. And so man is continually peopling his current in space with a world of his own, crowded with the offsprings of his fancies, desires, impulses, and passions; a current which reacts upon any sensitive or nervous organization which comes in contact with it, in proportion to its dynamic intensity. The Buddhist calls this his 'Skandha'; the Hindu gives it the name of 'Karma.' The adept evolves these shapes consciously; other men throw them off unconsciously. The adept, to be successful and preserve his power, must dwell in solitude, and more or less within his own soul. Still less does exact science perceive that while the building ant, the busy bee, the nidifacient bird, accumulates each in its own humble way as much cosmic energy in its potential form as a Haydn, a Plato, or a ploughman turning his furrow, in theirs; the hunter who kills game for his pleasure or profit, or the positivist who applies his intellect to proving that $+ \times + = ---$, are wasting and scattering energy no less than the tiger which springs upon its prey. They all rob Nature instead of enriching her, and will all, in the degree of their intelligence, find themselves accountable.

"Exact experimental science has nothing to do with morality, virtue, philanthropy—therefore, can make no claim upon our help until it blends itself with metaphysics. Being but a cold classification of facts outside man, and existing before and after him, her domain of usefulness ceases for us at the outer boundary of these facts; and whatever the inferences and results for humanity from the materials acquired by her method, she little cares. Therefore, as our sphere lies entirely outside hers—as far as the path of Uranus is outside the Earth's—we distinctly refuse to be broken on any wheel of her construction. Heat is but a mode of motion to her, and motion develops heat, but why the mechanical motion of the revolving wheel should be metaphysically of a higher value than the heat into which it is gradually transformed she has yet to discover. The philosophical and transcendental: (hence absurd) notion of the mediaeval Theosophist that the final progress of human labour, aided by the incessant discoveries of man, must one day culminate in a process which, in imitation of the sun energy —in its capacity as a direct motor—shall result in the evolution of nutritious food out inorganic matter, is unthinkable for men of science. Were the sun, the great nourishing father of or planetary system, to hatch granite chickens out of a boulder 'under test conditions' tomorrow, the (the men of science) would accept it as a scientific fact without wasting a regret that the fowls were not alive so as to feed the hungry and the starving. But let a *shaberon* cross the Himalayas in a time of famine and multiply sacks of rice for the perishing multitudes—as he could—and your magistrates and collectors would probably lodge him in jail make him confess what granary he had robbed. This is exact science and your realistic world. An though, as you say, you are impressed by the vast extent of the world's ignorance on every subject which you pertinently designate as a 'few palpable facts collected and roughly generalised, and a technical jargon invented to hide man's ignorance of all that lies behind these facts,' and though you speak of your faith in the infinite possibilities of Nature, yet you are content to spend your life in a work which aids only that same exact science.....

"Of your several questions we will first discuss, if you please, the one relating to the presumed failure of the 'Fraternity' to 'leave any mark upon the history of the world.' They ought, you think, to have been able, with their extraordinary advantages, to have 'gathered into their schools a considerable portion of the more enlightened minds of every race.' How do you know they have made no such mark? Are you acquainted with their efforts, successes, and failures? Have you any dock upon which to arraign them? How could your world collect proofs of the doings of men who have sedulously kept closed every possible door of approach by which the inquisitive would spy upon them? The prime condition of their success was that they should never be supervised or obstructed. What they have done they know; all that those outside their circle could perceive was results, the causes of which were masked from view. To account for these results, men have, in different ages, invented theories of the interposition of gods, special providences, fates, the benign or hostile influence of the stars. There never was a time within or before the so-called historical period when our predecessors were not moulding events and 'making history,' the facts of which were subsequently and invariably distorted by historians to suit contemporary prejudices. Are you quite sure that the visible heroic figures in the successive dramas were not often but their puppets? We never pretended to be able to draw nations in the mass to this or that crisis in spite of the general drift of the world's cosmic relations. The cycles must run their rounds. Periods of mental and moral light and darkness succeed each other as day does night. The major and minor yugas must be accomplished according to the established order of things. And we, borne along on the mighty tide, can only modify and direct some of its minor currents. If we had the powers of the imaginary Personal God, and the universal and immutable laws were but toys to play with, then, indeed, might we have created conditions that would have turned this earth into an arcadia for lofty souls. But having to deal with an immutable law, being ourselves its creatures, we have had to do what we could, and rest thankful. There have been times when a considerable portion of 'enlightened minds' were taught in our schools. Such times there were in India, Persia, Egypt, Greece, and Rome. But, as I remarked in a letter to Mr. Sinnett, the adept is the efflorescence of his age, and comparatively few ever appear in a single century. Earth is the battleground of moral no less than of physical forces, and the boisterousness of animal passion, under the stimulus of the rude energies of the lower group of etheric agents, always tends to quench spirituality. What else could one expect of men so nearly related to the lower kingdom from which they evolved? True also, our numbers are just now diminishing, but this is because, as I have said, we are of the human race, subject to its cyclic impulse, and powerless to turn that back upon itself. Can you turn the Gunga or the Bramaputra back to its sources; can you even dam it so that its piled-up waters will not overflow the banks? No; but you may draw the stream partly into canals, and utilise its hydraulic power for the good of mankind. So we, who cannot stop the world from going in its destined direction, are yet able to divert some part of its energy into useful channels. Think of us as demigods, and my explanation will not satisfy you; view us as simple men —perhaps a little wiser as the result of special study—and it ought to answer your objection.

"What good,' you say, 'is to be attained for my fellows and myself (the two are inseparable) by these occult sciences?' When the natives see that an interest is taken by the English, and even by some high officials in India, in their ancestral science and philosophies, they will themselves take openly to their study. And when they come to realise that the old 'divine' phenomena were not miracles, but scientific effects, superstition will abate. Thus, the greatest evil that now oppresses and retards the revival of Indian civilization will in time disappear. The present tendency of education is to make them materialistic and root out spirituality. With a proper understanding of what their ancestors meant by their writings and teachings, education would become a blessing, whereas now it is often a curse. At present the non-educated, as much as the learned natives, regard the English as too prejudiced, because of their Christian religion and modern science, to care to understand them or their traditions. They mutually hate and mistrust each other. This changed attitude towards the older philosophy, would influence the native princes and wealthy men to endow normal schools for the education of pundits; and old MSS., hitherto buried out of the reach of the Europeans, would again come to light, and with them the key to much of that which was hidden for ages from the popular understanding, for which your sceptical Sanscritists do not care, which your religious missionaries do not *dare*, to understand. Science would gain much, humanity everything. Under the stimulus of the Anglo-Indian Theosophical Society, we might in time see another golden age of Sanskrit literature.....

"If we look at Ceylon we shall see the most scholarly priests combining, under the lead of the Theosophical Society, in a new exegesis of Buddhistic philosophy; and at Galle, on the 15th of September, a secular Theosophical School for the teaching of Singhalese youth, opened with an attendance of over three hundred scholars; an example about to be imitated at three other points in that island. If the Theosophical Society, as at present constituted,' has indeed no 'real vitality,' and yet in its modest way has done so much practical good, how much greater results might not be anticipated from a body organised upon the better plan you could suggest?

"The same causes that are materialising the Hindu mind are equally affecting all Western thought. Education enthrones scepticism, but imprisons spirituality. You can do immense good by helping to give the Western nations a secure basis upon which to reconstruct their crumbling faith. And what they need is the evidence that Asiatic psychology alone supplies. Give this, and you will confer happiness of mind on thousands. The era of blind faith is gone; that of inquiry is here. Inquiry that only unmasks error, without discovering anything upon which the soul can build, will but make iconoclasts. Iconoclasm, from its very destructiveness, can give nothing; it can only raze. But man cannot rest satisfied with bare negation. Agnosticism is but a temporary halt. This is the moment to guide the recurrent impulse which must soon come, and which will push the age towards extreme atheism, or drag it back to extreme sacerdotalism, if it is not led to the primitive soul-satisfying philosophy of the Aryans. He who observes what is going on today, on the one hand among the Catholics, who are breeding miracles as fast as the white ants do their young, on the other among the freethinkers, who are converting, by masses, into Agnostics—will see the drift of things. The age is revelling at a debauch of phenomena. The same marvels that the spiritualists quote in opposition to the dogmas of eternal perdition and atonement, the Catholics swarm to witness as proof of their faith in miracles. The sceptics make game of both. All are blind and there is no one to lead them. You and your colleagues may help to furnish the materials for a needed universal religious philosophy; one impregnable to scientific assault, because itself the finality of absolute science, and a religion that is indeed worthy of the name since it includes the relations of man physical to man psychical, and of the two to all that is above and below them. Is not this worth a slight sacrifice? And if, after reflection, you should decide to enter this new career, let it be known that your society is no miracle-mongering or banqueting club, nor specially given to the study of phenomenalism. Its chief aim is to extirpate current superstitions and scepticism, and from long-sealed ancient fountains to draw the proof that man may shape his own future destiny, and know for a certainty that he can live hereafter, if he only wills, and that all 'phenomena', are but manifestations of natural law, to try to comprehend which is the duty of every intelligent being."

I have hitherto said nothing of the circumstances under which these various letters reached my hands; nor, in comparison with the intrinsic interest of the ideas they embody, can the phenomenal conditions under which some of them were delivered, be regarded as otherwise than of secondary interest for readers who appreciate their philosophy. But every bit of evidence which helps to exhibit the nature of the powers which the adepts exercise, is worth attention, while the rationale of such powers is still hidden from the world. The fact of their existence can only be established by the accumulation of such evidence, as long as we are unable to prove their possibility by a *priori* analysis of the latent capacities in man.

My friend to whom the last letter was addressed wrote a long reply, and subsequently an additional letter for Koot Hoomi, which he forwarded to me, asking me to read and then seal it up and send or give it to Madame Blavatsky for transmission, she being expected at about that time at my house at Allahabad on her way down country from Amritsur and Lahore, where, as I have already indicated, she had stayed for some little time after our household broke up for the season at Simla. I did as desired, and gave the letter to Madame Blavatsky, after gumming and sealing the stout envelope in which it was forwarded. That evening, a few hours afterwards, on returning home to dinner, I found that the letter had gone, and had come back again. Madame Blavatsky told me that she had been talking to a visitor in her own room, and had been fingering a blue pencil on her writing-table without noticing what she was doing, when she suddenly noticed that the paper on which she was scribbling was my letter that the addressee had duly taken possession of, by his own methods, an hour or two before. She found that she had, while talking about something else, unconsciously written on the envelope the words which it then bore, "Read and returned with thanks, and a few commentaries. Please open." I examined the envelope carefully, and it was absolutely intact, its very complete fastenings having remained just as I arranged them. Slitting it open, I found the letter which it had contained when I sent it, and another from Koot Hoomi to me, criticising the former with the help of a succession of pencil figures that referred to particular passages in the original letter—another illustration of the passage of matter through matter, which, for thousands of people who have had personal experience of it in Spiritualism, is as certain a fact of nature as the rising of the sun, and which I have now not only encountered at spiritual *séances*, but, as this record will have shown, on many occasions when there is no motive for suspecting any other agency than that of living beings with faculties of which we may all possess the undeveloped germs, though it is only in their case that knowledge has brought these to phenomenal fruition.

Sceptical critics, putting aside the collateral bearing of all the previous phenomena I have described, and dealing with this letter incident by itself alone, will perhaps say—of course Madame Blavatsky had ample time to open the envelope by such means as the mediums who profess to get answers to sealed letters from the spirit world are in the habit of employing. But, firstly, the Jhelum telegram proof, and the inherent evidence of the whole correspondence show that, the letters which come to me in that which I recognise as Koot Hoomi's handwriting, are not the work of Madame Blavatsky, at all events; secondly, let the incident I have just described be compared with another illustration of an exactly similar incident which occurred shortly afterwards under different circumstances Koot Hoomi had sent me a letter addressed to my friend to read and forward on. On the subject of this letter before sending it I had occasion to make a communication to Koot Hoomi . I wrote a note to him, fastened it up in an ordinary adhesive envelope, and gave it to Madame Blavatsky. She put it in her pocket, went into her own room, which opened out of the drawing room, and came out again almost instantly. Certainly she had not been away thirty seconds. She said "he" had taken it at once. Then she followed me back through the house to my office room, spoke for a few minutes in the adjoining room to my wife, and, returning into my office, lay down on a couch. I went on with my work, and perhaps ten minutes elapsed, perhaps less. Suddenly she got up. "There's your letter," she said, pointing to the pillow from which she had lifted her head; and there lay the letter I had just written, intact as regards its appearance, but with Koot Hoomi's name on the outside scored out and mine written over it. After a thorough examination I slit the envelope, and found inside, on the flyleaf of my note, the answer I required in Koot Hoomi's handwriting. Now, except for the thirty seconds during which she retired to her own room, Madame Blavatsky had not been out of my sight, except for a minute or two in my wife's room, during the short interval which elapsed between the delivery of the letter by me to her and its return to me as described. And during this interval no one else had come into my room. The incident was as absolute and complete a mechanical proof of abnormal power exercised to produce the result as any conceivable test could have yielded. Except by declaring that I cannot be describing it correctly, the most resolute partisan of the commonplace will be unable seriously to dispute the force of this incident. He may take refuge in idiotic ridicule, or he may declare that I am misrepresenting the facts. As regards the latter hypothesis I can only pledge my word, as I do hereby, to the exact accuracy of the statement.

In one or two cases I have got back answers from Koot Hoomi to my letters in my own envelopes, these remaining intact as addressed to him, but with the address changed, and my letter gone from the inside, his reply having taken its place. In two or three cases I have found short messages from Koot Hoomi written across the blank parts of letters from other persons, coming to me through the post, the writers in these cases being assuredly unaware of the additions so made to their epistles.

Of course I have asked Koot Hoomi for an explanation of these little phenomena, but it is easier for me to ask than for him to answer, partly because the forces which the adepts bring to bear upon matter to achieve abnormal results, are of a kind which ordinary science knows so little about that we of the outer world are not prepared for such explanations; and partly because the manipulation of the forces employed has to do, sometimes, with secrets of initiation which an occultist must not reveal. However, in reference to the subject before us, I received on one occasion this hint as an explanation.

"..........Besides, bear in mind that these my letters are not written, but *impressed*, or precipitated, and then all mistakes corrected."

Of course I wanted to know more about such precipitation; was it a process which followed thought more rapidly than any with which we were familiar? And as regards letters received, did the meaning of these penetrate the understanding of an occult recipient at once, or were they read in the ordinary way?

"Of course I have to read every word you write," Koot Hoomi replied, "otherwise I would make a fine mess of it. And whether it be through my physical or spiritual eyes, the time required for it is practically the same. As much may be said of my replies; for whether I precipitate or dictate them or write my answers myself, the difference in time saved is very minute. I have to think it over, to photograph every word and sentence carefully in my brain, before it can be repeated by precipitation. As the fixing on chemically prepared surfaces of the images formed by the camera requires a previous arrangement within the focus of the object to be represented, for otherwise—as often found in bad photographs—the legs of the sitter might appear out of all proportion with the head, and so on—so we have to first arrange our sentences and impress every letter to appear on paper in our minds before it becomes fit to be read. For the present it is *all* I can tell you. When science will have learned more about the mystery of the lithophyl (or litho-biblion), and how the impress of leaves comes originally to take place on stones, then I will be able to make you better understand the process. But you must know and remember one thing—we but follow and servilely copy Nature in her works."

In another letter Koot Hoomi expatiates more fully on the difficulty of making occult explanations intelligible to minds trained only in modern science.

"Only the progress one makes in the study of arcane knowledge from its rudimental elements brings him gradually to understand our meaning. Only thus, and not otherwise, does it, strengthening and refining those mysterious links of sympathy between intelligent men—the temporarily isolated fragments of the universal soul, and the cosmic soul itself—bring them into full rapport. Once this established, then only will those awakened sympathies serve, indeed, to connect *Man* with—what, for the want of a European scientific word more competent to express the idea, I am again compelled to describe as that energetic chain which binds together the material and immaterial kosmos—Past, Present, and Future, and quicken his perceptions so as to clearly grasp not merely all things of matter, but of spirit also. I feel even irritated at having to use the three clumsy words—Past, Present, and Future. Miserable concepts of the objective phases of the subjective whole, they are about as ill adapted for the purpose, as an axe for fine carving. Oh, my poor disappointed friend, that you were already so far advanced on THE PATH that this simple transmission of ideas should not be encumbered by the conditions of matter, the union of your mind with ours prevented by its induced incapabilities. Such is unfortunately the inherited and self-acquired grossness of the Western mind, and so greatly have the very phrases expressive of modern thoughts been developed in the line of practical materialism, that it is now next to impossible, either for them to comprehend or for us to express in their own languages anything of that delicate, seemingly ideal, machinery of the occult kosmos. To some little extent that faculty can be acquired by the Europeans through study and meditation, but—that's all. And here is the bar which has hitherto prevented a conviction of the theosophical truths from gaining currency among Western nations—caused theosophical study to be cast aside as useless and fantastic by Western philosophers. How shall I teach you to read and write, or even comprehend a language off which no alphabet palpable or words audible to you have yet been invented. How could the phenomena of our modern electrical science be explained to --- say a "Greek philosopher of the days of Ptolemy, were he suddenly recalled to life—with such an unbridged hiatus in discovery as would exist between his and our age? Would not the very technical terms be to him an unintelligible jargon, an abracadabra of meaningless sounds, and the very instruments and apparatuses used but miraculous monstrosities? And suppose for one instant I were to describe to you the lines of those colour rays that lie beyond the so-called visible spectrum-rays invisible to all but a very few even among us; to explain how we can find in space anyone of the so called subjective or *accidental* colours—the *complement* (to speak mathematically) *moreover' of any other given colour of a dichromatic body* (which alone sounds like an absurdity) could you comprehend, do you think, their optical effect, or even my meaning? And since you see them not—such rays—nor can know them, nor have you any names for them as yet in science, if I were to tell you......'without moving from your writing-desk, try search for, and produce before your eyes the whole solar spectrum decomposed into fourteen prismatic colour—(seven being complementary) as it is but with the help of that occult light that you can see me from a distance as I see you'—what think you would be your answer? What would you have to reply? Would you not be likely enough to retort by telling me that as there never, were but seven (now three) primary colours which, moreover, have never yet by any known physical process been seen decomposed further than the seven prismatic hues, my invitation was as unscientific as it was absurd? Adding that my offer to search for an imaginary solar complement, being no compliment to your knowledge of physical science—I had better, perhaps, go and search for my mythical dichromatic and solar 'pairs' in Tibet, for modern science has hitherto been unable to bring under any theory even so simple a phenomenon as the colours of all such dichromatic bodies. And yet truth knows these colours are objective enough.

"So you see the insurmountable difficulties in the way of obtaining not only *absolute*, but even primary knowledge in Occult Science, for one situated as you are. How could you make yourself understood, *command* in fact, those semi-intelligent forces, whose means of communicating with us are not through spoken words, but through sounds and colours in correlations between the vibrations of the two? For sound, light, and colour are the main factors in forming those grades of intelligences, these beings of whose very existence you have no conception, nor are you allowed to believe in them—Atheists and Christians, Materialists and Spiritualists, all bringing forward their respective arguments against such a belief-Science objecting stronger than either of these to such a degrading superstition.

"Thus, because they cannot with one leap over the boundary walls attain to the pinnacles of Eternity—because we cannot take a savage from the centre of Africa and make him comprehend at once the 'Principia' of Newton, or the 'Sociology' of Herbert Spencer, or make an unlettered child write a new "Iliad in old Achaian Greek, or an ordinary painter depict scenes in Saturn, or sketch the inhabitants of Arcturus—*because if all this our very existence is denied*. Yes, for this reason are believers in us pronounced impostors and fools, and the very science which leads to the highest goal of the highest knowledge, to the real tasting of the Tree of Life and Wisdom—is scouted as a wild flight of imagination."

The following passage occurs in another letter, but it adheres naturally enough to the extract just concluded.

"The truths and mysteries of occultism constitute, indeed, a body of the highest spiritual importance, at once profound and practical for the world at large. Yet it is not as an addition to the tangled mass of theory or speculation that they are being given to you, but for their practical bearing on the interests of mankind. The terms Unscientific, Impossible, Hallucination, Imposture, have hitherto been used in a very loose, careless way, as implying in the occult phenomena something either mysterious and abnormal, or a premeditated imposture. And this is why our chiefs have determined to shed upon a few recipient minds more light upon the subject, and to prove to them that such manifestations are as reducible to law as the simplest phenomena in the physical universe. The wiseacres say, 'the age of miracles is past', but we answer, 'it never existed.' While not unparalleled or without their counterpart in universal history, these phenomena must and *will* come with an overpowering influence upon the world of sceptics and bigots. They *have* to prove both destructive and constructive-destructive in the pernicious errors of the past, in the old creeds and superstitions which suffocate in their poisonous embrace, like the Mexican weed, nigh all mankind; but constructive of new institutions of a genuine, practical Brotherhood of Humanity, where all will become co-workers of Nature, will work for the good of mankind, *with* and *through* the higher *planetary spirits*, the only spirits we believe in. Phenomenal elements previously unthought of, undreamed of, will soon begin manifesting themselves day by day with constantly augmented force, and disclose at last the secrets of their mysterious workings. Plato was right. Ideas rule the world; and as men's minds will receive new ideas, leaving aside the old and effete, the world will advance, mighty revolutions will spring from them, creeds and even powers will crumble before their onward march, crushed by their Irresistible force. It will be just as impossible to resist their influence when the time comes as to stay the progress of the tide. But all this will come gradually on, and before it comes we have a duty set before us: that of sweeping away as much as possible the dross left to us by our pious forefathers. New ideas have to be planted on clean places, for these ideas touch upon the most momentous subjects. It is not physical phenomena, but these universal ideas, that we study; as to comprehend the former, we have first to understand the latter. They touch man's true position in the universe in relation to his previous and future births, his origin and ultimate destiny; the relation of the mortal to the immortal, of the temporary to the eternal, of the finite to the infinite; ideas larger, grander, more comprehensive, recognising the eternal reign of immutable law, unchanging and unchangeable, in regard to which there is only an ETERNAL Now; while to uninitiated mortals, time is past or future, as related to their finite existence on this material speck of dirt. This is what we study and what many have solved........ Meanwhile, being human, I have to rest. I took no sleep for over sixty hours."

Here are It few lines from Koot Hoomi's hand, in a letter not addressed to me, It fall conveniently into the present series of extracts.

"Be it as it may, we are content to live as we do, unknown and undisturbed by a civilization which rests so exclusively upon intellect. Nor do we feel in any way concerned about the revival of our ancient art and high civilization, for these are as sure to come back in their time, and in a higher form, as the Plesiosaurus and the Megatherium in theirs. We have the weakness to believe in ever-recurrent cycles, and hope to quicken the resurrection of what is past and gone. We could not impede it, even if we would. The new civilization will be but the child of the old one, and we have but to leave the eternal law to take its own course, to have our dead ones come out of their graves; yet we are certainly anxious to hasten the welcome event. Fear not, although we do 'cling superstitiously to the relics of the past', our knowledge will not pass away from the sight of man. It is, the 'gift of the gods,' and the most precious relic of all. The keepers of the sacred light did not safely cross so many ages but to find themselves wrecked on the rocks of modern scepticism. Our pilots are too experienced sailors to allow us to fear any such disaster. We will always find volunteers to replace the tired sentries, and the world, bad as it is in its present state of transitory period, can yet furnish us with a few men now and then."

Turning back to my own correspondence, and to the latest letter I received from Koot Hoomi before leaving India on the trip home during which I am writing these pages, I read:—

"I hope that at least *you* will understand that we (or most of us) are far from being the heartless morally dried-up mummies some would fancy us to be. Mejnour is very well where he is—as an ideal character of a thrilling, in many respects truthful story. Yet, believe me, few of us would care to play the part in life of a desiccated pansy between the leaves of a volume of solemn poetry. We may not be quite 'the boys' to quote ——'s irreverent expression when speaking of us, yet none of *our* degree are like the stern hero of Bulwer's romance. While the facilities of observation secured to some of us by our condition certainly give a greater breadth of view, a more pronounced and impartial, a more widely spread humaneness—for answering Addison, we might justly maintain that *it is* the business of "magic" to humanize our natures with compassion'—for the whole mankind as all living beings, instead of concentrating and limiting our affections to one predilected race—yet few of us (except such as have attained the final negation of Moksha) can so far enfranchise ourselves from the influence of our earthly connection as to be unsusceptible in various degrees to the higher pleasures, emotions, and interests of the common run of humanity. Of course the greater the progress towards deliverance, the less this will be the case, until, to crown all, human and purely individual personal feelings, blood-ties and friendship, patriotism and race predilection, will all give way to become blended into one universal feeling, the only true and holy, the only unselfish and eternal one-Love, an Immense Love for humanity as a whole. For it is humanity which is the great orphan, the only disinherited one upon this earth, my friend. And it is the duty of every man who is capable of an unselfish impulse to do something, however little, for its welfare. It reminds me of the old fable of the war between the body and its members; here, too, each limb of this huge 'orphan,' fatherless and motherless, selfishly cares but for itself, The body, uncared for, suffers eternally whether the limbs are at war or at rest. Its suffering and agony never cease; and who can blame it—as your materialistic philosophers do—if, in this everlasting isolation and neglect, it has evolved gods into whom 'it ever cries for help, but is not heard.' Thus—

> *'Since there is hope for man only in man,*
> *I would not let one cry whom I could save.'*

Yet I confess that I individually am not yet exempt from some of the terrestrial attachments. I am still attracted toward some men more than towards others, and philanthropy as preached by our great Patron

> *'..................The Saviour of the world,*
> *The teacher of Nirvana and the Law '*

has never killed in me either individual preferences of friendship, love for my next of kin, or the ardent feeling of patriotism for the country in which I was last materially individualised."

I had asked Koot Hoomi how far I was at liberty to use his letters in the preparation of this volume, and, a few lines after the passage just quoted, he says:—

"I lay no restrictions upon your making use of anything I may have written to you or Mr. ----- having full confidence in your tact and judgment as to what should be printed, and how it should be presented. I must only ask you..." and then he goes on to indicate one letter which he wishes me to withhold...... "As to the rest, I relinquish it to the mangling tooth of criticism."

---

1. This house at which the cigarette was found was Mr. O'Meara's. He is quite willing that this should be stated.
2. The theory is that a current of what can only be called magnetism, can be made to convey objects, previously dissipated by the same force, to any distance, and in spite of the Intervention of any amount of matter.
3. In the absence of my own letter, to which this Is a reply, the reader might think from this sentence that I had been animated by some unfriendly feeling for the representatives referred to—Madame Blavatsky and Colonel Olcott. This is far from having been the case; but, keenly alive to mistakes which had been made up to the time of, which I am writing, In the management of the Theosophical Society, Mr. ------and myself were under the impression that better public results might be obtained by commencing operations *de novo*, and taking, ourselves, the direction of the measures which might be employed to recommend the study of occultism to the modern world. This belief on our part was coexistent In both cases with a warm friendship based on the purest esteem for both the persons mentioned.
4. Many old Indians, and some books about the Indian Mutiny, take note of the perfectly incomprehensible way news of events transpiring at a distance would sometimes be found to have penetrated the native bazaars before It had reached the Europeans at such places by the quickest means of communication at their disposal. The explanation I have been informed, Is that the Brothers, who were anxious to save the British power at that time, regarding it as a better government for India than any system of native rule that could take its place, were quick to distribute information by their own methods when this could operate to quiet popular excitement and discourage new risings. The sentiment that animated them then, animates them still, and the influence of the Theosophical Society In India is one which the Government would do wisely to countenance and support. The suspicions directed against its founders in the first instance, misdirected as they were, were excusable enough, but now that the character of the whole movement is better understood, it would be well for the officers of the British Government in India who have any opportunity of the kind, to do whatever they can towards showing their sympathy with the promoters of the Society, who must, necessarily, have an uphill task to perform without such manifestations of sympathy.

TEACHINGS OF OCCULT PHILOSOPHY

AS AFFIRMED more than once already, Occult Philosophy in various countries and through different periods has remained substantially the same. At different times and places very different mythological efflorescences have been thrown off for the service of the populace; but, underlying each popular religion, the religious knowledge of the initiated minority has been identical. Of course, the modern Western conception of what is right in such matters will be outraged by the mere idea of a religion which is kept as the property of the few, while a "false religion," as modern phraseology would put it is served out to the common people. However, before this feeling is permitted to land us in too uncompromising disapproval of the ancient hiders of the truth, it may be well to determine how far it is due to any intelligent conviction that the common herd would be benefited by teaching, which must be in its nature too refined and subtle for popular comprehension, and how far the feeling referred to, may be due to an acquired habit of looking on religion as something which it is important to profess, irrespective of understanding it. No doubt, assuming that a man's eternal welfare depends upon his declaration, irrespective of comprehension, of the right faith, among all the faiths he might have picked out from the lucky bag of birth and destiny—then it would be the sovereign duty of persons conscious of possessing such a faith to proclaim it from the housetops. But, on the other hypothesis, that it cannot profit any man to mutter a formula of words without attaching sense to it, and that crude intelligences can only be approached by crude sketches of religious ideas, there is more to be advanced on behalf of the ancient policy of reserve than seems at first sight obvious. Certainly the relations of the populace and the initiates, look susceptible of modification in the European world of the present day. The populace, in the sense of the public at large, including the finest intellects of the age, are at least as well able as those of any special class to comprehend metaphysical ideas. These finer intellects dominate public thought, so that no great ideas can triumph among the nations of Europe without their aid, while their aid can only be secured in the open market of intellectual competition. Thus it ensues that the bare notion of an esoteric science superior to that offered in public to the scientific world, strikes the modern Western mind as an absurdity. With which very natural feeling it is only necessary at present here to fight, so far as to ask people not to be illogical in its application; that is to say, not to assume that because it would never occur to a modern European coming into possession of a new truth to make a secret of it, and disclose it only to a fraternity under pledges of reserve, therefore such an idea could never have occurred to an Egyptian priest or an intellectual giant of the civilization which overspread India, according to some not unreasonable hypotheses, before Egypt began to be a seat of learning and art. The secret society system was as natural, indeed, to the ancient man of science, as the public system is in our own country and time. Nor is the difference one of time and fashion merely. It hinges on to the great difference that is to be discerned in the essence of the pursuits in which learned men engage now, as compared with those they were concerned with in former ages. We have belonged to the material progress epoch, and the watchword of material progress has always been publicity. The initiates of ancient psychology belonged to the spiritual age, and the watchword of subjective development has always been secrecy. Whether in both cases the watchword is dictated by necessities of the situation is a question on which discussion might be possible; but, at all events, these reflections are enough to show that it would be unwise to dogmatize too confidently on the character of the philosophy and the philosophers who could be content to hoard their wisdom and supply the crowd with a religion adapted rather to the understanding of its recipients than to those eternal verities.

It is impossible now to form a conjecture as to the date or time at which occult philosophy began to take the shape in which we find it now. But though it may be reasonably guessed that, the last two or three thousand years have not passed over the devoted initiates who have held and transmitted it during that time, without their having contributed something towards its development, the proficiency of initiates belonging to the earliest periods with which history deals, appears to have been already so far advanced, and so nearly as wonderful as the proficiency of initiates in the present day, that we must assign a very great antiquity to the earliest beginnings of occult knowledge on this earth. Indeed the question cannot be raised without bringing us in contact with considerations that hint at absolutely startling conclusions in this respect.

But, apart from specific archaeological speculations, it has been pointed out that "a philosophy so profound, a moral code so ennobling, and practical results so conclusive and so uniformly demonstrable, are not the growth of a generation, or even a single epoch. Fact must have been piled upon fact, deduction upon deduction, science have begotten science, and myriads of the brightest human intellects have reflected upon the laws of Nature, before this ancient doctrine had taken concrete shape. The proofs of this identity of fundamental doctrine in the old religions are found in the prevalence of a system of initiation; in the secret sacerdotal castes, who had the guardianship of mystical words of power, and a public display of a phenomenal control over natural forces indicating association with preter-human beings. Every approach to the mysteries of all these nations, was guarded with the same jealous care, and in all the penalty of death was inflicted upon all initiates of any degree who divulged the secrets entrusted to them." The book just quoted shows this to have been the case with the Eleusinian and Bacchic Mysteries among the Chaldean Magi and the Egyptian Hierophants. The Hindu book of Brahminical ceremonies, the "Agrushada Parikshai," contains the same law, which appears also to have been adopted by the Essenes, the Gnostics, and the Theurgic Neo-Platonists. Freemasonry has copied the old formula, though its *raison d'être* has expired here with the expiration from among freemasons of the occult philosophy on which their forms and ceremonies are shaped to a larger extent than they generally conceive. Evidences of the identity spoken of may be traced in the vows, formulas, rites, and doctrines of various ancient faiths, and it is affirmed by those whom I believe qualified to speak with authority as to the fact, "that not only is their memory still preserved in India; but also that the secret association is still alive, and as active as ever."

As I have now, in support of the views just expressed, to make some quotations from Madame Blavatsky's great book, "Isis Unveiled," it is necessary to give certain explanations concerning the genesis of that work, for which the reader who has followed my narrative of occult experiences through the preceding pages, will be better prepared than he would have been previously. I have shown how, throughout the most ordinary incidents of her daily life, Madame Blavatsky is constantly in communication, by means of the system of psychological telegraphy that the initiates employ, with her superior "Brothers" in occultism. This state of the facts once realised, it will be easy to understand that in compiling such a work as "Isis," which embodies a complete explanation of 'all that can be told about occultism to the outer world, she would not be left exclusively to her own resources, The truth which Madame Blavatsky would be the last person in the world to wish disguised, is that the assistance she derived from the Brothers, by occult agency, throughout the composition of her book, was so abundant and continuous that she is not so much the author of "Isis" as one of a group of *collaborateurs*, by whom it was actually produced. I am given to understand that she set to work on "Isis" without knowing anything about the magnitude of the task she was undertaking, She began writing to dictation—the passages thus written not now standing first in the completed volumes—in compliance with the desire of her occult friends, and without knowing whether the composition on which she was engaged would turn out an article for a newspaper, or an essay for a magazine, or a work of larger dimensions. But on and on it grew. Before going very far, of course, she came to understand what she was about; and fairly launched on her task, she in turn contributed a good deal from her own natural brain. But the Brothers appear always to have been at work with her, not merely dictating through her brain as at first, but sometimes employing those methods of "precipitation" of which I have myself been favoured with some examples, and by means of which quantities of actual manuscript in other handwritings than her own were produced while she slept. In the morning she would sometimes get up and find as much as thirty slips added to the manuscript she had left on her table overnight. The book "Isis" is in fact as great a "phenomenon"—apart from the nature of its contents—as any of those I have described.

The faults of the book, obvious to the general reader, will be thus explained, as well as the extraordinary value it possesses for those who may be anxious to explore as far as possible the mysteries of occultism. The deific powers which the Brothers enjoy cannot protect a literary work which is the joint production of several—even among their minds, from the confusion of arrangement to which such a mode of composition inevitably gives rise. And besides confusion of arrangement, the book exhibits a heterogeneous variety of different styles, which mars its dignity as a literary work, and must prove both irritating and puzzling to the ordinary reader. But for those who possess the key to this irregularity of form, it is an advantage rather than otherwise. It will enable an acute reader to account for some minor incongruities of statement occurring in different parts of the book. Beyond this it will enable him to recognise the voice, as it were, of the different authors as they take up the parable in turn.

The book was written—as regards its physical production—at New York, where Madame Blavatsky was utterly unprovided with books of reference. It teems, however, with references to books of all sorts, including many of a very unusual character, and with quotations the exactitude of which may easily be verified at the great European libraries, as footnotes supply the number of the pages, from which the passages taken are quoted.

I may now go on to collect some passages from "Isis," the object of which is to show the unity of the esoteric philosophy underlying various ancient religions, and the peculiar value which attaches for students of that philosophy, to pure Buddhism, a system which, of all those presented to the world, appears to supply us with occult philosophy in its least adulterated shape. Of course, the reader will guard himself from running away with the idea that Buddhism, as explained by writers who are not occultists, can be accepted as an embodiment of their views. For example, one of the leading ideas of Buddhism, as interpreted by Western scholars, is that "Nirvana" amounts to annihilation. It is possible that Western scholars may be right in saying that the explanation of "Nirvana" supplied by exoteric Buddhism leads to this conclusion; but that, at all events, is not the occult doctrine.

"Nirvana," it is stated in "Isis," "means the certitude of personal immortality in *spirit*, not in *soul*, which, as a finite emanation, must certainly disintegrate its particles, a compound of human sensations, passions, and yearning for some objective kind of existence, before the immortal spirit of the Ego is quite freed, and henceforth secure against transmigration in any form. And how can man reach that state so long as the 'Upadana' that state of longing for life, more life, does not disappear from the sentient being, from the Ahancara clothed, however, in a sublimated body? It is the 'Upadana", or the intense desire that produces will, and it is will which develops force, and the latter generates matter, or an object having form. Thus the disembodied Ego, through this sole undying desire in him, unconsciously furnishes the conditions of his successive self-procreations in various forms, which depend on his mental, state, and 'Karma', the good or bad deeds of his preceding existence, commonly called 'merit' and 'demerit.'" There is a world of suggestive metaphysical thought in this passage, which will serve at once to justify the view propounded just now as regards the reach of Buddhistic philosophy as viewed from the occult standpoint.

The misunderstanding about the meaning of "Nirvana" is so general in the West, that before going on with explanations of the philosophy which this same misunderstanding has improperly discredited, it will be well to consider the following elucidation also:—

"Annihilation means with the Buddhistical philosophy only a dispersion of matter, in whatever form or semblance of form it may be; for every thing that bears a shape was created, and thus must sooner or later perish, *i.e.*, change that shape; therefore, as something temporary, though seeming to be permanent, it is but an illusion, 'Maya'; for as eternity has neither beginning nor end, the more or less prolonged duration of some particular form passes, as it were, like an instantaneous flash of lightning. Before we have the time to realise that we have seen it, it has gone and passed away forever; hence even our astral bodies, pure ether; are but illusions of matter so long as they retain their terrestrial outline. The latter changes, says the Buddhist, according to the merits or demerit of the person during his lifetime, and this is metempsychosis. When the spiritual entity breaks loose for ever from every particle of matter, then only it enters upon the eternal and unchangeable 'Nirvana'. He exists in spirit, in *nothing*; as a form, a shape, a semblance, he is completely annihilated, and thus will die no more; for spirit alone is no 'Maya' but the only reality in an illusionary universe of ever-passing forms... To accuse Buddhistical philosophy of rejecting a Supreme Being-God, and the soul's immortality—of Atheism, in short—on the ground that 'Nirvana' means annihilation, and 'Svabha vat' is not a person, but nothing, is simply absurd. The En (or Aym) of the Jewish Ensoph also means nihil, or *nothing*, that which is not (*quoad nos*), but no one bas ever ventured to twit the Jews with atheism. In both cases the real meaning of the term *nothing* carries with it the idea that God is *not a thing*, not a concrete or visible being to which a name expressive of *any* object known to us on earth may be applied with propriety."

Again: " 'Nirvana' is the world of *cause* in which all deceptive effects or illusions of our senses disappear. 'Nirvana' is the highest attainable sphere."The secret doctrines of the Magi of the pre-Vedic Buddhists, of the hierophants of the Egyptian Thoth or Hermes, were we find it laid down in "Isis"-identical from the beginning, an identity that applied equally to the secret doctrines of the adepts of whatever age or nationality, including the Chaldean Kabalists and the Jewish *Nazars*. "When we use the word Buddhists, we do not mean to imply by it either the exoteric Buddhism instituted by the followers of Gautama Buddha, or the modern Buddhistic religion, but the secret philosophy of Sakyamuni, which, in its essence, is certainly identical with the ancient wisdom—religion of the sanctuary—the pre-vedic Brahmanisn. The schism of Zoroaster, as it is called, is a direct proof of it: for it was no schism, strictly speaking, but merely a partially public exposition of strictly monotheistic religious truths hitherto taught only in the sanctuaries, and that he had learned from the Brahmans. Zoroaster, the primeval institution of sun-worship, cannot be called the founder of the dualistic system, neither was he the first to teach the unity of God, for he taught but what he had learned himself from the Brahmans, And that Zarathustra, and his followers the Zoroastrians, had been settled in India before they immigrated into Persia, is also proved by Max Muller. 'That the Zoroastrians and their ancestors started from India,' he says. 'during the Vaidic period, can be proved as distinctly as that the inhabitants of Massilia started from Greece........... Many of the gods of the Zoroastrians come out....... as mere reflections and deflections of the gods of the Veda.'

"If, now, we can prove, and we ban do so on the evidence of the

'Kabala,' and the oldest traditions of the wisdom religion, the philosophy of the old sanctuaries, that all these gods, whether of the Zoroastrians or of the *Veda*, are but so many personated occult powers of Nature, the faithful servants of the adepts of secret wisdom—magic—we are on secure ground.

"Thus; whether we say that Kabalism and Gnosticism proceeded from Masdeanism or Zoroastrianism, it is all the same, unless we meant the exoteric worship, which we do not. Likewise, and in this sense we may echo King, the author of the 'Gnostics,' and several other archaeologists, and maintain that both the former proceeded from *Buddhism*, at once the simplest and most satisfying of philosophies, and which resulted in one of the purest religions in the world... But whether among the Essenes or the Neo-Platonists, or again among the innumerable struggling sects born but to die, the same doctrine, identical in substance and spirit, if not always in form, are encountered. By *Buddhism*, therefore, we mean that religion signifying literally the doctrine of wisdom, and which by many ages antedates the metaphysical philosophy of Siddhartha Sakyamuni,"

Modern Christianity has, of course, diverged widely from its own original philosophy, but the identity of this with the original philosophy of all religions is maintained in "Isis" in the course of an interesting argument.

"Luke, who was a physician, is designated in the Syriac texts as *Asaia*, the Essaian or Essene. Josephus and Philo Judreus have sufficiently described this sect to leave no doubt in our mind that the Nazarene Reformer, after having received his education in their dwellings in the desert, and being duly initiated in the mysteries, preferred the free and independent life of a wandering *Nazaria*, and so separated, or *inazarenized*, himself, from them, thus becoming a travelling Therapeute, or Nazaria, a healer... In his discourses and sermons Jesus always spoke in parables, and used metaphors with his audience. This habit was again that of the Essenians and the Nazarenes; the Galileans, who dwelt in cities and villages, were never known to use such allegorical language. Indeed, some of his disciples, being Galileans as well as himself, felt even surprised to find him using with the people such a form of expression. 'Why speakest thou unto them in parables?' they often inquired. 'Because it is given unto you to know the mysteries of the kingdom of Heaven; but to them it is not given,' was the reply, which was that of an initiate. 'Therefore, I speak unto them in parables, because they seeing, see not, and hearing, they hear not, neither do they understand.' Moreover, we find Jesus expressing his thoughts... in sentences which are purely Pythagorean, when, during the Sermon on the Mount, he says, 'Give ye not that which is sacred to the dogs, neither cast ye your pearls before swine; for the swine will tread them under their feet, and the dogs will turn and rend you.' Professor A. Wilder, the editor of Taylor's 'Eleusillian

Mysteries,' observes a' like disposition on the part of Jesus and Paul to classify their doctrines as esoteric and exoteric—the mysteries of the Kingdom of God for the apostles, and parables for the multitude'. We speak wisdom, says Paul, 'among them that are *perfect*,' or 'initiated.' In the Eleusinian and other mysteries the participants were always divided in two classes, the *neophytes* and the *perfect*... The narrative of the Apostle Paul in his Second Epistle to the Corinthians, has struck several scholars well versed in 'the descriptions of the mystical rites of the initiation given by some classes as all ending most undoubtedly to the final Epopteia: 'I know a certain man—whether in body or outside of body I know not; God knoweth—who was rapt into Paradise, and heard things ineffable which it is not lawful for a man to repeat.' These words have rarely, so far as we know, been regarded by commentators as an allusion 'to the beatific visions of an initiated seer; but the phraseology is unequivocal'. These things which it is not lawful to repeat, are hinted at in the same words, and the reason assigned for it is the same as that which we find repeatedly expressed by Plato, Proclus, Jamblichus, Herodotus, and other classics. 'We speak wisdom only among them that are perfect,' says Paul; the plain and undeniable translation of the sentence being: 'We speak of the profounder or final esoteric doctrines of the mysteries (which are denominated wisdom), only among them who alone initiated. So in relation to the man who was rapt into Paradise—and who was evidently Paul himself—the Christian word Paradise having replaced that of Elysium."

The final purposes of occult philosophy is to show what Man was, is, and will be. "That which survives as an individuality," says 'Isis,' "after the death of the body is the actual soul, which Plato, in the *Timaeus* and *Gorgias* calls the mortal soul; for, according to the Hermetic doctrine, it throws off the more material particles at every progressive change into a higher sphere. The astral spirit is a faithful duplicate of the body in a physical and spiritual sense. The Divine, the highest immortal spirit, can be neither punished nor rewarded. To maintain such a doctrine would be at the same time absurd and blasphemous; for it is not merely a flame lit at the central and inextinguishable fountain of light, but actually a portion of it and of identical essence. It assures immortality to the individual astral being in proportion to the willingness of the latter to receive it. So long as the double man—*i.e.*, the man of flesh and spirit—keeps within the limits of the law of spiritual continuity; so long as the divine spark lingers in him, however faintly, he is on the road to an immortality in the future state. But those who resign themselves to a materialistic existence, shutting out the divine radiance shed by their spirit, at the beginning of their earthly pilgrimage, and stifling the warning voice of that faithful sentry the conscience, which serves as a focus for the light in the soul—such beings as these, having left behind conscience and spirit, and crossed the boundaries of matter, will, of necessity, have to follow its laws."

Again. "The secret doctrine teaches that man, if he wins immortality, will remain for ever the trinity that he is in life, and will continue so throughout all the spheres. The astral body, which in this life is covered by a gross physical envelope, becomes, when relieved of that covering by the process of corporeal death, in its turn the shell of another and more ethereal body. This begins developing from the moment of death, and becomes perfected when the astral body of the earthly form finally separates from it."

The passages quoted, when read by the light of the explanations I have given, will enable the reader, if so inclined, to take up "Isis" in a comprehending spirit, and find his way to the rich veins of precious metal which are buried in its pages. But neither in "Isis" nor in any other book on occult philosophy which has been or seems likely to be written yet awhile, must anyone hope to obtain a cut-and-dried, straightforward, and perfectly clear account of the mysteries of birth, death, and the future. At first, in pursuing studies of this kind, one is irritated at the difficulty of getting at what the occultists really believe as regards the future state, the nature of the life to come, and its general *mise en scène*. The well known religions have very precise views on these subjects, further rendered practical by the assurance some of them give that qualified persons, commissioned by churches to perform the duty, can shunt departing souls on to the right or the wrong lines, in accordance with consideration received. Theories of that kind have at any rate the merit of simplicity and intelligibility, but they are not, perhaps, satisfactory to the mind as regards their details. After a very little investigation of the matter, the student of occult philosophy will realise that on that path of knowledge he will certainly meet with no conceptions likely to outrage his purest idealisation of God and the life to come. He will soon feel that the scheme of ideas he is exploring is lofty and dignified to the utmost limits that the human understanding can reach. But it will remain vague, and he will seek for explicit statements on this or that point, until by degrees he realises that the absolute truth about the origin and destinies of the human soul may be too subtle and intricate to be possibly expressible in straightforward language. Perfectly clear ideas may be attainable for the purified minds of advanced scholars in occultism, who, by entire devotion of every faculty to the pursuit and prolonged assimilation of such ideas, come at length to understand them with the aid of peculiar intellectual powers specially expanded for the purpose; but it does not at all follow that with the best will in the world such persons must necessarily be able to draw up an occult creed which should bring the whole theory of the universe into the compass of a dozen lines. The study of occultism, even by men of the world, engaged in ordinary pursuits as well, may readily enlarge and purify the understanding, to the extent of arming the mind, so to speak, with tests that will detect absurdity in any erroneous religious hypotheses; but the absolute structure of occult belief is something which, from its nature, can only be built up slowly in the mind of each intellectual architect. And I imagine that a very vivid perception of this on their part explains the reluctance of occultists even to attempt the straight—forward explanation of their doctrines. They know that really vital plants of knowledge, so to speak, must grow up from the germ in each man's mind, and cannot be transplanted into the strange soil of an untrained understanding in a complete state of mature growth. They are ready enough to supply seed, but every man must grow his own tree of knowledge for himself. As the adept himself is not made, but becomes so,—in a minor degree, the person who merely aspires to comprehend the adept and his views of things must develop such comprehension for himself, by thinking out rudimentary ideas to their legitimate conclusions.

These considerations fit in with, and do something towards elucidating, the reserve of occultism, and they further suggest an explanation of what will at once seem puzzling to a reader of "Isis," who takes it up by the light of the present narrative. If great parts of the book, as I have asserted, are really the work of actual adepts, who know of their own knowledge what is the actual truth about many of the mysteries discussed, why have they not said plainly what they meant, instead of beating about the bush, and suggesting arguments derived from this or that ordinary source, from literary or historical evidence, from abstract speculation concerning the harmonies of Nature? The answer seems to be, firstly, that they could not well write, "We know that so and so is the fact," without being asked, "How do you know?"—and it is manifestly impossible that they could reply to this question without going into details, that it would be "unlawful," as a Biblical writer would say, to disclose, or without proposing to guarantee their testimony by manifestations of powers which it would be obviously impracticable for them to keep always at hand for the satisfaction of each reader of the book in turn. Secondly, I imagine that, in accordance with the invariable principle of trying less to teach than to encourage spontaneous development, they have aimed in "Isis," rather at producing an effect on the reader's mind, than at shooting in a store of previously accumulated facts. They have shown that Theosophy, or Occult Philosophy, is no new candidate for the world's attention, but is really a restatement of principles which have been recognised from the very infancy of mankind. The historic sequence which establishes this view is distinctly traced through the successive evolution's of the philosophical schools, in a manner which it is impossible for me to attempt in a work of these dimensions, and the theory laid down is illustrated with abundant accounts of the experimental demonstrations of occult power ascribed to various thaumaturgists. The authors of "Isis," have expressly refrained from saying more than might conceivably be said by a writer who was not an adept, supposing him to have access to all the literature of the subject and an enlightened comprehension of its meaning.

But once realise the real position of the authors or inspirers of "Isis," and the value of any argument on which you find them launched is enhanced enormously above the level of the relatively commonplace considerations advanced on its behalf. The adepts may not choose to bring forward other than exoteric evidence in favour of any particular thesis they wish to support, but if they wish to support it, that fact alone will be of enormous significance for any reader who, in indirect ways, has reached a comprehension of the authority with which they are entitled to speak.

LATER OCCULT PHENOMENA

[Added to the second English edition.]

I CANNOT let a second edition of this book appear without recording some, at least, of the experiences which have befallen me since its preparation. The most important of these, indeed, are concerned with fragmentary instruction I have been privileged to receive from the Brothers in reference to the great truths of cosmology which their spiritual insight has enabled them to penetrate. But the exposition even of the little, relatively, that I have learned on this head would exact a more elaborate treatise than I can attempt at present.[1] And the purpose of the present volume is to expound the outer facts of the situation rather than to analyse a system of philosophy. This is not entirely inaccessible to exoteric students, apart from what may be regarded as direct revelation from the Brothers. Though almost all existing occult literature is unattractive in its form, and rendered purposely obscure by the use of an elaborate symbology, it does contain a great deal of information that can be distilled from the mass by the application of sufficient patience. Some industrious students of that literature have proved this. Whether the masters of occult philosophy will ultimately consent to the complete exposition in plain language of the state of the facts regarding the spiritual constitution of Man, remains to be seen. Certainly, even if they are still reticent in a way that no ordinary observer can comprehend, they are more disposed to be communicative at this moment than they have been for a long time past.

But the first thing to do is to dissipate as much as possible the dogged disbelief that encrusts the Western mind as to the existence of any abnormal persons who can be regarded as masters of *True* Philosophy—distinguished from all the speculations that have tormented the world—and as to the abnormal nature of their faculties. I have endeavored already to point out plainly, but may as well here emphasise the reason why I dwell upon, the phenomena which exhibit these faculties. Rightly regarded, these are the credentials of the spiritual teaching which their authors supply. Firstly, indeed, *in themselves* abnormal phenomena accomplished by the willpower of living men must be intensely interesting for every one endowed with an honest love of science. They open out new scientific horizons. It is as certain as the sun's next rising that the forward pressure of scientific discovery, advancing slowly as it does in its own grooves, will ultimately, and probably at no very distant date, introduce the ordinary world to some of the superior scientific knowledge already enjoyed by the masters of occultism. Faculties will be acquired by exoteric investigation that will bring the outworks of science a step or two nearer the comprehension of some of the phenomena I have described in the present volume. And meanwhile it seems to me very interesting to get a glimpse beforehand of achievements which we should probably find engaging the eager attention of a future generation, if we really could, as Tennyson suggests—

> *"sleep through terms of mighty wars,*
> *And wake on science grown to more,*
> *On secrets of the brain, the stars,*
> *As wild as aught of fairy lore."*

But even superior to their scientific interest is the importance of the lesson conveyed by occult phenomena, when these distinctly place their authors in a commanding position of intellectual superiority as compared with the world at large. They show most undeniably that these men have gone far ahead of their contemporaries in a comprehension of Nature as exemplified in this world; that they have acquired the power of cognizing events by other means than the material senses; that while their bodies are at one place, their perceptions may be at another, and that they have consequently solved the great problem as to whether the Ego of man is a something distinct from his perishable frame. From all other teachers we can but find out what has been thought probable in reference to the soul or spirit of man; from them we can find out what is the fact; and if that is not a sublime subject of inquiry, surely it would be difficult to say what is. But we cannot read poetry till we have learned the alphabet; and, if the combinations b-a ba, and so on are found to be insufferably trivial and uninteresting, the fastidious person who objects to such foolishness will certainly never be able to read the "Idylls of the King."

So I return from the clouds to my patient record of phenomena, and to the incidents which have confirmed the experiences and conclusions set forth in the previous chapter of this book, since my return to India.

The very first incident which took place was in the nature of a pleasant greeting from my revered friend, Koot Hoomi. I had written to him (per Madame Blavatsky, of course) shortly before leaving London, and had expected to find a letter from him awaiting my arrival at Bombay. But no such letter had been received, as I found when I reached the headquarters of the Theosophical Society, where I had arranged to stay for a few days before going on to my destination up country. I got in late at night, and nothing remarkable happened then. The following morning, after breakfast, I was sitting talking with Madame Blavatsky in the room that had been allotted to me. We were sitting at different sides of a large square table in the middle of the room, and the full daylight was shining. There was no one else in the room. Suddenly, down upon the table before me, but to my right hand, Madame Blavatsky being to my left, there fell a thick letter. It fell "out of nothing", so to speak; it was materialised, or reintegrated in the air before my eyes. It was Koot Hoomi's expected reply—a deeply interesting letter, partly concerned with private matters and replies to questions of mine, and partly with some large, though as yet shadowy, revelations of occult philosophy, the first sketch of this that I had received. Now, of course, I know what some readers will say to this (with a self-satisfied smile)—"wires, springs, concealed apparatus," and so forth; but first all the suggestion would have been grotesquely absurd to anyone who had been present; and secondly, it is unnecessary to argue about objections of this sort all over again *ab initio* every time. There were no more wires and springs about the room I am now referring to, than about the breezy hilltops at Simla, where some of our earlier phenomena took place. I may add, moreover, that some months later an occult note was dropped before a friend of mine, a Bengal civilian, who has become an active member of the Theosophical Society, at a dak bungalow in the north of India; and that later again, at the headquarters of the Theosophical Society at Bombay, a letter was dropped, according to a previous promise, out in the open air in the presence of six or seven witnesses.

For some time the gift of the letter from Koot Hoomi in the way I have described was the only phenomenon accorded to me, and, although my correspondence continued, I was not encouraged to expect any further displays of abnormal power. The higher authorities of the occult world, indeed, had by this time put a very much more stringent prohibition upon such manifestations than had been in operation the previous summer at Simla. The effect of the manifestations then accorded was not considered to have been satisfactory on the whole. A good deal of acrimonious discussion and bad feeling had ensued; and I imagine that this was conceived to outweigh, in its injurious effect on the progress of the Theosophical movement, the good effect of the phenomena on the few persons who appreciated them. When I went up to Simla in August, 1881, therefore, I had no expectation of further events of an unusual nature. Nor have I any stream of anecdotes to relate which will bear comparison with those derived from the experience of the previous year. But nonetheless was the progress of a certain undertaking in which I became concerned—the establishment of a Simla branch of the Theosophical Society—interspersed with little incidents of a phenomenal nature. When this Society was formed, many letters passed between Koot Hoomi and ourselves which were *not* in every case transmitted through Madame Blavatsky. In one case, for example, Mr. Hume, who became president for the first year of the new Society—the Simla Eclectic Theosophical Society, as it was decided it should be called—got a note from Koot Hoomi inside a letter received through the post from a person wholly unconnected with our occult pursuits, who was writing to him in connection with some municipal business. I myself, dressing for the evening, have found an expected letter in my coat-pocket, and on another occasion under my pillow in the morning. On one occasion, having just received a letter by the mail from England which contained matter in which I thought she would be interested, I went up to Madame Blavatsky's writing-room and read it to her. As I read it, a few lines of writing, comment upon what I was reading, were formed on a sheet of blank paper which lay before her. She actually saw the writing form itself, and called to me, pointing to the paper where it lay. There I recognise Koot Hoomi's hand—and his thought, for the comment was to the effect, "Didn't I tell you so?" and referred back to something he had said in a previous letter.

By-the-by, it may be as well to inform the reader that during the whole of the visit to Simla, of which I am now speaking, for several months before it, and until several months later, Colonel Olcott was in Ceylon, where he was engaged in a very successful lecturing tour on behalf of the Theosophical Society, in reference to some of the phenomena which occurred at Simla in 1880, when both he and Madame Blavatsky were present. Ill-natured and incredulous people—when it would be glaringly absurd about some particular phenomenon to say that Madame Blavatsky had done it by trickery of her own—used to be fond of suggesting that the wire-puller must be Colonel Olcott. In some of the newspaper criticisms of the first edition of this book, even, it has been suggested that Colonel Olcott must be the writer of the letters that I innocently ascribe to Koot Hoomi, Madame Blavatsky merely manipulating their presentation. But inasmuch as all through the autumn of 1881, while Colonel Olcott was at Ceylon and I at Simla, the letters continued to come, alternating day by day sometimes with the letters we wrote, my critics, in future, must acknowledge that this hypothesis is played out.

For me myself—as I think it will also be for my appreciative readers—the most interesting fact connected with my Simla experience of 1881 was this:—During the period in question I got into relations with one other of the Brothers, besides Koot Hoomi. It came to pass that in the progress of his own development it was necessary for Koot Hoomi to retire for a period of three months into absolute seclusion, as regards not merely the body—which in the case of an Adept may be secluded in the remotest corner of the earth without that arrangement checking the activity of his "astral" intercourse with mankind—but as regards the whole potent Ego with whom we had dealings. Under these circumstances one of the Brothers with whom Koot Hoomi was especially associated agreed, rather reluctantly at first, to pay attention to the Simla Eclectic Society, and keep us going during Koot Hoomi's absence with a course of instruction in occult philosophy. The change which came over the character of our correspondence when our new master took us in hand was very remarkable. Every letter that emanated from Koot Hoomi had continued to bear the impress of his gently mellifluous style. He would write half a page at any, time rather than run the least risk of letting a brief or careless phrase hurt anybody's feelings. His hand writing, too, was always very legible and regular. Our new master treated us very differently: he declared himself almost unacquainted with our language, and wrote a very rugged hand which it was sometimes difficult to decipher. He did not beat about the bush with us at all. If we wrote out an essay on some occult ideas we had picked up, and sent it to him, asking if it was right, it would sometimes come back with a heavy red line scored through it, and "No" written on the margin. On one occasion one of us had written, "Can you clear my conceptions about so and so?" The annotation found in the margin when the paper was returned was, "How can I clear what you haven't got I" and so on. But with all this we made progress under M—, and by degrees the correspondence, which began on his side with brief notes, scrawled in the roughest manner on bits of coarse Tibetan paper, expanded into considerable letters sometimes. And it must be understood that while his rough and abrupt ways formed an amusing contrast with the tender gentleness of Koot Hoomi, there was nothing in these to impede the growth of our attachment to him as we began to feel ourselves tolerated by him as pupils a little more willingly than at first. Some of my readers, I am sure, will realise what I mean by "attachment" in this case. I use a colourless word deliberately to avoid the parade of feelings which might not be generally understood; but I can assure them that in the course of prolonged relations—even though merely of the epistolary kind—with a personage who, though a man like the rest of us as regards his natural place in creation, is elevated so far above ordinary men as to possess some attributes commonly considered divine, feelings are engendered which are too deep to be lightly or easily described.

It was by M‑‑‑‑‑‑‑‑‑ quite recently that a little manifestation of force was given for my gratification, the importance of which turned on the fact that Madame Blavatsky was entirely uninfluential in its production, and eight hundred miles away at the time. For the first three months of my acquaintance with him, M‑‑‑‑‑‑ had rigidly adhered to the principle he laid down when he agreed to correspond with the Simla Eclectic Society during Koot Hoomi's retirement. He would correspond with us, but would perform no phenomena whatever. This narrative is so much engaged with phenomena that I cannot too constantly remind the reader that these incidents were scattered over a long period of time, and that as a rule nothing is more profoundly distasteful to the great adepts than the production of wonders in the outside world. Ordinary critics of these, when they have been thus exceptionally accorded, will constantly argue, "But why did not the Brothers do so and so differently? then the incident would have been much more convincing." I repeat that the Brothers, in producing abnormal phenomena now and then, are *not* trying to prove their existence to an intelligent jury of Englishmen. They are simply letting their existence become perceptible to persons with a natural gravitation towards spirituality and mysticism. It is not too much to say that all the while they are scrupulously *avoiding* the delivery of direct proof of a nature calculated to satisfy the commonplace mind. For the present, at all events, they prefer that the crass, materialistic Philistines of the sensual, selfish world should continue to cherish the conviction that "the Brothers" are myths. They reveal themselves, therefore, by signs and hints which are only likely to be comprehended by people with some spiritual insight or affinity. True the appearance of this book is permitted by them—no page of it would have been written if a word from Koot Hoomi had indicated disapproval on his part—and the phenomenal occurrences herein recorded are really in many cases absolutely complete and irresistible proofs *for me*, and therefore for anyone who is capable of understanding that I am telling the exact truth. But the Brothers, I imagine, know quite well that, large as the revelation has been, it may safely be passed before the eyes of the public at large just because the herd, whose convictions they do not wish to reach, can be relied upon to reject it. The situation may remind the reader of the *farceur* who undertook to stand on Waterloo Bridge with a hundred real sovereigns on a tray, offering to sell them for a shilling apiece, and who wagered that he would so stand for an hour without getting rid of his stock. He relied on the stupidity of the passers-by, who would think themselves too clever to be taken in. So with this little book. It contains a straightforward statement of absolute truths, which, if people could only believe them, would revolutionise the world; and the statement is fortified by unimpeachable credentials. But the bulk of mankind will be blinded to this condition of things by their own vanity and inability to assimilate super-materialistic ideas, and none will be seriously affected but those who are qualified to benefit by comprehending.

Readers of the latter class will readily appreciate the way the phenomena that I have had to record have thus followed in the track of my own growing convictions, confirming these as they have in turn been inferentially constructed, rather than provoking and enforcing them in the first instance. And this has been emphatically the case with the one or two phenomena that have latterly been accorded by M------. It was in friendship and kindness that these were given, long after all idea of confirming my belief in the Brothers was wholly superfluous and out of date. M------ came indeed to wish that I should have the satisfaction of seeing him (in the astral body of course), and would have arranged for this in Bombay, in January, when I went down there for a day to meet my wife, who was returning from England, had the atmospherical and other conditions just at that period permitted it. But, unfortunately for me, these were not favourable. As M----- wrote in one of several little notes I received from him during that day and the following morning, before my departure from the headquarters of the Theosophical Society, where I was staying, even they, the Brothers, could not "work miracles;" and though to the ordinary spectator there may be but little difference between a miracle and anyone of the phenomena that the Brothers do sometimes accomplish, these latter are really results achieved by the manipulation of natural laws and forces, and are subject to obstacles which are sometimes practically insuperable.

But M------, as it happened, was enabled to show himself to one member of the Simla Eclectic Society, who happened to be at Bombay a day or two before my visit. The figure was clearly visible for a few moments, and the face distinctly recognised by my friend, who had previously seen a portrait of M-------.

Then it passed across the open door of an inner room in which it had appeared, in a direction where there was no exit; and when my friend, who had started forward in its pursuit, entered the inner room, it was no longer to be seen. On two or three other occasions previously, M----- had made his astral figure visible to other persons about the headquarters of the Society, where the constant presence of Madame Blavatsky and one or two other persons of highly sympathetic magnetism, the purity of life of all habitually resident there, and the constant influences poured in by the Brothers themselves, render the production of phenomena immeasurably easier than elsewhere.

And this brings me back to certain incidents which took place recently at my own house at Allahabad, when, as I have already stated, Madame Blavatsky herself was eight hundred miles off, at Bombay. Colonel Olcott, then on his way to Calcutta, was staying with us for a day or two in passing. He was accompanied by a young native mystic, ardently aspiring to be accepted by the Brothers as a *chela*, or pupil, and the magnetism thus brought to the house established conditions which for a short time rendered some manifestations possible. Returning home one evening shortly before dinner, I found two or three telegrams awaiting me, enclosed in the usual way, in envelopes securely fastened before being sent out from the telegraph office. The messages were all from ordinary people, on commonplace business; but inside one of the envelopes I found a little folded note from M-----. The mere fact that it had been thus transfused by occult methods inside the closed envelope was a phenomenon in itself, of course (like many of the same kind that I have described before); but I need not dwell on this point, as the feat that had been performed, and of which the note gave me information, was even more obviously wonderful. The note made me search in my writing-room for a fragment of a plaster bas-relief that M----- had just transported instantaneously from Bombay. Instinct took me at once to the place where I felt that it was most likely I should find the thing which had been brought—the drawer of my writing-table, exclusively devoted to occult correspondence; and there, accordingly, I found a broken corner from a plaster slab, with M——'s signature marked upon it. I telegraphed at once to Bombay, to ask whether anything special had just happened, and next day received back word that M----- had smashed a certain plaster portrait, and had carried off a piece. In due course of time I received a minute statement from Bombay, attested by the signatures of seven persons in all, which was, as regards all essential points, as follows:—

"At about seven in the evening the following persons" (five are enumerated, including Madame Blavatsky) "were seated at the dining-table, at tea, in Madame Blavatsky's veranda opposite the door in the red screen separating her first writing-room from the long veranda. The two halves of the writing-room were wide open, and the dining-table, being about two feet from the door, we could all see plainly everything in the room. About five or seven minutes after, Madame Blavatsky gave a start. We all began to watch. She then looked all round her, and said, 'What is he going to do?' and repeated the same twice or thrice without looking at or referring to any of us. We all suddenly heard a knock—a loud noise, as of something falling and breaking—behind the door of Madame Blavatsky's writing-room, when there was not a soul there at the time. A still louder noise was heard, and we all rushed in. The room was empty and silent; but just behind the red cotton door, where we had heard the noise, we found fallen on the ground a Paris plaster mould, representing a portrait, broken into several pieces. After carefully picking the pieces up to the smallest fragments, and examining it, we found the nail, on which the mould had hung for nearly eighteen months, strong as ever in the wall. The iron wire loop of the portrait was perfectly intact, and not even bent. We spread the pieces on the table, and tried to arrange them, thinking they could be glued, as Madame Blavatsky seemed very much annoyed, as the mould was the work of one of her friends in New York. We found that one piece, nearly square and of about two inches, in the right corner of the mould, was wanting. We went into the room and searched for it, but could not find it. Shortly afterwards, Madame Blavatsky suddenly arose and went into her room, shutting the door after her. In a minute she called Mr. ------ in, and showed to him a small piece of paper. We all saw and read it afterwards. It was in the same handwriting in which some of us have received previous communications, and the same familiar initials. It told us that the missing piece was taken by the Brother whom Mr. Sinnett calls, the Illustrious,'[2] To Allahabad, and that she should collect and carefully preserve the remaining pieces." The statement goes after this into some further details, which are unimportant as regards the general reader, and is signed by the four native friends who were with Madame Blavatsky at the time the plaster portrait was broken. A postscript, signed by three other persons, adds that these three came in shortly after the actual breakage, and found the rest of the party trying to arrange the fragments on the table.

It will be understood, of course, but I may s well explicitly state, that the evening to which the above narrative relates was the same on which I found Mr. ——'s note inside my telegram at Allahabad, and the missing piece of the cast in my drawer; and no appreciable time appears to have elapsed between the breakage of the cast at Bombay and the delivery of the piece at Allahabad, for though I did not note the exact minute at which I found the fragment—and, indeed, it may have been already in my drawer for some little time before I came home—the time was certainly between seven and eight, probably about half-past seven or a quarter to eight. And there is nearly half an hour's difference of longitude between Bombay and Allahabad, so that seven at Bombay would be nearly half-past at Allahabad. Evidently, therefore, the plaster fragment, weighing two or three ounces, was really brought from Bombay to Allahabad, to all intents and purposes, instantaneously. That it was veritably the actual piece missing from the cast broken at Bombay was proved a few days later, for all the remaining pieces at Bombay were carefully packed up and sent to me, and the fractured edges of my fragment fitted exactly into those of the defective corner, so that I was enabled to arrange the pieces all together again and complete the cast.

The shrewd reader—of the class of persons who would never have been "taken in" by the man who sold sovereigns on Waterloo Bridge—will laugh at the whole story. A lump of plaster of Paris sent a distance of eight hundred miles across India in the wink of an eye by the willpower of somebody Heaven knows where at the time—probably in Tibet! The shrewd person could not manage the feat himself, so he is convinced that nobody else could, and that the event never occurred. Rather believe that the seven witnesses at Bombay and the present writer are telling a pack of lies than that there can be anyone living in the world who knows secrets of Nature, and can employ forces 'of Nature that shrewd persons of the *Times*-reading, "Jolly Bank-holiday, three-penny 'bus young man" type know nothing about. Some friends of mine, criticising the first edition of this book, have found fault with me for not adopting a more respectful and conciliatory tone towards scientific scepticism when confronting the world with allegations of the kind these pages contain. But I fail to see any motive for hypocrisy in the matter. A great number of intelligent people in these days are shaking themselves free at once from the fetters of materialism forged by modern science and the entangled superstition of ecclesiastics, resolved that the Church herself, with all her mummeries, shall fail to make them irreligious; that science itself, with all its conceit, shall not blind them to the possibilities of Nature. These are the people who will understand my narrative and the sublimity of the revelations it embodies. But all people who have been either thoroughly enslaved by dogma, or thoroughly materialised by modern science, have finally lost some faculties, and will be unable to apprehend facts that do not fit in with their preconceived ideas. They will mistake their own intellectual deficiencies for inherent impossibility of occurrence on the part of the fact described; they will be very rude in thought and speech towards persons of superior intuition, who do find themselves able to believe and, in a certain sense, to understand; and it seems to me that the time has come for letting the commonplace scoffers realise plainly that in the estimation of their more enlightened contemporaries they do indeed seem a Beotian herd, in which the better educated and the lesser educated—the orthodox savant and the city clerk—differ merely in degree and not in kind.

The morning after the occurrence of the incident just detailed, B---- R-----, the young native aspirant for *chelaship*, who had accompanied Colonel Olcott, and was staying at my house, gave me a note from Koot Hoomi, which he found under his pillow in the morning. One which I had written to Koot Hoomi, and had given to B----- R----- the previous day, had been taken, he told me, at night, before he slept. The note from Koot Hoomi was a short one, in the course of which he said, "To force phenomena in the presence of difficulties magnetic or other is forbidden as strictly as for a bank cashier to disburse money which is only entrusted to him. Even to do this much for you so far from the headquarters would be impossible but for the magnetisms 0---- and B----- R——,—have brought with them—and I could do no more." Not fully realising the force of the final words in this passage, and more struck by a previous passage, in which Koot Hoomi wrote—" It is easy for us to give phenomenal proofs when we have necessary conditions"—I wrote next day, suggesting one or two things which I thought might be done to take additional advantage of the conditions presented by the introduction into my house of available magnetism different from that of Madame Blavatsky, who had been so much, however absurdly, suspected of imposing on me. I gave this note to B---- R----- on the evening of the 13th of March—the plaster fragment incident had taken place on the 11th—and on the morning of the 14th I received a few words from Koot Hoomi, simply saying that what I proposed was impossible, and that he would write more fully through Bombay. When in due time I so heard from him, I learned that the limited facilities of the moment had been exhausted, and that my suggestions could not be complied with; but the importance of the explanations I have just been giving turns on the fact that I did, after all, exchange letters with Koot Hoomi at an interval of a few hours, at a time when Madame Blavatsky was at the other side of India.

The account I have just been giving of the instantaneous transmission of the plaster of Paris fragment from Bombay to Allahabad forms a fitting prelude to a remarkable series of incidents I have next to record. The story now to be told has already been made public in India, having been fully related in "Psychic Notes,"[3] a periodical temporarily brought out at Calcutta, with the object especially of recording incidents connected with the spiritualistic mediumship of Mr. Eglinton, who stayed for some months at Calcutta during the past cold season. The incident was hardly addressed to the outside world; rather to spiritualists, who while infinitely closer to a comprehension of occultism than people still wrapped in the darkness of orthodox incredulity, about all super-material phenomena, are nevertheless to a large extent inclined to put a purely spiritualistic explanation on *all* such phenomena. In this way it had come to pass that many spiritualists in India were inclined to suppose that we who believed in the Brothers were in some way misled by extraordinary mediumship on the part of Madame Blavatsky. And at first the "spirit guides"who spoke through Mr. Eglinton confirmed this view. But a very remarkable change came over their utterances at last. Shortly before Mr. Eglinton's departure from Calcutta, they declared their full knowledge of the Brotherhood, naming the "Illustrious" by that designation, and declaring that they had been appointed to work in concert with the Brothers thenceforth. On this aspect of affairs, Mr. Eglinton left India in the steamship *Vega*, sailing from Calcutta, I believe, on the 16th of March. A few days later, on the morning of the 24th, at AIahabad, I received a letter from Koot Hoomi, in which he told me that he was going to visit Mr. Eglinton on board the *Vega* at sea, convince him thoroughly as to the existence of the Brothers, and if successful in doing this notify the fact immediately to certain friends of

Mr. Eglinton's at Calcutta. The letter had been written a day or two before, and the night between the 21st and 22nd was mentioned as the period when the astral visit would be paid. Now the full explanation of all the circumstances under which this startling programme was carried out will take some little time, but the narrative will be the more easily followed if I first describe the outline of what took place in a few words. 'The promised visit was *actually paid*, and not only that but a letter written by Mr. Eglinton at sea on the 24th describing it—and giving in his adhesion to a belief in the Brothers fully and completely—was transported instantaneously that same evening to Bombay, where it was dropped "out of nothing" like the first letter I received on my return to India before several witnesses; by them identified and tied up with cards written on by them at the time; then taken away again and a few moments later dropped down, cards from Bombay and all, among Mr. Eglinton's friends at *Calcutta* who had been told beforehand to expect a communication from the Brothers at that time. All the incidents of this series are authenticated by witnesses and documents, and there is no rational escape, for any one who looks into the evidence, from the necessity of admitting that the various phenomena as I have just described them have actually been accomplished, "impossible" as ordinary science will declare them.

For the details of the various incidents of the series, I may refer the reader to the account published in *Psychic Notes* of March 30, by Mrs. Gordon, wife of Colonel W. Gordon, of Calcutta, and authenticated with her signature.

Colonel Olcott, Mrs. Gordon explains in the earlier part of her statement, which for brevity's sake Icondense, had just arrived at Calcutta on a visit to Colonel Gordon and herself. A letter had come from Madame Blavatsky—

> "dated Bombay the 19th, telling us that something was going to be done, and expressing the earnest hope that she would not be required to assist, as she had had enough abuse about phenomena. Before this letter was brought by the post peon, Colonel Olcott had told me that he had had an intimation in the night from his Chohan (teacher) that K. H.[4] Had been to the *Vega* and seen Eglinton. This was at about eight o'clock on Thursday morning, the 23rd. A few hours later a telegram, dated at Bombay, 22nd day,21 hours 9 minutes, that is, say 9 minutes past 9 P.M. on Wednesday evening, came to me from Madame Blavatsky, to this effect: 'K. H. just gone to *Vega*.' This telegram came as a 'delayed' message, and was I to me from Calcutta, which accounts for its not reaching me until midday on Thursday. It corroborated, as will be seen, the message of the previous night to Colonel Olcott. We then felt hopeful of getting the letter by occult means from Mr. Eglinton. A telegram later on Thursday asked us to fix a "time for a sitting, so we named

9 o'clock Madras time, on Friday, 24th. At this hour we three—Colonel Olcott, Colonel Gordon, and myself—sat in the room which had been occupied by Mr. Eglinton.. We had a good light, and sat with our chairs placed to form a triangle, of which the apex was to the north. In a few minutes Colonel Olcott saw outside the open window the two 'Brothers' whose names are best known to us, and told us so; he saw them pass to another window, the glass doors of which were closed. He saw one of them point his hand towards the air over my head, and I felt something at the same moment fall straight down from above on to my shoulder, and saw it fall at my feet in the direction towards the two gentlemen. I knew it would be the letter, but for the moment I was so anxious to see the 'Brothers' that I did not pick up what had fallen. Colonel Gordon and Colonel Olcott both saw and heard the letter fall. Colonel Olcott had turned his head from the window for a moment to see what the I Brother' was pointing at, and so noticed the letter falling from a point about two feet from the ceiling. When he looked again the two 'Brothers' had vanished.

"There is no veranda outside, and the window is several feet from the ground.

"I now turned and picked up what had fallen on me, and found a letter in Mr. Eglinton's handwriting, dated on the *Vega* the 24th; a message from Madame Blavatsky, dated at Bombay the 24th, written on the backs of three of her visiting cards; also a larger card, such as Mr. Eglinton had a packet of, and used at his *séances*. On this latter card was the, to us, well-known handwriting of K. H., and a few words in the handwriting of the other 'Brother,' who was with him outside our window, and who is Colonel Olcott's chief. All these cards and the letter were threaded together with a piece of blue sewing silk. We opened the letter carefully, by slitting up one side, as we saw that some one had made on the flap in pencil three Latin crosses, and so we kept them intact for identification. The letter is as follows:—

"'S. S. *Vega*, Friday, 24th March, 1882.",

My DEAR MRS. GORDON,

—At last your hour of triumph has come! After the many battles we have had at the breakfast-table regarding K. H.'s existence, and my stubborn scepticism as to the wonderful powers possessed by the "Brothers," I have been forced to a *complete belief* in their being living distinct persons, and just in proportion to my scepticism will be my *firm unalterable opinion* respecting them. I am not allowed to tell you all I know, but K. H. *appeared* to me in person two days ago, and what he told me dumfounded me. Perhaps Madame B. will have already communicated the fact of K. H.'s appearance to you. The "Illustrious" is uncertain whether this can be taken to Madame or not, but he will try, notwithstanding the many difficulties in the way. If he does not I shall post it when I arrive at port. I shall read this to Mrs. B---- and ask her to mark the envelope; but *whatever happens*, you are requested by K. H. to keep this letter a profound secret until you hear from him though Madame. A storm of opposition is certain to be raised, and she has had so much to bear that it is hard she should have more.' Then follow some remarks about his health and the trouble which is taking him home, and the letter ends.

"In her note on the three visiting cards Madame Blavatsky says:— 'Headquarters, March 24th. These cards and contents to certify to my doubters that the attached letter addressed to Mrs. Gordon by Mr. Eglinton was just brought to me from the *Vega*, with another letter from himself to me, which I keep. K. H. tells me he saw Mr. Eglinton and had a talk with him, long and convincing enough to make him a believer in the "Brothers," as actual living beings, for the rest of his natural life. Mr. Eglinton writes to me: 'The letter which I enclose is going to be taken to Mrs. G. through your influence. You will receive it wherever you are, and will forward it to her in ordinary course. You will learn with satisfaction of my complete conversion to a belief in the "Brothers", and I have no doubt K. H. has already told you how he appeared to me two nights ago," etc., etc.. K. H. *told me all*. He does not, however, want me to forward the letter in "ordinary course", as it would defeat the object, but commands me to write this and send it off without delay, so that it would reach you all at Howrah tonight, the 24th. I do so...

H. P. Blavatsky.'

'The handwriting on these cards and signature are perfectly well known to us. That on the larger card (from Mr. Eglinton's packet) attached was easily recognised as coming from Koot Hoomi . Colonel Gordon and I know his writing as well as our own; it is so distinctly different from any other I have ever seen, that among thousands I could select it. He says, William Eglinton thought the manifestation could only be produced through H. P. B. as a "medium", and that the power would become exhausted at Bombay. We decided otherwise. Let this be a proof to all that the spirit of *living man* has as much potentiality in it (and often more) as a disembodied *soul*. He was anxious to *test her*, he often doubted; two nights ago he had the required proof and will doubt no more. But he is a good young man, bright, honest, and true as gold when once convinced...

'This card was taken from his stock today. Let it be an additional proof of his wonderful mediumship...

K. H.'

"This is written in blue ink, and across it is written in red ink a few words from the other 'Brother' (Colonel Olcott's Chohan or chief). This interesting and wonderful phenomenon is not published with the idea that anyone who is unacquainted with the phenomena of spiritualism will accept it. But I write for the millions of spiritualists, and also that a record may be made of such an interesting experiment. Who knows but that it may pass on to a generation which will be enlightened enough to accept such wonders?"

A postscript adds that since the above statement was written, a paper had been received from Bombay, signed by seven witnesses who saw the letter arrive there from the *Vega*.

As I began by saying, this phenomenon was addressed more to spiritualists than to the outer world, because its great value for the experienced observer of phenomena turns on the utterly unmediumistic character of the events. Apart from the testimony of Mr. Eglinton's own letter to the effect that he, an experienced medium, was quite convinced that the interview he had with his occult visitant was not an interview with such "spirits" as he had been used to, we have the three-cornered character of the incident to detach it altogether from mediumship either on his part or on that of Madame Blavatsky.

Certainly there have been cases in which under the influence or mediumship the agencies of the ordinary spiritual *séance* have transported letters half across the globe. A conclusively authenticated case in which an unfinished letter was thus brought from London to Calcutta will have attracted the attention of all persons who have their understanding awakened to the importance of these matters, and who read what is currently published about them, quite recently. But every spiritualist will recognise that the transport of a letter from a ship at sea to Bombay, and then from Bombay to Calcutta, with a definite object in view, and in accordance with a prearranged and pre-announced plan, is something quite outside the experience of mediumship.

Will the effort made and the expenditure of force, whatever may have been required to accomplish the wonderful feat thus recorded, be repaid by proportionately satisfactory effects on the spiritualistic world? There has been a great deal written lately in England about the antagonism between spiritualism and theosophy, and an impression has arisen in some way that the two *cultes* are incompatible. Now, the phenomena and the experiences of spiritualism are facts, and nothing can be incompatible with facts. But theosophy brings on the scene new interpretations of those facts, it is true, and sometimes these prove very unwelcome to spiritualists long habituated to their own interpretation. Hence, such spiritualists are now and then disposed to resist the new teaching altogether, and hold out against a belief that there can be anywhere in existence men entitled to advance it. This is consequently the important question to settle before we advance into the region of metaphysical subtleties. Let spiritualists once realise that the Brothers do exist, and what sort of people they are, and a great step will have been accomplished. Not all at once is it to be expected that the spiritual world will consent to revise its conclusions by occult doctrines. It is only by prolonged intercourse with the Brothers that a conviction grows up in the mind that as regards spiritual science they *cannot* be in error. At first, let spiritualists think them in error if they please; but at all events it will be unworthy of their elevated position above the Beotian herd if they deny the evidence of phenomenal facts; if they hold towards occultism the attitude which the crass sceptic of the mere Lankester type occupies towards spiritualism itself. So I cannot but hope that the coruscation of phenomena connected with the origin and adventures of the letter written on board the *Vega* may have flashed out of the darkness to some good purpose, showing the spiritualistic world quite plainly that the great Brother to whom this work is dedicated is, at all events, a living man, with faculties and powers of that entirely abnormal kind which spiritualists have hitherto conceived to inhere merely in beings belonging to a superior scheme of existence.

For my part, I am glad to say that I not only know him to be a living man by reason of all the circumstances detailed in this volume, but I am now enabled to realise his features and appearance by means of two portraits, which have been conceded to me under very remarkable conditions. It was long a wish of mine to possess a portrait of my revered friend; and some time ago he half promised that some time or other he would give me one. Now, in asking an adept for his portrait, the object desired is not a photograph, but a picture produced by a certain occult process which I have not yet had occasion to describe, but with which I had long been familiar by hearsay. I had heard, for example, from Colonel Olcott, of one of the circumstances under which his own original convictions about the realities of occult power were formed many years ago in New York, before he had actually entered on "the path." Madame Blavatsky on that occasion had told him to bring her a piece of paper which he would be certainly able to identify, in order that she might get a portrait precipitated upon it. We cannot, of course, by the light of ordinary knowledge form any conjecture about the details of the process employed; but just as an adept can, as I have had so many proofs, precipitate writing in closed envelopes, and on the pages of uncut pamphlets, so he can precipitate color in such a way as to form a picture. In the case of which Colonel Olcott told me he took home a piece of note-paper from a club in New York—a piece bearing a club stamp—and gave this to Madame Blavatsky. She put it between the sheets of blotting-paper on her writing-table, rubbed her hand over the outside of the pad, and then in a few moments the marked paper was given back to him with a complete picture upon it representing an Indian fakir in a state of *samadhi*. And the artistic execution of this drawing was conceived by artists to whom Colonel Olcott afterwards showed it to be so good that they compared it to the works of old masters whom they specially adored and affirmed that as an artistic curiosity it was unique and priceless. Now in aspiring to have a portrait of Koot Hoomi, of course I was wishing for a precipitated picture, and it would seem that just before a recent visit Madame Blavatsky paid to Allahabad, something must have been said to her about a possibility that this wish of mine might be gratified. For the day she came she asked me to give her a piece of thick white paper and mark it. This she would leave in her scrapbook, and there was reason to hope that a certain highly advanced *chela*, or pupil, of Koot Hoomi's, not a full adept himself as yet, but far on the road to that condition, would do what was necessary to produce the portrait.

Nothing happened that day nor that night. The scrapbook remained lying on a table in the drawing-room, and was occasionally inspected. The following morning it was looked into by my wife, and my sheet of paper was found to be still blank. Still the scrapbook lay in full view on the drawing-room table. At half-past eleven we went to breakfast; the dining-room, as is often the case in Indian bungalows, only being separated from the drawing-room by an archway and curtains, which were drawn aside. While we were at breakfast Madame Blavatsky suddenly showed, by the signs with which all who know her are familiar, that one of her occult friends was near. It was the *chela* to whom I have above referred. She got up, thinking she might be required to go to her room; but the astral visitor, she said, waved her back, and she returned to the table. After breakfast we looked into the scrapbook, and on my marked sheet of paper, which had been seen blank by my wife an hour or two before, was a precipitated profile portrait. The face itself was left white, with only a few touches within the limits of the space it occupied; but the rest of the paper all round it was covered with cloudy blue shading. Slight as the method was by which the result was produced, the outline of the face was perfectly well-defined, and its expression as vividly rendered as would have been possible with a finished picture.

At first Madame Blavatsky was dissatisfied with the sketch. Knowing the original personally, she could appreciate its deficiencies; but though I should have welcomed a more finished portrait, I was sufficiently pleased with the one I had thus received to be reluctant that Madame Blavatsky should try any experiment with it herself with the view of improving it, for fear it would be spoilt. In the course of the conversation, M---- put himself in communication with Madame Blavatsky, and said that he would do a portrait himself on another piece of paper. There was no question in this case of a "test phenomenon"; so after I had procured and given to Madame Blavatsky a (marked) piece of Bristol board, it was put away in the scrapbook, and taken to her room, where, free from the confusing cross magnetisms of the drawing-room, M---- would be better able to operate.

Now it will be understood that neither the producer of the sketch I had received, nor M-----, in the natural state, is an artist. Talking over the whole subject of these occult pictures, I ascertained from Madame Blavatsky that the supremely remarkable results have been obtained by those of the adepts whose occult science as regards this particular process has been superseded to ordinary artistic training. But entirely without this, the adept can produce a result which, for all ordinary critics, looks like the work of an artist, by merely realising very clearly in his imagination the result he wishes to produce, and then precipitating the coloring matter in accordance with that conception.

In the course of about an hour from the time at which she took away the piece of Bristol board—or the time may have been less—we were not watching it, Madame Blavatsky brought it me back with another portrait, again a profile, though more elaborately done. Both portraits were obviously of the same face, and nothing, let me say at once, can exceed the purity and lofty tenderness of its expression. Of course it bears no mark of age. Koot Hoomi, by the mere years of his life, is only a man of what we call middle age; but the adept's physically simple and refined existence leaves no trace of its passage; and while our faces rapidly wear out after forty—strained, withered, and burned up by the passions to which all ordinary lives are more or less exposed—the adept age, for periods of time that I can hardly venture to define, remains apparently the perfection of early maturity. M-----, Madame Blavatsky's special guardian still, as I judge by a portrait of him that I have seen, though I do not yet possess one, in the absolute prime of manhood, has been her occult guardian from the time she was a child; and now she is an old lady. He never looked, she tells me, any different from what he looks now.

I have now brought up to date the record of all external facts connected with the revelations I have been privileged to make. The door leading to occult knowledge is still ajar, and it is still permissible for explorers from the outer world to make good their footing across the threshold. This condition of things is due to exceptional circumstances at present, and may not continue long. Its continuance may largely depend upon the extent to which the world at large manifests an appreciation of the opportunity now offered. Some readers who are interested, but slow to perceive what practical action they can take, may ask what they can do to show appreciation of the opportunity. My reply will be modelled on the famous injunction of Sir Robert Peel: "Register, register, register!" Take the first steps towards making a response to the offer which emanates from the occult world—register, register, register; in other words, join the Theosophical Society—

the one and only association which at present is linked by any recognised bond of union with the Brotherhood of Adepts in Tibet. There is a Theosophical Society in London, as there are other branches in Paris and America, as well as in India. If there is as yet but little for these branches to do, that fact does not vitiate their importance. After a voter has registered, there is not much for *him* to do for the moment. The mere growth of branches of the Theosophical Society, as associations of people who realise the sublimity of adeptship, and have been able to feel that the story told in this little book, and more fully, if more obscurely, in many greater volumes of occult learning, is absolutely true—true, not as shadowy religious "truths" or orthodox speculations are held to be true by their votaries, but true as the "London Post-Office Directory" is true; as the Parliamentary reports people read in the morning are true; the mere enrolment of such people in a society under conditions which may enable them sometimes to meet and talk the situation over if they do no more, may actually effect a material result as regards the extent to which the authorities of the occult world will permit the further revelation of the sublime knowledge they possess. Remember, that knowledge is real knowledge of other worlds and other states of existence—not vague conjecture about hell and heaven and purgatory, but precise knowledge of other worlds going on at this moment, the condition and nature of which the adepts can cognize, as we can the condition and nature of a strange town we may visit. These worlds are linked with our own, and our lives with the lives they support; and will the further acquaintance with the few men on earth who are in a position to tell us more about them be superciliously rejected by the advance guard of the civilized world, the educated classes of England? Surely no inconsiderable group will be sufficiently spiritualized to comprehend the value of the present opportunity, and sufficiently practical to follow the advice already quoted, and—register, register, register.

---

1. Subsequently published as Esoteric Buddhism.
2. "My illustrious friend," was the expression I originally used in application to the Brother I have here called M—, and it got shortened afterwards into the pseudonym given in the statement. It is difficult sometimes to know what to call the Brothers, even when one knows their real names. The less these are promiscuously handled the better, for various reasons, among which is the profound annoyance which it gives their real disciples if such names get into frequent and disrespectful use among scoffers. I regret now that Koot Hoomi's name, so ardently venerated by all who have been truly subject to his influence, should ever have been allowed to appear in full in the text of the book.
3. Newton & Co., Calcutta.
4. We had got into the habit at this time of using these initials for the Mahatma's name.

APPENDIX

A

LATER acquaintance with the subject has done much to show me that the reserve hitherto maintained by the masters of occult science was inevitable. It is useless to offer any man information which his faculties are not sufficiently expanded to receive. Only a few hundred years after the physical science that has been absorbed by the last two or three generations with avidity would have been unwelcome and despised. Till quite recently the serious contemplation of psychic phenomena would have been resented as a relapse into superstition. No man can investigate causes till he is willing to observe facts, and it was only the other day that a disposition to observe facts lying outside the domain of physical causation would have alienated any prematurely developed enthusiast from the sympathies of all his contemporaries. The light of mere worldly wisdom may thus vindicate the reticence of the few and secluded custodians of the higher knowledge, but with far greater precision is their policy vindicated when with their own help we come at last to comprehend the scientific law of human intellectual development. The progress of the world is not rolling on under the direction of blind chance. Propelled though it is by the collective impulses of individual energy, it advances in a defined path, and the knowledge, the discoveries, the spiritual teaching, which breaks upon the world at each stage of its advancement, is precisely proportioned to the receptivity of mankind at that period of its evolution. The revelation of occult truth going on in the world just now in many ways and under various aspects—though as I most emphatically believe, under none more unequivocally or satisfactorily than in the case of the direct teaching of occult science I am instrumental in bringing to public notice—is the legitimate inheritance of this generation, and the good it may do in the world now could not have been done only a few decades ago. It is useless to try to take a photographic picture upon a non-sensitized plate; it is useless to present the subtle conceptions of spiritual science to minds on which no psychic collodion has previously been deposited. The Esoteric study in which some of us connected with the Theosophical Society have been privileged, during the last two or three years, to engage, has so effectually dispelled the discontent we first felt at the jealousy that had withheld this teaching from the world so long, that we recognise the message we are now commissioned to convey as addressed so far only to the most highly advanced and intuitive minds of our time. We are but beginning to put forward a doctrine which will only be appreciated in its full significance later on.

—June 7, 1884.

B.

It is interesting to observe that, in accordance with predictions made to me when I began to write on these subjects, the dawn of psychic truth has begun to brighten our sky from several directions at once. The psychological telegraphy here referred to was quite unheard of In the world at large in 1880. But for the last year or two the Psychic Research Society in London has been specially engaged on a long series of experiments in what it calls "thought transference," the phenomena of which contain the germs of the adepts' psychic telegraph. If anyone still doubts that thought impressions really can be conveyed from one mind to another, without the aid of speech or any sign or communication whatever having to do with the physical senses, he is unacquainted with the result of scientific enquiry in that direction. The transactions of the society referred to put the broad fact just noted beyond the reach of incredulity that can any longer be regarded as intelligent.

C

It is too late in the day now, when several editions of this book have already passed through the press, to affect any reserve about this name. But in truth I greatly regret now that I ever permitted it to become public property. All over India the disciples of the Brothers regard their Masters' names with the tenderest possible respect. The free and easy criticism to which this book has naturally been subject since its first appearance has often been associated with more or less disrespectful references to my revered correspondent, and this has given rise to great pain on the part of the regular *chelas* in India, the pupils of occult science; indeed, it is no longer necessary to go to India in search of persons whose sensibilities are liable to be disturbed seriously in the same way. In London a large and earnestly studious branch of the Theosophical Society has been formed, and long contact with the grand conceptions of Esoteric philosophy has developed on the part of its members a sentiment of reverence for the Mahatmas only second in intensity to that of the regular oriental initiates. It would spare all such persons a great deal of indignant distress, if the name I was unfortunately led to print in this work at full length had never been disclosed. To most Western readers the matter may seem very unimportant, but trouble and annoyance which I greatly deplore have ensued from the mistake thus committed. As a matter of fact, I may here observe that the original manuscript of my book, was written from end to end without the use of the name, instead of, which I had placed a mere initial, "H", but a letter I received from India shortly before the publication of the book authorised the use of the name, and I felt at that time that it was absurd to be *plus royaliste que le roi*. So the step came to be taken which cannot now be recalled. The name of the Mahatma here made use of, I may explain, in conclusion of this digression.

D

The necessity of reprinting this work for a fourth edition gives me an opportunity of noticing some discussion that has taken place in the spiritualistic press on the subject of a letter addressed to *Light*, of September 1st, 1883, by Mr. Henry Kiddle, an American spiritualist. The letter was as follows:

To THE EDITOR OF "*LIGHT*."

Sir,

—In a communication that appeared in your issue of July 21st, "'G. W., M.D.," reviewing "'Esoteric Buddhism," says: Regarding this Koot Hoomi, it is a very remarkable and unsatisfactory fact that Mr. Sinnett, although in correspondence with him for years, has yet never been permitted to see him."I agree with your corespondent entirely; and this is not the only fact that is unsatisfactory to me. On reading Mr. Sinnett's "Occult World," more than a year ago, I was very greatly surprised to find in one of the letters presented by Mr. Sinnett as having been transmitted to him by Koot Hoomi, in the mysterious manner described, a passage taken almost *verbatim* from an address on Spiritualislm by me at Lake Pleasant in August, 1880, and published the same month by the *Banner of Light*. As Mr. Sinnett's book did not appear till a considerable time afterwards (about a year, I think), it is certain that I did not quote, consciously or unconsciously, from its pages. How, then, did it get into Koot Hoomi's mysterious letter?

I sent to Mr. Sinnett a letter through his publishers, enclosing the printed pages of my address, with the part used by Koot Hoomi marked upon it, and asked for an explanation, for I wondered that so great a sage as Koot Hoomi should need to *borrow* anything from so humble a student of spiritual things as myself. As yet I have received no reply; and the query has been suggested to my mind—Is Koot Hoomi a myth? or, if not, is he so great an adept as to have impressed my mind with his thoughts and word while I was preparing my address?If the latter were the case he could not consistently exclaim: "'*Pereant qui ante nos nostra dixerunt.*"

Perhaps Mr. Sinnett may think it scarcely worth while to solve this little problem; but the fact that the existence of the brotherhood has not yet been proved may induce some to raise the question suggested by "G. W., M. D". Is there any such secret order? On this question, which is not intended to imply anything offensive to Mr. Sinnett, that other still more important question may depend. Is Mr. Sinnett's recently published book an exponent of Esoteric Buddhism? It Is, doubtless, a work of great ability, and its statements are worthy of deep thought; but the main question is, are they true, or how can they be verified?' As this cannot he accomplished except by the exercise of abnormal or transcendental faculties, they must be accepted, if at all, upon the *ipse dixit* of the accomplished adept, who has been so kind as to sacrifice his esoteric character or vow, and make Mr. Sinnett his channel of communication with the outer world, thus rendering his sacred knowledge exoteric. Hence, if this publication, with its wonderful doctrine of Shells,"overturning the consolatory conclusions of Spiritualists, is to be accepted, the authority must he established, and the existence of the adept or adepts—indeed, the facts of adeptship—must be proved. The first step in affording this proof has hardly yet, I think, been taken. I trust this book will be very carefully analysed, and the nature of its inculcations exposed, whether they are Esoteric Buddhism or not,

The following are the passages referred to, printed side by side[1]—for the sake of ready reference.

Extract from Mr. Kiddle's discourse, entitled "The Present Outlook of Spiritualism", delivered at Lake Pleasant Camp Meeting on Sunday, August 15, 1880.

"My friends, *ideas* rule the world; and as men's minds receive new ideas, laying aside the old and effete, the world advances. Society rests upon them; mighty revolutions spring from them; institutions crumble before their onward march. It is just as impossible to resist their influx, when the time comes, as to stay the progress of the tide.

And the agency called Spiritualism is bringing a new set of ideas into the world—ideas on the most momentous subjects, touching man's true position in the universe; his origin and destiny; the relation of the mortal to the immortal; of the temporary to the Eternal; of the finite to the Infinite; of man's deathless soul to the material universes in which it now dwells—ideas larger, more general, more comprehensive, recognising more fully the universal reign of law as the expression of the Divine will, unchanging and unchangeable in regard to which there is only an *Eternal Now*, while to mortals time is past or future, as related to their finite existence on this material plane; etc., etc., etc.,

New York, August 11th, 1883

Extract from Koot Hoomi's letter to Mr. Sinnett, in the "Occult World", 3rd Edition, page 102. The first edition was published in June 1881.

Ideas rule the world; and as men's minds receive new ideas, laying aside the old and effete, the world will advance, mighty revolutions will spring from them, creeds and even powers will crumble before their onward march, crushed by their irresistible force. It will be just as impossible to resist their influence when the time comes as to stay the progress of the tide. But all this will come gradually on, before it comes we have a duty set before us; that of sweeping away as much as possible the dross left to us by our pious forefathers. New ideas have to be planted on clean places, for these ideas touch upon the most momentous subjects. It is not physical phenomena, but these universal ideas that we study, as to comprehend the former, we have first to understand the latter. They touch man's true position in the universe in relation to his previous and future births, his origin and ultimate destiny; the relation of the mortal to the immortal, of the temporary to the Eternal, of the finite to the Infinite; ideas larger, grander, more comprehensive, recognising the eternal reign of immutable law, unchanging and unchangeable, in regards to which there is only an ETERNAL NOW; while to uninitiated mortals time is past or future as related to their finite existence on this material speck of dirt, etc., etc., etc.

HENRY KIDDLE.

The appearance of this letter puzzled, without very much disturbing, the equanimity of Theosophical students. If it had been published immediately after the first publication of the "Occult World," its effect might have been more serious, but in the interim the Brothers had by degrees communicated to the public through my agency such a considerable block of philosophical teaching, then already embodied in my second book, "*Esoteric Buddhism*," and scattered through two or three volumes of the *Theosophist*, that appreciative readers had passed beyond the stage of development in which it might have been possible for them to suppose that the principal author of this teaching could at any time have been under any intellectual temptation to borrow thoughts from a spiritualistic lecture. Various hypotheses were framed to account for the mysterious identity between the two passages cited, and people to whom the Theosophic teachings were unacceptable, as overthrowing conceptions to which they were attached, were greatly enchanted to find my revered instructor convicted, as they thought, of a commonplace plagiarism. A couple of months necessarily elapsed before an answer could be obtained from India on the subject, and meanwhile the "Kiddle incident," as it came to be called, was joyfully treated by various correspondents writing in the columns of *Light*, as having dealt a fatal blow at the authority of the Indian Mahatmas as exponents of esoteric truth.

In due course I received a long and instructive explanation of the mystery from Mahatma Koot Hoomi himself; but this letter reached me under the seal of the most absolute confidence. Rigidly adhering to the policy which had all along restrained within narrow limits the communication of their teaching to the world at large, the Brothers remained as anxious as ever to leave everybody full intellectual liberty to disbelieve in them, and reject their revelation if his spiritual intuitions were not of a kind to be readily kindled. In the same way that from the first they had refused me the overwhelming and irresistible proofs of their power, which I had sought for in the beginning as weapons with which I might successfully combat incredulity, they now shrank from interfering with the conclusions of any readers who might be found capable, after the rich assurances of the later teaching, of distrusting the Mahatmas on the strength of a suspicion which was ill founded in reality, plausible though it might seem. Debarred myself, however, from making any public use of the Mahatma's letter, some of the residents and visitors at the Headquarters of the Theosophical Society at Adyar, Madras, came into possession of the true facts of the case, and some communications appeared in the society's magazine which afforded everyone honestly desirous of comprehending the truth of the matter, all necessary information. In the December number of the *Theosophist*, Mr. Subba Row put forward a very cautiously worded article, hinting merely at the actual explanation of the identity of the passages cited by Mr. Kiddle, and concerned chiefly with an elaborate analysis of the "plagiarised" sentences, the object of which was to show that in truth we might have divined for ourselves, if we had been sharp enough in the beginning, that some mistake had been made, and that the Mahatma could not have intended to write the sentences just as they stood. The hint conveyed by Mr. Subba was as follows:—

> "Therefore from a careful perusal of the passage and its contents, any unbiased reader will come to the conclusion that somebody must have greatly blundered over the said passage, and will not be surprised to hear that it was unconsciously altered through the carelessness and ignorance of the *chela* by whose instrumentality it was 'precipitated.' Such alterations, omissions, and mistakes sometimes occur in the process of precipitation; and I now assert I know it for certain, from an inspection of the original precipitation proof, that such was the case with regard to the passage under discussion."

The same *Theosophist* in which this article appeared contained a letter from General Morgan in reply to various spiritualistic attacks on the Theosophical position, and in the course of his remarks he referred to the "Kiddle incident" as follows:—

> "Happily we have been permitted, many of us, to look behind the veil of the parallel passage mystery, and the whole affair is very satisfactorily explained to us; but all that we are permitted to say is that many a passage was entirely omitted from the letter received by Mr. Sinnett, its precipitation from the original dictation to the *chela*. Would our Great Master but permit us his humble followers to photograph and publish in the *Theosophist* the scraps shown to us, scraps in which whole sentences parenthetical and quotation marks are defaced and obliterated and consequently omitted in the *chela*' clumsy transcription—the public would be treated to a rare sight —something entirely unknown to modern science—namely, an *akasic* impression as good as a photograph of mentally expressed thoughts dictated from a distance."

A month or two after the appearance of these fragmentary hints, I received a note from the Mahatma relieving me of all restrictions previously imposed on the full letter of explanation he had previously sent me. The subject, by that time, however, seemed to have lost its interest for all persons in England whose opinions I valued. Within the London Theosophical Society, now already a large and growing body, the Kiddle incident was looked on as little more than a joke, and the notion that the

Mahatma who had inspired the teachings of Esoteric Buddhism, could have "plagiarised" from a spiritualistic lecture, as so absurd on the face of things that no appearances seeming to endorse that conception could have any importance. I did not feel disposed, therefore, to treat the suspicions some critics had entertained, with the respect that would have been involved in any appeal from me to the public to listen to what would have been represented as a defence—and a strangely postponed defence—of the Mahatma.

Now, however, that this new edition of the Occult World II is required, there is an obvious propriety in the course I now take. The new letter from the Mahatma constitutes in itself a correction of the letter from which I quote on pages 101-102, and apart from the interest of the explanation it furnishes in regard to the precipitation process, the thoughts it conveys are in themselves valuable and suggestive.

"The letter in question," writes the Mahatma, referring to the communication I originally received, "was framed by me while on a journey and on horseback. It was dictated mentally in the direction of and precipitated by a young *chela* not yet expert at this branch of psychic chemistry, and who had to transcribe it from the hardly visible imprint. Half of it, therefore, was omitted, and the other half more or less distorted by the 'artist.' When asked by him at the time whether I would look over and correct it, I answered—imprudently, I confess—"Anyhow will do, my boy; it is of no great importance if you skip a few words.'I was physically very tired by a ride of forty-eight hours consecutively, and (physically again) half asleep. Besides this, I had very important business to attend to psychically, and therefore little remained of me to devote to that letter. When I awoke I found it had already been sent on, and as I was not then anticipating its publication, I never gave it from that time a thought. Now I had never evoked spiritual Mr. Riddle's physiognomy, never had heard of his existence, was not aware of his name. Having, owing to our correspondence, and your Simla surroundings and friends, felt interested in the intellectual progress of the Phenomenalists, I had directed my attention, some two months previous, to the great annual camping movement of the American Spiritualists in various directions, among others to Lake or Mount Pleasant. Some of the curious ideas and sentences representing the general hopes and aspirations of the American Spiritualists remained impressed on my memory, and I remembered only these ideas and detached sentences quite apart from the personalities of those who harboured or pronounced them. Hence my entire ignorance of the lecturer whom I have innocently defrauded, as it would appear, and who raises the hue and cry. Yet had I dictated my letter in the form it now appears in print, it would certainly look suspicious, and however far from what is generally called plagiarism, yet in the absence of any inverted commas it would lay a foundation for censure. But I did nothing of the kind, as the original impression now before me clearly shows. And before I proceed any further I must give you some explanation of this mode of precipitation.

The recent experiments of the Psychic Research Society will help you greatly to comprehend the rationale of this mental telegraphy. You have observed in the journal of that body, how thought transference is cumulatively effected. The image of the geometrical or other figure which the active brain has had impressed upon it is gradually imprinted upon the recipient brain of the passive subject, as the series of reproductions illustrated in the cuts show. Two factors are needed to produce a perfect and instantaneous mental telegraphy—close concentration in the operator and complete receptive passivity in the reader subject. Given a disturbance of either condition, and the result is proportionately imperfect. The reader does not see the image as in the telegrapher's brain, but as arising in his own. When the latter's thought wanders, the psychic current becomes broken, the communication disjointed and incoherent. In a case such as mine the *chela* had, as it were, to pick up what he could from the current I was sending him, and, as above remarked, patch the broken bits together as best he might. Do not you see the same thing in ordinary mesmerism—the *maya* impressed upon the subject's imagination by the operator becoming now stronger, now feebler, as the latter keeps the intended illusive image more or less steadily before his own fancy. And how often the clairvoyants reproach the magnetiser for taking their thoughts off the subject under consideration. And the mesmeric healer will always bear you witness that if he permits himself to think of anything but the vital current he is pouring into his patient, he is at once compelled to either establish the current afresh or stop the treatment. So I, in this instance, having at the moment more vividly in my mind the psychic diagnosis of current spiritualistic thought, of which the Lake Pleasant speech was one marked symptom, unwittingly transferred that reminiscence more vividly than my own remarks upon it and deductions therefrom. So to say, the 'despoiled victim's'—Mr. Kiddle's—utterances came out as a high light, and were more sharply photographed (first, in the *chela*'s brain, and thence on the paper before him, a double process, and one far more difficult than thought reading simply), while the rest, my remarks thereupon and arguments—as I now find, are hardly visible and quite blurred on the original scraps before me. Put into a mesmeric subject's hand a sheet of bank paper, tell him it contains a certain chapter of some book that you have read, concentrate your thoughts upon the words, and see how—provided that he has himself not read the chapter, but only takes it from your memory, his reading will reflect your own more or less vivid successive recollections of your author's language. The same as to the precipitation by the *chela* of the transferred thought upon (or rather into) paper. If the mental picture received be feeble, his visible reproduction of it must correspond. And the more so in proportion to the closeness of attention he gives. He might—were he but merely a person of the true mediumistic temperament—be employed by his "Master" as a sort of psychic printing machine (producing lithographed or psychographed impressions of what the operator had in mind; his nerve system the machine, his nerve aura the printing fluid, the colors drawn from that exhaustless store-house of pigments (as of everything else) the akasa. But the medium and the *chela* are diametrically dissimilar, and the latter acts consciously, except under exceptional circumstances, during development not necessary to dwell upon here.

"Well, as soon as I heard of the change, the commotion among my defenders having reached me across the eternal snows, I ordered an investigation into the original scraps of the impression. At the first glance I saw that it was I the only and most guilty party, the poor boy having done hut that which he was told. Having now restored the characters and the lines omitted and blurred beyond hope of recognition by anyone but their original evolver, to their primitive color and places, I now find my letter reading quite differently, as you will observe. Turning to the 'Occult World', the copy sent by you, to the page cited, I was struck, upon carefully reading it, by the great discrepancy between the sentences, a gap, so to say, of ideas between part 1 and part 2, the plagiarised portion so called. There seems no connection at all between the two; for what has indeed the determination of our chiefs (to prove to a sceptical world that physical phenomena are as reducible to law as anything else) to do with Plato's ideas which 'rule the world,' or 'Practical Brotherhood of Humanity.' I fear that it is your personal friendship alone for the writer that has blinded you to the discrepancy and disconnection of ideas in this abortive precipitation even until now. Otherwise you could not have failed to perceive that something was wrong on that page, that there was a glaring defect in the connection. Moreover, I have to plead guilty to another sin: I have never so much as looked at my letters in print, until the day of the forced investigation. I had read only your own original matter, feeling it a loss of time to go over my hurried bits and scraps of thought. But now I have to ask you to read the passages as they were originally dictated by me, and make the comparison with the 'Occult World' before you...I enclose the copy verbatim from the restored fragments, underlining in red the omitted sentences for easier comparison.

"...Phenomenal elements previously unthought of... will disclose at last the secrets of their mysterious workings. Plato was right to *readmit every element of speculation which Socrates had discarded. The problems of universal being are not unattainable, or worthless if attained. But the latter can be solved only by mastering those elements that are now looming on the horizons of the profane. Even the Spiritualists, with their mistaken, grotesquely perverted views and notions, are hazily realising the new situation. They prophecy—and their prophecies are not always without a point of truth in them—or intuitional prevision, so to say. Hear some of them reasserting the old, old axiom that* 'ideas rule the world,' *and as men's minds receive new ideas, laying aside the old and effete, the world* will *advance, mighty revolutions* will *spring from them; institutions, aye, and even* creeds and powers, *they may add,* will crumble before their onward march, crushed by their *own inherent force,* not the irresistible force of the 'new ideas' *offered by the Spiritualists. Yes, they are both right and wrong. It will be 'just as impossible to resist their influence when the time comes as to stay the progress of the tide—to be sure. But what the Spiritualists fail to perceive, I see, and their spirits to explain (the latter knowing no more than what they can find in the brain of the former) is that all this* will *come gradually on, and that before it comes they, as well us ourselves,* have all a duty *to perform, a task* set before us—that of sweeping away as much as possible the dross left to us by our pious forefathers. New ideas have to be planted on clean places, for these ideas touch upon the most momentous subjects. It is not physical phenomena, *or the agency called Spiritualism,* but these universal ideas that *we have precisely to study; the noumenon, not the phenomenon*: for to comprehend the *latter* we have first to understand the *former.* They *do* touch man's true position in the universe, to be sure, *but only in* relation to his *future* not *previous* births. It is not *physical phenomena, however wonderful,* that can ever explain to *man* his origin, *let alone* his ultimate destiny, *or as one of them expresses it,* the relation of the mortal to the immortal, of the temporary to the eternal, of the finite to the infinite, etc. *They talk very glibly of what they regard as new ideas,* 'larger, more general, grander, more comprehensive,' *and at the same time they recognise instead* of the eternal reign of immutable law, *the universal reign of law and the expression of a Divine will. Forgetful of their "earlier beliefs, and that 'it repented the Lord that he had made man,'* these would-be philosophers and reformers would impress upon their hearers that the expression of the said Divine will *'is unchanging and unchangeable,* in regard to which there is only an Eternal Now, while to mortals[2] time is past or future as related to their finite existence on this material *plane,'—of which they know as little as of their spiritual spheres—a speck of dirt they have made the latter, like our own earth, a future life that the true philosopher would rather avoid than court. But I dream with my eyes open... At all events, this is not any privileged teaching of their own. Most of these ideas are taken piecemeal from Plato and the Alexandrian philosophers.* It is what we all study, and what many have solved, etc., etc.

"This is the true copy of the original document as now restored the 'Rosetta stone' of the Kiddle incident. And now, if you have understood my explanations about the process, as given in a few words further back, you need not ask me how it came to pass that, though somewhat disconnected, the sentences transcribed by the *chela* are mostly those that are now considered as plagiarised, while the missing links are precisely those phrases that would have shown the passages were simply reminiscences, if not quotations—the keynote around which came grouping my own reflections on that morning. For the first time in my life I had paid a serious attention to the utterances of the poetical 'media' of the so-called, 'inspirational' oratory of the English-American lecturers, its quality and limitations. I was struck with all this brilliant but empty verbiage, and recognised for the first time fully its pernicious intellectual tendency. It was their gross and unsavoury materialism, hiding clumsily under its shadowy spiritual veil, that attracted my thoughts at the time. While dictating the sentences quoted—a small portion of the many I have been pondering over for some days—it was those ideas that were thrown out *en relief* the most, leaving out my own parenthetical remarks to disappear in the precipitation."

I need only add a few words of apology to Mr. Kiddle for my accidental neglect of his original communication on this subject addressed to me in India. When his letter above quoted appeared in *Light*, I had no recollection, whatever of having received any letter from him while in India; but within the last few months going over, in London, and sorting papers brought back *en masse* from India, I have turned up the forgotten note. While in India, and the editor of a daily newspaper, my correspondence was such that letters requiring no immediate action on my part would inevitably sometimes be put aside after a hasty glance, and would unfortunately sometimes escape attention afterwards. And after the appearance of this book, I received letters of inquiry of various kinds from all parts of the world, which I was too often prevented by other calls on my time from answering as I should have wished. With the tone and spirit in which Mr. Kiddle made his very natural inquiry I have no fault to find whatever, and if his subsequent letter to *Light* betrayed some disposition on his part to construct unfavourable hypotheses on the basis of the parallel passages, even this second letter would hardly in itself have justified some of the indignant protests ultimately published on the other side. The spiritualists *pur sang*, eager to seize on an incident which seemed to cast discredit on the Theosophical teachings by which their views had been so seriously compromised, were responsible for handling the 'Kiddle incident', in such a way as to provoke the vehement rejoinders of some Theosophical correspondents writing in the columns of *Light* and elsewhere. In consideration, however, of the explanations to which it has eventually given rise, and of the further insight thus afforded us into some interesting details connected with the methods under which an adept's correspondence may sometimes be conducted, the whole incident need not altogether be regretted.

The relations with the "Occult World" that I have been fortunate enough to establish have so greatly expanded during the few years that have elapsed since this volume was written that I must refer my readers to my second book, "Esoteric Buddhism," for an account of their later development. It may be worth while, however, as directly connected with the main purpose of this earlier narrative, to insert here some papers I wrote quite recently for submission to Theosophical audiences in London on the main question discussed in this volume, the existence and sources of knowledge at the command of the adepts. The evidence on this subject has long since overshadowed in its amplitude and completeness the preliminary testimony afforded by my own experiences in India. I summed up some of this later evidence on one of the occasions just referred to, as follows:—

> All persons who become interested in any of the teachings which have found their way out into the world through the intermediation of the Theosophical Society very soon turn to the sanctions on which those teachings rest.
>
> Now the orthodox occult reply hitherto given to inquirers as to the authenticity of any small statements of occult science that have hitherto been put forth, has simply been this: —"Ascertain for yourself." That is to say, lead the pure spiritual life, cultivate the inner faculties, and by degrees these will be awakened and developed to the extent of enabling you to probe Nature for yourself. But that advice is not of a kind which great numbers of people have ever been ready to take, and hence knowledge concerning the truths of occult science has remained in the hands of a few.
>
> A new departure has now been taken. Certain proficients in occult science have broken through the old restrictions of their order, and have suddenly let out a flood of statements into the world, together with some information concerning the attributes and faculties they have themselves acquired, and by means of which they have learned what they now tell us.
>
> It, is very widely recognised that the teaching is interesting and coherent and even supported by analogies, but every new inquirer in turn must ask what assurance we can have that the persons from whom this teaching emanates are in a position to ascertain so much. Most people, I think, would be ready to admit that persons invested, as the Brothers of Theosophy are said to be invested with abnormal and extraordinary powers over Nature— even in the departments of Nature with which we are familiar—may very probably have faculties which enable them to obtain a deep insight into many of the generally hidden truths of Nature. But then come the primary question,

"What assurance can you give us that there really are behind the few people who stand forward as the visible representatives of the Theosophical Society, any such persons as the Adept Brothers at all?" This is an old question which is always recurring, and which must go on recurring as long as new comers continue to approach the threshold of the Theosophical Society. For many of us it has long been settled; for some new inquirers the existence of psychological Adepts seems so probable that the assurances of the leading representatives of the Society in India are readily accepted but for others again, the existence of the Brothers must first be established by altogether plain and unequivocal evidence before it will seem worth while to pay attention to the report some of us make as to the specific doctrine they teach.

I propose, therefore, to go over the evidence on this main question, which certainly underlies any with which the Theosophical Society, so far as it is concerned with the Indian teaching, can be engaged. Of course, I am not going to trouble you with any repetition of particular incidents already described in published writings. What I propose to do is briefly to review the whole case as it now stand, very greatly enlarged and strengthened as it has been during the last two years. The evidence, to begin with, divides itself into two kinds. First, we have the general body of current belief, which in India goes to show that such persons as Mahatmas or Adepts are *somewhere* in existence; secondly, the specific evidence which shows that the leaders of the Theosophical Society are in relation with, and in the confidence of, such Adepts.

As to the general body of belief, it would hardly be too much to say that the whole mass of the sacred literature of India rests on belief in the existence of Adepts and a very widely spread belief, covering great areas of space and time, can rarely be regarded as evolved from nothing—as having had no basis of fact. But passing over the Mahabharata and the Puranas and all they tell us concerning "Rishis or Adepts of ancient date, I may call your attention to a paper in the *Theosophist* of May 1882, on some relatively modern popular Indian books, recounting the lives of various "Sadhus," another word for saint, yogee, or Adept, who have lived within the last thousand years. In this article a list is given of over seventy such persons, whose memory is enshrined in a number of Marathi book", where the miracles they are said to have wrought are recorded. The historical value of their narratives may, of course, be disputed. I mention them merely as illustrations of the fact that belief in the persons having the power now ascribed to the Brothers is no new thing in India. And next we have the testimony of many modern writers concerning the very remarkable occult feats of Indian yogees and fakirs. Such people, of course, are immeasurably below the psychological rank of those whom we speak of as Brothers, but the faculties they possess, sometimes, will be enough to convince anyone who studies the evidence concerning them that living men can acquire powers and faculties commonly regarded as superhuman.

In Jaccolliot's books about his experiences in Benares and elsewhere, this subject is fully dealt with, and some facts connected with it have even forced their way into Anglo-Indian official records. The Report of an English resident at the court of Runjeet Singh describes how he was present at the burial of a yogee who was shut up in a vault, by his own consent, for a considerable period-six weeks, I think, but I have not got the report at hand just now to quote in detail—and emerged alive, at the end of that time, which he had spent in *Samadhi* or trance. Such a man would, of course be an "Adept" of a very inferior type, but the record of his achievements has the advantage of being very well authenticated as far as it goes. Again, up to within a few years ago, a very highly spiritualized ascetic and gifted seer was living at Agra, where he taught a group of disciples, and by their own statement has frequently reappeared amongst them since his death. This event itself was an effort of will accomplished at an appointed time. I have heard a good deal about him from one of his principal followers, a cultivated and highly respected native Government official, now living at Allahabad. His existence, and the fact that he possessed great psychological gifts, are quite beyond question.

Thus, in India, the fact that there are such people in the world as Adepts is hardly regarded as open to dispute. Most of those, of course, concerning whom one can obtain definite information, turn out on inquiry to be yogees of the inferior type, men who have trained their inner faculties to the extent of possessing various abnormal powers, and even insight into spiritual truths.' But none the less do all inquiries after Adepts superior to them in attainments provoke the reply that certainly there are such, though they live in complete seclusion, The general vague, indefinite belief, in fact, paves the way to the inquiry with which we are more immediately concerned—whether the leaders of the Theosophical Society are really in relation with some of the higher Adepts who do not habitually live amongst the community at large, nor make known the fact of their adeptship to any but their own regularly accepted pupils.

Now the evidence on this point divides itself as follows:

First, We have the primary evidence of witnesses who have personally seen certain of these Adepts, both in the flesh and out of the flesh, who have seen their powers exercised, and who have obtained certain knowledge as to their existence and attributes.

Secondly. The evidence of those who have seen them in the astral form, identifying them in various ways with the living men others have seen.

Thirdly. The testimony of those who have acquired circumstantial evidence as to their existence.

Foremost among the witnesses of the first group stand Madame

Blavatsky and Colonel Olcott themselves. For those who see reason to trust Madame Blavatsky, her testimony is, of course ample and precise, and altogether satisfactory. She has lived among the Adepts for many years. She has been in almost daily communication with them ever since. She has returned to them, and they have visited her in their natural bodies on several occasions since she emerged from Tibet after her own initiation. There is an intermediate alternative between the conclusion that her statements concerning the Brothers are broadly true, and the conclusion that she is what some American enemies have called her, "the champion impostor of the age." I am aware of the theory which some Spiritualists entertain to the effect that she may be a medium controlled by spirits whom she mistakes for living men, but this theory can only be held by people who are quite inattentive to nine-tenths of the statements she makes, not to speak yet of the testimony of others. How can she have lived under the roof of certain persons in Tibet for seven years and more, seeing them and their friends and relation" going about the business of their daily lives, instructing her by slow degrees in the vast science to which she is devoted, and be in any doubt as to whether they are living men or spirits. The conjecture is absurd. She is either speaking falsely when she tells us that she has so lived among them, or the Adepts who taught her are living men. The Spiritualists hypothesis about her supposed "controls" is built upon the statement she makes, that the Adepts appear to her in the astral form when she is at a distance from them. If they had never appeared to her in any other form there would be room to argue the matter from the Spiritualists' point of view, or there might be, but for other circumstances again. But her astral visitors are identical in all respects with the men she has lived and studied amongst, At intervals, as I have said, she has been enabled to go back again and see them in the flesh. Her astral communication with them merely fills up the gap of her personal intercourse with them, which has extended over a long series of years. Her veracity may of course be challenged, though I think it can be shown that it is most unreasonable to challenge this, but we might as reasonably doubt the living reality of our nearest relations, of the people we live amongst most intimately, as suppose that Madame Blavatsky can be herself mistaken in describing the Brothers as living men. Either she must be right, or has consciously been weaving an enormous network of falsehood in all her writings, acts, and conversations for the last eight or nine years And the plea that she may be a loose talker and given to exaggeration will no more meet the difficulty than the Spiritualists' hypothesis. Pare away as much as you like from the details of Madame Blavatsky's statement on account of possible exaggeration, and that which remains is a great solid block of residual statement which must be either true, or a structure of conscious falsehood. And even if Madame Blavatsky's testimony stood alone, we should have the wonderful fact of her self-sacrifice in the cause of Theosophy to make the hypothesis of her being a conscious impostor one of the most extravagant that could be entertained. At first, when we in India who specially became her friends pointed this out, people said, "But how do you know that she had anything to sacrifice? she may have been an adventurer from the beginning."We proved this conjecture as I have fully explained in my preface to the second edition of the "Occult World", and from some of the foremost people in Russia, her relations and affectionate friends, came abundant assurances of her personal identity. If she had not given up her life to Occultism she might have spent it in luxury among her own people, and in fact as a member of the aristocratic class.

Difficult as the hypothesis of her imposture thus becomes, we next find it in flagrant incompatibility with all the facts of Colonel Olcott's life. As undeniably as in the case of Madame Blavatsky, he has forsaken a life of worldly prosperity to lead the theosophical life, under circumstances of great physical self-denial, in India. And he also tells us that he has seen the Brothers, both in the flesh and in the astral form. By a long series of the most astounding thaumaturgic displays when he was first introduced to the subject in America, he was made acquainted with their powers. He has been visited at Bombay by the living man, his own special master, with whom he had first become acquainted by seeing him in the astral form in America. His life, for years, has been surrounded with the abnormal occurrences which Spiritualists again will sometimes conjecture—so wildly—to be Spiritualism, but which all hinge on to that continuous chain of relationship with the Brothers, which for Colonel Olcott has been partly a matter of occult phenomena, and partly a matter of waking intercourse between man and man. Again, in reference to Colonel Olcott, as in reference to Madame Blavatsky, I assert, fearlessly, that there is no compromises possible between the extravagant assumption that he is consciously lying in all he says about the Brothers, and the assumption that what he says establishes the existence of the Brothers as a broad fact, for remember that Colonel Olcott has now been a co-worker of Madame Blavatsky's and in constant intimate association with her for eight years. The notion the she has been able to deceive him all this while by fraudulent tricks, apart from its monstrosity in other ways, is too unreasonable to be entertained. Colonel Olcott, at all events, knows whether Madame Blavatsky is fraudulent or genuine, and he has given up his whole life to the service of the cause she represents in testimony of his conviction that she is genuine. Again the spiritualistic hypothesis comes into play. Madame Blavatsky may be a medium whose presence surrounds Colonel Olcott with phenomena; but then she is herself deceived by astral influences as to the true nature of the Brothers who are the head and front of the whole phenomenal display, and we have already seen reason, I think, to reject that hypothesis as absurd. There is logical escape from the conclusion that things are broadly as she and Colonel Olcott say, or they are both conscious impostors, rival champions of the age in this respect, both sacrificing everything that worldly minded people live for, to revel in this lifelong imposture which brings them nothing but hard living and hard words.

But the case for the authenticity of their statement, far from ending here, may in one sense be said to begin here. Our native Indian witnesses now come to the front. First, Damodar of whom the well known writer of "Hints on Esoteric Theosophy speaks as follows in that pamphlet:—

"You specially in a former letter referred to Damodar, and you asked how it could be believed that the Brothers would waste time with a half-educated slip of a boy like him, and yet absolutely refuse to visit and convince men like------ and ------, Europeans of the highest education and marked abilities. But do you know that this slip of a boy has deliberately given up high caste, family and friends, and an ample fortune, all in pursuit of the truth. That be has for years lived that pure, unworldly self-denying life which we are told is essential to direct intercourse with the Brothers? 'Oh, a monomaniac,' you say; 'of course he sees anything and everything. But do not you see whither this leads you? Men who do not lead the life do not obtain direct proof of the existence of the Brothers. A man does lead the life and avers that he has obtained such proof, and you straightaway call him a monomaniac, and refuse his testimony,.... quite a "heads I win, tails you lose, 'sort of position."

Damodar has seen some of the Brothers visit the headquarters of the Society in the flesh. He has repeatedly been visited by them in the astral shape. He has himself gone through certain initiations; he has acquired very considerable powers, for he has been rapidly developed as regards these, expressly that he might be an additional link of connection, independently of Madame Blavatsky, between the Brothers, his masters, and the Theosophical Society. The whole life be leads is impressive testimony to the fact that he also *knows* the reality of the Brothers. On another hypothesis we must include Damodar in the conscious imposture supposed to be carried on by Madame Blavatsky, for he has been her intimate associate and devoted assistant, sharing her meals, doing her work, living under her roof at Bombay for several years.

Shall we, then, rather than believe in the Brothers accept the hypothesis that Madame Blavatsky, Colonel Olcott, and Damodar are a band of conscious impostors? In that case Ramaswamy has to he accounted for. Ramaswamy is a very respectable, educated, English-speaking native of Southern India, in government service as a registrar of a court in Tinnevelly, I believe. I have met him several times. First, to indicate the course of his experience in a few words, —he sees the astral form of Madame Blavatsky's Guru, at Bombay; then he gets clairaudient communication with him, while many hundred miles away from all the Theosophists, at his own home in the South of India. Then he travels in obedience to that voice to Darjeeling; then be plunges wildly into the Sikkim jungles in search of the Guru, whom he has reason to believe in that neighbourhood, and after various adventures meets him, —the same man be has seen before in astral shape, the same man whose portrait Colonel Olcott has, and whom be has seen, the living speaker of the voice that has been leading him on from Southern India—He has a long interview with him, a waking, open-air, daylight interview, with a living man, and returns his devoted *chela*, as he is at this moment, and assuredly ever will be. Yet his master, who called him from Tinnevelly and received him in Sikkim, is of those who on the spiritualistic hypothesis are Madame Blavatsky's spirit controls.

Two more witnesses who personally know the Brothers next come to me at Simla, in the persons of two regular *chelas* who have been sent across the mountains on some business, and are ordered *en passant* to visit me and tell me about their master, my Adept correspondent. These men had just come, when I first saw them, from living with the Adepts. One of them, Dhabagiri Nath, visited me several days running, talked to me for hours about Koot Hoomi—with whom he had been living for ten years, and impressed me and one or two others who saw him as a very earnest, devoted, and trustworthy person. Later on, during his visit to India, he was associated with many striking occult phenomena directed to the satisfaction of native inquirers. He, of course, must be a false witness, invented to prop up Madame Blavatsky's vast imposture, if he is anything else than the *chela* of Koot Hoomi that he declares himself to be.

Another native, Mohini, soon after this, begins to get direct communication from Koot Hoomi independently altogether of Madame Blavatsky, and when hundreds of miles away from her. He also becomes a devoted adherent to the Theosophical cause; but Mohini must, as far as I am aware, be ranked in the second group of our witnesses, those who have had personal astral communication with the Brothers, but have not yet seen them in the flesh.

Bhavani Rao, a young native candidate for *chelaship*, who came once in company with Colonel Olcott, but at a time when Madame Blavatsky was in another part of India, to see me at Allahabad, and spent two nights under our roof there, is another witness who has had independent communication with Koot Hoomi, and more than that, who is able himself to act as a link of communication between Koot Hoomi and the outer world, For during the visit I speak of, he was enabled to pass a letter of mine to the master, to receive back his reply, to get off a second note of mine, and to receive back a little note of a few words in reply again. I do not mean that he did all this of his own power, but that his magnetism was such as to enable Koot Hoomi to do it through him. The experience is valuable because it affords a striking illustration of the fact that Madame Blavatsky is not an essential intermediary in the correspondence between myself and my revered friend. Other illustrations are afforded by the frequent passage of letters between Koot Hoomi and myself through the mediation of Damodar at Bombay, at a time when both Madame Blavatsky and Colonel Olcott were away at Madras, travelling about on a Theosophical tour, in the course of which their presence at various places was constantly mentioned in the local papers, I was at Allahabad, and I used, during that time, to send my letters for Koot Hoomi to Damodar at Bombay, and occasionally receive replies so promptly that it would have been impossible for these to have been furnished by Madame Blavatsky, then four or more days further from me in the course of post than Bombay.

In this way, my very voluminous correspondence is, demonstrably as regards portions of it, and therefore by irresistible inference as regards the whole, *not* the work of Madame Blavatsky, or Colonel Olcott, which, if the Brothers are not a reality, it must be, The correspondence is visible on paper, a considerable mass of it, How has it come into existence; reaching me at different places and times, and in different countries, and through different people? I do not quite understand what hypotheses can be framed by a nonbeliever in the Brothers about my correspondence. I can think of none which are not at once negatived by some of the facts about It.

It would be useless to copy out from statements that from time to time have been published in the *Theosophist* the names of native witnesses who have seen the astral forms of the Brothers—spectral shapes which they were informed were such—about the headquarters of the Society at Bombay. Quite a cloud of witnesses would testify to such experiences, and I myself, I may add, saw such an appearance on one occasion at the Society's present headquarters in Madras. But, of course, it might be suggested of such appearances that they were spiritualistic. On the other hand, in that case the argument travels back to the considerations already pointed out, which show that the occult phenomena surrounding Madame Blavatsky cannot be Spiritualism. They can be, in fact, nothing but what we who know her intimately and are now closely identified with the Society believe them to be with all conviction—viz., manifestations of the abnormal psychological powers of those whom we speak of as the Brothers.

As I write, Colonel Olcott and Mr. Mohini Mohun Chatterjee, mentioned above, are in London on a short visit, and many people have heard from their own lips the verification of what I have here stated—as far as it concerns them—and a great deal more besides. For during his recent tour in Northern India, Colonel Olcott had an opportunity of meeting the Mahatma Koot Hoomi personally in the flesh, and thus identifying his previous "astral" visitor. At the same time that this meeting took place, Mr. W. T. Brown, a young Scotchman who has recently become a devoted adherent to the Theosophical cause, also saw the Mahatma, and Mr. Lane Fox, who has gone out to India to follow up the clue afforded by the Theosophical Society, has been in receipt in India, by abnormal methods, of correspondence from Koot Hoomi, while Madame Blavatsky and Colonel Olcott have been in Europe. Taking into account, in fact, over and above the evidence collected in these pages, the abundant information connected with the adepts which has latterly been poured out through the pages of the *Theosophist*, the magazine of the Theosophical Society now published at Madras, the argument in the form in which it is here presented is really out of date. Anyone who may still think with Mr. Kiddle, if he remains of the opinion expressed in his letter to *Light*, that the allegations of my book concerning the existence of the adepts and the facts of adeptship still remain to be proved, must be inaccessible to the force of reason, or still unacquainted with the literature of the subject.

The second of the papers I wish to insert here, read like the first to a meeting of the Theosophists in London, dealt with the considerations which, after the *existence* of the Brothers is established, lead us to put confidence in the teaching they convey to us in regard to the origin and destinies of man and the whole problem of Nature. It is as follows:—

> Many people who approach the consideration of occult philosophy are inclined to lay great emphasis on the difference between believing in the existence of those whom we call "the Brothers," and believing in the vast and complicated body of teaching which has now been accumulated by their recent pupils. I think it can really be shown that there is no halting place at which a man who sets out on this enquiry can rationally pause and say, "Thus far will I go, and no farther". The chain of considerations which will lead anyone who has once realised the existence of the Adepts to feel sure that there can be no great error in a conception of nature obtained with their help, consists of many links, but is really unbroken in its continuity, and equally capable of bearing a strain at any point.
>
> It consists of many links, partly because no one at present among those who are in our position as students—who are living, that is to say, an ordinary worldly life all the while that they are intellectually studying Occultism—can ever obtain in his own person a complete knowledge of the Adepts. He cannot, that is to say, come to know of his own personal knowledge all about even any one Adept. The full elucidation of this difficulty leads to a proper comprehension of the principle on which the Adepts shroud themselves in a partial seclusion, a seclusion which has only become partial within a very recent period, and was so complete until then that the world at large was hardly aware of the existence of any esoteric knowledge from which it could be shut out. This is a matter that is all the

more important because experience has shown how the world at large has been quick to take offence at the hesitating and imperfect manner in which the Adepts have hitherto dealt with those who have sought spiritual instruction at their hands. Judging the occult policy pursued by comparison with inquiries on the plane of physical knowledge, the impatience of inquirers is very natural, but nonetheless does even a limited acquaintance with the conditions of mystic research show the occult policy to be reasonable likewise.

Of course, everyone will admit that Adepts are justified in exercising great caution in regard to communicating any peculiar scientific knowledge which would put what are commonly called magical powers within the reach of persons not morally qualified for their exercise. But the considerations that prescribe this caution do not seem to operate also in reference to the communication of knowledge concerning the spiritual progress of man or the grander processes of evolution. And in truth the Adepts have come to that very conclusion; they have undertaken the communication to the general public of their safe theoretical knowledge, and the effort they are making merely hangs fire, or may seem to do so to some observers, by reason of the magnitude of the task in hand, and the novel aspect it wears, as well for the teachers as for the students. For remember, if there has been that change of policy on the part of the Adepts to which I have just referred, it has been a change of such recent origin that it may almost be described as only just coming on. And if the question be then asked, Why has this safe theoretical knowledge not been communicated sooner, it seems reasonable to find a reply to that question in the actual state of the intellectual world around us at this moment. The freedom of thought of which English writers often boast is not very widely diffused over the world as yet; and hardly, at all events, in any generation before this, could the free promulgation of quite revolutionary tenets in religious matters have been safely undertaken in any country. Communities in which such an undertaking would still be fraught with peril are even now more numerous than those in which it could be set on foot with any practical advantage. One can thus readily understand how in the occult world the question has been one of debate up to our own time, whether it was desirable as yet to promote the dissemination of esoteric philosophy in the world at large at the risk of provoking the acrimonious controversies, and even more serious disturbances, liable to arise from the premature disclosure of truths which only a small minority would really be ready to accept. Keeping this in view, the mystery of the Adepts reserve, up till recently, can hardly be thought so astounding as to drive us on violent alternative hypotheses at variance with all the plain evidence concerning their present action. There is manifest reason why they should be careful in launching a body of newly-won disciples on to their general stream of human progress; and added to this, the force of their own training is such as to make them habitually cautious to a far greater extent than the utmost prudence of ordinary life would render ordinary men. "But," it will be argued, "granting all this, but assuming, that at last some of the Adepts, at all events, have come to the conclusion that some of their knowledge is ripe for presentation to the world, why do they not present as much as they do present, under guarantees of a more striking, irresistible, and conclusive kind than those which have actually been furnished?" I think the answer may be easily drawn from the consideration of the way in which it would be natural to expect that a change of policy amongst the Adepts in a matter of this kind would gradually be introduced. By the hypothesis we conceive them but just coming to the conclusion that it is desirable to teach mankind at large some portions of that spiritual science hitherto conveyed exclusively to those who give tremendous pledges in justification of their claim to acquire it. They will naturally advance, in dealing with the world at large, along the same lines they have learned to trust in dealing with aspirants for regular initiation. Never in the history of the world have they sought out such aspirants, courted them or advertised for them in any way whatever. It has been found an invariable law of human progress that some small percentage of mankind will always come into the world invested by Nature with some of the attributes proper to adeptship, and with minds so constituted as to catch conviction as to the possibilities of the occult life, from the least little sparks of evidence on the subject that may be floating about. Of persons so constituted some have always been found to press forward into the ranks of *chelaship*, to resort, that is to say, to any devices or opportunities that circumstances may afford them for fathoming occult knowledge. When thus besieged by the aspirant the Adept has always, sooner or later, disclosed himself. The change of policy now introduced prescribes that the Adept shall make one step towards the disclosure of himself in advance of the aspirant's demand upon him, but we can easily understand how the Adept, in first making this change, would argue that if many *chelas* have hitherto come forward in the absence of any spontaneous action from his side, it might be that an almost dangerous rush of ill qualified aspirants would be invited by any manifestation from him that should be more than a very slight one. At any rate, the Adept would say it would be premature to begin by too sensational a display of faculties inherent in advanced spiritual knowledge with which the world at large is as yet unfamiliar. It will be better at first to make such an offer as will only be calculated to inflame the imagination of persons only one step removed beyond those whose natural instincts would lead them into the occult life. This appears actually to have been the reasoning on which the Adepts have proceeded so far, and this may help us to understand how it is that, as I began by saying, no one person amongst those outer students, who have been called lay-*chelas*, has yet been enabled to say that of his own personal knowledge he knows all about any of the Adepts.

On the other hand, putting together the various scattered revelations concerning the Brothers which have been distributed amongst various people in India belonging to the Theosophical Society, so much can be learned about the Adepts as to put us in a very strong position in regard to estimating their qualifications for speaking with confidence as they do about the actual facts of Nature on the superphysical plane. These scattered revelations—if my reasoning in what has gone before may be accepted—have been broken up and thrown about in fragments designedly, in order that as yet it should only be possible to arrive at a full conviction concerning Adeptship after a certain amount of trouble spent in piecing together the disjointed proofs. But when this process is accomplished we are provided with a certain block of knowledge concerning the Adepts, out of which large inferences must necessarily grow. We find, to begin with, that they do unequivocally possess the power of cognizing event and facts on the physical plane of knowledge with which we are familiar, by other means than those connected with the five senses. We find also that they unequivocally possess the power of emerging from their proper bodies and appearing at distant places in more or less ethereal counterparts thereof which are not only agencies for producing impressions on others but habitations for the time being of the Adepts' own thinking principles, and thus in themselves, if the proof went no further, demonstration of the fact that a human soul is something quite independent of brain matter and nerve centres. I do not stop now to enumerate instances. The record of evidence must be dissociated from its manipulation in arguments like the present, but the records are abundant and accessible for all who will take the trouble of examining them. Now, if we know that the Adept's soul can pass at his own discretion into that state in which its perceptive faculties are independent of corporeal machinery, it is not surprising that he should be enabled to make, of his own knowledge, a great many statements concerning processes of Nature, reaching far beyond any knowledge that can be obtained by mere physical observation. Take for example, the Adepts' statement that certain other planets besides this earth, are concerned with the growth of the great crop of humanity of which we form a part. This is not advanced as a conjecture or inference. The Adepts tell us that once out of the body they find they can cognize events on some other planets as well as in distant parts of our own. This is not the exceptional belief of an exceptionally organised individual, who may be regarded by doubters as hallucinated; there is no room for doubting the fact that it is the concurrent testimony' of a considerable body of men engaged in the constant experimental exercise of similar faculties. In this way the fact becomes as much a fact of true science, as the fact that the great nebula

Orion, for instance, exhibits a gaseous spectrum, and is therefore a true nebula. All of us who have star spectroscope can ascertain that fact for ourselves, if we make use of a clear night when the conditions of observation are possible. To doubt it, would not be to show greater caution than is exercised by those who believe it, but merely an imperfect appreciation of the evidence. It is true that in regard to the condition of the other planets our acceptance of the Adepts' statement must be governed by our impressions concerning the *bona fides* of their intention in telling us that they have made such and such observations. So far it is a matter of inference with us whether the Adepts are saying what *they believe* to be true—when they speak of the septenary chain of planets to which the earth belongs—or consciously deluding us with a rigmarole of statements which they know to be false. I think it can be shown in a variety of ways, that the latter supposition is absurd. But an exhaustive examination of its absurdity would be a considerable task in itself. For the moment the position I am endeavouring to establish is one which does not depend upon the question whether the Adepts are telling us, in reference to the planets, what they know to be true, or something which they know to be untrue. My present position is that at all events the Adepts themselves know what is true In the matter, and that position, it will be observed, is not vitiated by the fact that, as yet, we, their most recent pupils, are unable to follow In their footsteps and repeat the experiments on which their teaching rests.

The same train of reasoning may be applied to the whole body of teaching which the Theosophical Society is now concerned in endeavouring to assimilate. As offered now to the uninitiated world, it can only take the form of a set of statement on authority. And that sort of statement is not one which is most agreeable to our methods or to the Adepts' habitual methods of teaching. For there is no chemical laboratory in England where the system of teaching Is more rigidly confined to the direction of the learner's own experiments, than that same system is adopted with occult *chelas* following the regular course of initiation. Step by step, as the regular *chela* is told that such and such is the fact in regard to the inner mysteries of Nature, he is shown how to apply his own developing faculties to the direct observation of such facts, But those developing faculties carry with them, as pointed out a while ago, fresh powers over Nature which can only be entrusted to those from whom the Adepts take the recognised pledges. In teaching outsiders as they are trying to do now, the Adepts *must* depart from their own habitual methods, —we must depart, if we wish to understand what they are willing to teach, from our habitual methods of inquiry. We must suspend our usual demand for proof of each statement made, in turn as it is advanced. We must rest our provisional trust in each statement on our broad general conviction which can be satisfied along familiar lines of demonstration, —that such men as the Adepts certainly exist, even though we cannot visit them at pleasure, that they must understand an enormous block of Nature's laws outside the range of those which the physical senses cognize, that in any statement they make to us they must be in a position to know absolutely whether that statement is or is not true.

This much fully realised, the truth is that each inquirer in turn becomes satisfied, *pari passu* with his realisation of the case so far, that reason revolts against the notion that the Adepts can be engaged in their present attempt to convey some of their own knowledge to the world at large in any other than the purest good faith. It may be concluded that we who have come to the conclusion that their teaching is altogether to be accepted, are rearing a large inverted pyramid upon a small base. But the logical strength of our position is not impaired by this objection. In every branch of human knowledge, inferences far transcend the observed facts out of which they grow. And even in the most exact science of all, a theorem is held to be proved if any alternative hypothesis is found, on examination to be irrational. Moreover, the doctrine even of legal testimony recognises the value of secondary evidence where in the nature of the case It is impossible that primary evidence can be forthcoming. That is exactly the state of the case in regard to the present attempt to bridge the gulf that separates the school of physical research from the from the school of spiritual knowledge. As long as we of this side were justified in doubting whether there was anywhere on earth such a thing as a school of spiritual knowledge, it may have been hardly worth while to worry ourselves with the stray fragments of its teaching which now and then broke loose in barely intelligible shapes. But to doubt the existence of such a school now is equivalent, really to doubting the statement about the nebula in Orion, according to the illustration I adduced just now. It can only arise from inattention to the facts of the whole case as these now stand, —from reluctance to take that *trouble* to examine these thoroughly, which still, as a sort of hedge, separates the Theosophical Society from the general community in the midst of which it is planted. Regarded in the light of an occult barrier, —as an obstacle which corresponds, in the case of the lay—*chela* to the really serious ordeals which have to be crossed by the regular *chela*, —the necessity of taking this trouble can hardly be regarded as a hedge that it is difficult to traverse. And on the other side there lies a wealth of information concerning the mysteries of Nature which clearly lights up vast regions of the past and future hitherto shrouded in total darkness for critical intelligences, and the prey for others of untrustworthy conjecture. For those who once thoroughly go into the matter, and obtain a complete mastery over all the considerations I have put forward, —who thus obtain full conviction the Brothers certainly exist, that they must be acquainted with the actual facts about Nature behind and beyond this life, that they are now ready to convey a considerable block of their knowledge to us, and that it is ridiculous to distrust their *bona fides* in doing this, —for all such true Theosophists of the Theosophical Society, nothing, at present, connected with spiritual success is comparable in importance with the study of the vast doctrine now in process of delivery Into our hands.

---

1. In the original book, but one after the other in this edition.
2. uninitiated

INVISIBLE HELPERS

By Charles W. Leadbeater

Charles Webster Leadbeater (1854–1934) was a high-ranking officer of the Theosophical Society and remained one of its leading members until his death, writing over 60 books and pamphlets and maintaining regular speaking engagements.

THE UNIVERSAL BELIEF IN THEM

It is one of the most beautiful characteristics of Theosophy that it gives back to people in a more rational form everything which was really useful and helpful to them in the religions which they have outgrown. Many who have broken through the chrysalis of blind faith, and mounted on the wings of reason and intuition to the freer, nobler mental life of more exalted levels, nevertheless feel that in the process of this glorious gain a something has been lost - that in giving up the beliefs of their childhood they have also cast aside much of the beauty and the poetry of life.

If, however, their lives in the past have been sufficiently good to earn for them the opportunity of coming under the benign influence of Theosophy, they very soon discover that even in this particular there has been no loss at all, but an exceeding great gain - that the glory and the beauty and the poetry are there in fuller measure than they had ever hoped before, and no longer as a mere pleasant dream from which the cold light of common-sense may at any time rudely awaken them, but as truths of nature which will bear investigation - which become only brighter, fuller and more perfect as they are more accurately understood.

A marked instance of this beneficent action of Theosophy is the way in which the invisible world (which, before the great wave of materialism engulfed us, used to be regarded as the source of all living help) has been restored by it to modern life. All the charming folk-lore of the elf, the brownie and the gnome, of the spirits of air and water, of the forest, the mountain and the mine, is shown by it to be no more meaningless superstition, but to have a basis of actual and scientific fact behind it. Its answer to the great fundamental question "If a man die, shall he live again?" is equally definite and scientific, and its teaching on the nature and conditions of the life after death throws a flood of light upon much that, for the Western world at least, was previously wrapped in impenetrable darkness.

It cannot be too often repeated that in this teaching as to the immortality of the soul and the life after death, Theosophy stands in a position totally different from that of ordinary religion. It does not put forward these great truths merely on the authority of some sacred book of long ago; in speaking of these subjects it is not dealing with pious opinions , or metaphysical speculations, but with solid, definite facts, as real and as close to us as the air we breathe or the houses we live in - facts of which many among us have constant experience - facts among which lies the daily work of some of our students, as will presently be seen.

Among the beautiful conceptions which Theosophy has restored to us stands pre-eminent that of the great helpful agencies of nature. The belief in these has been world-wide from the earliest dawn of history, and is universal even now outside the narrow domains of Protestantism, which has emptied and darkened the world for its votaries by its attempt to do away with the natural and perfectly true idea of intermediate agents, and reduce everything to two factors of man and deity - a device whereby the conception of deity has been infinitely degraded, and man has remained unhelped.

A moment's thought will show that the ordinary view of providence - the conception of an erratic interference by the central power of the universe with the result of his own decrees - would imply the introduction of partiality into the scheme, and therefore of the whole train of evils which must necessarily follow upon its heels. The Theosophical teaching, that a man can be thus specially helped only when his past actions have been such as to deserve this assistance, and that even then the help will be given through those who are comparatively near his own level, is free from this serious objection; and it furthermore brings back to us the older and far grander conception of an unbroken ladder of living beings extending down from the Logos Himself to the very dust beneath our feet.

In the East the existence of the invisible helpers has always been recognized, though the names given and the characteristics attributed to them naturally vary in different countries; and even in Europe we have had the old Greek stories of the constant interference of the gods in human affairs, and the Roman legend that Castor and Pollux led the legions of the infant republic in the battle of Lake Regillus. Nor did such a conception die out when the classical period ended, for these stories have their legitimate successors in medieval tales of saints who appeared at critical moments and turned the fortune of war in favour of the Christian hosts, or of guardian angels who sometimes stepped in and saved a pious traveler from what would otherwise have been certain destruction.

SOME MODERN INSTANCES

EVEN in this incredulous age, and amidst the full whirl of our nineteenth-century civilization, in spite of the dogmatism of our science and the deadly dullness of our Protestantism, instances of intervention inexplicable from the materialistic standpoint may still be found by anyone who will take the trouble to look for them; and in order to demonstrate this to the reader I will briefly epitomize a few of the examples given in one or other of the recent collections of such stories, adding thereto one or two that have come within my own notice.

One very remarkable feature of these more recent examples is that the intervention seems nearly always to have been directed towards the helping or saving of children.

An interesting case which occurred in London only a few years ago was connected with the preservation of a child's life in the midst of a terrible fire, which broke out in a street near Holborn, and entirely destroyed two of the houses there. The flames had obtained such hold before they were discovered that the firemen were unable to save the houses, but they succeeded in rescuing all the inmates except two - an old woman who was suffocated by the smoke before they could reach her, and a child about five years old, whose presence in the house had been forgotten in the hurry and excitement of the moment.

The mother of the child, it seems, was a friend or relative of the landlady of the house, and had left the little creature in her charge for the night, because she was herself obliged to go down to Colchester on business. It was not until everyone else had been rescued, and the whole house was wrapped in flame, that the landlady remembered with a terrible pang the trust that had been confided to her. It seemed hopeless then to attempt to get at the garret where the child had been put to bed, but one of the firemen heroically resolved to make the desperate effort, and, after receiving minute directions as to the exact situation of the room, plunged in among the smoke and flame.

He found the child, and brought him forth entirely unharmed; but when he rejoined his comrades he had a very singular story to tell. He declared that when he reached the room he found it in flames, and most of the floor already fallen; but the fire had curved round the room towards the window in an unnatural and unaccountable manner, the like of which in all his experience he had never seen before, so that the corner in which the child lay was wholly untouched, although the very rafters of the fragment of floor on which his little crib stood were half burnt away. The child was naturally very much terrified, but the fireman distinctly and repeatedly declared that as at great risk he made his way towards him he saw a form like an angel - here his exact words are given - something "all gloriously white and silvery, bending over the bed and smoothing down the counterpane." He could not possibly have been mistaken about it, he said, for it was visible in a glare of light for some moments, and in fact disappeared only when he was within a few feet of it.

Another curious feature of this story is that the child's mother found herself unable to sleep that night down in Colchester, but was constantly harassed by a strong feeling that something was wrong with her child, insomuch that at last she was compelled to rise and spend some time in earnest prayer that the little one might be protected from the danger which she instinctively felt to be hanging over him. The intervention was thus evidently what a Christian would call an answer to a prayer; a Theosophist, putting the same idea in more scientific phraseology, would say that her intense outpouring of love constituted a force which one of our visible helpers was able to use for the rescue of her child from a terrible death.

A remarkable case in which children were abnormally protected occurred on the banks of the Thames near Maidenhead a few years earlier than our last example. This time the danger from which they were saved arose not from fire but from water. Three little ones, who lived, if I recollect rightly, in or near the village of Shottesbrook, were taken out for a walk along the towing-path by their nurse. They rushed suddenly round a corner upon a horse which was drawing a barge, and in the confusion two of them got on the wrong side of the tow-rope and were thrown into the water.

The boatman, who saw the accident, sprang forward to try to save them, and he noticed that they were floating high in the water "in quite an unnatural way, like," as he said, and moving quietly towards the bank.

This was all that he and the nurse saw, but the children each declared that "a beautiful person, all white and shining," stood beside them in the water, held them up and guided them to the shore. Nor was their story without corroboration, for the bargeman's little daughter, who ran up from the cabin when she heard the screams of the nurse, also affirmed that she saw a lovely lady in the water dragging the two children to the bank.

Without fuller particulars than the story gives us, it is impossible to say with certainty from what class of helpers this "angel" was drawn; but the probabilities are in favour of its having been a developed human being functioning in the astral body, as will be seen when later on we deal with this subject from the other side, as it were - from the point of view of the helpers rather than the helped.

A case in which the agency is somewhat more definitely distinguishable is related by the well-known clergyman, Dr John Mason Neale. He states that a man who had recently lost his wife was on a visit with his little children at the country house of a friend. It was an old, rambling mansion, and in the lower part of it there were long, dark passages, in which the children played about with great delight. But presently they came upstairs very gravely, and two of them related that as they were running down one of these passages they were met by their mother, who told them to go back again, and then disappeared. Investigation revealed the fact that if the children had run but a few steps farther they would have fallen down a deep uncovered well which yawned full in their path, so that the apparition of their mother had saved them from almost certain death.

In this instance there seems no reason to doubt that the mother herself was still keeping a loving watch over her children from the astral plane, and that (as has happened in some other cases) her intense desire to warn them of the danger into which they were so heedlessly rushing gave her the power to make herself visible and audible to them for the moment - or perhaps merely to impress their minds with the idea that they saw and heard her. It is possible, of course, that the helper may have been someone else, who took the familiar form of the mother in order not to alarm the children; but the simplest hypothesis is to attribute the intervention to the action of the ever-wakeful mother-love itself, undimmed by the passage through the gates of death.

This mother-love, being one of the holiest and most unselfish of human feelings, is also one of the most persistent on higher planes. Not only does the mother who finds herself upon the lower levels of the astral plane, and consequently still within touch of the earth, maintain her interest in and her care for her children as long as she is able to see them; even after her entry into the heaven-world these little ones are still the most prominent objects in her thought, and the wealth of love that she lavishes upon the images which she there makes of them is a great outpouring of spiritual force which flows down upon her offspring who are still struggling in this lower world, and surrounds them with living centres of beneficent energy which may not inaptly be described as veritable guardian angels. An illustration of this will be found in the sixth of our Theosophical manuals, page 38.

Not long ago the little daughter of one of our English bishops was out walking with her mother in the town where they lived, and in running heedlessly across a street the child was knocked down by the horses of a carriage which came quickly upon her round a corner. Seeing her among the horses' feet, the mother rushed forward, expecting to find her very badly injured, but she sprang up quite merrily, saying, "Oh, mamma, I am not at all hurt, for something all in white kept the horses from treading upon me, and told me not to be afraid."

A case which occurred in Buckinghamshire, somewhere in the neighborhood of Burnham Beeches, is remarkable on account of the length of time through which the physical manifestation of the succouring agency seems to have maintained itself. It will have been seen that in the instances hitherto given the intervention was a matter of but a few moments, whereas in this a phenomenon was produced which appears to have persisted for more than half an hour.

Two of the little children of a small farmer were left to amuse themselves while their parents and their entire household were engaged in the work of harvesting. The little ones started for a walk in the woods, wandered far from home, and then managed to lose their way. When the weary parents returned at dusk it was discovered that the children were missing, and after enquiring at some of the neighbours' houses the father sent servants and labourers in various directions to seek for them.

Their efforts were, however, unsuccessful, and their shouts unanswered; and they had reassembled at the farm in a somewhat despondent frame of mind, when they all saw a curious light some distance away moving slowly across some fields towards the road. It was described as a large globular mass of rich golden glow, quite unlike ordinary lamplight; and as it drew nearer it was seen that the two missing children were walking steadily along in the midst of it. The father and some others immediately set off running towards it; the appearance persisted until they were close to it, but just as they grasped the children it vanished, leaving them in the darkness.

The children's story was that after night came on they had wandered about crying in the woods for some time, and had at last lain down under a tree to sleep. They had been roused, they said, by a beautiful lady with a lamp, who took them by the hand and led them home; when they questioned her she smiled at them, but never spoke a word. To this strange tale they both steadily adhered, nor was it possible in any way to shake their faith in what they had seen. It is noteworthy, however, that though all present saw the light, and noticed that it lit up the trees and hedges which came within its sphere precisely as an ordinary light would, yet the form of the lady was visible to none but the children.

A PERSONAL EXPERIENCE

ALL the above stories are comparatively well known, and may be found in some of the books which contain collections of such accounts - most of them in Dr Lee's *More Glimpses of the World Unseen*; but the two instances which I am now about to give have never been in print before, and both occurred within the last ten years - one to myself, and the other to a very dear friend of mine, a prominent member of the Theosophical Society, whose accuracy of observation is beyond all shadow of doubt.

My own story is a simple one enough, though not unimportant to me, since the interposition undoubtedly saved my life. I was walking one exceedingly wet and stormy night down a quiet back street near Westbourne Grove, struggling with scant success to hold up an umbrella against the savage gusts of wind that threatened every moment to tear it from my grasp, and trying as I laboured along to think out the details of some work upon which I was just then engaged.

With startling suddenness a voice which I know well - the voice of an Indian teacher - cried in my ear "Spring back!" and in mechanical obedience I started violently backwards almost before I had time to think. As I did so my umbrella, which had swung forward with the sudden movement, was struck from my hand and a huge metal chimney pot crashed upon the pavement less than a yard in front of my face. The great weight of this article, and the tremendous force with which it fell, make it absolutely certain that but for the warning voice I should have been killed on the spot; yet the street was empty, and the voice was that of one whom I knew to be seven thousand miles away from me, as far as the physical body was concerned.

Nor was this the only occasion upon which I received assistance of this supernormal kind, for in early life, long before the foundation of the Theosophical Society, the apparition of a dear one who had recently died prevented me from committing what I now see would have been a serious crime, although by the light of such knowledge as I then had it appeared not only a justifiable but even a laudable act of retaliation. Again, at a later date, though still before the foundation of this Society, a warning conveyed to me from a higher plane amid most impressive surroundings enabled me to prevent another man from entering upon a course which I now know would have ended disastrously, though I had no reason to suppose so at the time. So it will be seen that I have a certain amount of personal experience to strengthen my belief in the doctrine of invisible helpers, even apart from my knowledge of the help that is constantly being given at the present time.

The other case is a very much more striking one. One of our members, who gives me permission to publish her story, but does not wish her name mentioned, once found herself in very serious physical peril. Owing to circumstances which need not be detailed here, she was in the very centre of a dangerous street fracas, and seeing several men struck down and evidently badly hurt close to her, was in momentary expectation of a similar fate, since escape from the crush seemed quite impossible.

Suddenly she experienced a curious sensation of being whirled out of the crowd, and found herself standing quite uninjured and entirely alone in a small bye-street parallel with the one in which the disturbance had taken place. She still heard the noise of the struggle, and while she stood wondering what on earth had happened to her, two or three men who had escaped from the crowd came running round the corner of the street, and on seeing her expressed great astonishment and pleasure, saying that when the brave lady so suddenly disappeared from the midst of the fight they had felt certain that she had been struck down.

At the time no sort of explanation was forthcoming, and she returned home in a very mystified condition; but when at a later period she mentioned this strange occurrence to Madame Blavatsky she was informed that, her karma being such as to enable her to be saved from her exceedingly dangerous position, one of the Masters had specially sent some one to protect her in view of the fact that her life was needed for the work.

Nevertheless the case remains a very extraordinary one, both with regard to the great amount of power exercised and the unusually public nature of its manifestation. It is not difficult to imagine the *modus operandi*; she must have been lifted bodily over the intervening block of houses, and simply set down in the next street; but since her physical body was not visible floating in the air, it is also evident that a veil of some sort (probably of etheric matter) must have been thrown round her while in transit.

If it be objected that whatever can hide physical matter must itself be physical, and therefore visible, it may be replied that by a process familiar to all occult students it is possible to bend rays of light (which, under all conditions at present known to science, travel only in straight lines unless refracted) so that after passing round an object they may resume exactly their former course; and it will at once be seen that if this were done such an object would to all physical eyes be absolutely invisible until the rays were allowed to resume their normal course. I am fully aware that this one statement alone is sufficient to brand any remarks as nonsense in the eyes of the scientist of the present day, but I cannot help that; I am merely stating a possibility in nature which the science of the future will no doubt one day discover, and for those who are not students of occultism the remark must wait until then for its justification.

The process, as I say, is comprehensible enough to anyone who understands a little about the more occult forces of nature; but the phenomenon still remains an exceedingly dramatic one, while the name of the heroine of the story, were I permitted to give it, would be a guarantee of its accuracy to all my readers.

Another recent instance of interposition, less striking, perhaps, but entirely successful, has been reported to me since the publication of the first edition of this book. A lady, being obliged to undertake a long railway journey alone, had taken the precaution to secure an empty compartment; but just as the train was leaving the station, a man of forbidding and villainous appearance sprang in and seated himself at the other end of the carriage. The lady was much alarmed, thus to be left alone with so doubtful a character, but it was too late to call for help, so she sat still and commended herself earnestly to the care of her patron saint.

Soon her fears were redoubled, for the man arose and turned toward her with an evil grin, but he had hardly taken one step when he started back with a look of the most intense astonishment and terror. Following the direction of his glance, she was startled to see a gentleman seated directly opposite to her, gazing quietly but firmly at the baffled robber - a gentleman who certainly could not have entered the carriage by any ordinary means. Too much awed to speak, she watched him as though fascinated for a full half-hour; he uttered no word, and did not even look at her, but kept his eyes steadily upon the villain, who cowered trembling in the furthest corner of the compartment. The moment that the train reached the next station, and even before it came to a standstill, the would-be thief tore open the door and sprang hurriedly out. The lady, deeply thankful to be rid of him, turned to express her gratitude to the gentleman, but found only an empty seat, though it would have been impossible for any physical body to have left the carriage in the time.

The materialization was in this case maintained for a longer period than usual, but on the other hand it expended no force in action of any kind - nor indeed was it necessary that it should do so, as its mere appearance was sufficient to effect its purpose.

But these stories, all referring as they do to what would commonly be called angelic intervention, illustrate only one small part of the activities of our invisible helpers. Before, however, we can profitably consider the other departments of their work it will be well that we should have clearly in our minds the various classes of entities to which it is possible that these helpers may belong. Let that, then, be the portion of our subject to be next treated.

THE HELPERS

HELP, then, may be given by several of the many classes of inhabitants of the astral plane. It may come from devas, from nature-spirits, or from those whom we call dead, as well as from those who function consciously upon the astral plane during life - chiefly the adepts and their pupils. But if we examine the matter a little more closely we shall see that though all the classes mentioned may, and sometimes do, take a part in this work, yet their shares in it are so unequal that it is practically left almost entirely to one class.

The very fact that so much of this work of helping has to be done either upon or from the astral plane goes far in itself towards explaining this. To anyone who has even a faint idea of what the powers at the command of an adept really are, it will be at once obvious that for him to work upon the astral plane would be a far greater waste of energy than for our leading physicians or scientists to spend their time in breaking stones upon the road.

The work of the adept lies in higher regions - chiefly upon the arûpa levels of the devachanic plane or heaven-world, where he may direct his energies to the influencing of the true individuality of man, and not the mere personality which is all that can be reached in the astral or physical world. The strength which he puts forth in that more exalted realm produces results greater, more far-reaching and more lasting than any which can be attained by the expenditure of even ten times the force down here; and the work up there is such as he alone can fully accomplish, while that on lower planes may be at any rate to some extent achieved by whose feet are yet upon the earlier steps of the great stairway which will one day lead them to the position where he stands.

The same remarks apply also in the case of the devas. Belonging as they do to a higher kingdom of nature than ours, their work seems for the most part entirely unconnected with humanity; and even those of their orders - and there are some such - which do sometimes respond to our higher yearnings or appeals, do so on the mental plane rather than on the physical or astral, and more frequently in the periods between our incarnations than during our earthly lives.

It may be remembered that some instances of such help were observed in the course of investigations into the subdivisions of the devachanic plane which were undertaken when the Theosophical manual on the subject was in preparation. In one case a deva was found teaching the most wonderful celestial music to a chorister; and in another one of a different class was giving instruction and guidance to an astronomer who was seeking to comprehend the form and structure of the universe.

These two were but examples of many instances in which the great deva kingdom was found to he helping onward the evolution and responding to the higher aspirations of man after death; and there are methods by which, even during earth-life, these great ones may be approached, and an infinity of knowledge acquired from them, though even then such intercourse is gained rather by rising to their plane than by invoking them to descend to ours.

In the ordinary events of our physical life the deva very rarely interferes - indeed, he is so fully occupied with the far grander work of his own plane that he is probably scarcely conscious of this; and though it may occasionally happen that he becomes aware of some human sorrow or difficulty which excites his pity and moves him to endeavour to help in some way, his wider vision undoubtedly recognizes that at the present stage of evolution such interpositions would in the vast majority of cases be productive of infinitely more harm than good.

There was indubitably a period in the past - in the infancy of the human race - when it was much more largely assisted from outside than is at present the case. At the time when all its Buddhas and Manus, and even its more ordinary leaders and teachers, were drawn either from the ranks of the deva evolution or from the perfected humanity of a more advanced planet, any such assistance as we are considering in this treatise must also have been given by these exalted beings. But as man progresses he becomes himself qualified to act as a helper, first on the physical plane and then on higher levels; and we have now reached a stage at which humanity ought to be able to provide, and to some slight extent does provide, invisible helpers for itself, thus setting free for still more useful and elevated work those beings who are capable of it.

It becomes obvious then that such assistance as that to which we are here referring may most fitly be given by men and women at a particular stage of their evolution; not by the adepts, since they are capable of doing far grander and more widely useful work, and not by the ordinary person of no special spiritual development, for he would be unable to be of any use. Just as these considerations would lead us to expect, we find that this work of helping on the astral and lower mental planes is chiefly in the hands of the pupils of the Masters - men who, though yet far from the attainment of adeptship, have evolved themselves to the extent of being able to function consciously upon the planes in question.

Some of these have taken the further step of completing the links between the physical consciousness and that of the higher levels, and they therefore have the undoubted advantage of recollecting in waking life what they have done and what they have learnt in those other worlds; but there are my others who, though as yet unable to carry their consciousness through unbroken, are nevertheless by no means wasting the hours when they think they are asleep, but spending them in noble and unselfish labour for their fellow-men.

What this labour is we will proceed to consider, but before we enter upon that part of the subject we will refer to an objection which is very frequently brought forward with regard to such work, and we will also dispose of the comparatively rare cases in which the agents are either nature-spirits or men who have cast off the physical body.

People whose grasp of Theosophical ideas is as yet imperfect are often in doubt as to whether it is allowable for them to try to help some one whom they find in sorrow or difficulty, lest they should interfere with the fate which has been decreed for him by the absolute justice of the eternal law of karma. "The man is in his present position," they say in effect, "because he has deserved it; he is now working out the perfectly natural result of some evil which he has committed in the past; what right have I to interfere with the action of the great cosmic law by trying to ameliorate his condition, either on the astral plane or the physical.

Now the good people who make such suggestions are really, however unconsciously to themselves, exhibiting the most colossal conceit, for their position implies two astounding assumptions; first, that they know exactly what another man's karma has been, and how long it has decreed that his sufferings shall last; and secondly, that they - the insects of a day - could absolutely override the cosmic law and prevent the due working-out of karma by any action of theirs. We may be well assured that the great kârmic deities are perfectly well able to manage their business without our assistance, and we need have no fear that any steps we may take can by any possibility cause them the slightest difficulty or uneasiness.

If a man's karma is such that he cannot be helped, then all our well-meant efforts in that direction will fail, though we shall nevertheless have gained good karma for ourselves by making them. What the man's karma has been is no business of ours; our duty is to give help to the utmost of our power, and our right is only to the act; the result is in other and higher hands. How can we tell how a man's account stands? For all we know he may just have exhausted his evil karma, and be at this moment at the very point where a helping hand is needed to give relief and raise him out of his trouble or depression; why should not we have the pleasure and privilege of doing that good deed as well as another? If we *can* help him, then that fact of itself shows that he has deserved to be helped; but we can never know unless we try. In any case the law of karma will take care of itself, and we need not trouble ourselves about it.

The cases in which assistance is given to mankind by nature-spirits are few. The majority of such creatures shun the haunts of man, and retire before him, disliking his emanations and the perpetual bustle and unrest which he creates all around him. Also, except some of their higher orders, they are generally inconsequent and thoughtless - more like happy children at play under exceedingly favourable physical conditions than like grave and responsible entities. Still it sometimes happens that one of them will become attached to a human being, and do him many a good turn; but at the present stage of its evolution this department of nature cannot be relied upon for anything like steady co-operation in the work of invisible helpers. For a fuller account of the nature-spirits the reader is referred to the fifth of our Theosophical manuals.

Again, help is sometimes given by those recently departed - those who are still lingering on the astral plane, and still in close touch with earthly affairs, as (probably) in the above-mentioned case of the mother who saved her children from falling down a well. But it will readily be seen that the amount of such help available must naturally be exceedingly limited. The more unselfish and helpful a person is, the less likely is he to be found after death lingering in full consciousness on the lower levels of the astral plane, from which the earth is most readily accessible. In any case, unless he were an exceptionally bad man, his stay within the realm whence alone any interference would be possible would be comparatively short; and although from the heaven-world he may still shed benign influence upon those whom he has loved on earth, it will usually be rather of the nature of a general benediction than a force capable of bringing about definite results in a specific case, such as those which we have been considering.

Again, many of the departed who wish to help those whom they left behind, find themselves quite unable to influence them in any way, since to work from one plane upon an entity on another requires either very great sensitiveness on the part of that entity, or a certain amount of knowledge and skill on the part of the operator. Therefore, although instances of apparitions shortly after death are by no means uncommon, it is rare to find one in which the departed person has really done anything useful, or succeeded in impressing what he wished upon the friend or relation whom he visited. There are such cases, of course - a good many of them when we come to put them all together; but they are not numerous compared to the great number of ghosts who have succeeded in showing themselves. So that but little help is usually given by the dead - indeed, as will presently be explained, it is far more common for them to be themselves in need of assistance than to be able to accord it to others.

At present, therefore, the main bulk of the work which has to be done along these lines falls to the share of those living persons who are able to function consciously on the astral plane

THE REALITY OF SUPERPHYSICAL LIFE

IT seems difficult for those who are accustomed only to the ordinary and somewhat materialistic lines of thought of the nineteenth century, to believe in and realize fully a condition of perfect consciousness apart from the physical body. Every Christian, at any rate, is bound by the very foundations of his creed to believe that he possesses a soul; but if you suggest to him the possibility that that soul may be a sufficiently real thing to become visible under certain conditions apart from the body either during life or after death, the chances are ten to one that he will scornfully tell you that he does not believe in ghosts, and that such an idea is nothing but an anachronistic survival of an exploded medieval superstition.

If, therefore, we are at all to comprehend the work of the band of invisible helpers, and perchance ourselves to learn to assist in it, we must shake ourselves free from the trammels of contemporary thought on these subjects, and endeavour to grasp the great truth (now a demonstrated fact to many among us) that the physical body is in simple truth nothing but a vehicle or vesture of the real man. It is put off permanently at death, but it is also put off temporarily every night when we go to sleep - indeed the process of falling asleep consists in this very action of the real man in his astral vehicle slipping out of the physical body.

Again I repeat, this is no mere hypothesis or ingenious supposition. There are many among us who are able to perform (and *do* perform every day of their lives) this elementary act of magic in full consciousness - who pass from one plane to the other at will; and if that is clearly realized, it will become apparent how grotesquely absurd to them must appear the ordinary unreasoning assertion that such a thing is utterly impossible. It is like telling a man that it is impossible for him to fall asleep, and that if he thinks he has ever done so he is under a hallucination.

Now the man who has not yet developed the link between the astral and physical consciousness is unable to leave his denser body at will, or to recollect most of what happens to him while away from it; but the fact nevertheless remains that he leaves it every time he sleeps, and may be seen by any trained clairvoyant either hovering over it or wandering about at a greater or less distance from it, as the case may be.

The entirely undeveloped person usually floats close above his physical body, scarcely less asleep than it is, and comparatively shapeless and inchoate, and it is found that he cannot be drawn away from the immediate neighbourhood of that physical body without causing serious discomfort which would in fact awaken it. As the man evolves, however, his astral body grows more definite and more conscious, and so becomes a fitter vehicle for him. In the case of the majority of intelligent and cultured people the degree of consciousness is already very considerable, and a man who is at all spiritually developed is as fully himself in that vehicle as in this denser body.

But though he may be fully conscious on the astral plane during sleep, and able to move about on it freely if he wishes to do so, it does not yet follow that he is ready to join the band of helpers. Most people at this stage are so wrapped up in their own train of thought - usually a continuation of some line taken up in waking hours - that they are like a man in a brown study, so much absorbed as to be practically entirely heedless of all that is going on about them. And in many ways it is well that this is so, for there is much upon the astral plane which might be unnerving and terrifying to one who had not the courage born of full knowledge as to the real nature of all that he would see.

Sometimes a man gradually rouses himself out of this condition - wakes up to the astral world around him, as it were; but more often he remains in that state until someone who is already active there takes him in hand and wakens him. This is, however, not a responsibility to be lightly undertaken, for while it is comparatively easy thus to wake a man up on the astral plane, it is practically impossible, except by a most undesirable exercise of mesmeric influence, to put him to sleep again. So that before a member of the band of workers will thus awaken a dreamer, he must fully satisfy himself that the man's disposition is such that he will make good use of the additional powers that will then be put into his hands, and also that his knowledge and his courage are sufficient to make it reasonably certain that no harm will come to him as a result of the action.

Such awakening so performed will put a man in a position to join if he will the band of those who help mankind. But it must be clearly understood that this does not necessarily or even usually bring with it the power of remembering in the waking consciousness anything which has been done. That capacity has to be attained by the man for himself, and in most cases it does not come for years afterwards - perhaps not even in the same life. But happily this lack of memory in the body in no way impedes the work out of the body; so that, except for the satisfaction to a man of knowing during his waking hours upon what work he has been engaged during his sleep, it is not a matter of importance. What really matters is that the work should be done - not that we should remember who did it.

A TIMELY INTERVENTION

VARIED as is this work on the astral plane, it is all directed to one great end - the furtherance, in however humble a degree, of the processes of evolution. Occasionally it is connected with the development of the lower kingdoms, which it is possible slightly to accelerate under certain conditions. A duty towards these lower kingdoms, elemental as well as animal and vegetable, is distinctly recognized by our adept leaders, since it is in some cases only through connection with or use by man that their progress takes place.

But naturally by far the largest and most important part of the work is connected with humanity in some way or other. The services rendered are of many and various kinds, but chiefly concerned with man's spiritual development, such physical interventions as are recounted in the earlier part of this book being exceedingly rare. They do, however, occasionally take place, and though it is my wish to emphasize rather the possibility of extending mental and moral help to our fellow-men, it will perhaps be well to give two or three instances in which friends personally known to me have rendered physical assistance to those in sore need of it, in order that it may be seen how these examples from the experience of the helpers gear in with the accounts given by those who have received the supernormal aid - such stories, I mean, as those which are to be found in the literature of so-called "supernatural occurrences."

In the course of the recent rebellion in Matabeleland one of our members was sent upon an errand of mercy which may serve as an illustration of the way in which help upon this lower plane has occasionally been given. It seems that one night a certain farmer and his family in that country were sleeping tranquilly in fancied security, quite unaware that only a few miles away relentless hordes of savage foes were lying in ambush maturing fiendish plots of murder and rapine. Our member's business was in some way or other to arouse the sleeping family to a sense of the terrible danger which so unexpectedly menaced them, and she found this by no means an easy matter.

An attempt to impress the idea of imminent peril upon the brain of the farmer failed utterly, and as the urgency of the case seemed to demand strong measures, our friend decided to materialize herself sufficiently to shake the housewife by the shoulder and adjure her to get up and look about her. The moment she saw that she had been successful in attracting attention she vanished, and the farmer's wife has never from that day to this been able to find out *which* of her neighbours it was who roused her so opportunely, and thus saved the lives of the entire family, who but for this mysterious intervention would undoubtedly have been massacred in their beds half an hour later; nor can she even now understand how this friend in need contrived to make her way in, when all the windows and doors were found so securely barred.

Being this abruptly awakened, the housewife was half inclined to consider the warning a mere dream; however, she arose and looked around just to see that all was right, and fortunate it was that she did so, for though she found nothing amiss indoors she had no sooner thrown open a shutter than she saw the sky red with a distant conflagration. She at once roused her husband and the rest of the family, and owing to this timely notice they were able to escape to a place of concealment near at hand just before the arrival of the horde of savages, who destroyed the house and ravaged the fields indeed, but were disappointed of the human prey which they had expected. The feelings of the rescuer may be imagined when she read in the newspaper some time afterwards an account of the providential deliverance of this family.

THE "ANGEL STORY."

ANOTHER instance of intervention on the physical plane which occurred a short time ago makes a very beautiful little story, though this time only one life was saved. It needs, however, a few words of preliminary explanation. Among our band of helpers here in Europe are two who were brothers long ago in ancient Egypt, and are still warmly attached to one another. In this present incarnation there is a wide difference in age between them, one being advanced in middle life, while the other was at that time a mere child in the physical body, though an ego of considerable advancement and promise. Naturally it falls to the lot of the elder to train and guide the younger in the occult work to which they are so heartily devoted, and as both are fully conscious and active on the astral plane they spend most of the time during which their grosser bodies are asleep in labouring together under the direction of their common Master, and giving to both living and dead such help as is within their power.

I will quote the story of the particular incident which I wish to relate from a letter written by the elder of the two helpers immediately after it occurrence, as the description there given is more vivid and picturesque than any account in the third person could possibly be.

"We were going about quite other business, when Cyril suddenly cried, 'What's that?' for we heard a terrible scream of pain or fright. In a moment we were on the spot, and found that a boy of about eleven or twelve had fallen over a cliff on to some rocks below, and was very badly hurt. He had broken a leg and an arm, poor fellow, but what was still worse was a dreadful cut in the thigh, from which blood was pouring in a torrent. Cyril cried, 'Let us help him quick, or he'll die!'

"In emergencies of this kind one has to think quickly. There were clearly two things to be done; that bleeding must be stopped, and physical help must be procured. I was obliged to materialize either Cyril or myself, for we wanted physical hands at once to tie a bandage, and besides it seemed better that the poor boy should *see* someone standing by him in his trouble. I felt that while undoubtedly he would be more at home with Cyril than with me, I should probably be more readily able to procure help than Cyril would, so the division of labour was obvious.

"The plan worked capitally. I materialized Cyril instantly (he does not know yet how to do it for himself), and told him to take the boy's neckerchief and tie it round the thigh, and twist a stick through it. 'Won't it hurt him terribly? said Cyril; but he *did* it, and the blood stopped flowing. The injured boy seemed half unconscious, and could scarcely speak, but he looked up at the shining little form bending so anxiously over him, and asked, 'Be you an angel, master?' Cyril smiled so prettily, and replied, 'No, I'm only a boy, but I've come to help you;' and then I left him to comfort the sufferer while I rushed off to the boy's mother, who lived about a mile away.

"The trouble I had to force into that woman's head the conviction that something was wrong, and that she must go and see about it, you would never believe; but at last she threw down the pan she was cleaning, and said aloud, 'Well, I don't know what's come over me, but I must go and find the boy.' When she once started I was able to guide her without much difficulty, though at the time I was holding Cyril together by will-power, lest the poor child's angel should suddenly vanish from before his eyes.

"You see, when you materialize a form you are changing matter from its natural state into another - temporarily opposing the cosmic will, as it were; and if you take your mind off it for one half-second, back it flies into its original condition like a flash of lightning. So I could not give more than half my attention to that woman, but still I got her along somehow, and as soon as she came round the corner of the cliff I let Cyril disappear; but she had seen him, and now that village has one of the best-attested stories of angelic intervention on record!

"The accident happened in the early morning, and the same evening I looked in (astrally) upon the family to see how matters were going on. The poor boy's leg and arm had been set, and the great cut bandaged, and he lay in bed looking very pale and weak, but evidently going to recover in time. The mother had a couple of neighbours in, and was telling them the story; and a curious tale it sounded to one who knew the real facts.

"She explained, in very many words, how she couldn't tell what it was, but something came over her all in a minute like, making her feel something had happened to the boy, and she *must* go out and see after him; how at first she thought it was nonsense, and tried to throw off the feeling, 'but it warn't no use - she just had to go.' She told how she didn't know what made her go round by that cliff more than any other way, but it just happened so, and as she turned round the corner there she saw him lying propped up against a rock, and kneeling beside him was the 'beautifullest child ever she saw, dressed all in white and shining, with rosy cheeks and lovely brown eyes;' and how he smiled at her 'so heavenly like,' and then all in a moment he was not there, and at first she was so startled she didn't know what to think; and then all at once she felt what it was, and fell on her knees and thanked God for sending one of his angels to help her poor boy.

"Then she told how when she lifted him to carry him home she wanted to take off the handkerchief that was cutting into his poor leg so, but he would not let her, because he said the angel had tied it and said he was not to touch it; and how when she told the doctor this afterwards he explained to her that if she *had* unfastened it the boy would certainly have died.

"Then she repeated the boy's part of the tale - how the moment after he fell this lovely little angel came to him (he knew it *was* an angel because he knew there had been nobody in sight for half a mile round when he was at the top of the cliff just before - only he could not understand why it hadn't any wings, and why it said it was only a boy) - how it lifted him against the rock and tied up his leg, and then began to talk to him and tell him he need not be frightened, because somebody was gone to fetch mother, and she would be there directly; how it kissed him and tried to make him comfortable, and how its soft, warm, little hand held his all the time, while it told him strange, beautiful stories which he could not clearly remember, but he knew they were very good, because he had almost forgotten he was hurt until he saw his mother coming; and how then it assured him he would soon be well again, and smiled and squeezed his hand, and then somehow it was gone.

"Since then there has been quite a religious revival in that village! Their minister has told them that so signal an interposition of divine providence must have been meant as a sign to them, to rebuke scoffers and to prove the truth of holy scripture and of the Christian religion - and nobody seems to see the colossal conceit involved in such an astonishing proposition.

"But the effect on the boy had been undoubtedly good, morally as well as physically; by all accounts he was a careless enough young scamp before, but now he feels 'his angel' may be near him at any time, and he will never do or say anything rough or coarse or angry, lest it should see or hear. The one great desire of his life is that some day he may see it again, and he knows that when he dies its lovely face will be the first to greet him on the other side.

A beautiful and pathetic little story, truly. The moral dawn from the occurrence by the village and its minister is perhaps somewhat of a *non sequitur*; yet the testimony to the existence of at least something beyond this material plane must surely do the people more good than harm, and after all the mother's conclusion from what she saw was a perfectly correct one, though more accurate knowledge would probably have led her to express it a little differently.

An interesting fact afterwards discovered by the investigations of the writer of the letter throws a curious side-light upon the reasons underlying such incidents. It was found that the two boys had met before, and that some thousands of years ago the one who fell from the cliff had been the slave of the other, and had once saved his young master's life at the risk of his own, and had been liberated in consequence; and now, long afterwards, the master not only repays the debt in kind, but also gives his former slave a high ideal and an inducement to morality of life which will probably change the whole course of his future evolution. So true is it that no good deed ever goes unrewarded by karma, however tardy it may seem in its action - that

Though the mills of God grind slowly
Yet they grind exceeding small;
Though with patience stands
He waiting
With exactness grinds He all.

THE STORY OF A FIRE

ANOTHER piece of work done by the same boy Cyril furnishes an almost exact parallel to some of the stories from the books which I have given in earlier pages. He and his older friend, it seems, were passing along in the prosecution of their usual work one night, when they noticed the fierce glare of a big fire below them, and promptly dived down to see if they could be of any use.

It was a great hotel which was in flames, a huge caravanserai on the edge of a great lake. The house, many stories in height, formed three sides of a square round a sort of garden, planted with trees and flowers, while the lake formed the fourth side. The two wings ran right down to the lake, the big bay windows which terminated them almost projecting over the water, so as to leave only quite a narrow passage-way under them at the two sides.

The front and wings were built round inside wells, which contained also the lattice-work shafts of the lifts, so that when once the fire broke out, it spread with almost incredible rapidity, and before our friends saw it on their astral journey all the middle floors in each of the three great blocks were in flames. Fortunately the inmates - except one little boy - had already been rescued, though some of them had sustained very serious burns and other injuries.

This little fellow had been forgotten in one of the upper rooms of the left wing, for his parents were out at a ball, and knew nothing of the fire, while naturally enough no one else thought of the lad till it was far too late. The fire had gained such a hold on the middle floors of that wing that nothing could have been done, even if anyone had remembered him, as his room faced on to the inner garden which has been mentioned, so that he was completely cut off from all outside help. Besides, he was not even aware of his danger, for the dense, suffocating smoke had so gradually filled the room that his sleep had grown deeper and deeper, till he was all but stupefied.

In this state he was discovered by Cyril, who seems to be specially attracted towards children in need or danger. He first tried to make some of the people remember the boy, but in vain; and in any case it seemed scarcely possible that they could have helped him, so that it was soon evident that this was merely a waste of time. The older helper then materialized, Cyril, as before, in the room, and set him to work to awaken and rouse up the more than half-stupefied child. After a good deal of difficulty this was accomplished to some extent, but the boy remained in a half-dazed, semi-conscious condition through all that followed, so that he needed to be pushed and pulled about, guided and helped at every turn.

The two boys first crept out of the room into the central passage which ran through the wing, and then, finding that the smoke and the flames beginning to come through the floor made it impassable for a physical body, Cyril got the other boy back into the room again and out of the window on to a stone ledge, about a foot wide, which ran right along the block just below the windows. Along this he managed to guide his companion, half balancing himself on the extreme edge of the ledge, and half floating on air, but always placing himself outside of the other, so as to keep him from dizziness and prevent him from feeling afraid of a fall.

Towards the end of the block nearest the lake, in which direction the fire seemed less developed, they climbed in through an open window and again reached the passage, hoping to find the staircase at that end still passable. But it, too, was full of flame and smoke; so they crawled back along the passage, Cyril advising his companion to keep his mouth close to the ground, till they reached the latticed cage of the lift running down the long well in the centre of the block.

The lift of course was at the bottom, but they managed to clamber down the lattice work inside the cage till they stood on the roof of the elevator itself. Here they found themselves blocked, but luckily Cyril discovered a doorway opening from the cage of the lift on to a sort of *entresol* just above the ground floor. Through this they reached a passage, which they crossed, the little boy being half-stifled by the smoke; then they made their way through one of the rooms opposite, and finally, clambering out of the window, found themselves on the top of the veranda which ran along in front of the ground floor, between it and the garden.

There it was easy enough to swarm down one of the pillars and reach the garden itself; but even there the heat was intense, and the danger, when the walls should fall, very considerable. So Cyril tried to conduct his charge round the end first of one, then of the other wing; but in both cases the flames had burst through, and the narrow, overhung passages were quite impassable. Finally they took refuge in one of the pleasure boats which were moored to the steps of the quay at the side of the garden next the lake, and, casting loose, rowed out on to the water.

Cyril intended to row round past the burning wing and land the boy whom he had saved; but when they got some little way out, they fell in with a passing lake steamer, and were seen - for the whole scene was lit up by the glare of the burning hotel, till everything was as plain as in broad daylight. The steamer came alongside the boat to take them off; but instead of the two boys they had seen, the crew found only one - for his older friend had promptly allowed Cyril to slip back into his astral form, dissipating the denser matter which had made for the time a material body, and he was therefore now invisible.

A careful search was made, of course, but no trace of the second boy could be found, and so it was concluded that he must have fallen overboard and been drowned just as they came alongside. The child who had been rescued fell into a dead faint as soon as he was safe on board, so they could get no information from him, and when he did recover, all he could say was that he had seen the other boy the moment before they came alongside, and then knew nothing more.

The steamer was bound down the lake to a place some two days' sail distant, and it was a week or so before the rescued boy could be restored to his parents, who of course thought that he had perished in the flames, for though an effort was made to impress on their minds the fact that their son had been saved, it was found impossible to convey the idea to them, so it may be imagined how great was the joy of the meeting.

The boy is still well and happy, and is never weary of relating his wonderful adventure. Many a time he has regretted that the kind friend who saved him should have perished so mysteriously at the very moment when all the danger seemed over at last. Indeed, he has even ventured to suggest that perhaps he *didn't* perish after all - that perhaps he was a fairy prince; but of course this idea elicits nothing but tolerant smiles of superiority from his elders. The kârmic link between him and his preserver has not yet been traced, but no doubt there must be one somewhere.

MATERIALIZATION AND REPERCUSSION

ON meeting with a story such as this, students often enquire whether the invisible helper is perfectly safe amidst these scenes of deadly peril - whether, for example, this boy who was materialized in order to save another from a burning house was not himself in some danger - whether his physical body would not have suffered in any way by repercussion if his materialized form had passed through the flames, or fallen from the high ledge on the edge of which he walked so unconcernedly. In fact, since we know that in many cases the connection between a materialized form and a physical body is sufficiently close to produce repercussion, might it not have occurred in this case?

Now this subject of repercussion is an exceedingly abstruse and difficult one, and we are by no means yet in a position fully to explain its very remarkable phenomena; in order to understand the matter perfectly, it would probably be necessary to comprehend the laws of sympathetic vibration on more planes than one. Still, we do know by observation some of the conditions which permit its action, and some which definitely exclude it, and I think we are warranted in saying that it was absolutely impossible here.

To see why this is so we must first remember that there are at least three well-defined varieties of materialization, as anyone who has at all an extended experience of spiritualism will be aware. I am not concerned at the moment to enter upon any explanation as to how these three varieties are respectively produced, but am merely stating the indubitable fact of their existence.

There is the materialization which, though tangible, is not visible to ordinary physical sight. Of this nature are the unseen hands which so often clasp one's arm or stroke one's face at a *séance,* which sometimes carry physical objects through the air or make raps upon the table - though of course both these latter phenomena may easily be produced without a materialized hand at all.

There is the materialization which though visible is not tangible - the spirit-form through which one's hand passed as through empty air. In some cases this variety is obviously misty and impalpable, but in others its appearance is so entirely normal that its solidity is never doubted until some one endeavours to grasp it.

There is the perfect materialization which is both visible and tangible - which not only bears the outward semblance of your departed friend but shakes you cordially by the hand with the very clasp that you know so well.

Now while there is a good deal of evidence to show that repercussion takes place under certain conditions in the case of this third kind of materialization., it is by no means so certain that it can occur with the first or second class. In the case of the boy-helper it is probable that the materialization would not be of the third type, since the greatest care is always taken not to expend more force than is absolutely necessary to produce whatever result may be required, and it is obvious that less energy would be used in the production of the more partial forms which we have called the first and second classes. The probability is that only the arm with which the boy held his little companion would be solid to the touch, and that the rest of his body, though looking perfectly natural, would have proved far less palpable if it had been tested.

But, apart from this probability, there is another point to be considered. When a full materialization takes place, whether the subject be living or dead, physical matter of some sort has to be gathered together for the purpose. At a spiritualistic *séance* this matter is obtained by drawing largely upon the etheric double of the medium - and sometimes even upon his physical body also, since cases are on record in which his weight has been very considerably decreased while manifestations of this character were taking place.

This method is employed by the directing entities of the *séance* simply because when an available medium is within reach it is very much the easiest way in which a materialization can be brought about; and the consequence is that the very closest connection is thus set up between that medium and the materialized body, so that the phenomenon which (although very imperfectly understanding it) we call repercussion, occurs in its clearest form. If, for example, the hands of the materialized body be rubbed with chalk, that chalk will afterwards be found on the hands of the medium, even though he may have been all the time carefully locked up in a cabinet under circumstances which absolutely preclude any suspicion of fraud. If any injury be inflicted upon the materialized form, that injury will be accurately reproduced upon the corresponding part of the medium's body: while sometimes food of which the spirit-form has partaken will be found to have passed into the body of the medium - at least that happened in one case at any rate within my own experience.

It would be far otherwise, however, in the case which we have been describing. Cyril was thousands of miles from his sleeping physical body, and it would therefore be quite impossible for his friend to draw etheric matter from it, while the regulations under which all pupils of the great Masters of Wisdom perform their work of helping man would assuredly prevent him, even for the noblest purpose, from putting such a strain upon any one else's body. Besides, it would be quite unnecessary, for the far less dangerous method invariably employed by the helpers when materialization seems desirable would be ready to his hand - the condensation from the circumambient ether, or even from the physical air, of such an amount of matter as may be requisite. This feat, though no doubt beyond the power of the average entity manifesting at a *séance*, presents no difficulty to a student of occult chemistry.

But mark the difference in the result obtained. In the case of the medium we have a materialized form in the closest possible connection with the physical body, made out of its very substance, and therefore capable of producing all the phenomena of repercussion. In the case of the helper we have indeed an exact reproduction of the physical body, but it is created by a mental effort out of matter entirely foreign to that body, and is no more capable of acting upon it by repercussion than an ordinary marble statue of the man would be.

Thus it is that a passage through the flames or a fall from a high window-ledge would have had no terrors for the boy-helper, and that on another occasion a member of the band, though materialized, was able without any inconvenience to the physical body to go down in a sinking vessel.

In both the incidents of his work that have been described above, it will have been noticed that the boy Cyril was unable to materialize himself, and that the operation had to be performed for him by an older friend. One more of his experiences is worth relating, for it gives us a case in which by intensity of pity and determination of will he *was* able to show himself - a case somewhat parallel to that previously related of the mother whose love enabled her somehow to manifest herself in order to save her children's lives.

Inexplicable as it may seem, there is no doubt whatever of the existence in nature of this stupendous power of will over matter of all planes, so that if only the power be great enough, practically *any* result may be produced by its direct action, without any knowledge or even thought on the part of the man exercising that will as to *how* it is to do its work. We have had plenty of evidence that this power holds good in the case of materialization, although ordinarily it is an art which must be learnt just like any other. Assuredly an average man on the astral plane could no more materialize himself without having previously learnt how to do it than the average man on this plane could play the violin without having previously learnt it; but there are exceptional cases, as will be seen from the following narrative.

THE TWO BROTHERS

This story has been told by a pen of far greater dramatic capability than mine, and with a wealth of detail for which I have here no space, in *The Theosophical Review* of November, 1897, page 229. To that account I would refer the reader, since my own description of the case will be a mere outline, as brief as is consistent with clearness. The names given are of course fictitious, but the incidents are related with scrupulous accuracy.

Our *dramatis personae* are two brothers, the sons of a country gentleman - Lancelot, aged fourteen, and Walter, aged eleven - very good boys of the ordinary healthy, manly type, like hundreds of others in this fair realm, with no obvious psychic qualifications of any sort, except the possession of a good deal of Celtic blood. Perhaps the most remarkable feature about them was the intensity of the affection that existed between them, for they were simply inseparable - neither would go anywhere without the other, and the younger idolized the elder as only a younger boy can.

One unlucky day Lancelot was thrown from his pony and killed, and for Walter the world became empty. The child's grief was so real and terrible that he could neither eat not sleep, and his mother and nurse were at their wits' end as to what to do for him. He seemed deaf alike to persuasion and blame; when they told him that grief was wicked, and that his brother was in heaven, he simply answered that he could not be certain of that, and that even if it were true, he knew that Lancelot could no more be happy in heaven without him than he could on earth without Lancelot.

Incredible as it may sound, the poor child was actually dying of grief, and what made the case even more pathetic was the fact that, all unknown to him, his brother stood at his side all the time, fully conscious of his misery, and himself half-distracted at the failure of his repeated attempts to touch him or speak to him.

Affairs were still in this most pitiable condition on the third evening after the accident, when Cyril's attention was drawn to the two brothers - he cannot tell how. "He just happened to be passing," he says; yet surely the will of the Lords of Compassion guided him to the scene. Poor Walter lay exhausted yet sleepless - alone in his desolation, so far as he knew, though all the time his sorrowing brother stood beside him. Lancelot, free from the chains of the flesh, could see and hear Cyril, so obviously the first thing to do was to soothe his pain with a promise of friendship and help in communicating with his brother.

As soon as the dead boy's mind was thus cheered with hope, Cyril turned to the living one, and tried with all his strength to impress upon his brain the knowledge that his brother stood beside him, not dead, but living and loving as of yore. But all his efforts were in vain; the dull apathy of grief so filled poor Walter's mind that no suggestion from without could enter, and Cyril knew not what to do. Yet so deeply was he moved by the sad sight, so intense was his sympathy and so firm his determination to help in some way or other at any cost of strength to himself, that somehow (even to this day he cannot tell how) he found himself able to touch and speak to the heart-broken child.

Putting aside Walter's questions as to who he was and how he came there, he went straight to the point, telling him that his brother stood beside him, trying hard to make him hear his constantly repeated assurances that he was not dead, but living and yearning to help and comfort him. Little Walter longed to believe, yet hardly dared to hope; but Cyril's eager insistence vanquished his doubts at last, and he said, "Oh! I do believe you, because you're so kind; but if I could only see him, then I should *know*, then I should be quite sure; and if I could only hear his voice telling me he was happy, I shouldn't mind a bit his going away again afterwards."

Young though he was at the work, Cyril knew enough to be aware that Walter's wish was one not ordinarily granted, and was beginning regretfully to tell him so, when suddenly he felt a Presence that all the helpers know, and though no word was spoken it was borne in upon his mind that instead of what he had meant to say, he was to promise Walter the boon his heart desired. "Wait till I come back," he said, "and you shall see him then." And then - he vanished.

That one touch from the Master had shown him what to do and how to do it, and he rushed to fetch the older friend who had so often helped him before. This older man had not yet retired for the night, but on hearing Cyril's hurried summons, he lost no time in accompanying him, and in a few minutes they were back at Walter's bedside. The poor child was just beginning to believe it all a lovely dream, and his delight and relief when Cyril reappeared were beautiful to see. Yet how much more beautiful was the scene a moment later, when, in obedience to a word from the Master, the elder man materialized the eager Lancelot, and the living and the dead stood hand in hand once more!

Now in very truth for both the brothers had sorrow been turned into joy unspeakable, and again and again they both declared that now they should never feel sad any more, because they knew that death had no power to part them. Nor was their gladness damped even when Cyril explained carefully to them, at his older friend's suggestion, that this strange physical reunion would not be repeated, but that all day long Lancelot would be near Walter, even though the latter could not see him, and every night Walter would slip out of his body and be consciously with his brother once more.

Hearing this, poor weary Walter sank to sleep at once and proved its truth, and was amazed to find with what hitherto unknown rapidity he and his brother could fly together from one to another of their old familiar haunts. Cyril thoughtfully warned him that he would probably forget most of his freer life when he awoke next day; but by rare good fortune he did *not* forget, as so many of us do. Perhaps the shock of the great joy had somewhat aroused the latent psychic faculty which belongs to the Celtic blood; at any rate he forgot no single detail of all that had happened, and next morning he burst upon the house of mourning with a wondrous tale which suited it but ill.

His parents thought that grief had turned his brain, and, since he is now the heir, they have been watching long and anxiously for further symptoms of insanity, which happily they have not found. They still think him a monomaniac on this point, though they fully recognize that his "delusion" has saved his life; but his old nurse (who is a Catholic) is firm in her belief that all he says is true - that the Lord Jesus, who was once a child himself, took pity on that other child as he lay dying of grief, and sent one of His angels to bring his brother back to him from the dead as a reward for a love which was stronger than death. Sometimes popular superstition gets a good deal nearer to the heart of things than does educated skepticism!

Nor does the story end here, for the good work begun that night is still progressing, and none can say how far the influence of that one act may ramify. Walter's astral consciousness, once having been thus thoroughly awakened, remains in activity; every morning he brings back into his physical brain the memory of his night's adventures with his brother; every night they meet their dear friend Cyril, from whom they have learned so much about the wonderful new world that has opened before them, and the other worlds to come that lie higher yet. Under Cyril's guidance they also - the living and the dead alike - have become eager and earnest members of the band of helpers; and probably for years to come - until Lancelot's vigorous young astral body disintegrates - many a dying child will have cause to be grateful to these three who are trying to pass on to others something of the joy that they have themselves received.

Nor is it to the dead alone that these new converts have been of use, for they have sought and found some other living children who show consciousness on the astral plane during sleep; and one at least of those whom they have thus brought to Cyril has already proved a valuable little recruit to the children's band, as well as a very kind little friend down here on the physical plane.

Those to whom all these ideas are new sometimes find it very difficult to understand how children can be of any use in the astral world. Seeing, they would say, that the astral body of a child must be undeveloped, and the ego thus limited by childhood on the astral as well as the physical plane, in what way could such an ego be of use, or be able to help towards the spiritual, mental and moral evolution of humanity, which we are told is the chief concern of the helpers?

When first such a question was asked, shortly after the publication of one of these stories in our magazine, I sent it to Cyril himself, to see what he would say to it, and his answer was this:

"It is quite true, as the writer says, that I am only a boy, and know very little yet, and that I shall be much more useful when I have learnt more. But I am able to do a little even now, because there are so many people who have learnt nothing about Theosophy yet, though they may know very much more than I do about everything else. And you see when you want to get to a certain place, a little boy who knows the way can do more for you than a hundred wise men who don't know it."

It may be added that when a child had been awakened upon the astral plane the development of the astral body would proceed so rapidly that he would very soon be in a position upon that plane but little inferior to that of the awakened adult, and would of course be much in advance, so far as usefulness is concerned, of the wisest man who was as yet unawakened. But unless the ego expressing himself through the child-body possessed the necessary qualification of a determined yet loving disposition, and had clearly manifested it in his previous lives, no occultist would take the very serious responsibility of awakening him upon the astral plane. When, however their karma is such that it is possible for them to be thus aroused, children very often prove most efficient helpers, and throw themselves into their work with a whole-souled devotion which is very beautiful to see. And so is fulfilled once more the ancient prophecy "a little child shall lead them."

Another question that suggests itself to one's mind in reading this last story of the two brothers is this: Since Cyril was somehow able to materialize himself by sheer force of love and pity and strength of will, is it not strange that Lancelot, who had been trying so much longer to communicate, had not succeeded in doing the same thing.

Well, there is of course no difficulty in seeing why poor Lancelot was unable to communicate with his brother, for that inability is simply the normal condition of affairs, the wonder is that Cyril *was* able to materialize himself, not that Lancelot was *not*. Not only, however, was the feeling probably stronger in Cyril's case, but he also knew exactly what he wanted to do - knew that such a thing as materialization was a possibility, and had some general idea as to how it was done - while Lancelot naturally knew nothing of all this then, though he does now.

WRECKS AND CATASTROPHES

SOMETIMES it is possible for members of the band of helpers to avert impending catastrophes of a somewhat larger order. In more than one case when the captain of a vessel has been carried unsuspecting far out of his course by some unknown current or through some mistaken reckoning, and has thereby run into serious danger, it has been possible to prevent shipwreck by repeatedly impressing upon his mind a feeling that something was wrong; and although this generally comes through into the captain's brain merely as a vaguely warning intuition, yet if it occurs again and again he is almost certain to give it some attention and take such precautions as suggest themselves to him.

In one case, for example, in which the master of a barque was much nearer in to the land than he supposed, he was again and again pressed to heave the lead, and though he resisted this suggestion for some time as being unnecessary and absurd, he at last gave the order in a somewhat hesitating way. The result astounded him, and he at once put his vessel about and stood off from the coast, though it was not until morning came that he realized how very close he had been to an appalling disaster.

Often, however, a catastrophe is kârmic in its nature, and consequently cannot be averted; but it must not therefore be supposed that in such cases no help can be given. It may be that the people concerned are destined to die, and therefore cannot be saved from death; but in many cases they may still be to some extent prepared for it, and may certainly be helped upon the other side after it is over. Indeed, it may be definitely stated that wherever a great catastrophe of any kind takes place, there is also a special sending of help.

Two recent cases in which such help was given were the sinking of the *Drummond Castle* off Cape Ushant, and the terrible cyclone which devastated the city of St Louis in America. On both these occasions a few minutes' notice was given, and the helpers did their best to calm and raise men's minds, so that when the shock came upon them it would be less disturbing than it might otherwise have been. Naturally, however, the greater part of the work done with the victims in both these calamities was done upon the astral plane after they had left their physical bodies; but of this we shall speak later.

It is sad to relate how often when some catastrophe is impending the helpers are hindered in their kindly offices by wild panic among those whom the danger threatens - or sometimes, worse still, by a mad outburst of drunkenness among those whom they are trying to assist. Many a ship has gone to her doom with almost every soul on board mad with drink, and therefore utterly incapable of profiting by any assistance offered either before death or for a very long time afterwards.

If it should ever happen to any of us to find ourselves in a position of imminent danger which we can do nothing to avert, we should try to remember that help is certainly near us, and that it rests entirely with ourselves to make the helper's work easy or difficult. If we face the danger calmly and bravely, recognizing that the true ego can in no way be affected by it, our minds will then be open to receive the guidance which the helpers are trying to give, and this cannot but be best for us, whether its object be to save us from death or, when that is impossible, to conduct us safely through it.

Assistance of this latter kind has not infrequently been given in cases of accidents to individuals, as well as of more general catastrophes. It will be sufficient to mention one example as an illustration of what is meant. In one of the great storms which did so much damage around our coasts a few years ago, it happened that a fishing boat was capsized far out at sea. The only people on board were an old fisherman and a boy, and the former contrived to cling for a few minutes to the overturned boat. There was no physical help at hand, and even if there had been in such a raging storm it would have been impossible for anything to be done, so that the fisherman knew well enough that there was no hope of escape, and that death could only be a question of a few moments. He felt a great terror at the prospect, being especially impressed by the awful loneliness of that vast waste of waters, and he was also much troubled with thoughts of his wife and family, and the difficulties in which they would be left by his sudden decease.

A passing helper seeing all this endeavoured to comfort him, but finding his mind too much disturbed to be impressionable, she thought it advisable to show herself to him in order to assist him the better. In relating the story afterwards she said that the change which came over the fisherman's face at sight of her was wonderful and beautiful to see; with the shining form standing upon the boat above him he could not think that an angel had been sent to comfort him in his trouble, and therefore he felt that not only would he himself be carried safely through the gates of death, but his family would assuredly be looked after also. So, when death came to him a few moments later, he was in a frame of mind very different from the terror and perplexity which had previously overcome him; and naturally when he recovered consciousness upon the astral plane and found the "angel" still beside him he felt himself at home with her, and was prepared to accept her advice as regards the new life upon which he had entered.

Some time later the same helper was engaged in another piece of work of very similar character, the story of which she has since told as fellows: "You remember that steamer that went down in the cyclone at the end of last November; I betook myself to the cabin where about a dozen women had been shut in, and found them wailing in the most pitiful manner, sobbing and moaning with fear. The ship had to founder - no aid was possible - and to go out of the world in this state of frantic terror is the worst possible way to enter the next. So in order to calm them I materialized myself, and of course they thought I was an angel, poor souls; they all fell on their knees and prayed me to save them, and one poor mother pushed her baby into my arms imploring me to save that at least. They soon grew quiet and composed as we talked, and the wee baby went to sleep smiling, and presently they all fell asleep peacefully, and I filled their minds with thoughts of the heaven-world, so that they did not wake up when the ship made her final plunge downwards. I went down with them to ensure their sleeping through the last moments, and they never stirred as their sleep became death."

Evidently in this case, too, those who were thus helped had not only the enormous advantage of being enabled to meet death calmly and reasonably, but also the still greater one of being received on its farther shore by one whom they were already disposed to love and trust - one who thoroughly understood the new world in which they found themselves, and could not only reassure them as to their safety, but advise them how to order their lives under these much altered circumstances. And this brings us to the consideration of one of the largest and most important departments of the work of invisible helpers - the guidance and assistance which they are able to give to the dead.

WORK AMONG THE DEAD

IT is one of the many evils resulting from the absurdly erroneous teaching as to conditions after death which is unfortunately current in our western world, that those who have recently shaken off this mortal coil are usually much puzzled and often very seriously frightened at finding everything so different from what their religion had led them to expect. The mental attitude of a large number of such people was pithily voiced the other day by an English general, who three days after his death met one of the band of helpers whom he had known in physical life. After expressing his great relief that he had at last found someone with whom he was able to communicate, his first remark was: "But if I am dead, where am I? For if this is heaven I don't think much of it; and if it is hell, it is better than I expected."

But unfortunately a far greater number take things less philosophically. They have been taught that all men are destined to eternal flames except a favoured few who are superhumanly good; and since a very small amount of self-examination convinces them that they do not belong to *that* category, they are but too often in a condition of panic terror, dreading every moment that the new world in which they find themselves may dissolve and drop them into the clutches of the devil, in whom they have been sedulously taught to believe. In many cases they spend long periods of acute mental suffering before they can free themselves from the fatal influence of this blasphemous doctrine of everlasting punishment - before they can realize that the world is governed, not according to the caprice of a hideous demon who gloats over human anguish, but according to a benevolent and wonderfully patient law of evolution, which is absolutely just indeed, but yet again and again offers to man opportunities of progress, if he will but take them, at every stage of his career.

It ought in fairness to be mentioned that it is only among what are called protestant communities that this terrible evil assumes its most aggravated form. The great Roman Catholic Church, with its doctrine of purgatory, approaches much more nearly to a conception of the astral plane, and it devout members at any rate realize that the state in which they find themselves shortly after death is merely a temporary one, and that it is their business to endeavour to raise themselves out of it as soon as may be by intense spiritual aspiration, while they accept any suffering which may come to them as necessary for the wearing away of the imperfections in their character before they can pass to higher and brighter regions.

It will thus be seen that there is plenty of work for the helpers to do among the newly dead, for in the vast majority of cases they need to be calmed and reassured, to be comforted and instructed. In the astral, just as in the physical world, there are many who are but little disposed to take advice from those who know better than they; yet the very strangeness of the conditions surrounding them renders many of the dead willing to accept the guidance of those to whom these conditions are obviously familiar; and many a man's stay on that plane has been considerably shortened by the earnest efforts of this band of energetic workers.

Not, be it understood, that the karma of the dead man can in any way be interfered with; he has built for himself during life an astral body of a certain degree of density, and until that body is sufficiently dissolved he cannot pass on into the heaven-world beyond; but he need not lengthen the period necessary for that process by adopting an improper attitude.

All students ought clearly to grasp the truth that the length of a man's astral life after he has put off his physical body depends mainly upon two factors - the nature of his past physical life, and his attitude of mind after what we call death. During his earth life he is constantly influencing the building of matter into his astral body. He affects it directly by the passions, emotions and desires which he allows to hold sway over him; he affects it indirectly by the action upon it of his thoughts from above, and of the details of his physical life - his continence or his debauchery, his cleanliness or his uncleanliness, his food and his drink - from below.

If by persistence in perversity along any of these lines he is so stupid as to build for himself a coarse and gross astral vehicle, habituated to responding only to the lower vibrations of the plane, he will find himself after death bound to that plane during and long and slow process of that body's disintegration. On the other hand if by decent and careful living he gives himself a vehicle mainly composed of finer material, he will have very much less *post-mortem* trouble and discomfort, and his evolution will proceed much more rapidly and easily.

This much is generally understood, but the second great factor - his attitude of mind after death - seems often to be forgotten. The desirable thing is for him to realize his position on this particular little arc of his evolution - to learn that he is at this stage withdrawing steadily inward towards the plane of the true ego, and that consequently it is his business to disengage his thoughts as far as may be from things physical, and to fix his attention more and more upon those spiritual matters which will occupy him during his life in the heaven-world. By doing this he will greatly facilitate the natural astral disintegration, and will avoid the sadly common mistake of unnecessarily delaying himself upon the lower levels of what should be so temporary a residence.

But many of the dead very considerably retard the process of dissolution by clinging passionately to the earth which they have left; they simply will not turn their thoughts and desires upward, but spend their time in struggling with all their might to keep in full touch with the physical plane, thus causing great trouble to any one who may be trying to help them. Earthly matters are the only ones in which they have had any living interest, and they cling to them with desperate tenacity even after death. Naturally as time passes on they find it increasingly difficult to keep hold of things down here, but instead of welcoming and encouraging this process of gradual refinement and spiritualization they resist it vigorously by every means in their power.

Of course the mighty force of evolution is eventually too strong for them, and they are swept on in its beneficent current, yet they fight every step of the way, thereby not only causing themselves a vast amount of entirely unnecessary pain and sorrow, but also very seriously delaying their upward progress and prolonging their stay in astral regions to an almost indefinite extent. In convincing them that this ignorant and disastrous opposition to the cosmic will is contrary to the laws of nature, and persuading them to adopt an attitude of mind which is the exact reversal of it, lies a great part of the work of those who are trying to help.

It happens occasionally that the dead are earthbound by anxiety - anxiety sometimes about duties unperformed or debts undischarged, but more often on account of wife or children left unprovided for. In such cases as this it has more than once been necessary, before the dead man was satisfied to pursue his upward path in peace, that the helper should to some extent act as his representative upon the physical plane, and attend on his behalf to the settlement of the business which was troubling him. An illustration taken from our recent experience will perhaps make this clearer.

One of the band of pupils was trying to assist a poor man who had died in one of our western cities, but found it impossible to withdraw his mind from earthly things because of his anxiety about two young children whom his death had left without means of support. He had been a working man of some sort, and had been unable to lay by any money for them; his wife had died some two years previously and his landlady, though exceedingly kindhearted and very willing to do anything in her power for them, was herself far too poor to be able to adopt them, and very reluctantly came to the conclusion that she would be obliged to hand them over to the parish authorities. This was a great grief to the dead father, though he could not blame the landlady, and was himself unable to suggest any other course.

Our friend asked him whether he had no relative to whom he could entrust them, but the father knew of none. He had a younger brother, he said, who would certainly have done something for him in this extremity, but he had lost sight of him for fifteen years, and did not even know whether he was living or dead. When last heard of he had been apprenticed to a carpenter in the north, and he was then described as a steady young fellow who, if he lived, would surely get on.

The clues at hand were certainly very slight, but since there seemed no other prospect of help for the children, our friend thought it worth while to make a special effort to follow them up. Taking the dead man with him he commenced a patient search after the brother in the town indicated; and after a great deal of trouble they were actually successful in finding him. He was now a master carpenter in a fairly flourishing way of business - married, but without children though earnestly desiring them, and therefore apparently just the man for the emergency.

The question now was how the information could be conveyed to this brother. Fortunately he was found to be so far impressionable that the circumstances of his brother's death and the destitution of his children could be put vividly before him in a dream, and this was repeated three times, the place and even the name of the landlady being clearly indicated to him. He was immensely impressed by this recurring vision, and discussed it earnestly with his wife, who advised him to write to the address given. This he did not like to do, but was strongly inclined to travel down into the west country, find out whether there was such a house as that which he had seen, and if so make some excuse to call there. He was a busy man, however, and he finally decided that he could not afford to lose a day's work for what after all might well prove to be nothing but the baseless fabric of a dream.

The attempt along these lines having apparently failed, it was determined to try another method, so one of the helpers wrote a letter to the man detailing the circumstances of his brother's death and the position of the children, exactly as he had seen them in his dream. On receipt of this confirmation he no longer hesitated, but set off the very next day for the town indicated, and was received with open arms by the kind-hearted landlady. It had been easy enough for the helpers to persuade her, good soul that she was, to keep the children with her for a few days on the chance that something or other would turn up for them, and she has ever since congratulated herself that she did so. The carpenter of course took the children back with him and provided them with a happy home, and the dead father, now no longer anxious, passed rejoicing on his upward journey.

Since some Theosophical writers have felt it their duty to insist in vigorous terms upon the evils so frequently attendant upon the holding of spiritual séances, it is only fair to admit that on several occasions good work similar to that of the helper in the case just described has been done through the agency of a medium or of some one present at a circle. Thus, though spiritualism has too often detained souls who but for it would have attained speedier liberation, it must be set to the credit of its account that it has also furnished the means of escape to others, and thus opened up the path of advancement for them. There have been instances in which the defunct has been able to appear unassisted to his relatives or friends and explain his wishes to them; but these are naturally rare, and most souls who are earth-bound by anxieties of the kind indicated can satisfy themselves only by means of the services of the medium or the conscious helper.

Another case very frequently encountered on the astral plane is that of the man who cannot believe that he is dead at all. Indeed, most people consider the very fact that they are still conscious to be an absolute proof that they have not passed through the portals of death; somewhat of a satire this, if one thinks of it, on the practical value of our much vaunted belief in the immortality of the soul! However they may have labeled themselves during life, the great majority of those who die, in this country at any rate, show themselves by their subsequent attitude to have been to all intents and purposes materialists at heart; and those who on earth have honestly called themselves so are often no more difficult to deal with than others who would have been shocked at the very name.

A very recent instance was that of a scientific man who, finding himself fully conscious, and yet under conditions differing radically from any that he had ever experienced before, had persuaded himself that he was still alive, and merely the victim of a prolonged and unpleasant dream. Fortunately for him there happened to be among the band of those able to function upon the astral plane a son of an old friend of his, a young man whose father had commissioned him to search for the departed scientist and endeavour to render him some assistance. When after some trouble the youth found and accosted him, he frankly admitted that he was in a condition of great bewilderment and discomfort, but still clung desperately to his dream hypothesis as on the whole the most probable explanation of what he saw, and even went so far as to suggest that his visitor was nothing but a dream-figure himself!

At last, however, he so far gave way as to propose a kind of test, and said to the young man, "If you are, as you assert, a living person, and the son of my old friend, bring me from him some message that shall prove to me your objective reality." Now although under all ordinary conditions of the physical plane the giving of any kind of phenomenal proof is strictly forbidden to the pupils of the Masters, it seemed as though a case of this kind hardly came under the rules; and therefore, when it had been ascertained that there was no objection on the part of higher authorities, an application was made to the father, who at once sent a message referring to a series of events which had occurred before the son's birth. This convinced the dead man of the real existence of his young friend, and therefore of the plane upon which they were both functioning; and as soon as he felt this established, his scientific training at once reasserted itself, and he became exceeding eager to acquire all possible information about this new region.

Of course the message which he so readily accepted as evidence was in reality no proof at all, since the facts to which it referred might have been read from his own mind or from the records of the past by any creature possessed of astral senses! But his ignorance of these possibilities enabled this definite impression to be made upon him, and the Theosophical instruction which his young friend is now nightly giving to him will undoubtedly have a stupendous effect upon his future, for it cannot but greatly modify not only the heaven-state which lies immediately before him, but also his next incarnation upon earth.

The main work, then, done for the newly dead by our helpers is that of soothing and comforting them - of delivering them when possible from the terrible though unreasoning fear which but too often seizes them, and not only causes them much unnecessary suffering, but retards their progress to higher spheres - and of enabling them as far as may be to comprehend the future that lies before them.

Others who have been longer on the astral plane may also receive much help, if they will but accept it, from explanations and advice as to their course through its different stages. They may, for example, be warned of the danger and delay caused by attempting to communicate with the living through a medium, and sometimes (though rarely) an entity already drawn into a spiritualistic circle may be guided into higher and healthier life. Teaching thus given to persons on this plane is by no means lost for though the memory of it cannot of course be directly carried over to the next incarnation, there always remains the real inner knowledge, and therefore the strong predisposition to accept it immediately when heard again in the new life.

A rather remarkable instance of service rendered to the dead was the first achievement of a very recent recruit to the band of helpers - one who is hardly as yet a fully-fledged member. This young aspirant had not long before lost an aged relation for whom he had felt an especially warm affection; and his earliest request was to be taken by a more experienced friend to visit her in the hope that he might be of some service to her. This was done and the effect of the meeting of the living and the dead was very beautiful and touching. The older person's astral life was already approaching its end, but a condition of apathy, dullness and uncertainty prevented her from making any immediate progress.

But when the boy, who had been so much to her in earth-life, stood once more before her and dissolved by the sunlight of his love the grey mist of depression which had gathered around her, she was aroused from her stupor; and soon she understood that he had come in order to explain to her her situation, and to tell her of the glories of the higher life toward which her thoughts and aspirations ought now to be directed. But when this was fully realized, there was such an awakening of dormant feeling in her and such an outrush of devoted affection towards her earnest young helper, that the last fetters which bound her to the astral life were broken, and that one great outburst of love and gratitude swept her forthwith into the higher consciousness of the heaven-world. Truly there is no greater and more beneficent power in the universe than that of pure, unselfish love.

OTHER BRANCHES OF THE WORK

BUT turning back again now from the all-important work among the dead to the consideration of the work among the living, we must briefly indicate a great branch of it, without a notice of which our account of the labours of our invisible helpers would indeed be incomplete, and that is the immense amount which is done by suggestion - by simply putting good thoughts into the minds of those who are ready to receive them.

Let there be no mistake as to what is meant here. It would be perfectly easy - easy to a degree which would be quite incredible to those who do not understand the subject practically - for a helper to dominate the mind of any average man, and make him think just as he pleased, and that without arousing the faintest suspicion of any outside influence in the mind of the subject. But, however admirable the result might be, such a proceeding would be entirely inadmissible. All that may be done is to throw the good thought into the person's mind as one among the hundreds that are constantly sweeping through it; whether the man takes it up, makes it his own, and acts upon it, depends upon himself entirely. Were it otherwise, it is obvious that all the good karma of the action would accrue to the helper only, for the subject would have been a mere tool, and not an actor - which is not what is desired.

The assistance given in this way is exceedingly varied in character. The consolation of those who are suffering or in sorrow at once suggests itself, as does also the endeavour to guide toward the truth those who are earnestly seeking it. When a person is spending much anxious thought upon some spiritual or metaphysical problem, it is often possible to put the solution into his mind without his being at all aware that it comes from external agency.

A pupil too may often be employed as an agent in what can hardly be described otherwise than as the answering of prayer; for though it is true that any earnest spiritual desire, such as might be supposed to find its expression in prayer, is itself a force which automatically brings about certain results, it is also a fact that such a spiritual effort offers an opportunity of influence to the Powers of Good, of which they are not slow to take advantage; and it is sometimes the privilege of a willing helper to be made the channel through which their energy is poured forth. What is said of prayers is true to an even greater extent of meditation, for those to whom this higher exercise is a possibility.

Besides these more general methods of help there are also special lines open only to the few. Again and again such pupils as are fitted for the work have been employed to suggest true and beautiful thoughts to authors, poets, artists and musicians; but obviously it is not every helper who is capable of being used in this way.

Sometimes, though more rarely, it is possible to warn persons of the danger to their moral development of some course which they are pursuing, to clear away evil influences from about some person or place, or to counteract the machinations of black magicians. It is not often that direct instruction in the great truths of nature can be given to people outside the circle of occult students, but occasionally it is possible to do something in that way by putting before the minds of preachers and teachers a wider range of thought or a more liberal view of some question than they would otherwise have taken.

Naturally as an occult student progresses on the Path he attains a wider sphere of usefulness. Instead of assisting individuals only, he learns how classes, nations and races are dealt with, and he is entrusted with a gradually increasing share of the higher and more important work done by the adepts themselves. As he acquires the requisite power and knowledge he begins to wield the greater forces of the mental and the astral planes and is shown how to make the utmost possible use of each favourable cyclic influence. He is brought into relation with those great Nirmânakâyas who are sometimes symbolized as the Stones of the Guardian Wall, and he becomes - at first of course in the very humblest capacity - one of the and of their almoners, and learns how those forces are dispersed which are the fruit of their sublime self-sacrifice. Thus he rises gradually higher and higher until, blossoming at length into adeptship, he is able to take his full share of the responsibility which lies upon the Masters of Wisdom, and to help others along the road which he has trodden.

On the mental plane the work differs somewhat, since teaching can be both given and received in a much more direct, rapid and perfect manner, while the influences set in motion are infinitely more powerful, because acting on so much higher a level. But (though it is useless to speak of it in detail at present, since so few of us are yet able to function consciously upon this plane during life) here also - and even higher still - there is always plenty of work to be done, as soon as ever we can make ourselves capable of doing it; and there is certainly no fear that for countless æons we shall ever find ourselves without a career of unselfish usefulness open before us.

THE QUALIFICATIONS REQUIRED

HOW, it may be asked, are we to make ourselves capable of sharing in this great work? Well, there is no mystery as to the qualifications which are needed by one who aspires to be a helper; the difficulty is not in learning what they are, but in developing them in oneself. To some extent they have been already incidentally described, but it is nevertheless as well that they should be set out fully and categorically.

Single-mindedness. The first requisite is that we shall have recognized the great work which the Masters would have us do, and that it shall be for us the one great interest in our lives. We must learn to distinguish not only between useful and useless work, but between the different kinds of useful work, so that we may each devote ourselves to the very highest of which we are capable, and not fritter away our time in labouring at something which, however good it may be for the man who cannot yet do anything better, is unworthy of the knowledge and capacity which should be ours as Theosophists. A man who wishes to be considered eligible for employment on higher planes must begin by doing the utmost that lies in his power in the way of definite work for Theosophy down here.

Of course I do not for a moment mean that we are to neglect the ordinary duties of life. We should certainly do well to undertake no new worldly duties of any sort, but those which we have already bound upon our shoulders have become a kârmic obligation which we have no right to neglect. Unless we have done to the full the duties which karma has laid upon us we are not free for the higher work. But this higher work must nevertheless be to us the one thing really worth living for - the constant background of a life which is consecrated to the service of the Masters of Compassion.

Perfect self-control. Before we can be safely trusted with the wider powers of the astral life, we must have ourselves perfectly in hand. Our temper, for example, must be thoroughly under control, so that nothing that we may see or hear can cause real irritation in us, for the consequences of such irritation would be far more serious on that plane than on this. The force of thought is always an enormous power, but down here it is reduced and deadened by the heavy physical brain-particles which it has to set in motion. In the astral world it is far freer and more potent, and for a man with fully awakened faculty to feel anger against a person there would be to do him serious and perhaps even fatal injury.

Not only do we need control of temper, but control of nerve, so that none of the fantastic or terrible sights that we may encounter may be able to shake our dauntless courage. It must be remembered that the pupil who awakens a man upon the astral plane incurs thereby a certain amount of responsibility for his actions and for his safety, so that unless his neophyte had courage to stand alone the whole of the older worker's time would be wasted in hovering round to protect him, which it would be manifestly unreasonable to expect.

It is to make sure of this control of nerve, and to fit them for the work that has to be done, that candidates are always made, now as in days of old, to pass what are called the tests of earth, water, air and fire.

In other words, they have to learn with that absolute certainty that comes not by theory, but by practical experience, that in their astral bodies none of these elements can by any possibility be hurtful to them - that none can oppose any obstacle in the way the work which they have to do.

In this physical body we are fully convinced that fire will burn us, that water will drown us, that the solid rock forms an impassable barrier to our progress, that we cannot with safety launch ourselves unsupported into the ambient air. So deeply is this conviction ingrained in us that it costs most men a good deal of effort to overcome the instinctive action which follows from it, and to realize that in the astral body the densest rock offers no impediment to their freedom of motion, that they may leap with impunity from the highest cliff, and plunge with the most absolute confidence into the heart of the raging volcano or the deepest abysses of the fathomless ocean.

Yet until a man *knows* this - knows it sufficiently to act upon his knowledge instinctively and confidently - he is comparatively useless for astral work, since in emergencies that are constantly arising he would be perpetually paralyzed by imaginary disabilities. So he has to go through his tests, and through many another strange experience - to meet face to face with calm courage the most terrifying apparitions amid the most loathsome surroundings - to show in fact that his nerve may be thoroughly trusted under any and all of the varied groups of circumstances in which he may at any moment find himself.

Further, we need control of mind and of desire; of mind, because without the power of concentration it would be impossible to do good work amid all the distracting currents of the astral plane; of desire, because in that strange world to desire is very often to have, and unless this part of our nature were well controlled we might perchance find ourselves face to face with creations of our own of which we should be heartily ashamed.

Calmness. This is another most important point - the absence of all worry and depression. Much of the work consists in soothing those who are disturbed, and cheering those who are in sorrow; and how can a helper do that work if his own aura is vibrating with constant fuss and worry, or grey with the deadly gloom that comes from perpetual depression? Nothing is more hopelessly fatal to occult progress or usefulness than our nineteenth century habit of ceaselessly worrying over trifles - of eternally making mountains out of molehills. Many of us simply spend our lives in magnifying the most absurd trivialities - in solemnly and elaborately going to work to make ourselves miserable about nothing.

Surely we who are Theosophists ought, at any rate, to have got beyond this stage of irrational worry and causeless depression; surely we, who are trying to acquire some definite knowledge of the cosmic order, ought by this time to have realized that the optimistic view of everything is always nearest to the divine view, and therefore to the truth, because only that in any person which is good and beautiful can by any possibility be permanent, while the evil must by its very nature be temporary. In fact, as Browning said, "the evil is null, is naught, is silence implying sound," while above and beyond it all "the soul of things is sweet, the Heart of Being is celestial rest." So They who know maintain unruffled calm, and with Their perfect sympathy combine the joyous serenity which comes from the certainty that all will at last be well; and those who wish to help must learn to follow Their example.

Knowledge. To be of use the man must at least have some knowledge of the nature of the plane on which he has to work, and the more knowledge he has in any and every direction the more useful he will be. He must fit himself for this task by carefully studying Theosophical literature; for he cannot expect those whose time is already so fully occupied to waste some of it in explaining to him what he might have learnt down here by taking the trouble to read the books. No one who is not already as earnest a student as his capacities and opportunities permit, need begin to think of himself as a candidate for astral work.

Unselfishness. It would seem scarcely needful to assist upon this as a qualification, for surely everyone who has made the least study of Theosophy must know that while the slightest taint of selfishness remains in a man, he is not yet fit to be entrusted with higher powers, not yet fit to enter upon a work of whose very essence it is that the worker should forget himself but to remember the good of others. He who is still capable of selfish thought, whose personality is still so strong in him that he can allow himself to be turned aside from his work by feelings of petty pride or suggestions of wounded dignity - that man is not yet ready to show the selfless devotion of the helper.

Love. This, the last and greatest of the qualifications, is also the most misunderstood. Most emphatically it is *not* the cheap, namby-pamby backboneless sentimentalism which is always overflowing into vague platitudes and gushing generalities, yet fears to stand firm for the right lest it should be branded by the ignorant as "unbrotherly." What is wanted is the love which is strong enough *not* to boast itself, but to act without talking about it - the intense desire for service which is ever on the watch for an opportunity to render it, even though it prefers to do so anonymously - the feeling which springs up in the heart of him who has realized the great work of the Logos, and having once seen it, knows that for him there can be in the three worlds no other course but to identify himself with it to the utmost limit of his power - to become, in however humble a way, and at however great a distance, a tiny channel of that wondrous love of God which, like the peace of God, passeth man's understanding.

These are the qualities toward the possession of which the helper must ceaselessly strive, and of which some considerable measure at least must be his before he can hope that the Great Ones who stand behind will deem him fit for full awakening. The ideal is in truth a high one, yet none need therefore turn away disheartened, nor think that while he is still but struggling toward it he must necessarily remain entirely useless on the astral plane, for short of the responsibilities and dangers of that full awakening there is much that may safely and usefully be done.

There is hardly one among us who would not be capable of performing at least one definite act of mercy and good will each night while we are away from our bodies. Our condition when asleep is usually one of absorption in thought, be it remembered - a carrying on of the thoughts that have principally occupied us during the day, and especially of the last thought in the mind when sinking into sleep. Now if we make that last thought a strong intention to go and give help to some one whom we know to be in need of it, the soul when freed from the body will undoubtedly carry out that intention, and the help will be given. There are several cases on record in which, when this attempt has been made, the person thought of has been fully conscious of the effort of the would-be helper, and has even seen his astral body in the act of carrying out the instructions impressed upon it.

Indeed, no one need sadden himself with the thought that he can have no part nor lot in this glorious work. Such a feeling would be entirely untrue, for every one who can think can help. Nor need such useful action be confined to our hours of sleep. If you know (and who does not?) of some one who is in sorrow or suffering, though you may not be able consciously to stand in astral form by their bedside, you can nevertheless send them loving thoughts and earnest good wishes; and be well assured that such thoughts and wishes are real and living and strong - that when you so send them they do actually go and work your will in proportion to the strength which you have put into them. Thoughts are things, intensely real things, visible enough to those whose eyes have been opened to see, and by their means the poorest man may bear his part in the good work of the world as fully as the richest. In this way at least, whether we can yet function consciously upon the astral plane or not, we all can join, and we all ought to join, the army of invisible helpers.

But the aspirant, who definitely desires to become one of the band of astral helpers who are working under the direction of the great Masters of Wisdom, will make his preparation part of a far wider scheme of development. Instead of merely endeavouring to fit himself for this particular branch of their service, he will undertake with high resolution the far greater task of training himself to follow in their footsteps, of bending all the energies of his soul to attain even as they have attained, so that his power of helping the world may not be confined to the astral plane, but may extend to those higher levels which are the true home of the divine self of man.

For him the path has been marked out long ago by the wisdom of those who have trodden it in days of old - a path of self-development which sooner or later all must follow, whether they choose to adopt it of their own free will, or to wait until, after many lives and an infinity of suffering, the slow, resistless force of evolution drives them along it among the laggards of the human family. But the wise man is he who eagerly enters upon it immediately, setting his face resolutely toward the goal of adeptship, in order that, being safe for ever from all doubt and fear and sorrow himself, he may help others into safety and happiness also. What are the steps of this Path of Holiness, as the Buddhists call it, and in what order they are arranged, let us see in our next chapter.

THE PROBATIONARY PATH

EASTERN books tell us that there are four means by which a man may be brought to the beginning of the path of spiritual advancement: 1. By the companionship of those who have already entered upon it. 2. By the hearing or reading of definite teaching on occult philosophy. 3. By enlightened reflection; that is to say, that by sheer force of hard thinking and close reasoning he may arrive at the truth, or some portion of it, for himself. 4. By the practice of virtue, which means that a long series of virtuous lives, though it does not necessarily involve any increase of intellectuality, does eventually develop in man sufficient intuition to enable him to grasp the necessity of entering upon the path, and show him in what direction it lies.

When, by one or another of these means, he has arrived at this point, the way to the highest adeptship lies straight before him, if he chooses to take it. In writing for students of occultism it is hardly necessary to say that at our present stage of development we cannot expect to learn all, or nearly all, about any but the lowest steps of this path; whilst of the highest we know little but the names, though we may get occasional glimpses of the indescribable glory which surrounds them.

According to the esoteric teachings these steps are grouped in three great divisions:

The probationary period, before any definite pledges are taken, or initiations (in the full sense of the word) are given. This carries a man to the level necessary to pass successfully through what in Theosophical books is usually called the critical period of the fifth round.

The period of pledged discipleship, or the path proper, whose four stages are often spoken of in Oriental books as the four paths of holiness. At the end of this the pupil obtains adeptship - the level which humanity should reach at the close of the seventh round.

What we may venture to call the official period, in which the adept takes a definite part (under the great Cosmic Law) in the government of the world, and holds a special office connected therewith, Of course every adept - every pupil even, when once definitely accepted, as we have seen in the earlier chapters - takes a part in the great work of helping forward the evolution of man; but those standing on the higher levels take charge of special departments, and correspond in the cosmic scheme to the ministers of the crown in a well-ordered earthly state. It is not proposed to make any attempt in this book to treat of this official period; no information about it has ever been made public, and the whole subject is too far above our comprehension to be profitably dealt with in print. We will confine ourselves therefore to the two earlier divisions.

Before going into details of the probationary period it is well to mention that in most of the Eastern sacred books this stage is regarded as merely preliminary, and scarcely as part of the path at all, for they consider that the latter is really entered upon only when definite pledges have been given. Considerable confusion has been created by the fact that the numbering of the stages occasionally commences at this point, though more often at the beginning of the second great division; sometimes the stages themselves are counted, and sometimes the initiations leading into or out of them, so that in studying the books one has to be perpetually on one's guard to avoid misunderstanding.

This probationary period, however, differs considerably in character from the others; the divisions between its stages are less decidedly marked than are those of the higher groups, and the requirements are not so definite or so exacting. But it will be easier to explain this last point after giving a list of the five stages of this period, with their respective qualifications. The first four were very ably described by Mr Mohini Mohun Chatterji in the first Transaction of the London Lodge, to which readers may be referred for fuller definitions of them than can be given here. Much exceedingly valuable information about them is also given by Mrs. Besant in her books *The Path of Discipleship* and *In the Outer Court*.

The names given to the stages will differ somewhat, for in those books the Hindu Sanskrit terminology was employed, whereas the Pâli nomenclature used here is that of the Buddhist system; but although the subject is thus approached from a different side as it were, the qualifications exacted will be found to be precisely the same in effect even when the outward form varies. In the case of each word the mere dictionary meaning will first be given in parentheses, and the explanation of it which is usually given by the teacher will follow. The first stage, then is called among Buddhists.

Manodvâravajjana (the opening of the doors of the mind, or perhaps escaping by the door of the mind) - and in it the candidate acquires a firm intellectual conviction of the impermanence and worthlessness of mere earthly aims. This is often described as learning the difference between the real and the unreal; and to learn it often takes a long time and many hard lessons. Yet it is obvious that it must be the first step toward anything like real progress, for no man can enter whole-heartedly upon the path until he has definitely decided to "set his affection upon things above, not on things on the earth," and that decision comes from the certainty that nothing on earth has any value as compared with the higher life. This step is called by the Hindus the acquirement of Viveka or discrimination, and Mr. Sinnett speaks of it as the giving allegiance to the higher self.

Parikamma (preparation for action) - the stage in which the candidate learns to do the right merely because it is right, without considering his own gain or loss either in this world or the future, and acquires, as the Eastern books put it, perfect indifference to the enjoyment of the fruit of his own actions. This indifference is the natural result of the previous step; for when the neophyte has once grasped the unreal and impermanent character of all earthly rewards, he ceases to crave for them; when once the radiance of the real has shone upon the soul, nothing below that can any longer be an object of desire. This higher indifference is called by the Hindus Vairâgya.

Upachâro (attention or conduct) - the stage in which what are called "the six qualifications" (the Shatsampatti of the Hindus) must be acquired. These are called in Pâli:

a. Samo (quietude) - that purity and calmness of thought which comes from perfect control of the mind - a qualification exceedingly difficult of attainment, and yet most necessary, for unless the mind moves only in obedience to the guidance of the will it cannot be a perfect instrument for the Master's work in the future. This qualification is a very comprehensive one, and includes within itself both the self-control and the calmness which were described in chapter xiv. as necessary for astral work.

b. Damo (subjugation) - a similar mastery over, and therefore purity in, one's actions and words - a quality which again follows necessarily from its predecessor.

c. Uparti (cessation) - explained as cessation from bigotry or from belief in the necessity of any act or ceremony prescribed by a particular religion - so leading the aspirant to independence of thought and to a wide and generous tolerance.

d. Titikkhâ (endurance or forbearance) - by which is meant the readiness to bear with cheerfulness whatever one's karma may bring upon one, and to part with anything and everything worldly whenever it may be necessary. It also includes the idea of complete absence of resentment for wrong, the man knowing that those who do him wrong are but the instruments of his own karma.

 e. Samâdhâna (intentness) - one-pointedness involving the incapability of being turned aside from one's path by temptation. This corresponds very closely with the single-mindness spoken of in the previous chapter.

 f. Saddhâ (faith) - confidence in one's Master and oneself: confidence, that is, that the Master is a competent teacher, and that, however diffident the pupil may feel as to his own powers, he has yet within him that divine spark which when fanned into a flame will one day enable him to achieve even as his Master has done.

Anuloma (direct order or succession, signifying that its attainment follows as a natural consequence from the other three) - the stage in which is acquired that intense desire for liberation from earthly life, and for union with the highest, which is called by the Hindus Mumukshatva.

Gotrabhû (the condition of fitness for initiation); in this stage the candidate gathers up, as it were, his previous acquisitions, and strengthens them to the degree necessary for the next great step, which will set his feet upon the path proper as an accepted pupil. The attainment of this level is followed very rapidly by initiation into the next grade. In answer to the question, "Who is the Gotrabhû?" Buddha says, "The man who is in possession of those conditions upon which the commencement of sanctification immediately ensues - he is the Gotrabhû

The wisdom necessary for the reception of the path of holiness is called Gotrabhû-gñâna.

Now that we have hastily glanced at the steps of the probationary period, we must emphasize the point to which reference was made at the commencement - that the *perfect* attainment of these accomplishments and qualifications is not expected at this early stage. As Mr. Mohini says, "If all these are equally strong, adeptship is attained in the same incarnation." But such a result is of course extremely rare. It is in the direction of these acquirements that the candidate must ceaselessly strive, but it would be an error to suppose that no one has been admitted to the next step without possessing all of them in the fullest possible degree. Nor do they necessarily follow one another in the same definite order as the later steps; in fact, in many cases a man would be developing the various qualifications all at the same time - rather side by side than in regular succession.

It is obvious that a man might easily be working along a great part of this path even though he was quite unaware of its very existence, and no doubt many a good Christian, many an earnest freethinker is already far on the road that will eventually lead him to initiation, though he may never have heard the word occultism in his life. I mention these two classes especially, because in every other religion occult development is recognized as a possibility, and would certainly therefore be intentionally sought by those who felt yearnings for something more satisfactory than the exoteric faiths.

We must also note that the steps of this probationary period are not separated by initiations in the full sense of the word, though they will certainly be studded with tests and trials of all sorts and on all planes, and may be relieved by encouraging experiences, and by hints and help whenever these may safely be given. We are apt sometimes to use the word initiation somewhat loosely, as for example when it is applied to such tests as have just been mentioned; properly speaking it refers only to the solemn ceremony at which a pupil is formally admitted to a higher grade by an appointed official, who in the name of the One Initiator receives his plighted vow, and puts into his hands the new key of knowledge which he is to use on the level to which he has now attained. Such an initiation is taken at the entrance to the division which we shall next consider, and also at each passage from any one of its steps to the next.

THE PATH PROPER

IT is in the four stages of this division of the path that the ten Samyojana, or fetters which bind man to the circle of rebirth and hold him back from Nirvâna, must be cast off. And here comes the difference between this period of pledged discipleship and the previous probation. No partial success in getting rid of these fetters is sufficient now; before a candidate can pass on from one of the steps to the next he must be *entirely* free from certain of these clogs; and when they are enumerated it will be seen how far-reaching this requirement is, and there will be little cause to wonder at the statement made in the sacred books that seven incarnations are sometimes required to pass through this division of the path.

Each of these four steps or stages is again divided into four: for each has (1) its Maggo, or way, during which the student is striving to cast off the fetters; (2) its Phala (result or fruit) when he finds the results of his action in so doing showing themselves more and more; (3) its Bhavagga or consummation, the period when, the result having culminated, he is able to fulfil satisfactorily the work belonging to the step on which he now firmly stands; and (4) its Gotrabhû, meaning, as before, the time when he arrives at a fit state to receive the next initiation. The first stage is:

Sotâpatti or Sohan. The pupil who has attained this level is spoken of as the Sowani or Sotâpanna - "he who has entered the stream, - "because from this period, though he may linger, though he may succumb to more refined temptations and turn aside from his course for a time, he can no longer fall back altogether from spirituality and become a mere worldling. He has entered upon the stream of definite higher human evolution, upon which all humanity must enter by the middle of the next round, unless they are to be left behind as temporary failures by the great life-wave, to wait for further progress until the next chain of worlds.

The pupil who is able to take this initiation has therefore already outstripped the majority of humanity to the extent of an entire round of all our seven planets, and in doing so has definitely secured himself against the possibility of falling out of the stream in the fifth round. He is consequently sometimes spoken of as "the saved" or "the safe one." It is from a misunderstanding of this idea that there arises the curious theory of salvation promulgated by a certain section of the Christian community. The "æonian salvation" of which some of its documents speak is not, as has been blasphemously supposed by the ignorant, from eternal torture, but simply from wasting the rest of this æon or dispensation by falling out of its line of progress. This also is the meaning, naturally, of the celebrated clause in the Athanasian Creed, "Whosoever will be saved, before all things it is necessary that he hold the catholic faith" (See *The Christian Creed,* p.91). The fetters which he must cast off before he can pass into the next stage are:

Sakkâyaditthi - the delusion of self.

Vichikichchhâ - doubt or uncertainty.

Sîlabbataparâmâsa - superstition.

The first of these is the "I am I" consciousness, which as connected with the *personality* is nothing but an illusion, and must be got rid of at the very first step of the real upward path. But to cast off this fetter completely means even more than this, for it involves the realization of the fact that the individuality also is in very truth one with the All, that it can therefore never have any interests opposed to those of its brethren, and that it is most truly progressing when it most assists the progress of others.

For the very sign and seal of the attainment of the Sotâpatti level is the first entrance of the pupil into the plane next above the mental - that which we usually call the buddhic. It may be - nay, it will be - the merest touch of the lowest sub-plane of that stupendously exalted condition that the pupil can as yet experience, even with his Master's help; but even that touch is something that can never be forgotten - something that opens a new world before him, and entirely revolutionizes his feelings and conceptions. Then for the first time, by means of the extended consciousness of that plane, he truly realizes the underlying unity of all, not as an intellectual conception merely, but as a definite fact that is patent to his opened eyes; then first he really knows something of the world in which he lives - then first he gets some slight glimpse of what the love and compassion of the great Masters must be.

As to the second fetter, a word of caution is necessary. We who have been trained in European habits of thought are unhappily so familiar with the idea that a blind unreasoning adhesion to certain dogmas may be claimed from a disciple, that or hearing that occultism considers *doubt* as an obstacle to progress, we are likely to suppose that it also requires the same unquestioning faith from its followers as modern superstitions do. No idea could be more certainly false.

It is true that doubt (or rather uncertainty) on certain questions is a bar to spiritual progress, but the antidote to that doubt is not blind faith (which is itself considered as a fetter, as will presently be seen) but the certainty of conviction founded on individual experiment or mathematical reasoning. While a child doubted the accuracy of the multiplication table he would hardly acquire proficiency in the higher mathematics; but his doubts could be satisfactorily cleared up only by his attaining a comprehension, founded on reasoning or experiment, that the statements contained in the table are true. He believes that twice two are four, not merely because he has been told so, but because it has become to him a self-evident fact. And this is exactly the method, and the only method, of resolving doubt known to occultism.

Vichikichchhâ has been defined as doubt of the doctrines of karma and reincarnation, and of the efficacy of the method of attaining the highest good by this path of holiness; and the casting off of this Samyojana is the arriving at absolute certainty, based either upon personal first-hand knowledge or upon reason, that the occult teaching upon these points is true.

The third fetter to be got rid of comprehends all kinds of unreasoning or mistaken belief, all dependence on the efficacy of outward rites and ceremonies to purify the heart. He who would cast it off must learn to depend upon himself alone, not upon others, nor upon the outer husk of any religion.

The first three fetters are in a coherent series. The difference between individuality and personality being fully realized, it is then possible to some extent to appreciate the actual course of reincarnation, and so as to dispel all doubt on that head. This done, the knowledge of the spiritual permanence of the true ego gives rise to reliance on one's own spiritual strength, and so dispels superstition.

II. Sakadâgâmî. The pupil who has entered upon this second stage is spoken of as a Sakridâgâmin - "the man who returns but once" - signifying that a man who has reached this level should need but one more incarnation before attaining arahatship. At this step no additional fetters are cast off, but the pupil is occupied in reducing to a minimum those which still enchain him. It is, however, usually a period of considerable psychic and intellectual advancement.

If what are commonly called psychic faculties have not been previously acquired, they must be developed at this stage, as without them it would be impossible to assimilate the knowledge which must now be given, or to do the higher work for humanity in which the pupil is now privileged to assist. He must have the astral consciousness at his command during his physical waking life, and during sleep the heaven-world will be open before him - for the consciousness of a man when away from his physical body is always one stage higher than it is while he is still burdened with the house of flesh.

III. Anâgâmi. The Anâgâmin (he who does not return) is so called because, having reached this stage, he ought to be able to attain the next one in the life he is then living. He enjoys, while moving through the round of his daily work, all the splendid possibilities of progress given by the full possession of the priceless faculties of the heaven-world, and when he leaves his physical vehicle at night he enters once more into the wonderfully-widened consciousness that belongs to the buddhi. In this step he finally gets rid of any lingering remains of the two fetters of

Kâmarâga - attachment to the enjoyment of sensation, typified by earthly love, and

Patigha - all possibility of anger or hatred.

The student who has cast off these fetters can no longer be swayed by the influence of his senses either in the direction of love or hatred, and is free from either attachment to or impatience of physical plane conditions.

Here again we must guard against a possible misconception - one with which we frequently meet. The purest and noblest human love *never* dies away - is *never* in any way diminished by occult training; on the contrary, it is increased and widened until it embraces all with the same fervour which at first was lavished on one or two. But the student does in time rise above all considerations connected with the mere *personality* of those around him, and so is free from all the injustice and partiality which ordinary love so often brings in its train.

Nor should it for a moment be supposed that in gaining this wide affection for all he loses the especial love for his closer friends. The unusually perfect link between Ânanda and the Buddha, as between S. John and Jesus, is on record to prove that on the contrary this is enormously intensified; and the tie between a Master and his pupils is stronger far than any earthly bond. For the affection which flourishes upon the path of holiness is an affection between egos, and not merely between personalities; therefore it is strong and permanent, without fear of diminution or fluctuation, for it is that "perfect love which casteth out fear."

IV. Arahat (the venerable, the perfect). On attaining this level the aspirant constantly enjoys the consciousness of the buddhic plane, and is able to use its powers and faculties while still in the physical body; and when he leaves that body in sleep or trance he passes at once into the unutterable glory of the nirvânic plane. In this stage the occultist must cast off the last remains of the five remaining fetters, which are:

Rûparâga - desire for beauty of form or for physical existence in a form, even including that in the heaven-world.

Arûparâga - desire for formless life

Mâno - pride.

Uddhachcha - agitation or irritability.

10. Avijjâ - ignorance.

On this we may remark that the casting off of Rûparâga involves not only getting rid of desire for earthly life, however grand or noble that life may be, and astral or devachanic life, however glorious, but also of all liability to be unduly influenced or repelled by the external beauty or ugliness of any person or thing.

Arûparâga - desire for life either in the highest and formless planes of the heaven-world or in the still more exalted buddhic plane -would be merely a higher and less sensual form of selfishness, and must be cast off just as much as the lower. Uddhachcha really means "liability to be disturbed in mind," and a man who had finally cast off this fetter would be absolutely unruffled by anything whatever that might happen to him - perfectly impervious to any kind of attack upon his dignified serenity.

The getting rid of ignorance of course implies the acquisition of perfect knowledge - practical omniscience as regards our planetary chain. When all the fetters are finally cast off the advancing ego reaches the fifth stage - the stage of full adeptship - and becomes.

V. Asekha, "the one who has no more to learn," again as regards our planetary chain. It is quite impossible for us to realize at our present level what this attainment means. All the splendor of the nirvânic plane lies open before the waking eyes of the adept, while when he chooses to leave his body he has the power to enter upon something higher still - a plane which to us is the merest name. As Professor Rhys Davids explains, "He is now free from all sin; he sees and values all things in this life and their true value; all evil being rooted from his mind he experiences only righteous desires for himself and tender pity and regard and exalted love for others."

To show how little he has lost the sentiment of love, we read in the Metta Sutta of the state of mind of one who stands at this level: "As a mother loves, who even at the risk of her own life protects her only son, such love let there be toward all beings. Let goodwill without measure prevail in the whole world, above, below, around, unstinted, unmixed with any feeling of differing or opposing interests. When a man remains steadfastly in this state of mind all the while, whether he be standing or walking, sitting or lying down, then is come to pass the saying which is written, 'Even in this life has holiness been found.' "

WHAT LIES BEYOND

BEYOND this period it is obvious that we can know nothing of the new qualifications required for the still higher levels which yet lie before the perfect man. It is abundantly clear, however, that when man has become Asekha he has exhausted all the possibilities of moral development, so that further advancement for him can only mean still wider knowledge and still more wonderful spiritual powers. We are told that when man has thus attained his spiritual majority, whether in the slow course of evolution or by the shorter path of self-development he assumes the fullest control of his own destinies and makes choice of his future line of evolution among seven possible paths which he sees opening before him.

Naturally at our present level we cannot expect to understand much about these, and the faint outline of some of them which is all that can be sketched in for us conveys very little to the mind, except that most of them take the adept altogether away from our earth-chain, which no longer affords sufficient scope for his evolution.

One path is that of those who, as the technical phrase goes, "accept Nirvâna." Through what incalculable æons they remain in that sublime condition, for what work they are preparing themselves, what will be their future line of evolution, are questions upon which we know nothing; and indeed if information upon such points could be given it is more than likely that it would prove quite incomprehensible to us at our present stage.

But this much at least we may grasp - that the blessed state of Nirvâna is not, as some have ignorantly supposed, a condition of blank nothingness, but on the contrary of far more intense and beneficent activity; and that ever as man rises higher in the scale of nature his possibilities become greater, his work for others ever grander and more far-reaching, and that infinite wisdom and infinite power mean for him only infinite capacity for service, because they are directed by infinite love.

Another class chooses a spiritual evolution not quite so far removed from humanity, for though not directly connected with the next chain of our system it extends through two long periods corresponding to its first and second rounds, at the end of which time they also appear to "accept Nirvâna," but at a higher stage than those previously mentioned.

Others join the deva evolution, whose progress lies along a grand chain consisting of seven chains like ours, each of which to them is as one world. This line of evolution is spoken of as the most gradual and therefore the least arduous of the seven courses; but though it is sometimes referred to in the books as "yielding to the temptation to become a god." it is only in comparison with the sublime height of renunciation of the Nirmânakâya that it can be spoken of in this half-disparaging manner, for the adept who chooses this course has indeed a glorious career before him, and though the path which he selects is not the shortest, it is nevertheless a very noble one.

Yet another group are the Nirmânakâyas - those who, declining all these easier methods, choose the shortest but steepest path to the heights which still lie before them. They form what is poetically termed the "guardian wall," and, as *The Voice of the Silence* tells us, "protect the world from further and far greater misery and sorrow," not indeed by warding off from it external evil influences, but by devoting all their strength to the work of pouring down upon it a flood of spiritual force and assistance without which it would assuredly be in far more hopeless case than now.

Yet again there are those who remain even more directly in association with humanity, and continue to incarnate among it, choosing the path which leads through the four stages of what we have called above the official period; and among these are the Masters of Wisdom - those from whom we who study Theosophy have learnt such fragments as we know of the mighty harmony of evolving Nature. But it would seem that only a certain comparatively small number adopt this course - probably only so many as are necessary for the carrying on of this physical side of the work.

In hearing of these different possibilities, people sometimes exclaim rashly that there could of course be no thought in a Master's mind of choosing any but that course which most helps humanity - a remark which greater knowledge would have prevented them from making. We should never forget that there are other evolutions in the solar system besides our own, and no doubt it is necessary for the carrying out of the vast plan of the Logos that there should be adepts working on all the seven lines to which we have referred. Surely the choice of the Master would be to go wherever his work was most needed - to place his services with absolute selflessness at the disposal of the Powers in charge of this part of the great scheme of evolution.

This then is the path which lies before us, the path which each one of us should be beginning to tread. Stupendous though its heights appear we should remember that they are attained but gradually and step by step, and that those who now stand near the summit once toiled in the mire of the valleys, even as we are doing. Although this path may at first seem hard and toilsome, yet ever as we rise our footing becomes firmer and our outlook wider, and thus we find ourselves better able to help those who are climbing beside us.

Because it is at first thus hard and toilsome to the lower self, it has sometimes been called by the very misleading title of "the path of woe;" but, as Mrs. Besant has beautifully written, "through all such suffering there is a deep and abiding joy, for the suffering is of the lower nature, and the joy of the higher." When the last shred of the personality is gone all that can thus suffer has passed away, and in the perfected Adept there is unruffled peace and everlasting joy. He sees the end toward which all is working, and rejoices in that end, knowing that earth's sorrow is but a passing phase in human evolution.

"That of which little has been said is the profound content which comes from being on the path, from realizing the goal and the way to it, from knowing that the power to be useful is increasing, and that the lower nature is being gradually extirpated. And little has been said of the rays of joy which fall upon the path from loftier levels, the dazzling glimpses of the glory to be revealed, the serenity which the storms of earth cannot ruffle. To any one who has entered on the path all other ways have lost their charm, and its sorrows have a keeper bliss than the best joys of the lower world." (Vâhan, vol. v., No. 12.)

Let no man therefore despair because he thinks the task too great for him; what man has done man can do, and just in proportion as we extend our aid to those whom we can help, so will those who have already attained be able in their turn to help us. So from the lowest to the highest we who are treading the steps of the path are bound together by one long chain of mutual service, and none need feel neglected or alone, for though sometimes the lower flights of the great staircase may be wreathed in mist, we know that it leads up to happier regions and purer air, where the light is always shining.

REINCARNATION A STUDY IN HUMAN EVOLUTION

By Théophile Pascal

Théophile Pascal (1860-1909) was a French physician and General Secretary of the French Section of the Theosophical Society based in Adyar.

"Were an Asiatic to ask me for a definition of Europe, I should be forced to answer him:—It is that part of the world which is haunted by the incredible delusion that man was created out of nothing, and that his present birth is his first entrance into life."

— SCHOPENHAUER. *PARERGA AND PARALIPOMENA,*
VOL. 2, CHAP. 15

AUTHOR'S PREFACE

It will soon be: 1500 years since the decision of the Council of 543 a.d.[1] condemned to oblivion sublime teachings which ought to have been carefully preserved and handed down to future generations as a beacon amid social reefs; teachings that would have uprooted that frightful egoism which threatens to annihilate the world, and instilled patience into the hearts of such as were being crushed beneath the wheel of the cosmic law, by showing them the scales of Justice inclining to the side filled with their iniquities of bygone times; teachings which would have been welcomed by the masses, and the understanding of which would not have called for any lofty intellectual culture.

It was one of the greatest misfortunes that could have befallen the races of the West, more especially the European, that they were thus deprived for centuries of this indispensable knowledge. We look upon it as a duty, following on so many others, to offer it anew, this time in the clear, logical, illuminating form presented in theosophic teachings. The necessity thereof is all the more imperative when we consider the growth of scepticism and materialism amongst the more intellectual classes, whilst the mass of the people have forsaken their blind faith only to succumb to religious indifference.

To every awakened soul the question comes:

Why does evil exist?

So long as the enigma remains unsolved, Suffering remains a threatening sphinx, opposing God and ready to devour mankind.

The key to the secret lies in Evolution, which can be accomplished only by means of the continual return of souls to earth.

When once man learns that suffering is the necessary result of divine manifestation; that inequalities of conditions are due to the different stages which beings have reached and the changeable action of their will; that the painful phase lasts only a moment in Eternity, and that we have it in our power to hasten its disappearance; that though slaves of the past, we are masters of the future; that, finally, the same glorious goal awaits all beings —then, despair will be at an end; hatred, envy, and rebellion will have fled away, and peace will reign over a humanity made wise by knowledge.

Were this modest work to hasten forward this time by a few years, we should feel sufficiently rewarded.

The subject will be divided into four chapters :

- The Soul and the bodies.
- Reincarnation and the moral law.
- Reincarnation and science.
- Reincarnation and the religious and philosophical concensus of the ages.

---

1. This Council came to the following decision:—*Whosoever shall teach the pre-existence of the soul and the strange opinion of its returns to earth, let him be anathema!*

THE SOUL AND THE BODIES.

In a book dealing with the resurrection of bodies and the reincarnations of the Soul, a chapter must be devoted to the fundamental elements of the question.

We will give the name of *Soul* to abstract Being, to the Unknown, that unmanifested Principle which cannot be defined, for it is above all definition.

It is the Absolute of Western philosophers, the *Parabrahm* of the Hindus, the *Tao* of the ancient sages of China, the causeless Cause of all that has been or ever will be manifested in concrete time and space.

Some feeble idea of it may perhaps be obtained by comparing it with electricity, which, though the cause of various phenomena: heat, movement, chemical action, light, is not, *per se*, any one of these phenomena, undergoes no modification from their existence, and survives them when the apparatus through which they manifest disappears.

We shall set up no distinction between this Soul, which may be called the universal Soul, and the individual soul, which has often been defined as a ray, a particle of the total Soul, for logically one cannot imply parts to the Absolute; it is illusion, limitation on our part, which shows us souls in the Soul.

Bodies are "aspects" of the Soul, results of its activity—if, indeed, the Infinite can be said to be either active or passive; words fail when we attempt to express the Inexpressible. These bodies, or, more precisely, the varied forms assumed by force-matter[1] are aspects of the Soul, just as light or chemical action are aspects of electricity, for one cannot suppose anything outside of infinite Being, nor can anything be imagined which is not a manifestation of the abstract Whole.

Let us also define *Consciousness*.

Taken absolutely, it is Being, the Soul, God; the uncaused Cause of all the states which, in beings, we call states of consciousness.

This limited consciousness may be defined as the faculty a "centre of life" possesses of receiving vibrations from its surroundings. When, in the course of evolution, a being is sufficiently developed to become conscious of a separation between its "I" and the object which sends it vibrations, consciousness becomes self-consciousness. This *self*-consciousness constitutes the *human* stage; it appears in the higher animals, but as it descends the scale of being, gradually disappears in non-individualised consciousness.

In a word, absolute Consciousness is one, though, as in the above example, it is manifested differently, according to the differences in the vehicles which express it in the concrete world in which we live.

The Soul, *per se*, is beyond the reach of beings who have not finished the pilgrimage of evolution. To know it, one must have attained to the eternal Centre, the unmanifested Logos. Up to that point, one can only, in proportion as one ascends, feel it in oneself, or acknowledge it by means of the logic which perceives it through all its manifestations as the universal Mover of forms, the Cause of all things, the Unity that produces diversity by means of the various vehicles which serve it as methods of expression.

Science says that intelligence, or, to be more generic, consciousness, results from the action of matter. This is a mistake.

Consciousness does not change in proportion as the cells of the body are renewed; rather it increases with physical unconsciousness, as in somnambulism.

Thought is not the fruit of the brain; it offers itself to the latter, ready made, so to speak; the loftiest intellectual or artistic inspirations are flashes which strike down into the awaiting brain, when maintaining that passive expectant attitude which is the condition in which a higher message may be received.

The senses are not the thinking-principle. They need to be controlled by consciousness; thus, people blind from birth, when suddenly made to see, cannot judge either distance or perspective; like animals and primitive men, they see nothing but colours on a surface.

Science says also: the organ is created for the function it has to perform; again a mistake. The eyes of the fœtus are constructed in the darkness of the womb. The human germ, notwithstanding its unconsciousness and its simplicity of structure, develops a body that is complex and capable of a considerable degree of consciousness; though itself unintelligent, it produces prodigies of intelligence in this body; here, consequently, the effect would be greatly superior to the cause, which is absurd. Outside of the body and the germ is a supreme Intelligence which creates the models of forms and carries out their construction. This Intelligence is the Soul of the world.

If Consciousness *per se*, or the Soul, is above all direct proof at the present stage of human evolution, the vehicles through which it functions are more or less apparent to us provided they are capable of affecting the brain. At the present stage of human evolution, this is the case only with the astral body; the other bodies are too fine to manifest through the nervous system such characteristics as are calculated to furnish scientists with a proof of their existence; they can only be felt and proved in and by *Yoga*.[2]

It is not without importance, however, to set forth the proofs of the existence of a vehicle of consciousness immediately above the physical, for it affords us a wider horizon and throws far more light on the rest of the subject.

Proofs of the Astral Body.

Certain normal and abnormal or morbid phenomena in man have proved the existence of this vehicle, which we will call the *higher* consciousness, for it is far greater than normal, waking consciousness, that of the brain. In the somewhat rare cases in which this consciousness is expressed in the physical world, it is forced to make use of the brain. Now, in the majority of men, the latter is still incapable of vibrating harmoniously with the matter which forms the astral vehicle; this is because the density of the atoms of the brain cells which preside over thought is incapable of reproducing the rapid vibrations of the finer matter belonging to the body immediately above it. By special training (the *yoga* of the Hindus), by a particular constitution of body (*sensitiveness*), by certain special methods (*hypnotism*), or in certain maladies (*somnambulism*), the brain may become receptive to these vibrations, and receive from them an impression, though always an imperfect one. The rarity of this impression, its imperfection, and especially the necessity for the vibration of the physical brain that it may be manifested in our environment; all these have made it very difficult to prove the existence of this higher vehicle; still, there are certain considerations which show that it exists, and that it alone is capable of explaining the most characteristic phenomena of the higher consciousness.

Let us first define these two states of consciousness rather more completely, and fix their limits.

Normal consciousness is that which functions during waking hours, when the brain is in full physiological activity, freely and completely related to the outer physical world. This consciousness is more or less developed according to the individual, but its component parts—sensation, emotion, sentiment, reason, intelligence, will, intuition—do not exceed known limits; for instance, we do not find clairvoyance, the prophetic faculty, and certain other abnormal faculties, which we shall class under the higher consciousness.

The higher consciousness works in the astral body, whether externalised or not; it seldom manifests itself, and then incompletely; it is accompanied by the more or less complete inhibition of the senses, and by a kind of sleep in which the relations of the subject with the physical world are wholly or partially suspended. The characteristics of this state are greater keenness of the normal faculties, and the appearance of new ones, which are often inexplicable and extraordinary and the more remarkable in proportion as sleep is more profound, the brain calmer, or the physiological state more abnormal.

How can we explain the paradox that faculties shown by a brain in a state of inactivity cover an extent of ground which the brain in a state of activity cannot approach? The reason is that the brain, in this case, is not an instrument moved directly by the cause of consciousness, *the soul*, but a simple recipient, which the soul, then centred in the astral body, impresses *on returning to the physical body* (if it has been far away) or impresses directly when, whilst acting in the finer vehicle, the latter has not left the body.[3]

In other words, the brain, by reason of its functional inactivity, vibrates little or not at all in its higher centres; it plays the part of a sounding-board at rest, capable of vibrating sympathetically under the influence of a similar board placed by its side.

The necessity of cerebral quiet, if the higher consciousness is to make an impression, is now easy to understand; the finer vibration of the astral body cannot be impressed upon the brain when the latter is already strongly vibrating under the action of normal consciousness. For this reason also, the deeper the sleep of the physical body the better the higher consciousness manifests itself.

In ordinary man, organic quiet is scarcely ever complete during sleep; the brain, as we shall see shortly, automatically repeats the vibrations which normal consciousness has called forth during the waking state; this, together with an habitual density of the nervous elements, too great to respond to the higher vibration, explains the rarity and the confused state of the impression of astral consciousness on the brain.

The facts relating to the higher consciousness are as numerous as they are varied. We shall not enter into full details, but choose only a few phenomena quoted in well-known works.

Manifestations of the Higher Consciousness During the Different Kinds of Sleep.

Normal dream. During normal sleep there exists a special consciousness which must not be confounded either with waking consciousness or with that of the astral body. It is due to the automatic, cerebral vibration which continues during sleep, and which the soul examines on its return to the body—when awake. This dream is generally an absurd one, and the reason the dreamer notices it only on awaking is that he is absent from the visible body during sleep.

The proof of the departure of the astral body during sleep has been ascertained by a certain number of seers, but the absurdity of the commonplace dream is a rational proof thereof, one which must here be mentioned. As another rational proof of the existence of a second vehicle of consciousness, we must also notice the regular registering of the commonplace dream, because it takes place in the brain, and the habitual non-registering of the true dream experience, because this latter takes place in the externalised astral body.

Why does the astral body leave the physical during sleep? This question is beyond our power to answer, though a few considerations on this point may be advanced.

Sleep is characterised by the transfer of consciousness from the physical to the astral body; this transfer seems to take place normally under the influence of bodily fatigue. After the day's activity, the senses no longer afford keen sensations, and as it is the energy of these sensations that keeps the consciousness "centred" in the brain[4]; this consciousness, when the senses are lulled to sleep, centres in the finer body, which then leaves the physical body with a slight shock.

It is, however, of the real dream—which is at times so intelligent that it has been called lucid, and at all events is reasonable, logical, and co-ordinate—that we wish to speak. In most cases this dream consists of a series of thoughts due to the soul in action in the astral body; it is sometimes the result of seeing mental pictures of the future or else it represents quite another form of animistic activity, as circumstances and the degree of the dreamer's development permit.

It is in the lucid dream—whether belonging to normal or to abnormal sleep—that occur those numerous and well-known cases of visions past or future[5] to be found in so many of the books dealing with this special subject.

To these same states of higher consciousness are due such productions as Walter Scott's *Ivanhoe*. The author, suffering from fever, wrote this work whilst in a kind of delirious condition; *Ivanhoe* was printed before the recovery of the author, who, on reading it at a later date, had not the slightest recollection that it was his own production. (Ribot's *Maladies de la Mémoire*, p. 41.)

Walter Scott remembered nothing, because *Ivanhoe* was the fruit of the astral consciousness impressed upon a brain which fever had rendered temporarily receptive to the higher vibrations.

There are certain peculiarities of the real dream which prove almost mathematically the superior nature of the vehicle which gives expression to it. This dream, for instance, is never of a fatiguing nature, however long it may appear to last, because it is only an instantaneous impression made upon the brain by the astral body, when the latter returns to the physical body, on awaking. On the other hand, the cerebral ideation of the waking state is fatiguing if intense or prolonged, or if the nervous system of the thinker is deprived of its normal power of resistance (*in neurasthenia*); the commonplace (*brain*) dream is also fatiguing if prolonged or at all vivid.

Another peculiarity is that a dream—the real dream—which would require several years of life on earth for its realisation, can take place in a second. The dream of Maury (*Le Sommeil et le Rêve*, p. 161), who in half a second lived through three years of the French Revolution, and many other dreams of the same nature, are instances of this. Now, Fechner has proved, in his *Elemente der Psychophysik*, first, that a fraction of a second is needed for the sensorial contact to cause the brain to vibrate—this prevents our perceiving the growth of a plant and enables us to see a circle of fire when a piece of glowing coal is rapidly whirled round; secondly, that another fraction of a second is needed for the cerebral vibration to be transformed into sensation. We might add that a third fraction of a second is needed for sensation to be transformed into ideation, proving that in these special dreams there can have been no more than an instantaneous, mass impression of all the elements of the dream upon the brain[6], and that the dream itself has been produced by the imaginative action of the soul in the astral body, an extremely subtle one, whose vibratory power is such as to transform altogether our ordinary notions of time and space.

The death-bed dream. In dying people, the bodily senses gradually lose their vitality, and by degrees the soul concentrates itself within the finer vehicle. From that time signs of the higher consciousness appear, time is inordinately prolonged, visions present themselves, the prophetic faculty is sometimes manifested, and verified cases are related of removal to a distance, like that of the Alsatian woman dying on board ship. During the final coma she went to Rio de Janeiro and commended her child to the keeping of a fellow-countryman. (D'Assier's *L'humanité posthume*, p. 47) Similar instances are found in *The Night Side of Nature*, by C. Crowe, as well as in other works of the same kind.

The dream of intoxication. Under the influence of soporifics the same transfer of consciousness is produced, and we meet with more or less remarkable phenomena due to the higher consciousness. Opium smokers and eaters of hashish are able to form ideas with such rapidity that minutes seem to them to be years, and a few moments in dreamland delude them into the idea that they have lived through a whole life. (Hervey's *Les rêves et les moyens de les diriger*.)

The dream of asphyxia. During asphyxia by submersion the higher consciousness enters into a minute study of the life now running to its close. In a few moments it sees the whole of it again in its smallest details. Carl du Prel (*Philos. der Mystik*) gives several instances of this; Haddock (*Somnolism and Psychism*, p. 213) quotes, among other cases, that of Admiral Beaufort. During two minutes' loss of consciousness in a drowning condition, he saw again every detail of his life, all his actions, including their causes, collateral circumstances, their effects, and the reflections of the victim on the good and evil that had resulted therefrom.

Perty's account (*Die Mystischen Erscheinungen der Menschlichen Natur*) of Catherine Emmerich, the somnambulist nun, who, when dying, saw again the whole of her past life, would incline one to think that this strange phenomenon, which traditional Catholicism appears to have called the "Private Judgment," and which theosophy defines with greater preciseness, is not limited to asphyxia by submersion, but is the regular accompaniment of life's ending.

Manifestation of the Higher Consciousness in Various Cases of Mental Faculties Lost to Normal Consciousness.

A rather large number of people born blind have images in dreams, and can see with the higher consciousness, when placed in a state of somnambulism. This proves that the higher consciousness possesses the power of vision on its own plane, and can impress images thereof on the brain.

That this impression may be translated into the language of the physical plane[7], it must evidently take place in one of the physical centres of vision which make possible three-dimensional sight; these centres may be intact even when the external visual apparatus does not exist or is incapable of functioning.

A deaf and dumb idiot became intelligent and spoke during spontaneous somnambulism (Steinbach's *Der Dichter ein Seher*). This is a case which appears to us difficult to explain fully; indeed, if the impression of the higher vibration on that portion of the brain which presides over intelligence and thought can be understood, it is not easy to see how tongue and lips could suddenly utter precise sounds which they had never produced before. Another factor must have intervened here, as was the case with the child prophets of the Camisards. (V. Figuier's *Hist. du merveilleux, etc.*)

Young Hébert, who had gone mad as the result of a wound, regained full consciousness, the higher consciousness, during somnambulism. (Puysegur's *Journal du traitement du jeune Hébert.*)

Dr. Teste (*Manuel pratiq. du magnét. anim.*) came across madmen who became sane just before death, *i.e.*, when consciousness was passing into the astral body. He also mentions a servant girl, quite uneducated and of ordinary intelligence, who nevertheless became a veritable philosopher during mesmeric somnambulism and delivered learned discourses on lofty problems dealing with cosmogony.

This proves that the vibratory scale of the finer vehicle extends far beyond that of the physical, and that the soul cannot impress on this latter vehicle all that it knows when functioning in the former. By this we do not mean that it is omniscient as soon as it has left the visible body; this opinion, a current one, is contrary to the law of evolution, and will not bear examination.

Manifestations of the Higher Consciousness under the Form of Memory.

The memory that is lost by the brain is preserved in its entirety by the finer vehicle.

A musician, a friend of Hervey's, once heard a remarkable piece of music; he remembered it on awaking, and wrote it down, regarding it as his own inspiration. Many years afterwards, he found it in an old parcel of music where he knew it had been long before; he had totally forgotten it in his normal consciousness. (Hervey's *Dreams.*)

Coleridge tells of a servant girl who, when in a state of delirium, would recite long passages of Hebrew which she had formerly heard from the lips of a priest in whose service she had been. In the same way, she would repeat passages from Latin and Greek theological books, which she had heard under the same circumstances; in her normal state, she had no recollection whatever of all this. (Dr. Carpenter's *Mental Physiology*, p. 437, 1881 edition.)

Ricard (*Physiol. et Hygiène du Magnét.*, p. 183) relates the case of a young man, possessed of an ordinary memory, but who, in somnambulism, could repeat almost word for word a sermon he had heard or a book he had read.

Mayo, the physiologist, states that an ignorant young girl, in a state of somnambulism, wrote whole pages of a treatise on astronomy, including figures and calculations, which she had probably read in the *Encyclopædia Britannica*, for the treatise was afterwards found in that work. (*Truths in Popular Superstitions.*)

Ladame (*La Névrose hypnotique*, p. 105) mentions a woman who, having only on one occasion been to the theatre, was able, during somnambulism, to sing the whole of the second act of Meyerbeer's *L'Africaine*, an opera of which she knew nothing whatever in her waking state.

During experiments with the inhaling of protoxyde of azote, H. Davy said that normal consciousness disappeared, and was followed by a wonderful power of recalling past events. (Hibbert's *Philosophy of Apparitions*, p. 162.)

MANIFESTATIONS OF THE HIGHER CONSCIOUSNESS IN PHENOMENA OF DOUBLE CONSCIOUSNESS.

The "strata of memory" met with in many cases also prove the existence of the second vehicle of consciousness which we are trying to demonstrate.

Certain dreams continue night after night, beginning again just where they stopped the previous night; this is noticed in the case of those who talk in their sleep and in spontaneous or forced somnambulism.

The memory of one intoxicated, or in a state of fever delirium is lost when consciousness returns from the astral to the physical body; it comes back on the return of the delirium or the intoxication.

The same thing takes place in madness; at the termination of a crisis, the patients take up the past just where they left it. (Wienholt's *Heilkraft*.) Kerner relates that one of these unfortunate persons, after an illness lasting several years, remembered the last thing he did before the crisis happened, his first question being whether the tools with which he had been cutting up wood had been put away. During the whole of the interval he had been living in his higher consciousness.

Ribot (*Maladies de la Mémoire* p. 63) has noted the fact that the same thing happens with those who fall into a state of coma after having received a hurt or wound.

MANIFESTATIONS OF THE HIGHER CONSCIOUSNESS, INDICATING NOT ONLY THAT IT EXTENDS FARTHER THAN NORMAL CONSCIOUSNESS, BUT DOMINATES, AND IS SEPARATED FROM IT, RECOGNISING THAT ITS VEHICLE — THE BODY — IS NOTHING MORE THAN AN INSTRUMENT.

The Soul functioning in the finer body sees the physical body in a state of coma. Dr. Abercrombie relates the case of a child aged four, who was trepanned as the result of fracture of the skull, and whilst in a stale of coma. He never knew what happened. At the age of fifteen, during an attack of fever, the higher consciousness impressed itself upon the brain, and he remembered every detail of the accident; he described to his mother where he had felt the pain, the operation, the people present, their number, functions, the clothes they wore, the instruments used, etc. (Kerner, *Magikon*, vol. 3, p. 364.)

The Soul, in the finer body, during somnambulism, is separated both from the physical body and from normal consciousness, it calmly foresees the illness or the death of the denser body on which it sometimes imposes serious operations. Such facts were numerous in the case of magnetisers in olden days.

Deleuze (*Hist. crit. du magn. animal*, vol. 2, p. 173) had a patient who, in a state of somnambulism, held moral, philosophical, and religious opinions quite contrary to those of his waking state.

Charpignon (*Physiol., médecine et métaphys. du magnétisme*, p. 341) tells of a patient who, when awake, wished to go to the theatre, but during somnambulism refused to do so, saying: "*She* wants to go, but *I* don't want." On Charpignon recommending that she should try to turn *her* aside from her purpose, she replied: "What can I do? *She* is mad!"

Deleuze (*Inst. pratiq. s. le magét. anim.*, p. 121) says that many somnambulists look into their body when the latter is ill; that they are often indifferent to its sufferings, and sometimes are not even willing to prescribe remedies to cure it.

Chardel (*Esquisse de la nat. humaine expliq. p. le magn. anim.*, p. 282) relates that many somnambulists are unwilling to be awakened so as not to return to a body which is a hindrance to them.

There are many madmen who speak of their body in the third person. (Ladame, *La Névrose*, p. 43). They function in the non-externalised finer vehicle. Some explain their use of the third person as follows:—"*It* is the body; it is *I* who am the spirit."

Manifestation of the Higher Consciousness in the Phenomena of Possession and Materialisation.

In these strange phenomena, not only manifestations of the higher consciousness, analogous with or similar to those just cited, have been noted, but also a number of facts which prove, to some extent, the casual presence in a normal human body or in materialised abnormal forms, of beings other than that which constitutes the personality of the one possessed, or of the medium who conditions these materialisations. On this point, we would mention the well-known investigations of Sir W.

Crookes (*Katie King*), those of Colonel de Rochas (Vincent, *Un cas de changement de personnalité*, *Lotus Bleu* 1896), and similar experiments of other savants.

"Incarnation mediums" have often lent their physical bodies to disincarnated human entities, whose account of what happened or whose identity it has been possible to verify. Here I will mention only one case amongst several others, I heard it from my friend, D. A. Courmes, a retired naval captain, a man who is well-informed in these matters, thoroughly sincere, and of unquestioned veracity.

In 1895, he happened to be off Algiers, on a training vessel. A boat had sunk in the harbour, and a man was drowned. His body had not been recovered. On the evening of the accident, my friend, accompanied by a doctor, a professor, and the vice-president of the Court of Algiers, attended a spiritualistic meeting in the town. One of these "incarnation mediums" happened to be present. M. Courmes suggested that the drowned man should be called up. The latter answered to the call, entered the medium, whose voice and attitude immediately changed. He gave the following account of what had taken place: "When the boat sank, I was on the ladder. I was hurled down, my right leg passed between two bars, occasioning fracture of the leg, and preventing me from releasing myself. My body will be found caught in the ladder when the boat is brought to the surface. It is useless to seek elsewhere."

This account was shortly afterwards confirmed.

These phenomena are more frequent than one would imagine; a sufficient number might be given to show that, judging from the theory of probabilities, serious consideration should be given to them.

Manifestations of the Higher Consciousness in Apparitions.

A final group of phenomena to which I wish to call attention is the one which goes under the name of apparitions. A considerable number of these are to be found; we will confine ourselves, however, to referring the reader to a volume entitled *Phantasms of the Living*, due to the patient investigations of a distinguished body of foreign savants. Here we find, first of all, proof of the transmission of thought to a distance. An examination into the conditions under which most of these cases took place has convinced several students of the existence of the finer body which we are here endeavouring to demonstrate, as well as of the possibility of its instantaneous transference to a great distance. As the proofs afforded by apparitions are not mathematical, *i.e.*, indisputable, and as they give room for a variety of opinions, we will make no attempt to detail them, preferring to pass on to a final proof—the least important, perhaps, from a general point of view, since it is limited to the individual possessing it; the only absolute and mathematical one, however, to the man who has obtained it:—the personal proof.

There are persons—few in number, true—who, under divers influences, have been able to leave the physical body and see it sleeping on a couch. They have freely moved in an environment—the astral world—similar to our physical one in some respects, though different in many others, and have returned again to the body, bringing back the memory of their wanderings. These accounts have been given by persons deserving of credence and not subject to hallucinations.

There are other individuals, though not so numerous—of whom we have the pleasure of knowing some personally—who are able to leave their physical bodies and return at will. They travel to great distances with the utmost rapidity and bring back a complete memory of their journeyings. D'Assier gives a typical case in his work. (*L'Humanité posthume*, p. 59.)

Such is the proof we look upon as irrefutable, as complete and perfect. The man who can thus travel freely in his finer body knows that the physical body is only a vehicle adapted to the physical world and necessary for life in this world; he knows that consciousness does not cease to function, and that the universe by no means provides the conditions for a state of nothingness, once this body of flesh is laid aside.

At this stage of his evolution man can, in addition, make use of his astral body at will, and obtain on the astral plane, first by reason and intuition, afterwards by personal experience, proof of another vehicle of consciousness—the mental body. At a further stage he obtains the certainty of possession of the causal body, then of higher bodies, and from that time he can no longer doubt the teachings of the Elder Brothers, those who have entered the higher evolution, the worlds that are divine. He knows, beyond all possibility of doubt, that what the ordinary man expresses in such childish language regarding these lofty problems, what he calls the Absolute and the Manifested, God and the Universe, the soul and the body, are more vitally true than he imagined; he sees that these words are dense veils that conceal the supreme, ineffable, infinite Being, of whom manifested beings are illusory "aspects," facets of the divine Jewel[8].

With this introduction, we will plunge at once into the heart of the subject.

---

1. Which is nothing but an unknown "aspect" of abstract Divinity.
2. Present-day man possesses four bodies of increasing fineness, the elements of which interpenetrate. Proceeding from the most dense, these are: The physical, the astral, the mental, and the causal body. In certain conditions they are capable of dissociation, and they last for a longer or a shorter time. The astral body, also called the body of desire, animal soul

(Kâmarûpa, in Sanskrit) is the seat of sensation. Evolution has in store for us higher bodies stilt—the buddhic body, the atmic body, &c.... but these need only be mentioned at this point.

Yoga—Sanskrit, *union*—is a training of the different bodies of man by the will; its object is to make of those bodies complete and perfect instruments, capable of responding to the vibrations of the outer universe as well as to those of the individual soul. When this process is accomplished, man can receive, consciously and at will, in any one of his bodies, vibrations received by the soul primarily in one of the others; for instance, he may feel in the physical brain the direct action of his astral or higher bodies; he may also leave the physical, and feel directly in his astral body the action of the mental body, and so on.

3. When the astral body is externalised, the subject cannot speak; he must await its return; when only partially externalised or not at all, and consciousness is centred in it, the subject can speak and relate what he sees afar off, for astral vision is possible at enormous distances. Such cases as these are frequently met with.
4. In 1876, in a Leipzic hospital, there was a patient possessed of neither sensibility nor muscular sense. He had only sight in the right eye and hearing in the left ear. If this eye and ear were closed, the patient immediately fell asleep. Neither by being touched nor shaken could he be awakened; to effect this, it was necessary to open his eye and unstop his ear. (*Archiv. für die ges. Physiologie*, vol. 15, p. 573).
5. These pictures are often visible in the astral world; they explain the prophetic faculty of ordinary seers.
6. In such cases, by association of ideas or any other influence, the soul dramatises the physical impression which calls forth the dream, and creates the long phantasmagoria of this dream in so short a time as to be scarcely appreciable. Between the sleeping physical body and the externalised astral body there is so close a degree of sympathy that the latter is conscious of everything that takes place in the former. This explains why the astral body returns so rapidly to the physical when a noise, light, or any other sensation impresses this latter.
7. We say "language of the physical plane" because the soul, in the astral body, sees in four dimensions, *i.e.*, all the parts of an object at once, as though these parts were spread out on a two-dimensional plane. Consequently, the higher vision needs interpretation in order to be expressed on the physical plane.
8. There are other proofs of the existence of the causal body, the reincarnating vehicle; the principal one is given in the middle of Chapter 3. It is there shown that the physical germs explain only a very small portion of heredity, and that logic imperiously demands the existence of an invisible, durable body, capable of gathering up the germs which preserve the moral and intellectual qualities of man.

REINCARNATION AND THE MORAL LAW.

The Goodness, justice, and Omnipotence of God are the guarantees of Providence.

It is absolutely impossible that the faintest breath of injustice should ever disturb the Universe. Every time the Law appears to be violated, every time Justice seems outraged, we may be certain that it is our ignorance alone that is at work, and that a deeper knowledge of the net-work of evolution and of the lines of action created by human free will, sooner or later, will dissipate our error.

For all that, the whole universe appears to be the very incarnation of injustice. The constellations as they come into manifestation shatter the heavens with their titanic combats; it is the vampirism of the greatest among them that creates the suns, thus inaugurating egoism from the very beginning. Everywhere on earth is heard the cry of pain, a never-ending struggle; sacrifice is everywhere, whether voluntary or forced, offered freely or taken unwillingly. The law of the strongest is the universal tyranny. The vegetable kingdom feeds upon the mineral, and in its turn forms nourishment for the animal; the giants of the forests spread ruin in every direction, beneath their destructive influence the spent, exhausted soil can nourish nothing but weeds and shrubs of no importance. In the animal kingdom a war to the death is ever being waged, a terrible destruction in which those best armed for the fray pitilessly devour the weak and defenceless. Man piles up every kind and method of destruction, cruelty and barbarity of every sort; he tears away gold from the bowels of the earth, mutilates the mighty forests, exhausts the soil by intensive culture, harasses and tortures animals when unable to utilise their muscular strength, and, in addition, kills them when their flesh is eatable; his most careful calculations are the auxiliaries of his insatiable egoism, and, by might or cunning, he crushes everything that hinders or inconveniences him. Finally, from time to time, the Elements mingle their awful voice in this concert of pain and despair, and we find hurricanes and floods, fires and earthquakes pile up colossal wreck and ruin in a few hours, on which scenes of destruction the morrow's calm and glorious sun sheds his impassive beams.

And so, before reaching individual evil and apparent injustice, there rises up before us at the very outset the threatening spectre of universal evil and injustice. This problem is so closely bound up with our subject that we are compelled to spend a short time in considering it.

Why Does Pain Exist?

To admit, as do certain ignorant fatalists, that the Universe was created by the stroke of some magic wand, and that each planet, kingdom, and being is condemned, so to speak, to a definite crystallisation in the state in which it has pleased God to fix it; to admit that the mineral will remain a mineral throughout eternity, that the vegetable will ever reproduce the same types, that the animal will definitely be confined to his instincts and impulses, without the hope, some day, of developing the superior mentality of his torturers in human form; to admit that man will never be anything but man, *i.e.*, a being in whom the passions have full play whereas the virtues are scarcely born; to admit that there is no final goal—perfection, the divine state—to crown man's labour; all this is to refuse to recognise evolution, to deny the progress everywhere apparent, to set divine below human justice; blasphemy, in a word.

It has been said by unthinking Christians that evidently God created human suffering, so that those might gain Heaven who, but for this suffering, would have no right to it. To speak thus is to represent the Supreme Goodness in a very unworthy aspect and to attribute the most gratuitous cruelty to Divine Justice. When, too, we see that this absurd reasoning explains neither the sufferings of animals, which have no right to enjoy the felicity of heaven, they say, nor the fact[1] that "there are many called but few chosen," nor the saying that "outside the Church there is no salvation," although for ages past God has caused millions of men to be born in countries where the Gospel has not been preached, we shall not be astonished to find that those who arrogate to themselves a monopoly of Truth bring forward none but arguments of childish folly in support of their claims.

Generally, however, it is original sin that is advanced as the cause of suffering.

The absurdity of this doctrine is so apparent that it has lost all credence by enlightened members of the Christian faith. First of all, it does not explain the sufferings of animals, which have had no participation in this sin, nor does it account for the unequal distribution of pain amongst men themselves. This sin being the same for all at birth[2], punishment ought to have been equally severe for all, and we ought not to see such frightful disproportions as are to be found in the condition of children who have not attained to the age of reason, *i.e.*, of responsibility. Saint Augustine felt the weight of this consideration; he reflected long on this torturing problem:

"When I come to consider the sufferings of children," he says, "believe me, I am in a state of terrible perplexity. I have no wish whatever to speak only of the punishment inflicted on them after this life by eternal damnation to which they are of necessity condemned if they have left their bodies without receiving the sacrament of Christ, but of the pains they endure in this present life, under our very eyes. Did I wish to examine these sufferings, time would fail me rather than instances thereof; they languish in sickness, are torn by pain, tortured by hunger and thirst, weakened in their organs, deprived of their senses, and sometimes tormented by unclean beings. I should have to show how they can with justice be subjected to such things, at a time when they are yet without sin. It cannot be said that they suffer unknown to God or that God can do nothing against their tormentors, nor that He can create or allow unjust punishment. When men suffer, we say they are being punished for their crimes, but this can be applied only to adults. As children have in them no sin capable of meriting so terrible a punishment, tell me what answer can be given?"

The answer, indeed, cannot be made that original sin is capable of explaining this unequal retribution; but then, ought not the very absurdity of the consequences due to such sin to justify one in refusing to examine this argument? What soul could admit that the innocent should be punished for the guilty? Does human justice, in spite of its imperfection, punish the offspring of criminals? Can the millions of descendants of the mythical Adam have been chastised for a crime in which they have had no share? And would this chastisement, multiplied millions of times without the faintest reason, never have stirred the conscience of the Church? Saint Augustine could not make up his mind to accuse God of injustice; so, to avoid disputing the truth of the Christian teaching in which he wholly believed, he invented his famous theory of "generation," often called "translation."

Men suffer because of original sin, he says, but it would not be just of God to punish them for this, had they not shared therein[3]; this, indeed, they have done, for the soul of a man was not created directly, by God, at the moment of the birth of the body; it is a branch taken from the soul of his father, as the latter's comes from that of his parents; thus, ascending the genealogical chain, we see that all souls issue from that of the common father of mankind: Adam.[4]

So that Saint Augustine preferred to deny the creation of souls and to derive them from the soul of Adam, through a successive progeny of human vehicles, rather than to allow God to be charged with injustice. We are not called upon to demonstrate the falsity of his hypothesis, which the Church has been forced to condemn, though without replacing it with a better theory; all the same, if human souls suffer from a sin in which they have not individually and consciously participated—and such is the case, for even granting that translation be a fact, these souls existed in Adam only potentially, as unconscious, undeveloped germs, when the sin took place—their punishment is none the less arbitrary and revolting. Saint Augustine believed he was justifying Providence; he succeeded only in deceiving his own reason and revolted sense of justice, but he preferred by suggestion to deceive himself to such an extent as to believe in the reality of his desire rather than enrol himself against the Church.

In order to reconcile divine Justice with the injustice of punishing all for the fault of one alone, the theologians also said: "Adam sinned, his sin has been distributed over the whole of his race, but God, by sending down his son, instituted baptism; and the waters of the sacrament wash the stains of original sin from the souls of men."

This reply is as childish as the former. As a matter of fact, according to the Church, about four thousand years intervened between the sin of Adam and the coming of the Redeemer, and so only after that interval did the souls of the just, who were waiting in the Life Beyond for the coming of the Messiah, enter Paradise!

Would not this delay in itself be an injustice? Ought not baptism to have been instituted immediately after the sin, and should it not have been placed within the reach of all? Besides, do we not see that even in our days, two thousand years after the coming of the Christ, millions of human beings are born and die without ever having heard of the existence of this sacrament. This part of the argument is too puerile to dwell upon at length, but we will spend a few moments on it to show definitely how powerless this theory is to explain evil.

Before teaching the doctrine of "Limbo," the Church accepted the idea of the damnation of children who died without being baptised, as we have just seen in the case of Saint Augustine.[5] Bossuet, with incredible blindness, also accepted it; and, sad to relate, his reason did not feel called upon to furnish an explanation which would justify Providence, as was the case with Saint Augustine. He rejected "translation," and discovered nothing with which to veil the blasphemy.

On this point the following is a faithful *résumé* of his letter to Pope Innocent XII.:

> The damnation of children who have died without being baptised must be firmly believed by the Church. They are guilty because they are born under the wrath of God and in the power of Darkness. Children of wrath by nature, objects of hatred and aversion, hurled into Hell with the rest of the damned, they will remain there for all eternity punished by the horrible vengeance of the Demon.
>
> Such also are the decisions of the learned Denis Pétau, the most eminent Bellarmin, the Councils of Lyons, of Florence, and of Trent; for these things are not decided by human considerations, but by the authority of tradition and of the Scriptures.

Such logic makes one really doubt human reason, and reminds one of the spirit with which the courts of the Holy Inquisition were inspired. Where in Nature can there be found such lack of proportion between cause and effect, crime and punishment? Have such arguments ever been justified by the voice of conscience?

Official Christianity remains powerless to explain suffering. Let us see what we can learn from the philosophies and religions of the past and the greatest of modern philosophers, as well as from the admirable *résumés* of Teachers of theosophy.

The problem of suffering is one with that of life, *i.e.*, with that of evolution in general. The object of the successive worlds is the creation of millions of centres of consciousness in the germinal state (*souls*) and the transformation of these germs into divinities similar to their father, God. This is the divine multiplication, creating innumerable "gods," in God.

To produce divine germs, homogeneous Unity must limit its immensity and create within itself the diversity of matter, of form. This can be obtained by the creation of "multiplicity" and by the "limitation" of what might be called a portion of Divinity. Now, limitation implies imperfection, both general and individual, *i.e.*, suffering; and multiplicity implies diversity of needs and interests, forced submission to the general law *i.e.*, suffering again. That the divine germs may evolve, their potentialities must be awakened by their surroundings; in other words, by the action of the "opposites," and sensation must come into being; the action of the opposites on sensation is also a cause of pain.

Outside of the unknown Being—which will be known at the end of evolution—nothing can *be*. Everything is in Him. He is all; the worlds, time and space are "aspects" which He assumes from time to time[6]; for this reason it has been said that the Universe is an illusion, which may be expressed more clearly by saying that it is an illusion to believe that what exists is not one form of divine activity, an "aspect" of God.

That anything may exist, or rather that aspects of God may appear, there must be manifested in Him a special mode of being, to call forth what we designate as multiplicity.

That multiplicity[7] may be manifest, differences must be produced in Unity; these differences in the world are the "pairs of opposites"—the contraries. These contraries are everywhere.

Matter is the fulcrum of force—both of these terms being "aspects" of God—and without a fulcrum no force can manifest itself; there is no heat without cold, and when it is summer in the northern hemisphere it is winter in the southern. There is no movement that does not depend upon a state of rest, no light without shadow, no pleasure without the faculty of pain, no freedom that is not founded upon necessity, no good that does not betoken an evil.

The following are a few examples of duality taken from nature. The current of electricity is polarised into a positive and a negative current. It is the same with the magnet; though you break a bar into a hundred pieces, you bring into being a hundred small magnets, each possessing its positive and negative side; you will not have destroyed the "duality," the opposites.

Like the magnet, the solar spectrum forms two series, separated by a neutral point, the blue series and the red one, united by the violet.[8]

Violet.
Indigo.   Yellow.
Blue.   Orange.
Green.   Red.

The terms of the two series are respectively complimentary to each other; the violet dominates the two groups of opposites and is a visible member of the axis formed by the colours that might be called neutral.

Duality appears in every shape and form.

Symbolically, we may say with the Hindus that the Universe begins and ends with two opposite movements: an emanation from Brahmâ, it is born when the breast of God sends forth the heavenly outbreathing, it dies, reabsorbed, when the universal inbreathing takes place. These movements produce attraction and repulsion, the aggregation and dissolution to be found everywhere. It is the attraction of a force-centre, the "laya centre" of Theosophy, which permits of the atomic condensation that gives it the envelope whose soul it is; when its cycle of activity ends, attraction gives place to repulsion, the envelope is destroyed by the return of its constituent elements to the source from which they were drawn, and the soul is liberated until a future cycle of activity begins.

Even the rhythm of pulmonary respiration, the contraction and dilation (systole and diastole) of the heart, the ebb and flow of the tides, as also day and night, sleeping and waking, summer and winter, life and death, are all products of that law of contraries which rules creation.

These "opposites" are the very essence of cosmic life, the twin pillars of universal equilibrium; they have been represented in Solomon's symbolical temple—here, the Universe—by Jakin and Boaz, the white and the black columns; they are also the interlaced triangles of "Solomon's Seal," the six-pointed star, the two Old Men of the Kabbalah, the white Jehovah and the black Jehovah; Eros and Anteros, the serpents of Mercury's caduceus, the two Sphinxes of the car of Osiris, Adam and Eve, Cain and Abel, Jacob and Esau, the Chinese "Yang" and "Yin," the goblet and staff of Tarot, man and woman. All these images represent the same law.

Multiplicity, the fruit of the contraries, makes its appearance in the forms born in infinite, homogeneous Being; its goal is the goal of creation; the production, in infinite Being, of centres which are developed by evolution and finally become gods in God. These centres, or "souls," these points in the supreme Point, are divine in essence, though, so far, they have no share at all in the perfection "manifested" by God; they are all "centres," for God is a sphere, whose centre is everywhere and circumference nowhere, but they have not developed consciousness which is as yet only potential in them. Like cuttings of willow which reproduce the mother-tree, these points, veritable portions of God, are capable of germinating, growing up, and becoming "I's," self-conscious beings, intelligent and endowed with will-power, and finally gods, having developed the entire potentialities of the All by their repeated imprisonment in the series of forms that make up the visible and invisible kingdoms of nature.

Every form, *i.e.* aggregate of substance-force, reflects within itself one of these points of Divinity. This point is its Monad, its centre of consciousness, or soul; it is the cause which is manifested as qualities in the envelopes, and these give it the illusion of separateness for a certain period[9], just as a soap-bubble momentarily acquires a fictitious individuality and appears separate from the atmosphere—of which it forms part—so long as its illusory envelope endures.

Thus do men imagine themselves separate from one another, when all the time their soul is nothing more than a drop of the divine Ocean, hidden momentarily in a perishable body.

The "contraries" are the anvil and the hammer which slowly forge souls by producing what might be called sensation in general, and sensation is a fertile cause of suffering each time the vehicles of consciousness receive vibrations that greatly exceed their fundamental capacity of sensation. Without sensation however—consequently without suffering—the body could neither walk,[10] nor see, nor hear, nor show any disturbance brought to bear upon it; there would exist no possible relation between the Universe and the "I," between the All and the parts, between bodies and souls; there would be no consciousness, or sensation of being, since no vibration from without would find an echo in the incarnated "centres" of life; no knowledge would be possible; man would be, as it were, in a state of nothingness; and, without suspecting it, his body might at any moment be crushed to the ground by the forces of Nature.

But these material necessities are not by any means the only ones that demand sensation; without it, one of the principal objects of evolution—the development of "Egos"—would be impossible. As an example borrowed from the domain of physical sensation, we need only call to memory a well-known experience in childhood.

All who have been at a boarding school know how heavy and fetid is the atmosphere of a dormitory in the early winter morning, when fifty boys have been breathing the same air again and again during the whole of the night. And yet, who suspected this until he had gone out for a few minutes and then returned to the bed-room? It needed the "contrary," the pure outside air, to make known the state of the atmosphere inside. The contrast produced sensation—that nauseous, suffocating impression of foul, mephitic air; suffering[11] generated knowledge of the vitiated air; as the result of this influence, the "centre of consciousness" felt itself an "I" distinct from its surroundings, and its "self-consciousness" received a slight increase.

What might be called passional sensibility—desire, emotion, impulse—is, like physical sensation, another indispensable factor in evolution; it is the special element in the development of the animal kingdom as well as of the less evolved portion of the human kingdom.

The young souls of mankind must receive the comparatively simple lessons of sensation, desire, and passion, before beginning the far more complicated study of mentality. But for desire, a host of needs could not be manifested, numberless functions would remain inactive; the body would not feed itself, and would die, were it not for hunger; danger would not be fled from, but for the instinct of self-preservation; nor without this would there be any propagation of the species. None the less is this life of sensation the source of many evils; desire and passion amongst human beings create terrible misery, fill prisons and hospitals, and are at the root of all kinds of moral suffering. In its turn, intelligence—that sensation so characteristic of the human state—is both an indispensable necessity and the most fertile source of evil, so long as it has not experienced a yearning for that inner "divinity," deep in the heart of man, which calls to it. A powerful lever of progress, it might convert this earth into a paradise, whereas it is the weapon which the strong, in their egoism, use to crush the feeble, a terrible weapon which either creates or intensifies all the evils under which the people writhe in despair. Once it becomes the instrument of a regenerate humanity, that is to say, when men have become compassionate, loving, and devoted, then the social question will cease to exist, and the old instrument of torture will become a pledge of general happiness.

Even spiritual sensibility is a cause of suffering to some noble souls who have developed it, for however deep the joy of loving and giving oneself, intense too is the pain of witnessing the cruel drama of life, that fratricidal struggle in which passion strikes without mercy, whilst illusion and ignorance deal blows even more terrible, for into the wounds they make they instil the poison of revolt and despair.

The action of multiplicity, and of its creators, the "contraries," engenders still other causes of suffering. Every being lives both for others and at their expense. For instance, physical bodies are obliged to replace with food and nourishment those particles which the various functions of life cause them to lose. The vegetable kingdom takes its constituent elements from the mineral kingdom, and itself serves as food for large portions of the animal kingdom; up to this point physical pain has not manifested itself, though there is a momentary arrest of evolution for the animistic essence which represents the individual in the destroyed vegetable. A portion of the animal kingdom feeds on its own members; man, too, extorts from this same kingdom a very heavy tribute; here, the arrested evolution of the victims is all the more important, inasmuch as their stage of evolution is higher, and the existence of a nervous system brings the possibility of suffering, suffering which certain influences[12] either diminish or suppress altogether, when caused by animal destructiveness, but which may become intense when it is man who is the sacrificer.

Among the causes of pain, arising from multiplicity there is also the physical, mental, and moral action exercised by the solidarity of all beings. By exchanging, with those that come into contact with us, the products thrown off by our visible and invisible bodies, we are the dispensers of good or ill-health. Everyone, for instance, is aware of the far-reaching effects of an evil intellectual and moral example; physical contagion, in spite of the torture it inflicts, is far less to be dreaded than moral contagion. The spiritual qualities alone do not form a leaven of evil; they are not the double-edged instruments we meet with elsewhere. The reason of this is that they belong to the plane of Unity. But it is none the less true that, though the presence of a highly developed soul is a help to younger souls within its reach and influence, its powerful vibrations may, from certain points of view, prove fatiguing to those still at the foot of the ladder of evolution. This is one of the many reasons that have given rise to the saying that it is dangerous prematurely to enter the "circle of the ascetics."

But the most powerful causes of pain, due to multiplicity, are the ignorance and the will of beings who have reached the human stage. Man can employ his mental faculties for good or evil, and so long as he does not know definitely that he is the brother of all beings, *i.e.*, until his divine faculties have been developed, and love and the spirit of sacrifice have taken possession of his heart, he remains a terrible egoist, more to be dreaded than the criminal dominated by a momentary burst of passion, for he acts in cold blood, he evades or refuses to recognise the law of humanity, he dominates and destroys. This man is at the stage of ingratitude; he no longer possesses the harmlessness of childhood, nor has he yet acquired the wisdom of advanced age. Our Western race has reached this critical stage, whereof the menacing demands of the suffering masses are a striking testimony. Here, too, God could not do otherwise; He might create bodies blindly obedient to his law, mere automata, but it would be impossible for Him to cause divine germs to evolve into "gods" without pulling them through the school of evolution which teaches them, first, of the "ego," the root of all egoism, then knowledge by ignorance, liberty by necessity, good by evil, and the perfect by the imperfect.

It may at this point just be mentioned that though human egoism appears to have free play and to be unrestrained in its cruelty, divine Law never allows innocence to suffer for the errors of evolving souls, it punishes only the guilty, whether their faults or misdeeds be known or unknown, belonging to the present life or to past ones.

Such, briefly, is the cause of pain and suffering in evolution; in the following pages we will set forth the causes of the unequal distribution of this suffering.

The Problem of the Inequality Of Conditions.

If suffering in general is the child of Necessity—since it is born of multiplicity and the limitation of the Infinite, without which the Universe could not exist—it would seem that we ought to find it falling upon all beings without distinction, in uniform, regular, and impartial fashion. Instead of this, it is every moment losing its character of impersonality; it respects those who are guilty on a large scale; and, without any visible cause, strikes fiercely the most innocent of persons; noble souls are born in the families of criminals, whilst criminals have fathers of the utmost respectability; we find parricides, and brothers hostile to each other; millionaires die of surfeiting alongside of paupers dying of hunger; we find giants by the side of dwarfs; the healthy and well-formed near the crippled or those wasted away by terrible diseases; Apollos contrast with Quasimodos; men of genius are met with, cheek by jowl with idiots; some children are stillborn, others blind or deaf and dumb from birth. Extremely different races people the earth—on the one hand, unintelligent and cannibal negroes; on the other, the proud, handsome, and intelligent, though selfish and cruel white race. Again, from a moral standpoint, who can explain congenital tendencies to crime, the vicious by birth, the wicked by nature, the persons with uncontrollable passions? Wherefore are thrift and foresight lacking in so many men, who are consequently condemned to lifelong poverty and wretchedness? Why this excess of intelligence, used mainly for the exploiting of folly? It is useless to multiply examples, one has only to look around at hospitals and prisons, night-shelters, palaces and garrets; everywhere suffering has taken up its abode. Can no reply be given to this terrible charge brought against Divinity? Is man to remain in a state of dejection and discouragement, as though some irreparable catastrophe had befallen him?

According to the Church, all this is the work of the soul which God gives at the birth of a man—a soul that is good or bad, prudent or foolish, one which damns or saves itself according as its will can, or cannot, dominate its passions, its intelligence discover the way to heaven or not; according as grace or rejection predestine it to heaven or to hell.

Is it not the depth of profanity to represent God as watching over conceptions in order to create souls so unfairly endowed, most of whom will never hear the Gospel message, and consequently cannot be saved, whilst the rest are destined to animate the bodies of savages and cannibals, devoid of moral consciousness? Is it not an act of sacrilege thus to convert God, Who is all Wisdom and Love, into a kind of accomplice of adulterers and lewd persons or the sport of Malthusian insults. Unconscious blasphemers are they who would offer this Dead Sea fruit as the true manna of Life!

There is also another theory, often advanced in certain quarters, on which we must say a few words, for though it contains only a minimum of truth, and consequently cannot withstand serious examination, it has led astray more than one earnest thinker. Inequalities of suffering, it has been said, arise from inequalities of social conditions. Intelligence, morality, will, in fact all human faculties, develop more or less according to their environment; men are born equal; they become unequal as the result of different environment; pay the same care and attention to all and they will remain equal, and if they are equal, the theory seems to imply, evil will disappear from the face of the earth.

This is not so.

Inequality of suffering does not result from inequality of condition. Many a poor tiller of the fields enjoys a degree of peace and happiness that those favoured by birth or fortune would envy. Disease visits poor and rich alike; moral suffering is more especially the appanage of the so-called higher classes, and if obscurity and poverty render certain troubles specially severe, wealth and rank play the same *rôle* in afflictions of another kind; there is a dark side to every picture. More than this, inequality of condition is one of the fundamental factors of social equilibrium; without it, many urgent and even indispensable functions would be neglected, numerous general needs would remain unsatisfied; so-called menial work, which, in a state of society that is still imperfect and consequently selfish, is performed only in the hope of remuneration, would never be done at all; every man would have to provide for the whole of his necessities; no one could find time for self-improvement or for flinging himself entirely into those divers branches of activity which, if personal interest were absent, would make life infinitely better and progress extremely rapid. The partisans of this theory rely on diversity of tastes to fill the diversity of functions that are necessary in social life: another illusion. The inferior, painful, or difficult tasks will never find sufficient workers, whilst easy or honourable posts will always be overcrowded. To believe the contrary would be to shut one's eyes to the present imperfection of men; it would mean the belief that they were noble and lofty beings, eager for self-sacrifice, demanding only to work for the happiness of all, without a single thought of their personal preferences; it would mean seeing, in present-day humanity, that of the future in which each individual has attained to such a degree of perfection that not a single idle, ill-disposed, or stupid person is to be found amongst them, for each one would regard himself as the brother and helper of all, and the universal standard of life would be: Each for all and all for each! How ardently we desire that this were so; how eagerly we pray for that future, so far away, when we shall have grown to this nobler stature, and the present fratricidal struggle shall have given place to a lasting peace, the offspring of a higher, spiritual, universal love. Anxiously do we await it; like lost travellers, we fix our eyes on the dark horizon to catch the first faint streaks of light, harbingers of the dawn. We greet with joy and gratitude all such as believe in that blessed future and endeavour to hasten its coming, all who impersonally and in sincerity aim at the social Unity towards which the heart aspires, and especially those whose aim it is to advance in accordance with that continuous, progressive evolution based on the physical, moral, mental, and spiritual amelioration of men, for it is they who have learned the secret of Nature. Indeed, evolution shows us that, the more souls grow, the nearer they approach that perfection to which progress destines them, and happiness exists only in perfection.

To return to other aspects of the subject.

Men are born equal, we are told.

A single glance at the differences in the moral and intellectual qualities of races and individuals, at the differences between young children, even at the differences in the instincts of infants at the breast, is sufficient to prove the contrary.

There are savages in whom no trace whatever of the moral sense can be discovered. Charles Darwin in one of his works relates a fact, which Mrs. Besant has quoted, in illustration of this. An English missionary reproached a Tasmanian with having killed his wife in order to eat her. In that rudimentary intellect, the reproach aroused an idea quite different from that of a crime; the cannibal thought the missionary imagined that human flesh was of an unpleasant flavour, and so he replied: "But she was very good!"

Is it possible to attribute to the influence of surroundings alone a degree of moral poverty so profound as this?

Many a mother has been able to find out that souls are not equal, in other words, that they are of different ages, by the discovery of diametrically opposite qualities and tendencies in two children born under the same conditions; in twins, for instance.

Every schoolmaster has noticed the same fact in the pupils under his charge. Mrs. Besant says that amongst the 80,000 children who came under her inspection in the London schools she would often find side by side with gentle, affectionate little beings others who showed criminal tendencies from birth.

Looking at the question from another point of view, are we not continually finding in schools and educational establishments pupils who, for no explicable reason, show a disposition for one branch of instruction only? They shine in this, but are dunces in every other subject.

As a final example, do not infant prodigies prove that men are not born equal? Young, who discovered the undulatory theory of light, could read with wonderful rapidity at the age of two, whilst at eight he had a thorough knowledge of six languages.

Sir W. R. Hamilton began to learn Hebrew when he was three, and knew it perfectly four years later. At the age of thirteen he knew thirteen languages.

Gauss, of Brunswick—the greatest mathematician in Europe, according to Laplace—solved problems in arithmetic when only three.

No, men are not born equal. Nor does environment cause the inequalities we find; it favours or checks the development of qualities, but has no part in their creation. Still, its influence is sufficiently important for us to give it due consideration.

We are linked to one another by the closest bonds of solidarity, whether we wish it and are conscious thereof or not. Everything absorbs and throws off, breathes in and breathes out, and this universal exchange, if at times bad, is none the less a powerful factor in evolution. The atom of carbon, on entering into the combinations of the human body, is endowed with a far higher power of combining than the one which has just left the lump of ore; to obtain its new properties, this atom has had to pass through millions of vegetable, animal, and human molecules. Animals brought into close contact with man develop mentally to a degree that is sometimes incredible, by reason of the intellectual food with which our thoughts supply them. The man who lives alone is, other things being equal, weaker physically, morally, and mentally than he who lives in a large social environment; it is for this reason that the mind develops far more rapidly in large centres of life than in the country. And what is true of good is, unfortunately, true also of evil qualities.

Consequently, environment has an undeniable influence, and it is perfectly true to say that the social conditions under which individuals are born favour or impede the development of their faculties. There its influence stops; it can intensify inequality, but does not create it.

Inequality of condition arises, above all else, from the continuity of what might be called creation. Atoms are incessantly being formed in the womb of the Virgin Mother,[13] by the might of the divine vortex perceived by seers in ecstatic vision, and which theosophy has named the Great Breath; ceaselessly are these atoms entering into multitudes of organisms, ceaselessly is the plan of evolution being worked—some ending, others beginning the great Pilgrimage. It is the existence of this circuit which creates and keeps complete the hierarchy of beings, brings into existence and perpetuates the known and the unknown kingdoms of Nature; souls ascend slowly from one kingdom to another, whilst the places they leave are filled by new-comers, by younger souls.

A second cause of human inequality is the difference in effort and deed accomplished by the will of human beings who have reached a certain point in evolution. As soon as this will is guided by intelligence and the moral sense, it hastens or delays individual evolution, makes it easy when it acts in harmony with divine Law—by doing what is called "good"—or disturbs evolution by pain, when it opposes this Law, by doing "evil." By modifying the direction of the Law, the Soul engenders beneficent or maleficent forces, which, after having played in the universe within the limit the law has imposed on them, return to their starting point—man. From that time, one understands that the balance of the scales in different individuals becomes unequal. These effects of the will influence to a noticeable degree the life during which they have originated; they are preserved in a latent condition after death, and appear again in future returns to earth.

Thus are men born laden with the results of their past and in possession of the capacities they have developed in the course of their evolution. Those whom the difficulties of life have filled with energy in the past return to existence on earth possessed of that might which the world admires; now it is perseverance or courage; now patient calm or violence, which is the stronger, according to the aspect of the energy developed. Others, again, are born feeble and devoid of energy; their former lives have been too easy. Men are philosophers or mathematicians, artists or *savants*, from the very cradle.

Objections have been brought against the doctrine of Rebirth by opponents who have looked only on one side of the individual life, and so have been unable to explain apparent anomalies, especially in those cases where it is seen that the effect does not immediately follow the cause. In reality, every force that emerges from a centre of will[14] describes an ellipse, so to speak, which travels through a net-work of other ellipses generated by thousands of other centres of energy, and is accelerated or retarded in its course, according to the direction and nature of the forces with which it is connected. It is for this reason that certain actions meet with their reward or their punishment almost immediately. Then the people say: "It is the finger of God!" In other cases, again, and these are the most numerous, the reaction is postponed; the noble-hearted man, who has made sacrifices the whole of his life, seems to receive in exchange nothing but misfortune and pain, whilst close by the wicked, selfish man prospers and thrives exceedingly. Thereupon the ignorant say: "There is no God, for there is no justice."

Not so! It is impossible to defeat Justice; though, in the interests of evolving beings, it may allow the forces around to accelerate or retard its progress. Nothing is ever lost; causes that have not fructified remain potential; and, like the grain of corn gathered thousands of years ago, grow and develop as soon as favourable soil and environment are offered them. Debts are still recorded, when the perishable sheaths of our physical bodies have been cast off; they come up for future payment, often in the next life. But this next life may not wipe off the whole of the liabilities, so the process is continued for several successive existences, and this has given rise to the saying that the sins of the parents[15] are visited upon the children[16] unto the seventh generation.[17]

Such is the truth.

Souls, equal in potentialities whilst dormant as germs in the womb of Being, become unequal, as soon as they are born into existence in the manifested Universe, for they find predecessors, elder souls in front of them; inequality is intensified when they have reached the human stage, where intelligence and will come into play, for henceforth, inequality in the actions of individuals, variations of what might be called merit and demerit, set up a second factor in the inequality of conditions. Evolution treasures up the causes that have not been able to germinate in one existence, and, by successive returns to earth, realises the aims and ends of that Justice which governs the Universe, the designs of that Love which makes for progress and leads to perfection.

OBJECTION.

An apparently serious objection to the doctrine of Rebirth is constantly being made. It is unjust and useless, people say, to be punished for misdeeds that are forgotten. As this objection has reference to moral proofs, we must deal with it here.

Does forgetfulness efface faults or destroy their consequences? Could the assassin, who has lost all memory of the crime committed the previous evening, change his deed or its results in the slightest degree? Rebirths are nothing more than the morrows of former lives, and though the merciful waters of Lethe have effaced their memory, the forces stored up in the soul, during the ages, perform their work all the same in the future.

On the other hand, injustice would exist, and that under a very cruel aspect, were memory to continue; for the painful vision of a past always full of weaknesses, even when free from the stain of crime, would be a continual one. And if, too—as our opponents would prefer—man knew why he was punished, *i.e.*, if he knew that each of these past errors and faults, ever present before his eyes, would carry with it a particular fruit, and that strict payment would be exacted at every step in his new life, would not the punishment be far greater than the sin? Would there not rise from every human heart an outcry of blasphemy against a God who, by means of memory, transformed life into an endless torment, destroying all activity or initiative in the anxiety of expectancy, in a word, stifling the present beneath the heavy nightmare of the past?

Men, though so unjust and little disposed to pity, have always refused to inflict on a man condemned to death the torture of anticipation; only at the last moment is he informed of the rejection of his appeal for mercy. Could divine Law be less compassionate than human law?

Is it not rash for us, in our profound ignorance, to criticise the workings of a boundless Wisdom? He who takes only a few steps along the pathway of Knowledge, or enters, however slightly, into the secret of the works of God, obtains the proof that Providence leaves no part of the Cosmos, no being anywhere, deprived of its fatherly care and protection. When, in our blindness, we imagine injustice, a void or an imperfection of any kind, a radiant beam of light shows us the omnipresent Life, bestowing love on all its children without distinction, from the slumbering atom to the glorious planetary Spirit, whose consciousness is so vast as to enfold the Universe.

It is more especially after death that the soul, set free from its illusory sheaths, makes an impartial review of its recent incarnation, attentively following its actions and their consequences, noting its errors and failures, along with their motives and causes. In this school it grows in knowledge and power; and when, in a future incarnation, the same difficulties present themselves anew, it is better equipped for the struggle; what has been learned, is retained within the soul; it knows, where formerly it was ignorant, and by the "voice of conscience," tells the personality[18] what its duty is. This wisdom, sifted from the panorama of a thousand past images, is the best of all memories, for on those numerous occasions when a decision must be arrived at on the spur of the moment it would not be possible to summon forth from the depths of the past such groups of memories as refer to the decision to be reached, to see the events over again, and deduce therefrom a line of conduct. The lesson must have been learnt and thoroughly assimilated during the enlightened peace and calm of the Hereafter; then only is the soul ready to respond without delay, and its command is distinct; its judgment, sure; do this, avoid that.

When a soul, in the course of evolution, has succeeded in impressing its vibration—its thought—on a brain which it has refined and made responsive by a training which purifies the entire nature of the man, it is able to transmit to the incarnated consciousness the memory of its past lives; but this memory then ceases to be painful or dangerous, for the soul has not only exhausted the greater part of its karma of suffering, it also possesses the strength necessary to sustain its personality, whenever a foreboding of what we call misfortune comes upon it.

In the divine work everything comes in its own time, and we recognise the perfection of the Creator by the perfect concatenation of all creation.

Reincarnation is so intimately bound up with the Law of Causality, and receives from it such powerful support, that this chapter would be left in a very incomplete form were we not to say a few words on Karma.

THE LAW OF CAUSALITY (KARMA).[19]

Karma is the Law of the Universe, the expression of divine Will. Its seemingly essential attributes are Justice and Love; it neither punishes nor rewards, but adjusts things, restores disturbed balance and harmony, brings back evolving souls to the right path and teaches them Law.

When a man acts against the Law, he is like a swimmer, struggling against the current of a rapid river; his strength fails, and he is borne away.

So does God bear away, in spite of all their efforts, those who, whether ignorantly or consciously, fight against the Law, for it is His love that wills evolution, *i.e.*, the making human beings divine; so he brings them back to the path, in spite of themselves, every time they wander astray.

"God is patient because He is eternal," it has been said. The sentence is incomplete and must be changed, since it attributes to Divinity a vindictive nature. The Law is patient because it is perfect in Wisdom, Power, and Love.

This Law is the divine Will which moves all things and vibrates everywhere; it is the music of the spheres, the song of glory and harmony, which murmurs in the heart like the rippling of a waterfall, the chant of life and joy that eternally triumphs in its never-ending creation of beings, who, after revolving for a moment in the universe, have become perfect.

Its glorious strains resound in the heart of man, when the soul has found peace in the Law, and we are told that, when once heard, its divine accents continue for ever, like an ineffable whisper which brings us back to hope and faith, when we are sunk in the depths of despair.

God limited himself in order to become incarnate in the Universe: He is the Soul of the world. His will is exerted everywhere, it finds its reflection in every creature; and man, a portion of divinity in course of evolution, possesses a germ of will that is infinite in its essence, and consequently capable of limitless development; God respects this will in His creatures, and submits to violence, in order to teach them His will, which is supreme Love. Like a stone that falls into a tranquil lake, a human action creates, all round, concentric ripples which continue to the very shores or limits of the Universe; then the wave is thrown back upon itself, returns to its starting-point, and the man who began the first movement receives a recoil exactly equivalent to the original impetus. Reaction is equal to action; obstacles on the way may delay its return or break up its energy, but the time comes when the fractions return to the centre that generates the disturbance, which thus receives from the Law a perfectly just retribution.

The principal element in actions is thought. Every thought is a form in a state of vibration—a ray of intelligence which unites itself with subtle matter[20] and forms a being, of which this matter is the body, and thought, the soul. This being, often called a "thought-form," possesses form, duration, and strength that bear a strict relation to the energy of the thought that created it; if it embodies a soul of hatred, it will react on the man who harbours this thought, and on all who come into contact with him, as a leaven of destruction, but if it is guided by love it will be, as it were, the incarnation of some beneficent power.

In certain cases its action is expressed visibly and rapidly; for instance, a venomous thought may[21] cause the death of the person against whom it is directed—this is one aspect of the "evil eye"—as also it may[22] return to its starting-point and kill the one who generated it, by the recoil. Every mental projection of a criminal nature, however, by no means necessarily reaches the object aimed at; a sorcerer, for instance, could no more injure one who was positive, consciously and willingly good, than he could cause a grain of corn to sprout on a block of granite; favourable soil is needed to enable the seed of evil to take root in a man's heart; otherwise, the evil recoils with its full force upon the one who sent it forth and who is an irresistible magnet, for he is its very "life-centre."

Thoughts cling to their creator and attract towards this latter those of a similar nature floating about in the invisible world, for they instinctively come to vitalise and invigorate themselves by contact with him; they radiate around him a contagious atmosphere of good or evil, and when they have left him, hover about, at the caprice of the various currents, impelling those they touch towards the goal to which they are making. They even recoil on the visible form of their generator; it is for this reason that physical is closely connected with moral well-being, and most of our diseases are nothing else than the outer expression of the hidden leaven of passion. When the action of this latter is sudden and powerful, diseases may be the immediate consequence thereof; blinded by materialism, certain doctors seldom acknowledge their real cause; and yet instances of hair turning white in a single night are too numerous to be refuted, congestion of the brain brought on by a fit of anger, jaundice and other grave maladies caused by grief and trouble, are to be met with continually.

When the mental forces which disturb the physical organs meet with obstacles which prevent their immediate outlet, they accumulate, like the electric fluid in a condenser, until an unexpected contact produces a discharge; this condensation often persists for a whole life in a latent condition, and is preserved intact for a future incarnation; this is the cause of original vices, which, incorporated in the etheric double, react upon the organic texture of the body. This also explains why each individual possesses an *ensemble* of pathological predispositions often radically different from those heredity should have bequeathed to him; it is also, to some extent, the key to physiognomy, for every single feature bears either the stamp of our passions or the halo of our virtues.

Thought creates lasting bonds between human beings; love and hatred enchain certain individuals to one another for a whole series of incarnations; many a victim of the past is to be found again in those unnatural sons who send a thrill of horror through society when it hears of some heinous crime—they have become the torturers of their former oppressors. In other cases, it is love which attracts and unites in renewed affection those who formerly loved one another—they return to earth as brothers, sisters, fathers, mothers, husbands or wives.

But if we are the slaves of the past, if fate compels us to reap what we have sown, we yet have the future in our hands, for we can tear up the weeds, and in their place sow useful plants. Just as, by means of physical hygiene, we can change within a few years the nature of the constituents that make up our bodies, so also, by a process of moral hygiene, we can purify our passions and then turn their strength in the direction of good. According as we will, so do we actually become, good or bad; every man who has taken his evolution in hand notices this rapid transformation of his personality, and sees his successive "egos" rise step by step, so to speak, throughout his whole life. Speaking generally, the first part of life is the expression of the distant past—of former lives—the second is a mixture of the past and of the energies of the present incarnation; the end of life is nothing but a sinking into an ever-deepening rut for those who crystallise in only one direction; the force of habit sets up its reign, and man finds himself bound by the chains he himself has forged. This is the reason an old man does not like the present times; he has stopped whilst time has advanced, and he is now being carried along like the flotsam and jetsam of a wreck; the very tastes and habits of his contemporaries violently clashing with his beloved past. Speak not to him of progress or evolution, he has brought himself into a state of complete immobility, and he will discover no favourable field of action nor will he acquire real energy until he has drunk of the waters of Lethe in a rest-giving Hereafter and a new body supplies his will with an instrument having the obedient suppleness of youth.

H. P. Blavatsky, in the *Secret Doctrine*, has well described this progressive enmeshing of man in the net he himself is weaving.

"Those who believe in Karma have to believe in destiny, which, from birth to death, every man is weaving, thread by thread, around himself, as a spider his web; and this destiny is guided either by the heavenly voice of the invisible prototype outside of us, or by our more intimate *astral* or inner man, who is but too often the evil genius of the embodied entity called man. Both these lead on the outward man, but one of them must prevail; and from the very beginning of the invisible affray the stern and implacable *Law of Compensation* steps in and takes its course, faithfully following the fluctuations of the fight. When the last strand is woven, the man is seemingly enwrapped in the net-work of his own doing, then he finds himself completely under the empire of this *self-made* destiny...."

She adds shortly afterwards:

"An Occultist or a philosopher will not speak of the goodness or cruelty of Providence; but, identifying it with Karma-Nemesis, he will teach that nevertheless it guards the good and watches over them in this as in future lives; and that it punishes the evil-doer, aye, even to his seventh rebirth, so long, in short, as the effect of his having thrown into perturbation even the smallest atom in the Infinite World of harmony, has not been finally readjusted. For the only decree of Karma—an eternal and immutable decree—is absolute Harmony in the world of matter as it is in the world of Spirit. It is not, therefore, Karma that rewards or punishes, but it is we who reward or punish ourselves, according to whether we work with, through, and along with nature, abiding by the laws on which that Harmony depends, or—break them.

"Nor would the ways of Karma be inscrutable, were men to work in union and harmony instead of disunion and strife. For our ignorance of those ways—which one portion of mankind calls the ways of Providence, dark and intricate, while another sees in them the action of blind Fatalism, and a third, simple chance, with neither gods nor devils to guide them—would surely disappear, if we would but attribute all these to their correct cause...."

"We stand bewildered before the mystery of our own making, and the riddle of life that we will not solve, and then accuse the great Sphinx of devouring us. But verily, there is not an accident in our lives, not a misshapen day or a misfortune, that could not be traced back to our own doings in this or in another life...."

On the same subject, Mrs. Sinnett says in *The Purpose of Theosophy*:

"Every individual is making Karma either good or bad in every action and thought of his daily round, and is at the same time working out in this life the Karma brought about by the acts and desires of the last. When we see people afflicted by congenital ailments, it may be safely assumed that these ailments are the inevitable results of causes started by the same in a previous birth. It may be argued that, as these afflictions are hereditary, they can have nothing to do with a past incarnation; but it must be remembered that the ego, the real man, the individuality, has no spiritual origin in the parentage by which it is re-embodied, but is drawn by the affinities which its previous mode of life attracted round it into the current that carries it, when the time comes for re-birth, to the home best fitted for the development of those tendencies....

"This doctrine of Karma, when properly understood, is well calculated to guide and assist those who realise its truth to a higher and better mode of life; for it must not be forgotten that not only our actions, but our thoughts also, are most assuredly followed by a crowd of circumstances that will influence for good or for evil our own future; and, what is still more important, the future of many of our fellow-creatures. If sins of omission and commission could in any case be only self-regarding, the effect on the sinner's Karma would be a matter of minor consequence. The fact that every thought and act through life carries with it, for good or evil, a corresponding influence on the members of the human family renders a strict sense of justice, morality, and unselfishness so necessary to future happiness and progress. A crime once committed, an evil thought sent out from the mind, are past recall—no amount of repentance can wipe out their results on the future....

"Repentance, if sincere, will deter a man from repeating errors; it cannot save him or others from the effects of those already produced, which will most unerringly overtake him either in this life or in the next rebirth."

We will also quote a few lines from E. D. Walker in *Reincarnation*:

"Briefly, the doctrine of Karma is that we have made ourselves what we are by former actions, and are building our future eternity by present actions. There is no destiny but what we ourselves determine. There is no salvation or condemnation except what we ourselves bring about.... Because it offers no shelter for culpable actions and necessitates a sterling manliness, it is less welcome to weak natures than the easy religious tenets of vicarious atonement, intercessions, forgiveness, and death-bed conversions....

"In the domain of eternal justice, the offence and the punishment are inseparably connected as the same event, because there is no real distinction between the action and its outcome.

"It is Karma, or our old acts, that bring us back into earthly life. The spirit's abode changes according to its Karma, and this Karma forbids any long continuance in one condition, because it is always changing. So long as action is governed by material and selfish motives, just so long must the effect of that action be manifested in physical rebirths. Only the perfectly selfless man can elude the gravitation of material life. Few have attained this, but it is the goal of mankind."

The danger of a too brief explanation of the law of Causality consists in the possibility of being imperfectly understood, and consequently of favouring the doctrine of fatalism.

"Why act at all, the objection will be urged, if everything is foreseen by the Law? Why stretch out a hand to the man who falls into the water before our very eyes? Is not the Law strong enough to save him, if he is not to die; and if he is, have we any right to interfere?...

"Such reasoning arises from ignorance and egoism.

"Yes, the law is powerful enough to prevent the man from drowning, and also to prevent the possibility of his being saved by some passer-by, who has been moved to pity by the sight; to doubt this were to doubt the power of God. In the work of evolution, however, God does more than supply man with means of developing his intelligence; in order to enrich his heart, he offers him opportunities of sacrificing himself. Again, the innumerable problems set by duty are far from being solved for us; with difficulty can we distinguish a crime from a noble action; very often we do wrong, thinking we are doing right, and it not unfrequently happens that good results from our evil deeds; this is why God sends us experiences which are to teach us our duty.

"The soul learns not only during its incarnations, but even more after leaving the body,[23] for life after death is largely spent in examining the consequences of deeds performed during life on earth.

"Whenever, then, an opportunity for action offers itself, let us follow the impulse of the heart, the cry of duty, and not the sophisms of the lower nature, the selfish "ego," the cold brain, which knows neither compassion nor devotion. Do your duty, whatever happens, says the Law, *i.e.*, do not allege, as your excuse for being selfish, that God, if He thinks it best, will help your brother in his trouble; why do you not fling yourself into the fire, with the thought that, if your hour has not yet come, God will prevent the flames from burning you? Does not the man, who commits suicide, himself push forward the hand on the dial of life, setting it at the fatal hour?

"The threads of karmic action are so wonderfully interwoven, and God, in order to hasten evolution, makes such marvellous use of human forces, both good and bad, that the first few glances cast at the *mêlée* of events are calculated to trouble the mind rather than reveal to it the marvels of adjustment effected by divine Wisdom, but no sooner does one succeed in unravelling some of the entanglements of the karmic forces, and catching a glimpse of the harmony resulting from their surprising co-operation, than the mind is lost in amaze. Then, one understands how the murderer is only an instrument whose passions are used by God in carrying out the karmic decree which condemned the victim long before the crime was committed; then, too, one knows that capital punishment is a legal crime of which divine Justice makes use—yes, a crime, for none but God can judge; every being has a right to live, and does live, until God condemns him.

"But man, by making himself, even ignorantly, the instrument of Karma, acts against the universal law, and is preparing for himself that future suffering which results from every attack made on the harmony of the whole."[24]

On the other hand, Destiny is not an immutable mass of forces; will can destroy what it has created, that is a question of time or energy; and when these are unable, within a given period, to bring about the total destruction of a barrier belonging to the past, none the less does this barrier lessen day by day, for the "resultant" of this system of opposing forces changes its direction every moment, and the final shock, when it cannot be avoided, is always diminished to a greater or less degree.

In the case of those who have attained to a perfect reading of the past, their knowledge of the hostile forces is complete, and the neutralisation of these forces immensely facilitated. They can seek out, in this world or in the next, those they wronged in the past, and thus repair the harm done; they can see the source of those thoughts of hatred that are sent against them, and destroy them by the intervention of love;[25] they can find out the weak points of their personal armour and strengthen them: it is this that in theosophical language is called the burning of Karma in the fire of "Wisdom."

None the less, there are two points in the law of Causality, which appear to favour the idea of fatalism, though in reality, they are merely corollaries of Karma. According to the first, every force is fatal, in the sense that, if left to itself, it is indestructible. This is not fatality, for the force can be modified by meeting with forces differing in character, and if no such encounter takes place, it finally unites with the cosmic Law, or else is broken to pieces upon it, according as it moves with evolution or against it.[26] Only in one sense, then, is it fatal; it cannot be destroyed save by an opposing force of the same momentum. For instance, in order to annihilate an obstructive force, created in the past, the soul must expend an amount of energy that is equal and opposite to that force; it meanwhile cannot devote itself to any other work, thus causing, in one sense, a useless production of energy; in other words, evolution will suffer delay,[27] but, we must repeat, that is not fatality.

Now to the second point.

Thought, by repetition, gains ever-increasing energy, and when the forces which thoughts accumulate have become as powerful as those of the will of the Ego which created them, a final addition of energy—another thought—alone is needed for the will to be overcome and the heavier scale of the balance to incline; then the thought is fatally realised in the action. But so long as dynamic equilibrium has not been reached, the will remains master, although its power is ever diminishing, in proportion as the difference in the forces becomes smaller. When equilibrium is reached, the will is neutralised; it becomes powerless, and feels that a fall is only a question of moments, and, with a fresh call of energy, the thought is fatally realised on the physical plane; the hour of freedom has gone and the fatal moment arrived. Like some solution that has reached saturation point, obedient to the last impulse, this thought crystallises into an act.

Many a criminal thus meets, in a single moment, the fatality he has created in the course of several incarnations; he no longer sees anything, his reason disappears; in a condition of mental darkness his arm is raised, and, impelled by a blind force, he strikes automatically. "What have I done?" he immediately exclaims in horror. "What demon is this that has taken possession of me?"

Then only is the crime perpetrated, without there being time for the will to be consulted, without the "voice of conscience" having been invited to speak. The whole fatality of automatism is in the deed, which has been carried through without the man suspecting or being conscious of it; his physical machine has been the blind instrument of the force of evil he has himself slowly accumulated throughout the ages. But let there be no mistake; every time a man, who is tempted, has time to think, even in fleeting fashion, of the moral value of the impulse which is driving him onward, he has power to resist; and if he yields to this impulse, the entire responsibility of this final lapse is added on to that incurred by past thoughts.

Among the victims of these actions that have become fatal are often to be found those who are near the stage of initiation, for before being exposed to the dangers of the bewildering "Path," which bridges the abyss —the abyss which separates the worlds of unity from the illusory and transitory regions of the Universe—they are submitted to the most careful tests.

There may even be found souls that tread this path[28], bearing within themselves[29] some old surviving residue which has not yet been finally thrown into the physical plane, and must consequently appear for the last time before falling away and disappearing for ever.[30] Mankind, incapable of seeing the man—the divine fragment gloriously blossoming forth in these beings—often halts before these dark spots in the vesture of the great soul, these *excreta* flung off from the "centre," belonging to the refuse of the vehicle, not to the soul, and in its blindness pretends to see, in its folly to judge, loftily condemning the sins of a brother more evolved than itself!

The future will bring men greater wisdom, and teach them the greatness of their error.[31]

At the conclusion of this important chapter, let us repeat that Karma—divine Will in action—is Love as well as justice, Wisdom as well as Power, and no one ought to dread it. If at times it uses us roughly and always brings us back to the strait way when folly leads us astray, it is only measuring its strength against our weakness, its delicate scales balance the load according to our strength, and when, in times of great anguish or terrible crisis, man is on the point of giving way, it suddenly lifts the weight, leaves the soul a moment's respite, and only when it has recovered breath is the burden replaced. The righteous Will of God is always upon us, filling our hearts with its might; His Love is ever about us, enabling us to grow and expand, even through the suffering he sends, for it is ourselves who have created this suffering.

---

1. Fortunately, this is a fact only in the imagination of those who are blinded by faith.
2. Before men had sinned individually on earth.
3. *De corruptione et gratia*, chap. 7, No. 19; *Cont. Jul. Pelag.*, Book 4, chap. 3, No. 16, et *De Peccat. merit. et remiss.*, Book 3, chap. 4, No. 7.
4. "Omnes illae unus homo fuerunt." *De Peccat. merit. et remiss.*, Book 1, chap. 10, No. 11.
    Theologians pass over St. Augustine's adoption of this theory, giving one to understand that he abandoned his error shortly before his death. (*Dictionnaire de Théol.*, by Abbé Berger; volume VIII., article X., "*Traduciens*.")
5. See also, on this subject, his letter to Sixtus, before the latter became Pope. Chap. VII., No. 31, and chap. VI., No. 27.
6. The movements of "creation" and "absorption," which are called in Hindu symbolism the outbreathing and the inbreathing of Brahmâ.
7. Creation.

8. After violet and red there stretches quite another spectrum, invisible to the human eye; it is because violet is at the beginning of our known spectrum, that one might think it was not the neutral point thereof.
9. The soul believes itself distinct from the All, because it is subjected to the illusion engendered by its body.
10. Without the aid of the eyes, walking is impossible to those suffering from plantar anæsthesia.
11. Pleasure, like every other form of sensation, produces the same results, though perhaps with less force.
12. A magnetic effect or an emotion. All travellers who have escaped from the attacks of wild beasts mention this effect of inhibition, manifested by the absence of fear and pain at the moment of attack.
13. Primordial matter which has not yet entered into any combination and is not differentiated.
14. A soul.
15. In these cases, the soul.
16. The personalities or new bodies created by the soul, on each return to earth.
17. That is to say, the seventh incarnation.
18. Waking consciousness.
19. See *Karma*, by A. Besant.
20. Those who have studied thought know that it is capable of being incorporated in diverse states of astral and mental matter.
21. If the divine law allows it.
22. If the divine law has not allowed the action to take place.
23. Man, after death, loses in succession his astral and mental bodies.
24. *La Théosophie en quelques chapitres*, by the author, pages 31 to 34.
25. "Hatred is destroyed only by love," said the Buddha. "Return good for evil," said Jesus.
26. It is this that causes the universal force of opposition—*the Enemy* or *demon*—to become evil only when ignorance or the human will make use of it to oppose evolution: apart from such cases, it is only the second pillar necessary for the support of the Temple, the stepping-stone of the good.
27. Perhaps this is only an apparent delay, for, on every plane, force is correlative, and knowledge is the fruit of many different kinds of energy. The only real cases in which there is delay of individual evolution are probably those in which *evil is done in return for evil*. Of course, we are speaking in relative terms and from a relative standpoint.
28. When human evolution is completed, man passes the "strait gate" leading to superhuman evolution, to the spiritual life, which develops the next higher principle, *Buddhi*; this is *the Path*. Human evolution develops the mental principle, *Manas*; Super-human evolution develops the spiritual body, *Buddhi*.
29. Here we are dealing with faults of a more or less venial nature.
30. For ever, in this case, for the soul is above these residues, and, so to speak, has given them no vitality for ages past.
31. In completion of this chapter on the Law of Causality, we refer the reader to A. Besant's book: *Karma*.

REINCARNATION AND SCIENCE.

The secret of the Universe lies in observation; it is for man to develop his senses and patiently to search into the hidden things of Nature.

All science proceeds thus, and the reason that savants have not unearthed the precious object for which they seek with such wonderful perseverance is that the physical senses, even when aided by the most delicate instruments, are able to cognise only a portion of the physical Universe—the denser portion. This is proved by the fact that when man has succeeded in directing into a channel some subtle force, he remains as ignorant of its essence as he was before chaining it down, so to speak; he has not the slightest knowledge of it. He can utilise but he cannot dominate it, for he has not discovered its source. This source is not in the physical world, but on the finer planes of being, which will remain unknown to us, so long as our senses are incapable of responding to their vibrations.

Because physical observation reveals only the bark, the outer crust of the Cosmos, man sees nothing but the surface of the world, and remains in ignorance of the heart and vital plexus that give it life; consequently, he calls the disintegration following upon disincarnation by the senseless name of "death."

He who has lifted the veil of Isis sees divine Life everywhere, the Life that animates forms, builds them up, uses them, and finally breaks them to pieces when they have ceased to be of use; and this Life—God—thus spread about in numberless forms, by means of its many rays, develops in itself centres—souls—which gradually grow and awaken their infinite potentialities[1] in the course of these successive incarnations.

Still, though the eye of the god-man alone can penetrate this wonderful mechanism and study it in all its astonishing details, the savant whose mind is unprejudiced can judge of the concealed mechanism by examining its outer manifestations, and it is on this ground we now place ourselves with the object of setting forth another series of proofs of reincarnation.

The Evolutionary Series.

If we look attentively at the totality of beings we perceive a progressive series of forms expressing a parallel series of qualities and states of consciousness. The portion of this scale we are able to compass extends from the amorphous state[2]—which represents the minimum of consciousness—up to those organic complexities which have allowed of a terrestrial expression being given to the soul of the Saviours of the world. In this glorious hierarchy each step forms so delicate a transition between the one preceding and the one following that on the borders of the different kingdoms it becomes impossible to trace a line of demarcation between different beings; thus one does not know whether such or such a family should be classed among minerals, or vegetables or animals. It is this that science has called the evolutionary series.[3]

The Cyclic Process of Evolution.

Another fact strikes the observer: the cyclic march of evolution. After action comes reaction; after activity, rest; after winter, summer; after day, night; after inspiration—the breath of life during which universal Movement works in a molecular aggregate and there condenses in the form of vitality—expiration—the breath of death, which causes the individualised life to flow back into the ocean of cosmic energy; after the systole, which drives the blood into every part of the body, comes the diastole, which breathes back the vital liquid into the central reservoir; after the waking state comes sleep; life here and life hereafter; the leaves sprout and fall away periodically, with the rising and descending of the sap; annual plants die at the end of the season, persisting in germinal state within a bulb, a rhizome, or a root before coming again to the light; in "metamorphoses," we find that the germ (*the egg*) becomes a larva (*a worm*), and then dies as a chrysalis, to be reborn as a butterfly.

Ideas also have their successive cycles of glory and decadence; is not the present theosophical movement the renaissance of the Neoplatonic movement which brought the light to Greece and Egypt fifteen hundred years ago? In 1875 H. P.

Blavatsky restored it to life, whilst its previous birth took place in the time of Ammonius Saccas, the theosophist, in the Schools of Alexandria. Those who have acquired the power to read the cosmic records[4] will easily recognise amongst the present pioneers of theosophy many a champion who in a former age struggled and fought in the same sublime cause.

Races are born and grow up, die and are born again; pass through a state of childhood, of youth, of maturity, and of old age. They flourish in all their splendour when the vital movement which animates them is at its height; when it leaves them and passes to other portions of the globe, they gradually fall into old age; then the more developed Egos—those incarnated in these races during their maturity—come down into the advanced nations, living on the continents animated by the "life-wave," whilst the less evolved go to form the so-called degenerate races vegetating in obscure parts of the world. Look now at the adolescence of Russia, the youth of America, the old age of France, and the decrepitude of Turkey. Look backwards at the glorious Egypt of bygone ages; nothing remains but deserts of sand on which imperishable structures still testify to the greatness of her past; the race that witnessed the majesty of the Hierophants and the divine Dynasties is now inhabiting other lands.

Continents submit to the same law; history and science show how they pass through a series of immersions and emersions; after Lemuria, which bore the third race, came Atlantis, the mother of the fourth; Europe and America now hold the various branches of the fifth; and later on, when this old land of ours is again sunk beneath the waters, new lands will have emerged from the ocean depths to bear the future race, the sixth.

The very planets, too, come under this law; issuing as nebulæ from the great womb of the Universe at the beginning of the evolution of a solar system they are absorbed back again when the hour of their dissolution strikes. Finally, the very Universes go forth from the breast of Brahmâ when he out-breathes, and return to him when he in-breathes again.

Everything, then, in appearance is born and dies. In reality, each thing springs from its germ, makes an effort—the effort of the divine Will incarnated in this germ—develops its potentialities up to a certain step in the ladder of evolution, then garners the acquired qualities and again returns to activity in continuous cycles of life until its full development is reached.

Progress.

The observer of Nature makes a third discovery. Every fresh cycle of life is characterised by an advance on the preceding cycle; every stage brings the end nearer. This represents progress, and it is seen everywhere; when it does not appear, it is because our limited vision cannot pierce its veil.

Minerals slowly develop in the bowels of the earth, and miners well know when the ore is more or less "ripe,"[5] and that certain portions, now in a transition stage, will in a certain number of centuries have become pure gold; experiments[6] have proved that metals are liable to "fatigue" from excessive tension; and that, after a rest, they acquire greater power of resistance than before; magnets "are fed," *i.e.*, they increase their power of attraction, by exercise; cultivation improves and sometimes altogether transforms certain species of vegetables; the rapid mental development of domestic animals by contact with man is a striking instance of the heights to which progress may attain when it is aided, whilst the influence of teaching and education on the development of individuals as well as of races is even more striking.[7]

The Goal of Evolution.
The Formation of Centres of Consciousness that become "Egos."

Through innumerable wanderings this general progress traces a clear, unwavering line. Those capable of following evolution on the planes of finer matter at once perceive, as it were, wide-spreading centres forming in the sea of divine Essence, which is projected by the Logos into the Universe. As the ages pass, these centres are sub-divided into more restricted centres, into clearer and clearer "blocks" in which consciousness, that is, the faculty of receiving vibrations from without, is gradually developed, and when this consciousness within them reaches its limit, they begin to differentiate from their surroundings, to feel the idea of the "I" spring up within them. From that time, there is added to the power of receiving vibrations consciously, that of generating them voluntarily; no longer are they passive centres, but rather beings that have become capable of receiving and giving freely, individualities recognising and affirming themselves more day by day; "I's," who henceforth regard themselves as separated from the rest of the Universe; this stage is that of the Heresy of Separateness. Regarding this heresy, however, one may well say: *Felix culpa.*

Fortunate error, indeed, for it is the condition, *sine quâ non* of future divinity, of salvation. It is self-consciousness; man is born; man, the centre of evolution, set midway between the divine fragment which is beginning and that which is ending its unfoldment, at the turning point of the arc which leads the most elementary of the various kingdoms of Nature to the most divine of Hierarchies. This stage is a terrible one, because it is that which represents egoism, *i.e.* combat, the cause of every evil that afflicts the world, but it is a necessary evil, for there can be no *individual* wisdom, power, and immortality without the formation of an "I." This ego is nothing but the first shoot, or bud, of the individual soul; it is only one of its first faculties; the finest show themselves subsequently. This bud is to blossom into a sweet-smelling flower; love and compassion, devotion, and self-sacrifice will come into manifestation, and the "centre of consciousness," after passing through the primitive stages—often called the elemental kingdoms—after being sheathed in mineral, vegetable, and animal forms, after having thought, reasoned, and willed in human forms and looked upon itself as separated from its fellow-creatures, comes finally to understand that it is only a breath of the spirit, momentarily clad in a frail garment of matter, recognises its oneness with all and everything, passes into the angelic state, is born as Christ and so ends as a finished, perfected soul—a World-Saviour.

Such is the Goal of life, the wherefore of the Universes, the explanation of these startling evolutions of souls in the various worlds, the solution of the problem regarding the diversity in the development of beings, the justification of Providence before the blasphemy of the inequality of conditions.

A Few Deductions.
The Germ.

From the facts established in the course of this comprehensive view of the Universe, we are enabled to draw important deductions.

For instance, as the basis of every "cycle of life" is found the egg or germ, that strange microcosm which appears to contain within itself the entire organism from which it proceeds and which seems capable of manifesting it in its entirety. The first embryologic discovery we make as the result of this study—a discovery of the utmost importance—is that germs are one in essence, and are all endowed with the same possibilities and potentialities. The only difference that can be found in them is that the more evolved have acquired the power of developing, in the same cycle, a greater number of links, so to speak, in the chain of forms that proceeds from the atom to the sheath, or envelope, of the Gods-Men. Thus, the highest germ which the microscope enables us to follow—the human ovule—is first a kind of mineral represented by the nucleus (the point, unity) of its germinal cell; then it takes the vegetable form—a radicle, crowned by two cotyledons (duality); afterwards it becomes a fish (multiplicity), which is successively transformed into a batrachian, then a bird, afterwards assuming more and more complex animal forms, until, about the third month of fœtal life, it appears in the human form.

The process of transformation is more rapid when Nature has repeated it a certain number of times; it then represents a more extensive portion of the ladder of evolution, but, be it noted, the process is the same for all, and for all the ladder is composed of the same number of steps; beings start from the same point, follow the same path and halt at the same stages; nothing but their age causes their inequalities. They are more than brothers, they are all representatives of the One, that which is at the root of the Universe, Divinity, supreme Being.

We also see that progress, the result of the conservation of qualities, offers us repeated instances of these stages in the reappearance, at each step of the ladder, of the forms preceding it in the natural series. In the course of its evolution, the germ of an animal passes through the mineral and vegetable forms; if the animal is a bird, its final embryological form will be preceded by the animal forms, which, in the evolutionary series, make their appearance before the avian type; if we are dealing with a mammifer, the animal will be the summit of all the lower types; when it is the human germ that we are following in its development, we see that it also has contained within itself and is successively reproducing the potentialities of the whole preceding series. The microscope is able to show only clearly marked stages and the most characteristic types, for evolution runs through its initial stages with a rapidity defying the closest physical observation. If only Nature would slacken her pace in order to humour our incapacity, we should see in an even more striking fashion that she preserves everything she has attained and develops the power of reconstruction with ever-increasing rapidity and perfection.

True, each cycle of incarnation realises only an infinitesimal fraction of the total progress made, each being advances only one step at a time along this interminable series; but then, are not these minor "cycles" in the course of which brings grow and advance towards the final Goal, the visible, material expression, the tangible and indisputable proof of the strict, the inexorable Law of Rebirths?

What the Germ contains.

Now let us examine a little more carefully this process of physical germination and attempt to discover an important secret from it; let us see whether the material germ contains the whole being, or whether, as the ancient wisdom teaches, the vehicles of the divine Spark in evolution are as numerous as the germs which respectively effect their development and preservation.

Although here, too, the doctrine of the Christian churches is inadequate, we cannot altogether pass it by in silence. We will, therefore, state it, recommending the reader to compare it with the theory of science and the teachings of theosophy.

The Churches deny evolution. They say: one single body, one single state of development for each human being. For the lower kingdoms a state of nothingness before birth and after death, whatever may have been the fate of these beings during the short life imposed upon them; for man a single body for which God creates a single soul and to which He gives a single incarnation on a single planet,[8] the Earth.

It is our ardent wish that the signs of the growing acceptance of the idea of evolution now manifesting themselves in Christian teaching may increase, and that the Church, whatever be the influence that induces her to take the step, will in the end loyally hold out her hand to Science. Instead of remaining hostile, the two will then help each other to mount the ladder of Truth; and divine Life, the light of all sciences, philosophies, and religions, will illumine the dark path they are treading, and guide their steps towards that One Truth which is both without and within them.

Scientific materialism says:

Yes, everything is born again from its germ—thus is progress made, but that is the limit of my concessions. Everything is matter; the soul has no existence. There is evolution of matter, for matter, and by matter. When a form is destroyed, its qualities, like its power of rebirth, are stored away in a latent condition, within the germs it has produced during its period of activity. Along with the disappearance of matter, everything disappears—qualities, thoughts, "ego"—and passes into a latent slate within the germ; along with the return of the form, qualities and attributes gradually reappear without any hypothetical soul whatever having any concern in the matter. So long as the form is in its germ stage, the being is nothing more than a mass of potentialities; when fully developed its faculties reappear, but they remain strictly attached to the form, and if the latter changes, the faculties echo the change, so to speak, with the utmost fidelity. Matter is the parent of intelligence, the brain manufactures thought, and the heart distills love, just as the liver secretes bile; such is the language of present-day science.

This theory accepts the idea of universal injustice in its entirety; we shall shortly prove that, notwithstanding its apparent logic, it explains only one side of evolution, and that if matter is the condition *sine quâ non* of the manifestation of spirit, it is at least curious that the latter acts so powerfully upon it, and is, beyond the possibility of a doubt, its real master.[9]

Modern Theosophy, as well as the Wisdom of old, says in its turn:

Spirit is the All, the one Being, the only Being that exists.

Force-matter[10] is nothing but the product of the spirit's activity; in it we find many and divers properties—density, weight, temperature, volume, elasticity, cohesion, &c., because we judge it from our sense perceptions; but in reality, we know it so little, that the greatest thinkers have called it "a state of consciousness," *i.e.*, an impression produced by it within ourselves.[11] It is the result of the will of the supreme Spirit, which creates "differences" (forms) in unfathomable homogeneous Unity, which is incarnated in them and produces the modifications necessary for the development of its powers, in other words, for the accomplishment of their evolution. As this evolution takes place in the finite—for the Infinite can effect its "sacrifice," *i.e.* its incarnation,[12] only by limiting itself—it is progressive, proceeding from the simple to the complex. Each incarnate, divine "fragment"[13] at first develops the simpler qualities and acquires the higher ones only by degrees; these qualities can appear only by means of a vehicle of matter, just as the colour-producing properties of a ray of light only become manifest with the aid of a prism. Form plays the part of the revealer of the qualities latent in the divine germ (the soul); the more complex this form becomes, the more atomic divisions it has in a state of activity; the greater the number of senses it has awake, the greater the number of qualities it expresses.

In this process, we see at work, three main factors; *Spirit*,[14] awakening within itself *vibrations*,[15] which assume *divers appearances*.[16] These three factors are one; force-matter and form cannot exist without the all-powerful, divine Will (Spirit), for this is the supreme Being, who, by his Will, creates force matter, by his Intelligence gives it a form, and animates it with his Love.

Force-matter is the blind giant, who, in the Sankhya philosophy, carries on his shoulders the lame man who can see—a giant, for it is activity itself; and blind, because this activity is directed only by the intelligent Will of the Spirit. The latter is lame, because when it has not at its disposal an instrument of form-matter, it cannot act, it cannot appear, it is no longer manifested, having disappeared with the great periodical dissolution of things which the poetical East calls the inbreathing of Brahmâ.

Form—all form—creates a germ which reproduces it. The germ is an aggregate containing, in a very high state of vitalisation, all the atomic types that will enter into the tissues of the form it has to build up. These types serve as centres of attraction for the atoms which are to collect round them when, under the influence of the "vital fire,"[17] creative activity has been roused in the germ. Each atomic type now attracts from the immediate surroundings the atoms that resemble it, the process of segmentation which constitutes germination begins, and the particular tissues represented by the different atomic types are formed; in this way the fibrous, osseous, muscular, nervous, epithelial, and other tissues are reproduced.

The creative activity that builds up tissues, if left to itself, could create nothing but formless masses; it must have the help of the intelligence to organise the atoms into molecules, the molecules into tissues, and these again into organs capable of a corporate life as a single organism, supplied with centres of sensation and action. This intelligence cannot proceed from the mind bodies of the various beings, for the latter manifest their qualities only when they possess a fully-developed form—which is not the case with the germs; moreover, the lower kingdoms show nothing but instinct, and even the superior animals possess only a rudimentary form of mentality. The most skilful human anatomist knows nothing more than the eye can teach him regarding the forms he dissects, though even if he were acquainted with their whole structure, he would none the less be quite incapable of creating the simplest sense organ. The Form is the expression of cosmic intelligence, of God incarnated in the Universe, the Soul of the world, which, after creating matter, aggregates it into divers types, to which it assigns a certain duration. The type of the form varies with the stage of development of the being (*the soul*) incarnated therein, for the instrument must be adapted to the artist's capacity; the latter could not use an instrument either too imperfect or too perfect for his degree of skill. What could the rudimentary musician of a savage tribe do if seated before the complex organ of one of our cathedrals; whilst, on the other hand, what kind of harmony could a Wagner produce from a shepherd's pipe? The Cosmic intelligence would appear to have created a single, radical form-type, which gradually develops and at each step produces an apparently new form, until its series has reached the finished type of evolution. It stops the evolutionary process of each germ at the requisite point in the scale; in the case of the most rudimentary souls it allows a single step to be taken, thus supplying an instrument that possesses the requisite simplicity; the process is continued longer for the more advanced souls, but stops just when the form has become a suitable instrument. When it does not furnish the fecundated germ with the "model" which is to serve as a ground-plan for atomic deposits, segmentation takes place in a formless mass, and in this the tissues are shown without organisation; it is then a môle, a false conception.

It is the same cosmic Intelligence that derides the period during which the form shall remain in a state of activity in the world. Until a soul has learnt the lesson that incarnation in a form must teach it, this form is necessary, and is given to it again and again until the soul has assimilated the experience that form had to supply; when it has nothing more to learn from the form, on returning to incarnation it passes into one that is more complex. The soul learns only by degrees, beginning with the letters of the alphabet of Wisdom, and gradually passing to more complex matter; thus the stages of evolution are innumerable and the transition from one to the other imperceptible; modern science states this fact, though without explaining it, when she says that "Nature makes no leaps."

The building up of forms is effected by numerous Beings, forming an uninterrupted chain that descends from the mighty Architect, God, to the humblest, tiniest, least conscious of the "builders."[18] God, the universal Spirit, directs evolution, and could accomplish every detail of it directly; but it is necessary, for their own development, that the souls, whatever stage they have reached, should work in the whole of creation, and therein play the part, whether consciously or unconsciously, that they are fitted to play. Consequently they are employed at every stage; and, in order to avoid mistakes, their activity is guided by more advanced souls, themselves the agents of higher cosmic Entities, right on up to God, the sovereign controller of the hierarchies. Consequently there are no mistakes—if, indeed, there are any real ones at all—in Nature, except those that are compatible with evolution and of which the results are necessary for the instruction of souls; but the Law is continually correcting them in order to restore the balance. Such, in general outline, is the reason for the intervention of beings in the evolutionary process.

So far as man is concerned, the highest of these Beings supply the ideal type of the form which is to give the soul, when reincarnated, the best means of expression; others take charge of these models and entrust them to entities whose sole mission is to keep them before their mental eyes and guide the thousands of "builders" who build round them the atoms which are to form the tabernacle of flesh in its minutest details; these Liliputian builders may be seen at work by the inner eye; they are as real as the workmen who construct material edifices in accordance with an architect's plans.

That everything may be faithfully reproduced in form the entity that controls the building must not lose sight of the model for a single moment. Nor does it do so, generally speaking, for one may say that this being is, as it were, the soul of the model, being one with it and conscious only of the work it has to perform. In many cases, however, it receives certain impressions before birth from the mother's thoughts: an influence capable either of forwarding or hindering its work. The ancient Greeks were well acquainted with this fact when they assisted Nature to create beautiful forms by placing in the mother's room statues of rare plastic perfection, and removing from her sight every suggestion of ugliness. More than this; certain intense emotions of the pregnant woman are capable of momentarily effacing the image of the model which the builder has to reproduce, and replacing certain of its details with images arising from the mother's imagination. If these images are sufficiently vivid, the being follows them; and if they endure for a certain length of time they are definitely incorporated in the building of the body. In this fashion, many birth marks (*naevi materni*) are produced; strawberries or other fruit, eagerly desired at times when they cannot be procured, have appeared on the child's skin; divers objects that have left a vivid impression on the imagination may have the same effect. The clearness and perfection of the impression depend on the intensity and continuance of the mental image; the part where it is to appear depends on the sense impressions of the mother coinciding with the desire which forms the image—for instance, a spot on the body touched rather sharply at the moment.

This has given rise to the idea that the "longing" is impressed on that part of the body which the mother is touching during her desire. When the image is particularly strong and persistent considerable modifications of the body have been obtained; in such cases, children are born with animal-like heads, and treatises on teratology relate the case of a fœtus born with the head detached from the trunk, because the mother, after witnessing an execution, had been horribly impressed by the sight of the separated heads of the victims. Malebranche, in his *Recherche de la Vérité*, tells of a child that was born with broken limbs because his mother had seen the torture of the wheel. In this case, the image must have been of enormous vibratory power and of considerable persistence.[19]

A general or even a local arrest of development is almost always due to the phenomenon of mental inhibition experienced by the same being; it definitely ceases to see the plan, evolution stops, and the embryo, expelled before the time takes on the form of the evolutionary stage it had reached at that moment; if it ceases to deal with a single detail only that detail remains in *statu quo*, and is often embedded in portions of the organism quite away from the point where it would have been found had it continued to evolve; certain cysts belong to this class.

The third factor, the Spirit, the Soul—or, to be more exact, the incarnated divine ray—follows a line of evolution parallel to that of the matter which constitutes its form, its instrument; this parallelism is so complete that it has deceived observers insufficiently acquainted with the wonders of evolution. It is thus that scientific materialism has taken root. We will endeavour to set forth the mistake that has been made, and call to mind the correctness of the Vedantin symbol, which represents the soul as lame, incapable of acting without the giant, force-matter; though the latter, without the guidance of the former, could not advance along the path of evolution.

This soul is a "no-thing," which, in reality, is everything; a ray of the spiritual sun (*God*), a divine spark incarnated in the vibration (*matter*) produced by the supreme Being, it is a "centre," capable of all its Father's potentialities. These potentialities, which may be grouped together under three general heads—power, love, and wisdom—we may sum up in the one word: consciousness. It is, indeed, a "centre of consciousness" in the germinal state, that is about to blossom forth, realising all its possibilities and becoming a being fully aware of its unity with the Being from which it comes and which it will then have become.

In this development the vibrations of outer matter play the part of the steel, which, on striking flint, causes the life latent within the latter to dart forth. Each vibration which strikes the soul arouses therein a dormant faculty, and when all the vibrations of the universe have touched it, this soul will have developed as many faculties as that universe admits of, until, in the course of successive worlds, it becomes increasingly divine in the one Divine Being. In order that all the vibrations of which a universe is capable may reach the soul the latter must surround itself with all the different types of atoms that exist in the world, for every vibration is an atomic movement, and the nature of the vibration depends on the quality of the atoms in motion. Now, the first part of evolution consists in condensing round vital centres[20] (*souls*) atoms aggregated in combinations of a progressively increasing density, on to those that make up the physical plane; when the soul has thus clothed itself with the elements of all the planes, the resulting form is called a "microcosm"—a small Cosmos—for it contains, in reality, all the elements contained in the Universe. During this progressive development, the soul, which thus effects its "fall" into matter, receives from all the planes through which it passes and from all the forms in which it incarnates, varied vibrations which awake within it correspondingly responsive powers and develop a non-centred, diffused, non-individualised consciousness.

In the second phase of evolution, the forms are limited, the vibrations they receive are transmitted by specialised sensorial groups, and the soul, hitherto endowed with a diffused consciousness, begins to feel varieties of vibrations that grow ever more numerous, to be distinguished from the surrounding world, to separate itself, so to speak, from everything around; in a word, to develop self-consciousness. This separation first takes place on the physical plane; it is made easier by hard, violent contacts, and the forms, in their turn, become more complex, varied, and specialised in proportion as the soul is the more perfectly individualised. When it has developed all the self-conscious responsive powers in the physical body, it begins to develop those faculties which have as their organs of transmission the finer bodies, and as planes of vibration the invisible worlds.

In our planetary system the number of the invisible planes is seven.[21] Each of them in turn supplies the soul with a form; thus, when evolution—which in its second phase successively dematerialises matter, *i.e.*, disassociates the atoms from their combinations, beginning with the denser ones—has dissolved the physical plane, the human soul will utilise, as its normal body, a finer one which it is at present using as a link between the mental and the physical bodies. Before this dissolution is effected, however, human beings will have developed, to some extent, several finer bodies, already existing, though hitherto not completely organised.

The first of these bodies, the astral—a very inappropriate name, though here used because it is so well known—is a copy, more or less, of the physical form in its general aspect; the resemblance and clearness of the features are pronounced in proportion to the intellectual development of the person, for thought-vibration has great influence over the building up of the centres of force and of sensation in this body.[22]

The second is an even finer aggregate, composed of mental substance and assuming, during incarnation, the form of a smaller or larger ovoid—the causal body—surrounding the physical form.[23] At its centre, and plunged in the astral body during incarnation, is another kind of ovoid not so large and composed of denser substance—the mental body.[24]

Above these states of matter, at the present stage there appears no form to the consciousness of human beings, though perfect seers can perceive, within the causal body, still higher grades of matter, which will only subsequently become centres of self-consciousness.

During incarnation, the soul, in the majority of men, is clearly conscious of itself and of its surroundings only when it is functioning through the nervous system (the brain); when it leaves the denser body, during sleep, its consciousness is in the astral body, and there it thinks,[25] but without being conscious of what is taking place around it. After disincarnation, it generally becomes highly conscious in its astral body, where it passes its purgatorial life; and this latter endures until the soul leaves the astral body. As soon as the latter is thrown off, consciousness centres in the mental body; this is the period of *Devachan* or Heaven. When the mental body is put off, paradise is at an end, and the soul, sheathed only in the causal body, finds itself on a very lofty plane, but here, consciousness is vague, when we are dealing with a man of average development. Instead of laying aside this garment, as so far it has done with the rest, it recommences, after the lapse of a certain time, another descent into the matter of the lower planes and a new incarnation begins.

To the centre of the causal body are drawn atoms from the inner mental plane; these represent a new mental body.[26] When this latter has been formed, there are attracted to it atoms of the astral plane, and these form a new astral body; the soul, clothed in these two sheaths, if one may so express it, is brought into conscious or unconscious relation, according to its degree of development, with the two corresponding planes, lives there generally for a short time, and is directed to a mother's womb, in which is created the visible body of flesh within the centre of its astral body.

This force of atomic attraction has its centre in the causal body, a kind of sensitive plate on which are registered all those vibrations which disturb or affect human vehicles during incarnation. This body is, in effect, the present abode of the soul, it represents the terminal point of human consciousness,[27] the real centre of man.[28] It receives all the impressions of the plane on which it finds itself, as well as those which come to it from the lower planes, and responds to them the more readily as it has now attained a fuller development. It possesses the power to attract and to repel; a microcosm, it has its outbreathing and inbreathing, as has the Macrocosm; like Brahmâ, it creates its bodies and destroys them, although in the vast majority of mankind it exercises this power more or less unconsciously and under the irresistible impulsion of the force of evolution—the divine Will. When it attracts, it causes to recur within itself the vibrations it has received and registered—like a phonographic roll—during the past incarnations; these vibrations reverberate in the outer world, and certain of them attract from this world[29]—in this case the mental world—the atoms capable of responding to them. When they have created the mental body, other vibrations can be transmitted through this body to the astral world and attract atoms which will form the body bearing the same name—the astral—and finally other vibrations, making use of these two bodies as a means of transmission, will affect the physical plane and attract atoms which will assist in the building up of the denser body.

Everywhere the formative power of vibration is guided by cosmic intelligence, but it is effected far more easily in the reconstruction of the higher bodies, that precedes incarnation properly so-called, than in the creation of the now physical body. Indeed, in the astral and mental bodies, nothing is produced but an atomic mass, the many elements of which will be aggregated into complete organisms only during incarnation properly so-called, whilst the construction of the visible body admits of a mass of extremely delicate and important details. It is for this reason that we have seen this work of construction entrusted to special Beings who prepare, control and watch over it unceasingly.

It is because the causal body registers every vibration the personality[30] has generated or received in the course of its series of incarnations, that the vices and virtues are preserved, as is the case with the faults or the good qualities of the physical body. The man who has created for himself a coarse astral body by feeding the passions and thoughts which specially vivify the coarser matter of this body will on returning to earth find a new astral body composed of the same elements, though then in a dormant state. He who, by the cultivation of a lofty intellect, has built up a refined mental body, will return to incarnation with a like mental body, whilst the one who, by meditation and the practice of devotion which bring into being the noblest qualities of the heart, has set vibrating the purest portions of the causal body and of the divine essence (Âtmâ-Buddhi, as it is named in Sanskrit), with which it is filled, will return to birth endowed with those qualities which make apostles and saints, the Saviours of the world.

In other words:

Matter has more remote boundaries than science recognises; the numberless grades of atoms of which it consists, their powers of aggregation, the multiplicity and duration of the bodies they form, are not even suspected by materialism.

Materialism sees nothing but the part played by matter; it denies that intelligence plays any part, and will by no means admit—in spite of evolution and progress—that above man there exists an almost endless chain of higher and higher Beings, whilst below him are kingdoms of an increasingly restricted range of consciousness. By refusing to believe in the multiplicity of the vehicles which the human soul uses, it is unable to understand individual survival or to solve the problem of heredity. Indeed, evolution is only partially explained by the physical germ; the latter, in order to act alone and of itself in the development of the human embryo should possess a degree of intelligence considerably superior to that of man. This is the opposite of what we find, however, and we are brought face to face with the absurd fact of a cause vastly inferior to its effect. Indeed, the intelligence shown by the germ is not its own; it is that of the cosmic Mind reflected by mighty Beings, its willing servants. Besides, this germ contains only the qualities that belong to physical matter, and, as we shall show, the moral, mental, and spiritual qualities are preserved by the finer—the causal—body, which represents the real man at the present time.

The Problem of Human Heredity.

If materialism were the whole truth, it ought to explain the whole of heredity; instead of that it clashes with almost all the problems of life. Physical substance offers for analysis none but physical phenomena: attraction, repulsion, heat, electricity, magnetism, vital movement; the anatomical constitution of the highest—the nerve—tissue, presents only the slightest differences in the animal series, if these differences are compared with the enormous distinctions in the qualities it expresses. Differences of form, visible to the microscope, are at times important, we shall be told, and those that affect the atomic activity and groupings[31] are perhaps even more important. That is true, especially in whatever concerns man.

Intelligence cannot always be explained by the complexity of the brain —though this complexity is the condition of faculty, as a rule—insects such as ants, bees, and spiders, whose brains are nothing but simple nerve ganglia, display prodigies of foresight, architectural ability and social qualities; whilst along with these dwarfs of the animal kingdom, we see giants that manifest only a rudimentary mind, in spite of their large, convoluted brains. Among the higher animals, there is not one that could imitate the beaver—which, all the same, is far from being at the head of the animal series—in building for itself a house in a river and storing provisions therein.

There is a vast gulf, in the zoological series, before and after these insects, as there is before and after the beaver; whilst an even wider gulf separates the highest specimens of the animal world from man himself.

Nor do the weight and volume of the brain afford any better explanation of the difference in intellect than does its structural complexity.

The weight relations between the brain and the body of different animals have been estimated as follows by Debierre (*La Moëlle et l' Encéphale*):—

- Rabbit 1 of brain for 140 of body.
- Cat 1 of brain for 156 of body.
- Fox 1 of brain for 205 of body.
- Dog 1 of brain for 351 of body.
- Horse 1 of brain for 800 of body.

If matter were the only condition *sine quâ non* of intelligence, we should have to admit that the rabbit was more intelligent than the cat, the fox, the dog, and even than the horse.

In the same work the following figures express the average size of the brain in different races of men.

- Pariahs of India 1332 cubic centimetres.
- Australians 1338 "
- Polynesians 1500 "
- Ancient Egyptians 1500 "
- Merovingians 1537 "
- Modern Parisians 1559 "

This would prove that the people who built Karnac and the Pyramids, who raised to an elevation of about 500 feet blocks of granite, one of which would require fifteen horses to drag it along a level road, who placed these enormous stones side by side without mortar or cement of any kind and with almost invisible joints, who possessed the secret of malleable glass and of painting in colours that have not faded even after the lapse of centuries ... that such a race of men were inferior to the rude, uncultured Merovingians, and scarcely the equals of the Polynesians!

Science also tells us that in a child five years of age the human brain weighs, on an average, 1250 grammes—this, too, would bear no relation whatever with the intellectual and moral development of a child of that age and that of an adult man.

Though Cuvier's brain weighed 1830 grammes, and Cromwell's 2230, that of Tiedemann, the great anatomist, when placed on the scales, weighed no more than 1254, and that of Gambetta only 1246.

The physical body of itself can give no reason for a host of psychological phenomena on which, however, a flood of light is shed if one recognises the existence of other vehicles of consciousness possessing more far-reaching vibrations, and consequently capable of expressing higher faculties. During sleep, for instance, which is characterised by the Ego having left his physical body, reason is absent, and what we call dreams are generally nothing but a tissue of nonsense, at which the dreamer feels astonishment only when returning to his body on awaking. On the other hand, as we have seen in Chapter I., when the Ego succeeds in imprinting on the brain the vibrations of the higher consciousness, it is able to regain the memory of facts long forgotten and to solve problems that could not be solved during the waking state. There are madmen who have ceased to be mad during somnambulism; persons of rudimentary intelligence have proved themselves to be profound thinkers during the mesmeric trance; when under somnambulism vision is possible to those born blind and certain people can see things that are happening a great distance away, and their reports have been proved correct; certain phenomena of double-consciousness cannot be explained without the plurality—the duality, at all events—of the vehicles of consciousness.

To return to the *rôle* played by the germ in the question of heredity, we repeat that the physical germ, of itself alone, explains only a portion of man; it throws light on the physical side of heredity, but leaves in as great darkness as ever the problem of intellectual and moral faculty. If it represented the whole man, one would expect to find in any individual the qualities manifested in his progenitors or parents—never any other; these qualities could not exceed the amount possessed by the parents, whereas we find criminals from birth in the most respectable families and saints born to parents who are the very scum of society. You may come across twins, *i.e.*, beings born from the same germs, under the same conditions of time and environment, one of whom is an angel and the other a demon, though their physical forms closely resemble each other.

Child prodigies are sufficiently numerous to frequently trouble the thinker with the problem of heredity. Whence came that irresistible impulse towards poetry in Ovid which showed itself from his earliest youth and in the end overcame the vigorous opposition of his parents?

Pascal in his youth met with keen opposition from his parents, who forbade him to think of mathematics and geometry. He besought his father to tell him, at all events, "what was that science of which he was forbidden to think, and what it treated of." The answer was given to him that "it is the method of making correct figures and finding out the proportions they bear to each other." With nothing more than this information and the aid of reflection, he discovered for himself the first thirty-two propositions of Euclid by means of "circles and lines" traced in secret.

Mozart, at the age of three, learnt the clavecin by watching his sister play; a year afterwards he composed admirably, at the age of seven he played the violin at first sight without having had any teacher, and proved himself a composer of genius before he reached his twelfth birthday.

Pepito Ariola, the little Spaniard, was only three years of age when, about ten years ago, he filled with astonishment the Court of Madrid by his wonderful playing on the piano.

In the lineage of these prodigies has there been found a single ancestor capable of explaining these faculties, as astonishing as they are premature? If to the absence of a cause in their progenitors is added the fact that genius is not hereditary, that Mozarts, Beethovens, and Dantes have left no children stamped from birth as prodigies of genius, we shall be forced to the conclusion that, within the limits it has taken up, materialism is unable to explain heredity.

A few more words must be said on physical heredity to explain why moral qualities in men of average development are often on a par with the same in their parents.

In reality, the physical germs only multiply the organic elements of the ovule, and as this latter contains the cell-types of all the tissues, it follows that these cell-types will possess the qualities of the tissues that exist in the parents. For instance, germs of sufferers from arterio-sclerosis will supply a vascular apparatus predisposed to arterio-sclerosis; tuberculous subjects will supply germs in which the vital vibrations and cellular solidity will be below the normal, and bring about those degenerate tendencies which characterise the tuberculous subject; those of sanguine constitution will transmit a faculty for vital assimilation and considerable corpuscular production, and so on.[32]

In this transmission there are two main factors: the male and the female germs. The former represents force, it imprints on the ovule the initial vital vibration which is to be that of each of the cells of the organism in course of construction. The function of this germ may be studied more easily in animals, because their heredity is not complicated by the individual differences due to the mental vehicle. The stallion supplies the vital qualities—the blood, *i.e.*, the vivacity, *brio*, pace; physical resistance comes from the mare. To sum up, the modalities of matter are supplied by the feminine germ.

Peculiarities of form proceed from several causes. Phrenology and physiognomy are sciences, though the studies hitherto known by these names are almost valueless because they have not been carried on with the necessary scientific precision. Doubtless Gall and Lavater possessed the gift of penetrating both mind and heart, as was also the case with Mlle. Lenormand Desbarolles and the genuine graphologists; but this gift was not the result of mathematical deduction, but rather a psychometric or prophetic faculty; for this reason neither they nor their books have produced pupils worthy of the name. The main features and lines only of the human form have a known meaning—and not always a very precise one—for every physical, passional, mental, or spiritual force possesses an organ of expression in the visible body, and the varieties of form of this organ enable one to judge of the degrees of force they express on the earth plane. On this basis, peculiarities of form mainly stand; and the intensity of certain defects or qualities is at times expressed so strongly that it completely modifies the tendencies it would seem that heredity ought to pass on. The similarity of form between parent and child is not exact, because it proceeds from the peculiarities of the individual in incarnation far more than from the collective tendencies of the embryonic cells in process of proliferation.

The being charged with building the body can, in turn, considerably modify its form, copying specially striking features found in the mother's thought; certain characteristic family traits, the Bourbon nose, for instance; those belonging to strangers in continual relationship with the mother, and those that a babe, fed and brought up away from home, takes from his nurse or from the sur roundings amid which he lives; all these probably leave their impress in the same way. In this case, indeed, the "builder"—who, it must be added, ceases the work of construction only when it is on its way to completion, which happens about the age of seven—is influenced by the forms of the new surroundings, and at times copies them, more or less, and we may ask ourselves if the unexplained fact of negro children being born to a white woman—the widow of a negro—remarried to a white man is in no way connected with the reproduction of a mental image of the coloured children of a former marriage.

Another fact: observers have noticed that almost all great men have had as their mother a woman of lofty character. This preponderance of the maternal influence will be understood if we remember that the cellular mass that composes the child's body belongs to the mother, not only because this mass originates from the proliferation of the ovule, and, consequently, is only the multiplication of the maternal substance, but also because the materials that have formed it and have been transmuted into flesh have been supplied by her; indeed, everything comes from this cellular mass, the elements drawn from the amniotic fluid and the blood, the milk, which, after birth, continues for long months to build up the child's body and the magnetic fluid, the "atoms of life," which are continually escaping from it and which the babe absorbs whilst receiving incessant attention from his mother.

This exchange of atoms is of the utmost importance, for these ultra-microscopic particles are charged with our mental and moral tendencies as well as with the physical qualities; personally, I have had many direct proofs of this, but the most striking came at a critical period of my life. One day, when nervous exhaustion, steadily increased by overwork, had reached an extreme stage, a great Being—not a Mahatma, but a Soul at a very lofty stage of evolution—sent to me by destiny at the time, poured into my shattered body a portion of his physical life. Shortly afterwards a real transformation took place, far more of a moral than of a physical nature, and for a few hours I felt myself the "copy" or counterpart of that great Soul, and the divine influence lasted twenty-four hours before it gradually died away.

I then understood, better than by any other demonstration, the influence of the physical upon the moral nature and the method of the subtle contagion often effected by mesmerism. *A man is known by the friends he keeps* is an old proverb.

If atoms of life can have so marked an influence upon a man nearly forty years of age, *i.e.*, at a period when he is in full possession of himself, how much more powerful is this influence when exercised upon the child—a delicate, sensitive body, almost entirely lacking the control of the soul? This is the reason hired nurses often transmit to the child their own physical features and countless moral tendencies which last some time after weaning; orphans, too, morally, often resemble the strangers who have brought them up. Like physical tendencies these moral propensities disappear only by degrees, according to change of environment, and especially to the degree in which the body is controlled by the reincarnated soul.[33]

The most important, however, of the moral influences at work on the being again brought into touch with earth-life is connected with the emotions, the passions and thoughts of those around. The child—and under this name must be included the embryo and the fœtus—possesses bodies the subtle elements of which are in a dormant state; his mental and sense organisms are scarcely more than masses of substance that have not yet been vitalised—a sort of collection of germs of good or of evil, which will yield fruit when they awake. The passional and mental vibrations of the parents play on the matter capable of responding to them in the invisible bodies of the child; they vivify it, attract atoms of the same nature taken from the finer atmosphere around, and awake in it passional and mental centres which, but for them, might have remained latent, or, at all events, would only have developed at a later stage, when the Ego, master of its vehicles, would be in a position to struggle against the outer evil influences and not permit them to have effect save within the limits imposed by will. In this way, it is possible to bring to birth evil instincts in a child, and intensify them to a considerable extent, before a single virtue has succeeded in expressing itself on the new instrument in course of development. This mental action is so strong that it colours vividly, if not altogether, the morality of the little ones living beneath its influence, and even older children are still so sensitive to it that whole classes are seen to reflect the moral character of the teacher who has charge of them. This influence, too, does not cease with childhood, it weighs—though far less heavily—on the man during the whole of his life; and families, nations, nay, even races, each see through the prism of their own special atmosphere. Mighty and subtle is this illusion which man, in the course of his pilgrimage towards divine Unity, must succeed in piercing and finally entirely dissipating.

Our responsibility towards children is all the more serious in that, to the deep impression which thought makes on the subtle, plastic, and defenceless mental bodies of the little ones, is added the fact that, could one prevent the development of the germs of evil in the course of one incarnation, these germs, not having fructified, would transmit nothing to the *causal body* after death, and would disappear[34] with the disintegration of the matter of which they were composed. Consequently, with regard to children especially, we should cultivate none but noble emotions and lofty thoughts, so as to create centres of pure and worthy activity within their vehicles in course of reconstruction, and to turn their early impulses in the direction of good, their first actions towards duty and their first aspirations towards the lofty and luminous heights of spirituality.

One may see from this rapid sketch how numerous and important are the influences added to and blended with those of physical heredity. This group of influences, some maleficent, some beneficent, is chosen by the Beings who control destiny and give to each Ego, on reincarnation, the body and environment it has merited, or rather that are needed, for the harmonious development of its faculties. A young soul[35] still at the mercy of the animal impulses—necessary impulses at the outset of human development—of its kâmic, *i.e.*, desire, vehicle, is sent to parents who will be able to supply its body with material elements of a particular density without which these impulses could not manifest themselves. An Ego that is approaching maturity will be drawn to a family that is physically and morally pure, in which it will receive both the finer physical vehicle it needs and that lofty environment which, when it enters upon earth life, will develop the centres of expression for its nobler faculties. Those who are named in the mystic phraseology of the East, the "Lords of Karma," in their choice of the race, the family, and the environment in which the reincarnated soul is to appear, seek to give this latter the most favourable conditions for its evolution. An Ego whose artistic side needs to be developed will often be born in a family which will supply it with a nervous system accustomed to the kind of vibrations required, and an environment favourable to the early development of the physical centres of these faculties; to assist a being whose scientific, mystical, or metaphysical side needs to be developed, other environment and parentage will be chosen, and it is this relative parallelism existing between the moral qualities of the parents and those of the children which has deceived observers insufficiently instructed in the mystery of heredity, and made them believe in the influence of the physical germ alone.

It is an easy matter to supply an Ego of average development with a vehicle; an ordinary body is all that is needed. There may be extreme difficulty, however, when a new instrument has to be found for a lofty soul, and when we think that, in pressing instances when the fortune of humanity is at stake and the hour of destiny has struck, certain great Souls accept very imperfect bodies for want of better ones, we shall no longer be astonished at finding that any particular Messenger, in his compassion for the humanity he has to enlighten and to direct to the ancient, eternal Source of Truth, has clothed himself with a body of flesh the ancestry of which was far from being adapted to the expression of his lofty faculties; courageous Souls are well able to put on the robe of pain and to submit to slander and calumny when the world's salvation can only be achieved at such a cost. We know scarcely anything of the conditions that control the return to earth of the Avataras, the "Sons of God," except that sometimes great Initiates, after purifying their bodies, voluntarily hand them over to the "gods," who come down to earth—a sublime sacrifice which, like that of the Saviours who consent to come amongst us, shows forth that supreme characteristic of divinity; the gift of oneself.

Nor is heredity always realised; many a physical characteristic is not reproduced; in families tainted with dangerous physiological defects, many children escape the evil, and the diseased tendencies of the tissues remain latent in them, although they often afflict their descendants. On the other hand, as already stated, extremely divergent mental types are often met with in the same family, and many a virtuous parent is torn with grief on seeing the vicious tendencies of his child. Here, as elsewhere, the hand of Providence, as Christianity calls it—the Intelligence that brings about evolution, the Justice that controls and the Love that animates it—the hand of God or of those who, having become divine, collaborate in the divine plan, comes to make up for the imperfection of the vehicles, and they permit only what is necessary to come to each one—only what he has deserved, as is generally said: this hand can create a physical or a psychic malady even where heredity and environment could not supply it, just as it can preserve a pure soul from the moral infection of the surroundings into which it is thrown.[36] This is the reason we find that heredity and environment either fail to fulfil their promise or else give what was not their's to give.

Objection.

Reincarnation is not necessary, it has been alleged; the soul's evolution is continued after death in the invisible worlds in finer bodies; consequently it is needless to return to the denser bodies of earth.

In our opinion, the trials of life, so exhausting to the will, must have given rise to this theory, for not only have those who advance it never given the slightest proof of its truth, but it is utterly opposed to the law of evolution.

In a world which prefers the flights of imagination to logical reasoning we are too accustomed to regard man as a being apart in Nature; we are only too prone to make exceptions on his behalf. The patient scientific researches of all ages have laid down this universally accepted axiom: *Nature does not proceed by leaps*. It has not so far entered anyone's mind—we think not at all events—to teach that the development of the mineral, the vegetable, and even of the animal kingdom, comes to a sudden halt on this planet, once the forms in these kingdoms are dispersed, to be completed in finer worlds; but regarding man other thoughts have prevailed, as though his intelligence and his heart had learnt all the lessons this earth is capable of teaching! From the most undeveloped of savages up to those glorious Spirits that have been the Manu, the Buddha, and the Christ, we find every step occupied on the long ladder of humanity. In the lower kingdoms all the stages exist also and are utilised, each link receiving something from its neighbours and giving them something in return, thus expressing on the visible plane that gracious unity which is divine Love: love that is instinctive and imperative in beings of a low degree of evolution; obeyed by those who, without loving it, understand its good services, and actually lived by such souls as have entered upon the path of sacrifice—souls that comprehend the Unity of beings. If this earth has been capable of teaching the Saviours of the world, why should divine Wisdom send thereon only for one short life this mass of imperfect men, to hurl them afterwards on to other worlds, like careless butterflies flitting from flower to flower?

Can the evolutionary effort be so easy and simple; is divine energy of such slight value that it can thus be squandered to no purpose; is the process of creation the sport of an infant God; is the Logos, sacrificing himself in order to give life to the Universe, a prodigal, working without rhyme or reason, sending forth His intelligence and might in aimless sport and leaving evolution at the mercy of His caprice; did not Brahmâ, by means of meditation, which, as the Oriental scriptures tell us, preceded creation, practise the gentlest, the most rapid, and the easiest method of guiding beings to the Goal? Is it not sheer blasphemy to attribute such folly to the Soul of the world? Does not the study of Nature, at each step, belie this insensate waste, of which no human being would be guilty? Everywhere with the minimum of force, Nature produces the maximum of effect; everywhere energy is consolidated with one end in view; and yet, amid the general order around, is the evolution of man to form a solitary, an incomprehensible exception?

No, we cannot believe it for a moment. American spiritists,[37] however —for it is they who have given out this hypothesis—are not in agreement with the school of Allan Kardec on this fundamental point, and this fact is by no means calculated to strengthen, the authority for this doctrine. Did we not know that disincarnate beings are as ignorant in the life beyond as they were on earth; that they tend to group themselves, as they did here below, with those who think as they do, whilst remaining aloof from such as profess hostile opinions; that the Hindu remains a Hindu, the Christian a Christian, and the Mussulman a Mussulman; that sceptics are still sceptics; and atheists, atheists; we should think that spirit "communications" with their incessant contradictions were unparalleled nonsense, since the "spirits" are by no means agreed on the very things regarding which they pretend to pronounce a judgment from which there is no appeal.

Fortunately, there is a reason for these divergences. Death neither lifts the veil of Isis nor brings the soul into the presence of omniscient Light; man remains what he was, with all his former beliefs, opinions, passions, qualities, sympathies, and antipathies. True, he knows a little more than he did upon earth; no more has he doubts as to the after-life, he regains a precise memory of the whole of his life here, and the recollection of many a forgotten fact comes back to him; he understands better, for his intelligence is being served by a much finer body—but that is all. Therefore "spirits" reflect both the morality and the mentality of the nation to which they belonged on earth, and in the other life are to be found friends and enemies, believers and unbelievers, reincarnationists and non-reincarnationists.

Rebirths can be established only by personal proof, by memory; now, the soul that has entered the life beyond, after disincarnation, has not reached the end of its pilgrimage; it is learning that it must, by self-purification, pass from world to world until it attains to a state of supreme and final rest; but when this latter has been reached, it has lost its lower sheaths and the memory they gave it, and when the Law brings it back to earth, it puts on new bodies, which, having had no participation in preceding events, are ignorant of the past.

Remembrance, we shall see later on, is preserved in the cosmic Memory, but until the soul has readied a sufficient development, it cannot summon it forth, and even could it do so, it would succeed in leaving its impress on the brain only when the physical, the astral, and the mental bodies have submitted to a process of purification which harmonises[38] them and binds them closely together. Then only does man know that Reincarnation is true, and takes place on earth until this latter passes into a slate of obscuration[39], or, at all events, until the development of the soul enables it to utilise for its evolution some environment on the planet, other than the physical one.[40]

We shall be told that we are now proving what we before denied. No, we are simply stating an exception which happens in very few cases and only then to the pioneers of the race—an exception which is nothing but an apparent one and finds its place in the progressive order which unifies all the beings in the planetary chain to which we belong.

---

1. Each part possesses in a potential state the properties of the whole.
2. The kingdoms that are invisible to physical sight are as interesting as those we see, but we have no occasion to speak of them here. Logic compels us to acknowledge them until the time comes when human development enables them to be discovered and affords direct proof of their existence.
3. We do not mean to affirm that evolutionists have not committed serious errors in their theory of development. But the law they have set prominently forth is one of the fundamental expressions of the working of God in the Universe.
4. The vibratory impressions that constitute the memory of the Universe. See in Chapter 4, the final *Objection*.
5. See *L'or et la Transmutation des métaux*, by Tiffereau.
6. Such as the one with the magnet which, if too great a weight is suspended to its armature, loses strength, and this it only regains by degrees when "fed" with successively stronger charges. A steel spring that has borne too great a weight loses strength, and may break if subjected anew to the same weight that "fatigued" it. Pieces of iron break after being "fatigued" by a weight they easily carried before. Professor Kennedy made very useful experiments regarding the "fatigue" of metals at the time when metallic bridges were continually breaking, thus causing great perplexity in the engineering world.
7. There has been much discussion as to the causes of Evolution.

    In his *Progress and Poverty*, Henry George endeavours to show that Evolution is in no way brought about by individual or collective heredity. He says that the factors of Progress are: First, the mind, which causes the advance of civilisation when not exercised solely in the "struggle for life," or in frequent conflicts between nation and nation; second, association or combination, which ensures all the benefits to be derived from division of work; third, justice, which harmonises the units of the social body, and without which civilisation decays and dies.

    H. George saw only these elements in evolution; consequently, he could neither solve the problem of progress nor explain the rise and fall of empires. Indeed, egoism and war are in no way, as he says they are, the sole causes of the fall of races: the soil cannot feed a great nation for an indefinite period even if the country is prevented by emigration from becoming over-populated; the very nature itself of the civilisation of the time prevents it from continuing for ever. Modern western races, for instance, have for centuries past been developing energy and intelligence; a limit must be fixed to that particular line of progress, under penalty of destroying equilibrium both in the individual and the race.

If, indeed, man is to learn strength and intelligence, he must also develop love, or he will fail. The Elder Brothers behind Evolution control the advance of the races in accordance with the plan of God, whose servants they are.

The real cause of evolution does not lie in environment, as H. George and his school would have it: it is in the divine Will, incarnate in the Universe. It is God who creates the world, God who fills it with life, guides it and permits its development. All the laws of Nature are the expression of the supreme Intelligence; all progress is nothing but the realisation of the possibilities of the divine Will.

The evolutionary edifice is based on solidarity, and here environment is undoubtedly an indispensable factor in development; still, it only acts as the field or soil, and soil without seed remains barren.

The mind is also a powerful lever in evolution, but it affects only one side of the matter. Association or co-operation facilitates only the growth of certain faculties whilst checking the development of others. Justice calls forth only certain individual and social forces, and leaves many of them in a state of stagnation.

In a word, H. George forgets that there is no useless force in the whole of Nature; that they all collaborate in the general task, and finally that there would be no progress, were it not for the existence of opposing forces. If, *e.g.*, egoism were non-existent, those still incapable of working without the hope of personal gain would lack a powerful incentive to action. True is the saying that evil is the stepping-stone to good.

Were the Law of Rebirths known, it would prove to be an explanation of the problems of evolution.

8. A few theologians have feebly affirmed the possibility of human life on other planets than the Earth, but their voices have either been stifled or have met with no echo.

At the Congress of Fribourg, in Switzerland, August, 1897, evolution was adopted by an assembly of 700 eminent Catholics—laymen and clergy. Dr. Zahn said that *although creation is possible a priori, it is a posteriori so very improbable that it ought to be rejected; that those who believe in this creation rely upon the literal interpretation of Genesis, whilst the contemporary students of the Bible affirm that the book is allegorical, that God, in the beginning created the elements and gave them power to evolve in all the forms that characterise the organic and inorganic worlds.* One voice alone was raised in protest, but it was drowned beneath the refutations of the rest. The question, however, might be asked: How is the transition made from one kingdom to another? What is the missing link? Who is to interpret the Bible if it is an allegorical book? Is it the Church which has always imposed *the letter* of the Bible and condemned all who have attempted to set forth *its spirit*?

9. In hypnosis, indeed, the thought suggested is strong enough to modify organic life and bring about hematic extravasion (stigmata), burnings, vomiting, etc.... In certain ecstatic cases, fixity of thought produces analogous effects. No one who has studied these questions can have the slightest doubt that mind dominates matter.

10. We say force-matter, for there is no force without matter, they are the two poles of the same thing. Moreover, what is considered force in relation to dense matter plays the *rôle* of matter to subtler forces; electricity, *e.g.*, is force-matter, probably capable of serving as a vehicle for subtler force-matter, just as it plays the *rôle* of force in relation to its conductors. Force is born and dies with matter and *vice versâ*; both alike arise from the activity of God.

11. The sensations it calls forth vary with the forms. That which burns us, gives life to other beings; water, which suffocates us, enables fishes to live; whilst air suffocates creatures that live in the water, etc.

12. All this must be taken figuratively. God does not incarnate Himself. He is the All. To our limited conceptions, He seems to limit Himself, in order to be the Life of a Universe.

13. Here, too, we are speaking relatively; in reality, there are no fragments of the Absolute. We describe the process as it seems to us in the world of illusion.

14. Being: Divinity.

15. Force-matter.

16. Forms.

17. The movement given to the germ by the union of its positive and negative forces.

18. The "builders" are inferior beings utilised by Nature in every process of germination and development. To certain readers, this will perhaps appear to be an aberration of the theosophic imagination, in which case we recommend them to supply us with a better theory

and to believe in that, until the time comes when the functioning of the "inner senses" takes place in them, and enables them to perceive these beings in action.
19. Teratological phenomena attributable to the imagination of the mother are so numerous that they cannot be refuted. The case mentioned here is taken from Van Helmont's *De Injectis Materialibus*. The woman in question had been present at the decapitation of thirteen soldiers, condemned to death by the Duc d'Alva. In the same work are two other instances which occurred under similar circumstances: in the first, the fœtus at birth was lacking a hand; and in the second, it was the whole arm that was missing; whilst, what is perhaps even stranger than this, neither arm, nor hand, nor head were found, they had been absorbed by the body of the mother.
20. To be strictly logical, one should say round the only centre, the one Being, but looked upon from the side of manifestation, evolution appears as stated.
21. Hellenbach, in his book, *Magie der Zahlen*, says regarding the number seven.

"*The law governing the phenomena on which our knowledge is based decrees that the vibrations of sound and light regularly increase in number, that they are grouped in seven columns, and that the vibratory elements of each column have so close a relation to one another that not only can it be expressed in figures, but it is even confirmed by practice in music and chemistry.*

"*The fact that this variation and periodicity are governed by the number seven cannot be disputed; it is not a matter of chance: there is a cause and we ought to discover it.*"

In his table of the elements grouped according to atomic weight, Mendelejef also acknowledges that the number seven controls what he calls the *Law of periodical function*. He reaches conclusions similar to those of Hellenbach.

Dr. Laycock, in his Articles on the *Periodicity of Vital Phenomena* (Lancet) 1842, sums up as follows:—

"*It is, I think, impossible to come to any less general conclusion than this, that, in animals, changes occur every 3-1/2, 7, 14, 21 or 28 days, or at some definite period of weeks.*"
22. See *Man and his Bodies*, by A. Besant.
23. The size of the causal body varies according to its development. It has been named *causal*, because it contains within itself the causes or germs of all the other bodies, with the exception of the denser part of the physical. We say denser because the physical body is double: its etheric part belongs to the causal body, its visible part comes from the parents.
24. The mental body, which is, as it were, an ephemeral flower of the causal, is born and developed in each incarnation, disintegrating after the *devachanic* (heavenly) life.
25. It moves more or less freely on the astral plane, according to the development of the astral body. In men of low development, this body cannot be separated from the physical, under penalty of a nightmare which brings about a waking condition.
26. The atoms interpenetrate in consequence of their differences of tenuity.
27. Later on, the centre of consciousness passes from the human to the superhuman state and ascends unceasingly until it reaches the centre of the Divinity incarnate in the world.
28. When this centre is fixed in one of the higher bodies, the buddhic for instance, the man has passed into the superhuman stage.
29. As sand, placed on a plate in a state of vibration, assumes varying forms.
30. The soul acting in the mental, the astral, and more especially—in the average man—the physical body. The Individuality is the soul acting in the causal body.
31. See the diagram in the chapter on the Atom in *The Ancient Wisdom*, by A. Besant.
32. We have seen that the organs formed by these tissues are the special work of a particular being controlled by lofty Intelligences.
33. As the building of the body is reaching completion, the Ego (the Soul) begins to make use of the new instrument. It is at about the age of seven years that the development of the nerve centres becomes sufficiently advanced to allow of the brain receiving the vibrations of the soul; up to this point, the real man has scarcely had any influence upon the body, although the mental projection (the mental body) which he has formed can express itself to a certain extent much earlier, from the seventh month of fœtal life; up to this time, the instinctive energies of the astral body alone affect the embryo.
34. In Kâmaloka (Purgatory). The desires, in purgatory, cannot be satisfied, because there is no physical body to express them, and this causes a state of suffering which has been compared to a burning fire. This fire burns up the passions and leaves behind only the "germs," which the causal body takes up and bequeaths to the future astral body. But for this providential burning away, the passions would exist from early childhood in the future incarnation, *i.e.*, at a time when the Ego has no hold whatever upon the new

personality, and when the latter would be terribly affected by this influx of the forces of evil.
35. Souls are of different ages: the savage is not so old as the civilised man, while the latter is the younger brother of those strong and wise Souls who compose the vanguard of humanity.
36. It is impossible for heredity and environment to supply *all* the conditions that a soul's evolution calls for, and *nothing but these conditions*; that is the reason Providence intervenes in the interests of justice.
37. It is in this great body, with which we are in sympathy, though we claim the right to dispute their theories when we regard them as erroneous, that this hypothesis is met with more especially. True, certain schools of lower occultism teach it also, but they form a minority, and are of no importance.
38. Harmony is established when there is vibratory synchronism of all the states of matter of the different bodies *i.e.*, when each slate of matter in a body vibrates in unison with the analogous states of matter of all the other bodies.
39. When the "life wave" has ended its cycle on this earth, it passes in succession over the other planets of our chain and leaves the earth in a state of slumber. This slumber ceases with the return of the "life wave"; it becomes death when the evolution of the chain is accomplished. See A. P. Sinnett's *Esoteric Buddhism.*
40. At a certain stage on the *Path,* return to earth is no longer obligatory.

REINCARNATION AND THE RELIGIOUS AND PHILOSOPHIC CONSENSUS OF THE AGES.

In the rapid review we are now about to make of the religion and philosophy of the past, we shall find that, under many and divers names and veils, the doctrine of Rebirths has been taught from the farthest antiquity right up to the present time. There is not a nation that has not preserved clear traces of this doctrine; not a religion that has not taught it, either openly or in secret, or, at all events, retained the germ of the teaching; and if we count only those peoples of whose national religion it forms part, *i.e.*, Hindus and Buddhists, the number of believers in Reincarnation may be summed up in round figures at 540 millions of the present population of 1400 millions throughout the world. The greatest of philosophers, both ancient and modern, have regarded palingenesis as the basis of life, but whereas in the past the pledge of initiation prevented its details from being promulgated, in our days, along with the flood of light which this cycle has brought us, the veil of secrecy has been partially lifted, and theosophy has been privileged to set forth this glorious teaching in its main outlines and its most important details.

INDIA.

Northern India was the cradle of the present race—the fifth—the Eden of our humanity, our physical, moral, mental, and spiritual mother.[1] From her womb issued the emigrant hordes that peopled Europe after spreading over Egypt, Asia Minor, and Siberia; it was her code of ethics that civilised Chaldæa, Greece, Rome, and the whole of the East; our own code is full of traces of the Laws of Manu, whilst both the Old and New Testament are, in many respects, an abridged and often almost a literal copy of the sacred Books of ancient Aryavarta.

The presence of the doctrine of reincarnation in the Vedic hymns has been disputed; this proves nothing more than the present fragmentary condition of the Vedas. Nothing, indeed, could be more absurd than to find that the sacred Scriptures of India had maintained silence on a doctrine which, along with that of Karma, form the two main columns of the Hindu temple; for the Brâhman as well as for the Buddhist—who is only a member of a powerful offshoot of Hinduism—these two laws rule throughout the whole Universe, from the primordial kingdoms up to the gods, including man; and the principal, nay, the only goal of human life is Moksha—salvation, in Christian terminology—liberation from the chain of rebirths.

In this land, in which, along with strict obedience to the rules of conduct set forth by its great Teachers, there existed the most complete freedom of opinion, and where the most divergent and numerous philosophic sects consequently developed, there has always been perfect unanimity regarding the doctrine of rebirth, and in that inextricable forest of metaphysical speculations two giant trees have always overtopped the rest: the tree of Karma and the tree of Reincarnation.

In spite of the intentional obscurity in which we are left as to the teachings regarding rebirth from the time of the decadence of India, it is no difficult matter, with the aid of theosophy, to discover its main points. Thus we find in them the return of the "life-atoms"[2] and animal souls[3] to existence in new physical bodies; the rebirths of the human Egos are indicated in their main phases; but here, the deliberate omission of certain points which had long to remain incomprehensible—and consequently dangerous—to the masses, makes obscure, and at times absurd, certain aspects of transmigration. I have heard a great Teacher clearly explain these points to some of the most enlightened of the Hindu members of the Theosophical Society, but I do not feel authorised to repeat these explanations, and so will leave this portion of the subject under a veil, which the reader will, with the aid of intuition, be able to lift after reflecting on the following pages.

The Sages of ancient India, then, teach three distinct phases in the return-to-birth process: Resurrection, Transmigration or Metempsychosis and Reincarnation properly so-called.

RESURRECTION.

The human body is a species of polyp colony, a kind of coral island like those that emerge above the waves of the Pacific, by reason of the collective efforts of lower organisms.

The most numerous of the compounds of the human aggregate are known to physiology as microbes, bacteria, and bacilli; but amongst them our microscopes discover only comparative monsters, "those that are to the ordinary infinitesimal organisms as the elephant is to the invisible infusorium."[4]

Each cell is a complete being; its soul is a vital ray of the general life of our planet; its body consists of molecules that are attracted and then repelled, whilst the cellular soul remains immutable in the ceaseless fluctuations of its corporeal elements.

The molecules, too, are animated by a vital soul, connected with the cellular soul, which, in turn, is subordinate to a higher[5] unit of the collective life of the human body.

The most infinitesimal of these beings—often called "lives"—penetrate the body freely; they circulate in the aura[6] and in each plexus of the organism; there they are subjected to the incessant impact of the moral, menial, and spiritual forces, and become impregnated with a spirit of good or of evil, as the case may be. They enter the cells and leave them with intense rapidity, for their cycles of activity as well as of passivity are being incessantly repeated.

We are all the time emanating millions of "lives," which are at once drawn into the different kingdoms of Nature to which they carry the energies they have gathered in us; they impress on their new organisms the tendencies we have given them, and in this way become ferments of regeneration or of decay; they aid or retard, pollute or purify, and it is for this reason that it is not a matter of indifference whether one lives in town or country, with men or animals, the temperate or the intemperate, the wicked or the good. The animal gains from association with human beings, man loses from association with animals; the disciples of the great schools of initiation, at a certain stage of their discipline, are carefully isolated from any inferior contact.

It is these subtle forces that are at play in the physical accomplishment of an action.[7] "For material sins," says Manu, "one[8] passes into mineral and vegetable forms." When, at death, the outer sheath of man disintegrates, these "life atoms" are thrown back into the general surroundings of the earth, where they are subjected to the magnetic currents around; these currents either attract or repel them, and thus bring about that wise selection, which directs them to organisms in affinity with them.

The doctrine of metempsychosis[9] is true only for the atoms or emanations sent out by man after death or during the whole course of life. The hidden meaning of the passage from Manu, where we read that "he who slays a Brâhman enters into the body of a dog, a bear, an ass, a camel, &c.," does not apply to the human Ego, but only to the atoms of his body, *i.e.*, to the lower triad[10] and its fluidic emanations, as H. P. Blavatsky says, and she adds:

"The Hîna-yana, the lowest form of transmigration of the Buddhist, is as little comprehended as the Mahâ-yâna, its highest form, and, because Sâkya Muni—the Buddha—is shown to have once remarked to his Bhikkus—Buddhist monks—while pointing out to them a broom, that it had formerly been a novice who neglected to sweep out the Council room, hence was reborn as a broom,(!) therefore the wisest of all the world's sages stands accused of idiotic superstition. Why not try and understand the true meaning of the figurative statement before criticising? Is or is not that which is called magnetic effluvia a something, a stuff or a substance, invisible and imponderable though it be?... The mesmeric or magnetic fluid which emanates from man to man, or even from man to what is termed an inanimate object, is far greater. Indeed, it is 'life atoms' that a man in a blind passion throws off unconsciously. Let any man give way to any intense feeling such as anger, grief, &c., under or near a tree, or in direct contact with a stone, and many thousands of years after that any tolerable psychometrist will see the man and sense his feelings from one single fragment of that tree or stone that he has touched. Why then should not a broom, made of a shrub, which grew most likely in the vicinity of the building where the lazy novice lived—a shrub, perhaps, repeatedly touched by him while in a state of anger, provoked by his laziness and distaste of his duty—why should not a quantity of his life atoms have passed into the materials of the future broom, and therein have been recognised by Buddha owing to his superhuman (not supernatural) powers?"[11]

Such is the meaning of the Resurrection of the body, taught in the Christian church in a form that is repellent to reason, for it kills the spirit of the doctrine and leaves this latter like a corpse from which the life has gone.

METEMPSYCHOSIS.

After the disintegration of the body, the kâmic[12] elements continue for some time, us a "shade"[13] or a "phantom,"[14] in the finer and invisible atmosphere;[15] then they, in turn, become disintegrated by the various forces of this environment[16], and are lost in the strata of matter from which they have been taken. Like the physical elements (*life-atoms*), they whirl about in their environment and there submit to the same law of attraction and repulsion as that which controls universal selection; they are drawn towards the kâmic elements of men and animals, and it is here that we ought to place the list of those misdeeds, by reason of which these elements pass into bodies of animals or men of inferior development. "A drunken priest becomes a worm," says Manu, "a stealer of corn, a rat; the murderer of a Brâhman, a dog, a tiger, or a serpent"—and this means that those elements which, in man, serve as a basis for the passions, at death, pass over into the bodies of animals that possess the same passions or experience the same needs.

The transmigration of human souls into the bodies of animals is still generally accepted amongst the less intelligent Hindus; it has contributed, perhaps more than anything else, to that wonderful respect for life one meets with all over India. The thought that some ancestor or other might happen to be in the body of an animal prevents its destruction; even the sacrifice of his life offered by a man to one of his brothers in the animal world is regarded as a sublime virtue, and legend tells us of the Buddha, the Lord of Compassion, giving himself up as food for a famishing tigress, that she and her cubs might not perish of hunger.

REINCARNATION.

The process of disintegration[17] which, after disincarnation, destroys the physical, astral, and mental bodies of the man leaves the Soul—or, to be more exact, the causal body, for the soul is not the causal body any more than it is any of the other human vehicles—intact. Indeed, the causal body is at present the only vehicle that resists the cyclic dissolution of the human compound; this it will be subjected to only when the divine spark which constitutes the Soul—an eternal spark in its essence, since it is a fragment of God, and immortal as an "ego," once it has attained to individualisation, the goal of evolution—has formed for itself a new and superior body with the substance of the finer planes above the mental; but ages will pass before the masses of mankind reach this point.

After thus throwing off, one after the other, all its sheaths, the Ego finds that it has ended a "life-cycle," and is preparing to put on new bodies, to return to reincarnation on earth. On Reincarnation properly so called, the Hindu scriptures are so precise and complete, so generally accepted, than it is unnecessary to quote from them in detail. A few extracts will suffice.

These we will take from the *Bhagavad Gîtâ*, that glorious episode in the mighty civil war which shattered India, and left her defenceless against the successive invaders who were to complete her fall. This great epic poem introduces to us Arjuna, a noble prince, about to take part in the strife. The two armies, arrayed for battle, are on the point of engaging, arrows have already begun to pierce the air. In the opposing ranks Arjuna sees cherished relatives, dear friends, and revered teachers, whom destiny has placed in hostile array, thus giving to the battle all the horrors of parricide and fratricide. Overwhelmed with grief and pity, his heart moved to its inmost depths, Arjuna drops his bow on the ground and thus addresses his Teacher, the divine Krishna:

"Seeing these my kinsmen arrayed, O Krishna, eager to fight,

"My limbs fail and my mouth is parched, my body quivers and my hair stands on end.

"Gândîva (Arjuna's bow) slips from my hand, and my skin burns all over; I am not able to stand, and my mind is whirling.

"And I see adverse omens, O Keshava (hairy one). Nor do I foresee advantage by slaying kinsmen in battle.

"For I desire not victory, O Krishna, nor kingship nor pleasures; what is kingship to us, O Govinda (Thou who knowest all that is done by our senses and organs), what enjoyment or even life?

"Those for whose sake we desire kingship, enjoyments, and pleasures, they stand here in battle, abandoning life and riches.

"Teachers, fathers, sons, as well as grandfathers, mothers' brothers, fathers-in-law, grandsons, brothers-in-law, and other relatives.

"These I do not wish to kill, though (myself) slain, O Madhusûdana (slayer of Madhu, a demon), even for the sake of the kingship of the three worlds (the habitations of men, gods, and semi-divine beings); how then for earth?

... "I will not do battle."

The divine Krishna then smiled upon his well-beloved disciple, and said to him:

"Thou grievest for those that should not be grieved for, and speakest words of wisdom (words that sound wise but miss the deeper sense of wisdom). The wise grieve neither for the living nor for the dead.

"Nor at any time verily was I not, nor thou, nor these princes of men, nor verily shall we ever cease to be hereafter.

"As the Dweller in the body seeketh in the body childhood, youth, and old age, so passeth he on to another body; the well-balanced grieve not thereat....

"These bodies of the Embodied One, who is eternal, indestructible, and boundless, are known as finite. Therefore fight, O Bhârata.

"He who regardeth This (the Dweller in the body) as a slayer, and he who thinketh it is slain, both of them are ignorant. It slayeth not, nor is it slain....

"Who knoweth It indestructible, perpetual, unborn, undiminishing; how can that man slay, O Pârtha, or cause to be slain?

"As a man casting off worn-out garments, taketh new ones, so the

Dweller in the body, casting off worn-out bodies, entereth into others that are new.

"Weapons cleave It not, nor fire burneth It, nor waters wet It, nor wind drieth It away...."

"Further, looking upon thine own Dharma,[18] thou shouldst not tremble, for there is nothing more welcome to a Kshattriya than righteous war."

Here are other extracts of this wonderful teaching:

"Many births have been left behind by Me and by thee, O Arjuna. I know them all, but thou knowest not thine, Parantapa."

"He who thus knoweth My divine birth and action, in its essence, is not born again, having abandoned the body, but he cometh unto Me, O Arjuna."

"Having attained to the worlds of the pure-doing, and having dwelt there for eternal years, he who fell from Yoga is reborn in a pure and blessed house.... There he obtaineth the complete yogic wisdom belonging to his former body, and then again laboureth for perfection, O joy of the Kurus!"

"But the Yogî, verily, labouring with assiduity, purified from sin, fully perfected through manifold births, he treadeth the supreme Path.... He who cometh unto Me, O Kaunteya, verily he knoweth birth no more."

The daily life of Hindu and Buddhist is so entirely based on Reincarnation and on its foundation, the law of Causality, that this faith gives them patience in the present and hope for the future; for it teaches that man, every moment he lives, is subject to the circumstances he has created, and that, though bound by the past, he is yet master of the future.

Why cannot we, in this troubled Europe of ours, accept this belief as the solution of the distressing problem of the inequality of conditions, for to the weak in rebellion against oppression it would come as a soothing balm, whilst the strong would find in it a stimulus to devoted pity such as wealth owes to poverty and happiness to misfortune? Herein lies the solution of the whole social problem.

Egypt.

If we pass from India to Egypt, the land of mystery, we again find the world-wide doctrine of palingenesis hidden beneath the same veil.

According to Egyptian teaching, the theory of the "fall of the angels" was accepted; the fallen angels were human souls[19] who had to become reincarnated till they reached a state of purification; fallen into the flesh, subjected to its vicissitudes and passions, these souls had to evolve, in successive rebirths, until they had developed all their faculties, obtained complete control over the lower nature, and won back their original purity; then this latter would no longer be the unconscious purity of youthful innocence, but the conscious purity of mature age, *i.e.*, of the soul that has known both good and evil in the course of its experiences, has overcome the serpent of matter, the tempter, and voluntarily chosen the life of virtue.

The "Judgment" of the after-life is determined by the degree of purity that has been attained; if insufficient, the soul returns to earth, there to inhabit a human, an animal, or a vegetable form, in accordance with its merits or demerits.

These lines prove that Egyptian teaching has come down to us, covered with gross dross and slag, as it were, which must be subjected to careful sifting; when this is done, we see that it also sets forth the transmigrations to which the elements of the various vehicles are subjected,[20] the physical ternary[21] rises from the dead, the animal man[22] transmigrates; and man, properly so-called,[23] reincarnates, but the details of these processes have been so confused in such fragments of Egyptian palingenesis as we possess that it is no easy matter to find the traces of this classification.

For instance. Herodotus tells us:

"The Egyptians were the first to hold the opinion that the soul of man is immortal and that when the body dies it enters into the form of an animal which is born at the moment, thence, passing on from one animal into another until it has circled through the forms of all the creatures which tenant the earth, the water, and the air, after which it enters again into a human form and is born anew. The whole period of the transmigration is (they say) three thousand years."[24]

This passage evidently refers to the resurrection of the "life atoms." H. P. Blavatsky, in the *Theosophist*, vol. 4, pages 244, 286, confirms this in the following words:

"We are taught that for 3000 years, at least, the 'mummy,' notwithstanding all the chemical preparations, goes on throwing off to the last invisible atoms, which, from the hour of death, re-entering the various vortices of being, go indeed 'through every variety of organised life forms.' But it is not the soul, the fifth,[25] least of all, the sixth[26] principle, but the life atoms of the Jiva,[27] the second principle. At the end of the three thousand years, sometimes more, sometimes less, after endless transmigrations, all these atoms are once more drawn together, and are made to form the new outer clothing or the body of the same monad (the real soul) which they had already been clothed with two or three thousands of years before. Even in the worst case, that of the annihilation of the conscious personal principle,[28] the monad, or individual soul,[29] is ever the same, as are also the atoms of the lower principles,[30] which, regenerated and renewed in this ever-flowing river of being, are magnetically drawn together owing to their affinity and are once more reincarnated together...."

Certain authors have stated that belief in Resurrection was the origin of embalming, because it was thought that after three thousand years the soul returned to the same body, that it immediately rose again, when the body had been preserved, whereas if such had not been the case, it entered wherever it could, sometimes even into the body of a lower creature. Herodotus, however, says that after the cycle of three thousand years the soul enters a new body, not the mummified one,[31] and this would lead one to imagine that there were other reasons for the process of embalming. Indeed, it became general only during the decline of Egypt; at the beginning, it was reserved for the hierophants alone, with the object of allowing their physical molecular elements to pass into the still coarse bodies of the masses and help forward ordinary souls by the powerful influence of the magnetic potency with which they were charged. It is also for this reason that the body of a Yogî, in India, is interred, whilst in the case of other men cremation is the rule.

On the other hand, among the multitude of beliefs left in Egypt by degenerate traditions, there were found some which hinted, more or less clearly, at occult truths, and which might have perpetuated or generalised this practice. It was supposed, according to Servius, that the transmigrations[32] began only when the magnetic bond between the soul and its remains had been broken by the complete disintegration of the corpse; consequently they did all in their power to preserve this latter.

This belief may readily be connected with theosophic teaching which says that the affinity existing between the visible corpse and the soul clad in its kâmic (astral) body, the animal soul in Kâmaloka (Purgatory), is capable, in certain cases, of detaining this soul on earth, after its disincarnation, and thus delaying, for a longer or shorter period, the disintegration of the elements of the passional body. It is these elements, not the soul, that pass over into animal bodies, and, contrary to the opinions set forth in Egyptian exotericism, it is to the interest of the soul to free itself from terrestrial attraction and from its kâmic (astral) vehicle, and not to remain bound down to earth. Consequently, embalming was a mistaken action, the result of an error of doctrine, or at all events of teachings that were incomplete, imperfectly transmitted, and misunderstood.

Egypt multiplied her symbols of palingenesis. Resurrection—in the sense of re-birth in general—was symbolised by the toad which then became the goddess Hiquet. This animal was chosen because it lives in air and in water,[33] because it can remain imprisoned a very great number of years without either air or food[34] and afterwards come back to life. G. Maspero, in his *Guide du Visiteur au Musée de Boulac*, tells us that the early Christians in Egypt had adopted this symbolism, and that the lamps in their churches were formed in the shape of a toad, and bore the inscription, "I am the Resurrection," in the Greek language. This goddess-toad may still be seen in the museum of Boulac.

The Scarabeus, or beetle[35], symbolised the "personality," the expansion of the mental substance, projected, so to speak, by the higher mental body, at each incarnation, into the new kâmic (astral) body; a certain number of them were always deposited with the mummies, and the beetle was represented standing on an ear of corn, a symbol of the attainments acquired during the past earth life. Indeed, the development of the Ego is effected by that of the personality it sends on to the earth each incarnation; it is the new mental body which controls the new astral and physical bodies of each incarnation, and which is, in very truth, the flower and the fruit of the labour of life.

Sacred Egyptology tells us that the scarabeus requires to be "osirified," united to its "living soul," or Ego, which sent it forth. I will now give the reason for this emanation.

When, after disincarnation, the purgatorial life begins, the Ego endeavours to throw off the kâmic (astral) body, to pass into the higher world—the mental plane—which is its home, there to enjoy the delights of heaven. Thereupon a veritable battle begins. On the one hand, the Ego endeavours to withdraw the mental body, which, at the beginning of the incarnation, it sent into the kâmic body, and to take it to itself; on the other hand, the passional body[36]—which instinctively feels its life bound to that of the mental element, which gives it its strength, vital activity, and personal characteristics—tries to keep back this centre of individual life, and generally succeeds in doing so up to a certain point. When desire, during incarnation, has regularly gained the victory over the will, the passional body, or Kâma, maintains the supremacy beyond the grave, and the Ego, in endeavouring to rescue its mental projection from the kâmic bonds, yields up a more or less considerable fragment thereof, and this fragment is restored to liberty only when the passional body of the deceased has become disintegrated by the forces of the astral world. This has been called the *fire* of purgatory.

On the other hand, when the Ego, during life, has always refused the appeals of the lower nature, it easily withdraws, after death, from the net of passion, the substance it has infused therein, and passes with this substance into that part of the mental plane which is called "heaven."

Such is the struggle that Egypt committed to her annals when she inscribed upon papyrus or engraved upon stone the journeyings of the soul into the world of shades. The soul—the mental personality—which demands "osirification," and invokes the Ego, its god and projector, beseeching him to draw it to himself that it may live with him, is the lower "I." This "I" has not exhausted the "desire to live" on earth; its desire is impressed on the germs it has left in the causal body, and brings the Ego back to incarnation; this is the reason it prays and desires the resurrection[37] of its "living soul," the Ego. Denon, in his *Journeyings in Egypt*, has made known to us the Sha-En (the book of metamorphoses), written in hieratic signs and republished in Berlin, by Brugsch, in the year 1851. Explicit mention is here made of reincarnations, and it is stated that they are very numerous.

The third part of the *Book of the Dead* sets forth a detailed account of the resurrection of an Osiris; the identification of the departed one with Osiris, God of Light, and his sharing in the life, deeds, and power of the God; in a word, it is the final reintegration of the human soul with God.

The loftiest and most suggestive of Egyptian palingenetic symbols is unquestionably that of the egg. The deceased is "resplendent in the egg in the land of mysteries." In Kircher's *Œdipus Egyptiacus*[38] we have an egg—the Ego freed from its vehicles—floating over the mummy; this is the symbol of hope and the promise of a new birth to the soul, after gestation in the egg of immortality.[39]

The "winged globe," so widely known in Egypt, is egg-shaped, and has the same meaning; its wings indicate its divine nature and prevent it from being confused with the physical germ. "Easter eggs" which are offered in spring, at the rebirth of Nature, commemorate this ancient symbol of eternal Life in its successive phases of disincarnation and rebirth.

CHALDÆA.

It is said that the Magi taught the immortality of the soul and its reincarnations, but that they considerably limited the number of these latter, in the belief that purification was effected after a restricted number of existences on the soul returning to its heavenly abode.

Unfortunately we know nothing definite on this special point in Chaldæan teaching, for some of the most important sources of information were destroyed when the library of Persepolis was burnt by the Macedonian vandal, Alexander the Great, whilst Eusebius—whom Bunsen criticises so harshly[40]—made such great alterations in the manuscripts of Berosus, that we have nothing to proceed upon beyond a few disfigured fragments.[41] And yet Chaldæism comprises a great mass of teachings; he whom we know as "the divine Zoroaster" had been preceded by twelve others, and esoteric doctrine was as well known in Chaldæa as in Egypt.

The descendants of the Chaldæans—Fire-worshippers, Mazdeans, Magi, Parsees—according to the names they received at different periods —have preserved the main points of palingenetic instruction up to the present, and, from time to time, have set them forth in the most charming style of Oriental poetry. Book 4 of the great Persian poem, *Masnavi i Ma'navi*, deals with evolution and its corollary, reincarnation, stating that there is one way of remembering past existences, and that is by attaining to spiritual illumination, which is the crown of human evolution and brings the soul to the threshold of divinity.

"If your purified soul succeeds in escaping from the sea of ignorance, it will see, with eyes now opened, 'the beginning' and 'the end.' Man first appeared in the order of inorganic things; next, he passed therefrom into that of plants, for years he lived as one of the plants, remembering naught of his inorganic state, so different from this, and when he passed from the vegetable to the animal state he had no remembrance of his state as a plant.... Again the great Creator, as you know, drew man out of the animal into the human state. Thus man passed from one order of nature to another, till he became wise and intelligent and strong as he is now. Of his first soul he has now no remembrance, and he will be again changed from his present soul. In order to escape from his present soul, full of lusts, he must rise to a thousand higher degrees of intelligence.

"Though man fell asleep and forgot his previous states, yet God will not leave him in this self-forgetfulness; and then he will laugh at his own former state, saying: 'What mattered my experiences when asleep, when I had forgotten the real state of things, and knew not that the grief and ills I experienced were the effect of sleep and illusion and fancy?'"

These lines are concise, but they sum up the whole of evolution, and render it unnecessary to quote at greater length from Chaldæan tradition on this point. Still, those who desire other passages relating to the same doctrine may find them in the "Desatir."[42]

THE CELTS.

Sacerdotal India—and perhaps also Atlantis—in early times sent pioneers into the West to spread religious teachings amongst their energetic inhabitants; those who settled in Gaul and the British Isles were the Druids. "I am a serpent, a druid," they said. This sentence proves that they were priests, and also the Atlantæan or Indian origin of their doctrines; for the serpent was the symbol of initiation in the sacred mysteries of India, as also on the continent of Atlantis.

We know little of their teaching, which was entirely oral, though it covered so much ground that, according to Cæsar, not less than thirty years of study were needed to become a druid. The Roman conquest dispersed them by degrees; then it was that their disciples, the bards, committed to writing more or less imperfect and mutilated fragments of the teachings of their masters. Their "triads"[43] are undoubtedly akin to

Hindu teachings; Evolution results from the manifestation of the Absolute, it culminates in man, who possesses a maximum of individualisation, and terminates in the personal, conscious union of the beings thus created with the ineffable All.

The Absolute is "Ceugant"; manifestation, or the Universe, is "Abred"; the divine state of freed souls is in "Gwynvyd"; these are in the three circles.[44]

In "Ceugant" there is only the Unknowable, the rootless Root. Souls are born and develop in "Abred," passing into the different kingdoms; "Amwn" is the state through which beings pass only once, which means that the "I," when once gained, continues for ever. "Gwynvyd" is the world of perfect and liberated souls, eternal Heaven, great Nirvâna.

During this long pilgrimage, the Monad—the divine fragment in a state of incarnation—undergoes an endless number of rebirths, in myriads of bodies.

"I have been a viper in the lake," said Taliesin, the bard[45]; "a spotted adder on the mountain, a star, a priest. This was long, long ago; since then, I have slept in a hundred worlds, revolved in a hundred circles."

It was their faith in rebirth that gave the Gauls their indomitable courage and extraordinary contempt of death:

"One of their principal teachings," said Cæsar,[46] "is that the soul does not die, but passes at death into another body—and this they regard as very favourable for the encouragement of valour and for inculcating scorn of death."

Up to a few years ago, belief in the return of the soul to earth was still prevalent in those parts of Brittany in which civilisation had not yet exercised its sceptical, materialising influence; there even existed druids—probably degenerate ones—in Great Britain and France; in the Saône-et-Loire district, they seem to have been called the "Adepts of the White Religion"[47]; both in them and in their ancestors, belief in rebirth remained unshakable.

ANCIENT GREECE (MAGNA GRÆCIA).

In Greece, the doctrine of Rebirths is met with in the Orphic tradition, continued by Pythagoras and Plato. Up to the present time, this tradition has probably found its best interpreter in Mr. G. R. S. Mead, an eminent theosophist and a scholar of the first rank. We recommend our readers to study his *Orpheus*, if they desire a detailed account of this tradition.

Its origins are lost in antiquity, only a few obscure shreds remaining; Pherecydes, however,[48] when speaking of the immortality of the soul, refers to the doctrine of Rebirths; it is also presented very clearly by both Pythagoras and Plato.

According to the Pythagorean teaching, the human soul emanates from the Soul of the World, thus affirming, at the outset, the divine nature of the former. It teaches subsequently that this soul assumes successive bodies until it has fully evolved and completed the "Cycle of Necessity."[49]

Pythagoras, according to Diogenes of Laertius,[50] was the first in Greece to teach the doctrine of the return of souls to earth. He gave his disciples various details of his past lives; he appears to have been the initiate Œthalides, in the times of the Argonauts; then, almost immediately afterwards, Euphorbus, who was slain by Menelaus at the siege of Troy; again he was Hermotimus of Clazomenæ, who, in the temple of Juno at Argos,[51] recognised the shield he was carrying when his body was slain as Euphorbus, and which Menelaus had given as an offering to the goddess[52]; at a later date he was Pyrrhus, a fisherman of Delos, and, finally, Pythagoras.

In all likelihood this genealogy is not correct in every detail, it comes to us from the disciples of the sage of Samos, who were not very trustworthy in their reports.

Empedocles, one of the early disciples of Pythagoras, said that he inhabited a female body in his preceding existence. Saint Clement of Alexandria quotes a few lines of his, in which we find the philosopher of Agrigentum teaching the general evolution of forms.

"I, too, have been a boy, a maiden, a star, a bird, a mute fish in the depths of the sea."

Iarchas, the Brâhman chieftain, said to the great Apollonius:

"In bygone ages thou wert Ganga, the famous monarch, and, at a later date, captain of an Egyptian vessel."[53]

The Emperor Julian said that he had been Alexander the Great.[54] Proclus affirmed that he had been Nichomachus the Pythagorean.[55]

The works of Plato are full of the idea of rebirth, and if the scattered fragments of the teaching are gathered together and illumined with the torch of theosophy, a very satisfactory *ensemble* will be the result.

Souls are older than bodies, he says in *Phædo*; they are ever being born again from *Hades* and returning to life on earth; each man has his daimon,[56] who follows him throughout his existences, and at death takes him to the lower world[57] for Judgment.[58] Many souls enter Acheron[59], and, after a longer or shorter period, return to earth to be incarnated in new bodies. Unpardonable sins fling the soul into Tartarus.[60]

"Know that if you become worse you will go to the worse souls, or if better to the better, and in every succession of life and death you will do and suffer what like may fitly suffer at the hands of like...."[61]

According to Plato, the period between two incarnations is about a thousand years.[62] Man has reminiscences of his past lives that are more or less distinct; they are manifested rather by an intuitive impression than by a definite memory, but they form part of the individual[63], and at times influence him strongly. "Innate ideas" are only one aspect of memory, often it is impossible to explain them by heredity, education, or environment; they are attainments of the past, the store which the soul takes with it through its incarnations, which it adds to during each sojourn in heaven.

There can be no doubt that Plato would appear to have taught metempsychosis, *i.e.*, the possibility of a human soul passing into the body of an animal:

"Men who have followed after gluttony and wantonness and drunkenness, and have had no thought of avoiding them, would pass into asses and animals of that sort. And those who have chosen the portion of injustice and tyranny and violence will pass into wolves or hawks or kites, and there is no difficulty in assigning to all of them places according to their several natures and propensities."[64]

Under the heading of *Neoplatonism*, we shall show that, beneath these coarse symbols, Plato concealed truths which it was then necessary to keep profoundly secret; which, even nowadays, it is not permitted to reveal to all.

OLD TESTAMENT.

H. P. Blavatsky tells us that the *Old Testament* is not a homogeneous composition; that *Genesis* alone is of immense antiquity; that it is prior to the time when the Libra of the Zodiac was invented by the Greeks, for it has been noticed that the chapters containing the genealogies have been touched up so as to adapt them to the new zodiac, and this is the reason that the rabbis who compiled them twice repeated the names of Enoch and Lamech in the Cain list. The other parts seem to be of a comparatively recent date and to have been completed about 150 b.c.

The first part of the *Book of God*—as the Scriptures were then called—was written by Hilkiah, jointly with the prophetess Huldah; this disappeared at a later date, and Ezra had to begin a new one which was finished by Judas Maccabæus. This was recopied some time after, with the object of changing the pointed letters into square ones, and in this way was quite disfigured. The Masoretes ended by mutilating it completely. The result is that the text we now possess is one not more than nine hundred years old, bristling with premeditated omissions, interpolations, and perverted interpretations.[65]

By the side of this initial difficulty we find another, quite as important. Almost every page of the *Old Testament* contains veiled meanings and allegories, as is frankly confessed by the rabbis themselves.

"We ought not to take literally that which is written in the story of the Creation, nor entertain the same ideas of it as are held by the vulgar. If it were otherwise, our ancient sages would not have taken so much pains to conceal the sense, and to keep before the eyes of the uninstructed the veil of allegory which conceals the truth it contains...."[66]

Does not Saint Paul, speaking of the hidden meaning of the Bible, say that Agar is Mount Sinai?[67] Origen and Saint Augustine are of the opinion that the *Old Testament* must be regarded as symbolical, as otherwise it would be immoral; the Jewish law forbade anyone to read it who had not attained the age of thirty years; Fénelon would have liked it to be thrust away in the recesses of the most secret libraries; the Cardinal de Noailles says that Origen, so full of zeal on behalf of the Holy Scriptures, would not allow anyone to read the *Old Testament*, unless he were firmly anchored in the practice of a virtuous life; he affirms too that Saint Basilius, in a letter to Chilon, the monk, stated that the reading of it often had a harmful influence; for the same reasons, the *Index expurgatorius* forbids the publication of the Bible in the vulgar tongue, and orders that no one be allowed to read it without the written permission of his confessor.[68]

A third difficulty arises from the fact that the Old Testament—its dead "letter" and its commandments, at all events—is no longer suitable to our own race. It was intended for a nation that was composed of young souls, at a low stage of evolution, for whom nothing more than the rudiments of instruction were necessary, and on whom stern rules of morality, suitable for advanced souls, ought not to be imposed. This is why divorce[69], polygamy[70], slavery[71], retaliation, *lex talionis*[72], the blood of sacrifice[73] are instituted; it is the reason God is represented as a being to be dreaded, punishing those who do not obey him, wicked, jealous, bloodthirsty.[74] Bossuet understood all this when he said that the primitive Hebrew race was not sufficiently advanced to have the immortality of the soul taught to it. This, too, is the only explanation we can find for the sensual materialism of *Ecclesiastes*[75]. Consequently one need not be astonished to find that the Old Testament nowhere deals—directly, at all events—with the doctrine of Rebirth.

All the same, here and there we come across a few passages that point in this direction. For instance, we read in *Genesis*, chapter 25, regarding the birth of Jacob and Esau:

"And the children (of Rebecca) struggled together within her.

"And the Lord said unto her: Two nations are in thy womb, and two manner of people shall be separated from thy bowels, and the one people shall be stronger than the other people; and the elder shall serve the younger.

"And when her days to be delivered were fulfilled, behold there were twins in her womb."

This passage has been the occasion of lengthy commentaries on the part of certain Fathers of the Church—more especially of Origen. Indeed, either we must acknowledge divine injustice, creating, without any cause, two hostile brothers, one of whom must submit to the rule of the other, and who begin to strive together even before birth, or we must hark back to the pre-existence of the human soul and to a past Karma which had created inequality in condition.

David begins the ninetieth *Psalm* with a verse which only a belief in reincarnation can explain:

"Lord, thou hast been our dwelling-place in all generations...."

The dwelling-place of the soul, at death, is in heaven, whence it returns to earth when the hour of rebirth has struck; thus, in all generations, that is, from life to life, "the Lord is our dwelling-place."

In Chapter 8 of the *Book of Wisdom*, Solomon says in more explicit language:

"For I was a witty child, and had a good spirit, yea, rather, being good, I came into a body undefiled."

This clearly points to the pre-existence of the soul and the close relation that exists between the conditions of its rebirth and the merits or demerits of its past.

Verse 5 of the first chapter of *Jeremiah* is similar to verse 23 of the twenty-fifth chapter of *Genesis*:

"Before I formed thee in the belly I knew thee, and before thou camest forth out of the womb I sanctified thee, and I ordained thee a prophet unto the nations...."

It is the deeds done in the past lives of Jeremiah that accompany him on his return to earth; God could not, in an arbitrary fashion, have conferred on him the gift of prophecy had he not acquired it by his efforts in a past life; unless, here too, we altogether abandon reason and go back to a capricious or unjust—consequently altogether impossible—God.

THE KABALA.

Contact with the Babylonians, during the Captivity, brought about a rapid development in the Hebrews, who were at that time far more advanced souls than those that animated the bodies of their fathers,[76] and taught them many important details of religious instruction. It was then that they learned the doctrine of rebirth and that the Kabala came into being.[77]

In it the cycle of rebirths is called Gil'gool'em[78] or the "revolving of the Incorporeal" in search of the "promised land." This promised land, the Christian Paradise, or Buddhist Nirvâna, was symbolised by Palestine; the soul in its pilgrimage was brought to this abode of bliss,[79] and, according to the allegory, "the bodies of Hebrews buried in a foreign land contained an animistic principle which only found rest when, by the 'revolving of the Incorporeal,' the immortal fragment had returned to the promised land."[80]

There are other aspects from which this "revolution of souls" may be regarded. Certain Kabalists speak of it as a kind of purgatory in which, by means of this "revolving," the purging of the soul is brought about before it enters paradise.

In this connection, H. P. Blavatsky states that in the language of the Initiates the words "soul" (âme) and "atom" were synonyms, and were frequently used for each other. She says that the "revolution of souls" was in reality only the revolving of the atoms of the bodies which are continually transmigrating from one body to another throughout the various kingdoms of nature. From this point of view, it would seem that "Gil'gool'em" is more especially the cycle of atomic transmigration: *Resurrection*.

The doctrine of the reincarnation of the human soul, however, is clearly set forth in the *Zohar*:

"All souls are subjected to the tests of transmigration; men know not the designs of the Most High with regard to them; they know not how they are being at all times judged, both before coming into this world and when they leave it; they have no knowledge of the mysterious transformations and sufferings they must undergo, or how numerous are the spirits who coming; into this world never return to the palace of their divine King; they are ignorant of the revolutions to which they are subjected, revolutions similar to those of a stone when it is being hurled from a sling. And now the time has come when the veil shall be removed from all these mysteries.... Souls must in the end be plunged back into the substance from which they came. But before this happens, they must have developed all the perfections the germs of which are implanted within them; if these conditions are not realised in one existence, they must be born again until they reach the stage that makes possible their absorption in God."[81]

According to the Kabala, incarnations take place at long intervals; souls completely forget their past, and, far from being a punishment, rebirth is a blessing which enables men to develop and to attain to their final goal.

The Essenes taught reincarnation and the immortality of the soul. Ernst von Bunsen[82] speaking of this sect, says:

"Another marked peculiarity of the doctrine of the Essenes was the doctrine concerning the pre-existence of souls. They exist originally in the purest ether, which is their celestial home. By a natural attraction they are drawn towards the earth and are enclosed in human bodies, as in a prison. The death of the body causes the return of the soul to its heavenly abode. The Essenes can, therefore, not have believed in the resurrection of the body, but of the soul only, or, as Paul says, of the 'spiritual body.' This is positively asserted by Josephus."[83]

Rome.

Although Rome, above all else, was a warlike republic, and religion principally a State cult, that allowed but slight opportunity for the outer expression of spirituality, none the less did it inherit the beliefs of Egypt, Greece, and Persia; the Bacchic mysteries, previous to their degradation, were a copy of the Orphic and Eleusinian mysteries. In the reign of Pompey, Mithraism, a cult borrowed from Persia, was spread throughout the empire. Consequently, we need not be surprised at finding the doctrine of Rebirth mentioned by the great Latin writers.

We will quote only from Virgil and Ovid.

In the speech addressed by Anchises to Æneas, his son, the Trojan prince deals with the life beyond death, the tortures endured by souls in expiation of their misdeeds, their purification, their passing into Tartarus,[84] into the Elysian Fields[85], then their return to earth after having drunk of the river of forgetfulness. In Book VI. of the *Æneid*, we find Æneas visiting the lower regions:

"After having for a thousand years turned the wheel (of existence), these souls come forth in a mighty troop to the Lethean stream to which God calls them that they may lose the memory of the past, see the higher regions[86], and begin to wish to return into bodies."

Ovid, in his *Metamorphoses* also deals with the teaching of Pythagoras, his master, on the subject of palingenesis:

> *"Then Death, so-called, is but old matter drest*
> *In some new figure, and a varied vest;*
> *Thus all things are but alter'd, nothing dies,*
> *And here and there th' embodied spirit flies,*
> *By time, or force, or sickness dispossest,*
> *And lodges, when it lights, in man or beast.*
> *Th' immortal soul flies out in empty space*
> *To seek her fortune in some other place."*

New Testament.

The *New Testament* is far more explicit than the *Old*, even though we find the teachings of reincarnation indicated in only a vague, indirect fashion. All the same, it must not be forgotten that the canonical Gospels have suffered numerous suppressions and interpolations. On the other hand, there can be no doubt that the early Fathers of the Church made use of gospels that are now either lost or have become apocryphal.[87] It has been proved that neither Jesus nor his disciples wrote a single word, and that no version of the Gospels appeared earlier than the second century.[88] It was at that time that religious quarrels gave birth to hundreds of gospels, the writers of which signed them with the name of an apostle or even with that of Jesus, after forging them in more or less intelligent fashion.

Celsus, Jortin, Gibbons, and others have shown that Christianity is directly descended from Paganism; it was by combining the doctrines of Egypt, Persia, and Greece with the teachings of Jesus that the Christian doctrine was built up. Celsus silenced all the Christian doctors of his time by supplying evidence of this plagiarism; Origen, the most learned doctor of the age, was his opponent, but he was no more fortunate than the rest, and Celsus came off victorious. Thereupon recourse was had to the methods usual in those days; his books were burnt.

And yet it is evident that the author of the *Revelation* was a Kabalist; and the writer of the *Gospel of Saint John* a Gnostic or a Neoplatonist. The *Gospel of Nicodemus* is scarcely more than a copy of the *Descent of Hercules into the Infernal Regions*; the *Epistle to the Corinthians* is a distinct reminiscence of the initiatory Mysteries of Eleusis; and the Roman Ritual, according to H. P. Blavatsky, is the reproduction of the Kabalistic Ritual.

One gospel only was authentic, the secret or Hebrew *Gospel of Matthew*, which was used by the Nazareans, and at a later date by Saint Justin and the Ebionites. It contained the esoterism of the One-Religion, and Saint Jerome, who found this gospel in the library of Cæsarea about the end of the fourth century, says that he "received permission to translate it from the Nazareans of Berœa."

These considerations prove that interested and narrow-minded writers selected from the mass of existing traditions whatever seemed to them of a nature to support their spiritual views as well as their material interests, and that they constructed therefrom not only what has come down to us as the four canonical gospels, but also the whole edifice of Christian dogma.

Consequently, we need not be surprised to find in the *New Testament* only unimportant fragments dealing with reincarnation; but even these are not to be despised, for they prove that the doctrine was, to a certain extent at all events, known and accepted in Palestine.

Reincarnation in the Gospels.

Saint Mark, Chapter 6.
v. 14. And King Herod heard of him; and he said, That John the Baptist was risen from the dead....

v. 15. Others said, That it is Elias; and others said, That it is a prophet, or as one of the prophets.

v. 16. But when Herod heard thereof, he said, It is John whom I beheaded; he is risen from the dead.

Saint Matthew, Chapter 14.

v. 1. At that time, Herod the tetrarch heard of the fame of Jesus.

v. 2. And said unto his servants, This is John the Baptist; he is risen from the dead....

Saint Luke, Chapter 9.

v. 7. Now Herod the tetrarch heard of all that was done by him; and he was perplexed because it was said of some that John was risen from the dead.

v. 8. And of some, that Elias had appeared; and of others, that one of the old prophets was risen again.

v. 9. But Herod said, John have I beheaded; but who is this of whom I hear such things?

The account here given proves that the people as well as Herod believed in reincarnation, and that it applied, at all events, "to the prophets" and to those like them.

Saint Matthew, Chapter 16.

v. 13. When Jesus came into the coasts of Cæsarea Philippi, he asked his disciples, saying, Whom do men say that I, the Son of man, am?

v. 14. And they said, Some say that thou art John the Baptist; some, Elias; and others, Jeremias, or one of the prophets.

The same account is given in *Saint Luke*, chapter 9, verses 18, 19.

Saint Matthew, Chapter 17.

v. 12. But I say unto you, That Elias is come already, and they knew him not, but have done unto him whatsoever they listed. Likewise shall also the Son of man suffer of them.

v. 13. Then the disciples understood that he spake unto them of John the Baptist.

He continued in *Saint Matthew*, Chapter 11.

v. 7. Jesus began to say unto the multitudes concerning John, What went ye out into the wilderness to see? A reed shaken with the wind?

v. 8. But what went ye out for to see? A man clothed in soft raiment? Behold, they that wear soft clothing are in kings' houses.

v. 9. But what went ye out for to see? A prophet? Yea, I say unto you, and more than a prophet.

v. 14. And if ye will receive it, this is Elias which was for to come.

Here we have a distinct declaration: Reincarnation is a fact; John is the rebirth of Elias.[89]

Judging from these texts, one might be tempted to think that reincarnation was confined to the prophets or to people of importance, but Saint

John shows us that the Jews, though perhaps ignorant that it was a law of universal application, recognised, at any rate, that it might happen in the case of any man.

Saint John, Chapter 9.

v. 1. And as Jesus passed by, he saw a man which was blind from his birth.

v. 2. And his disciples asked him, saying: Master, who did sin, this man or his parents, that he was born blind?

v. 3. Jesus answered, Neither hath this man sinned nor his parents; but that the works of God should be made manifest in him.

Here we are dealing with a man *blind from birth*, and the Jews ask Jesus if he was blind because he sinned; this clearly indicates that they were referring to sins committed in the course of a former existence[90]; the thought is, therefore, quite a natural, straightforward one, referring to something well known to everyone and needing no explanation.

As one well acquainted with this doctrine of Rebirth, without combating it as an error or as something doubtful which his disciples ought not to believe, Jesus simply replies:

"Neither hath this man sinned nor his parents; but that the works of God should be made manifest in him."

And yet it appears as though this answer must have been distorted, as so many others have been, otherwise it would mean that the only reason for this man's blindness was the caprice of the Deity.

Reincarnation in the Apocalypse.

The *Apocalypse*, an esoteric book *par excellence*, confirms the doctrine of Reincarnation, and throws considerable light on it:

"Him that overcometh will I make a pillar in the temple of my God, and he shall go no more out...."[91]

In another verse it is stated that to him who overcometh "I will give the morning star."[92] In the language of theosophy, this means: He who has overcome the animal soul, shall, by mystic Communion, be united to the divine soul, which, in the *Apocalypse*, is the symbol of the Christ:

"I, Jesus, am the bright and morning star."[93]

Another verse clearly characterises the nature and the cost of victory:

"To him that overcometh will I give to eat of the hidden manna, and I will give him a *white stone*, and in the stone a new *name* written, which no man knoweth saving he that receiveth it."[94]

The hidden manna is the ambrosia of the Greeks, the *kyteon* of the mysteries of Eleusis, the *soma* of the Hindus, the eucharist of the Christians, the sacred drink offered to the disciples at Initiation, which had the

Moon as its symbol, conferred the gift of divine clairvoyance and separated the soul from the body.

The "white stone" is none other than the *alba petra*, the white cornelian, the chalcedony, or stone of Initiation. It was given to the candidate who had successfully passed through all the preliminary tests.[95] The "Word" written on the stone is the *sacred Word*, the "lost Word" which Swedenborg said was to be sought for amongst the hierophants of Tartary and Tibet, whom theosophists call the Masters.

"He who overcometh" is, therefore, the disciple ready for initiation; it is of him that "a pillar in the temple of God" will be made. In esoteric language, the column signifies Man redeemed, made divine and free, who is no longer to revolve on the wheel of Rebirths, who "shall no more go out," as the *Apocalypse* says, *i.e.*, shall not again leave Heaven.

If we examine the text of both *Old* and *New Testament* by the light of esoteric teaching, the dead letter, often absurd and at tunes repellent and immoral, would receive unexpected illumination, and would fully justify the words of the great rabbi, Maimonides, quoted a few pages back.[96]

Origen, the most learned of the Fathers of the Church, adds in his turn:

"If we had to limit ourselves to the letter, and understand after the fashion of the Jews or the people, what is written in the Law, I should be ashamed to proclaim aloud that it was God who gave us such laws; I should find more dignity and reason in human laws, as, for instance, in those of Athens, Rome, or Sparta...." (*Homil 7. in Levit.*)

Saint Jerome, in his *Epistle to Paulinus*, continues in similar fashion:

"Listen, brother, learn the path you must follow in studying the Holy Scriptures. Everything you read in the divine books is shining and light-giving without, but far sweeter is the heart thereof. He who would eat the nut must first break the shell."

It is because they have lost the Spirit of their Scriptures that the Christians—ever since their separation from the Gnostics—have offered the world nothing more than the outer shell of the World Religion.

Neoplatonism.

The great philosophic body that formed a bridge, as it were, between the Old World and the New was the famous School of Alexandria, founded about the second century of our era by Ammonius Saccas and closed in the year 429 a.d. through the intolerance of Justinian. Theosophical in its origin, this school had received from Plato the esoteric teaching of Egypt and the East, and the dogma of Rebirth was secretly taught in its entirety, though its meaning may have been travestied by the ignorance of the masses to whom only the grosser aspects of the teaching were given.

"It is a dogma recognised throughout antiquity," says Plotinus[97],"that the soul expiates its sins in the darkness of the infernal regions, and that afterwards it passes into new bodies, there to undergo new trials."

"When we have gone astray in multiplicity[98], we are first punished by our wandering away from the path, and afterwards by less favourable conditions, when we take on new bodies."[99]

"The gods are ever looking down upon us in this world, no reproach we bring against them can be justifiable, for their providence is never-ending; they allot to each individual his appropriate destiny, one that is in harmony with his past conduct, in conformity with his successive existences."[100]

The following is a quotation from the same philosopher, dealing with metempsychosis, and which, when compared with the foregoing sentences, appears strangely absurd. We make no comment here, as this obscure question will be dealt with a few pages farther on.

"Those who have exercised human faculties are reborn as men; those who have lived only the life of the senses pass into animals' bodies, especially into the bodies of wild beasts if they have given way to excesses of anger ... those who have sought only to satisfy their lust and gluttony, pass into the bodies of lascivious and gluttonous animals ... those who have allowed their senses to become atrophied, are sent to vegetate in trees ... those who have reigned tyranically become eagles, if they have no other vice."[101]

Porphyry says:

"The souls that are not destined for the tortures of hell (*Tartarus*), and those that have passed through this expiation, are born again, and divine Justice gives them a new body, in accordance with their merits and demerits."[102]

The following remarkable lines are from Iamblichus:

"What appears to us to be an accurate definition of justice does not also appear to be so to the Gods. For we, looking at that which is most brief, direct our attention to things present, and to this momentary life, and the manner in which it subsists. But the powers that are superior to us know the whole life of the Soul, and all its former lives; and, in consequence of this, if they inflict a certain punishment in obedience to the entreaties of those that invoke them, they do not inflict it without justice, but looking at the offences committed by souls in former lives: which men, not perceiving, think that they unjustly fall into the calamities which they suffer."[103]

Proclus gave out the same teaching; he affirmed that he had been incarnated in Nichomachus, the Pythagorean.

In his commentary on the *Golden Verses of Pythagoras*, Hierocles expresses himself thus:

"The ways of the Lord can be justified only by metempsychosis."[104]

Damascius and Hermias, as also their masters, proclaimed their belief in Rebirth.

Here a short explanation must be given of what has been said regarding transmigration or metempsychosis, in order that all misunderstanding may be removed.

Neither Pythagoras nor Plotinus nor any of the great Teachers of the past believed in metempsychosis, as it has been described; all their disciples have affirmed if, and these affirmations, set over against a line of teaching which seems to contradict them, because it is incomplete and intended for the less intelligent portion of society at that time, ought to have reminded its opponents that there might be hidden reasons capable of explaining the paradox.

We must first remember that a veil of strictest secrecy was flung over the noblest and most sublime spiritual teachings of the day. According to Bossuet, the teaching of the immortality of the soul seems not to have been deemed suitable for the Hebrew race, and, indeed, it is easy to understand that no double-edged truth should be taught except under conditions that would safeguard it. Ptolemy Philadelphus exiled Hegesias[105], whose eloquent fanaticism had caused some of his disciples to commit suicide, at Cyrene, after a lesson on immortality. Ptolemy ordered those schools of philosophy to be closed which continued teaching this doctrine, for in the case of a people insufficiently developed, the instinct which binds to physical life, and the dread of the torture that awaits guilty souls in the Hereafter, are preferable to doctrines of immortality deprived of the safeguards with which they should be surrounded.

The doctrine of Rebirths called for even stricter secrecy than that of immortality, and this secrecy was accorded it in ancient times; after the coming of the Christ, it grew less rigorous, and the Neoplatonists, though obliged to keep the esoteric teaching to themselves, were permitted to throw light on certain points.

Timæus of Locris, one of the masters of Plotinus, hinted at the existence of a more profound doctrine in the following words:

"Just as by the threat of punishment imperfectly evolved souls are prevented from sinning, so the transmigration of the souls of murderers into the bodies of wild beasts, and of the souls of unchaste persons into the bodies of swine, was taught; and the previous punishment of these souls in the infernal regions was entrusted to Nemesis (Karma)."

Certain modern commentators—though imperfectly instructed in the teachings of palingenesis—have also seen that the masters of philosophy in the past could not possibly have made a mistake which less far-seeing minds would have avoided. Dacier[106] says:

"A sure token that Pythagoras never held the opinion attributed to him lies in the fact that there is not the faintest trace of it in the symbols we have left of him, or in the precepts his disciple, Lysis, collected together and handed down as a summary of the master's teachings."

Jules Simon also speaks as follows regarding Plotinus[107]:

"Here we have the doctrine of metempsychosis which Plotinus found all around, among the Egyptians, the Jews, the Neoplatonists, his predecessors, and finally in Plato himself. Does Plato take metempsychosis seriously, as one would be tempted to believe after reading the *Republic*? Did he mention it only to ridicule the superstitions of his contemporaries, as seems evident from the *Timæus*?[108]

"However important Plato may have considered metempsychosis, it can scarcely be imagined that Plotinus took it seriously.... Even granting that this doctrine were literally accepted by Plotinus, the question would still have to be asked whether the human soul really does dwell in the body of an animal, or simply enters a human body, which, in its passions and vices, recalls the nature of that particular animal."

The reasons mentioned by Dacier and Jules Simon form only a trifling portion of the whole explanation, but if they are added to the constant protests raised by the disciples of the Masters of the Pythagorean and Platonic traditions, against those who said that their instructors taught metempsychosis in all its crudeness, they assume considerable importance, and show that, although the restrictions of esoteric teaching travestied by the ignorance of the masses may have caused it to be believed that the contrary was the case, none the less the Initiates, from the very beginning, denied that human transmigration into the bodies of animals ever took place.

On this question many of them have frequently said that it is the soul which, in such cases, changes its nature, and assumes the passions of animals into which, as is said exoterically, it transmigrates, though it does not enter into their bodies.

"He who believes that he transmigrates, after death, into the body of a beast or a plant," says Hierocles[109], "is grossly mistaken; he is ignorant of the fact that the essential form of the soul cannot change, that it is and it remains human, and only, metaphorically speaking, does virtue make of it a god, and vice an animal."

"A human soul," adds Hermes, "cannot go back into the body of an animal; it is preserved from such pollution, for all time, by the will of the gods."[110]

Mrs. Besant says as follows in a letter dealing with Theosophy and Reincarnation (*The Theosophist*, April, 1906):

"Even with the wealth of detail given in the Hindu Shâstras, thousands of facts of the invisible world are omitted, because their statement would hopelessly bewilder the public mind.

"If all the details are given, ere the main principles are grasped, hopeless confusion is caused to the beginner.

"When an Ego, a human soul, by vicious appetite or otherwise, forms a very strong link of attachment to any type of animal, the astral body (Kâmarûpa) of such a person shows the corresponding animal characteristics, and in the astral world, where thoughts and passions are visible as forms, may take the animal shapes; thus, after death, in *Pretaloka*, the soul would be embodied in an animal vesture, resembling or approximating to the animal whose qualities had been encouraged during earth-life. Either at this stage, or when the soul is returning towards reincarnation, and is again in the astral world, it may, in extreme cases, be linked by magnetic affinity to the astral body of the animal it has approached in character, and will then, through the animal's astral body, be chained as a prisoner to that animal's physical body. Thus chained, it cannot go onwards to *Svarga*, if the tie be set up while it is a *Preta*; nor go onwards to human birth, if it be descending towards physical life. It is truly undergoing penal servitude, chained to an animal; it is conscious in the astral world, has its human faculties, but it cannot control the brute body with which it is connected, nor express itself through that body on the physical plane. The animal organisation does not possess the mechanism needed by the human Ego for self-expression; it can serve as a jailor, not as a vehicle. Further, the "animal soul" is not ejected, but is the proper tenant and controller of its own body. S'rî Shankarâchârya hints very clearly at the difference between this penal imprisonment and becoming a stone, a tree, or an animal. Such an imprisonment is not "reincarnation," ... the human Ego "cannot reincarnate as an animal," cannot "become an animal."

"In cases where the Ego is not degraded enough for absolute imprisonment, but in which the astral body has become very animal, it may pass on normally to human re-birth, but the animal characteristic will be largely reproduced in the physical body—as witness the "monsters" who in face are sometimes repulsively animal, pig-faced, dog-faced, &c. Men, by yielding to the most bestial vices, entail on themselves penalties more terrible than they, for the most part, realise; for Nature's laws work on unbrokenly and bring to every man the harvest of the seed he sows. The suffering entailed on the conscious human entity, thus cut off from progress and from self-expression, is very great, and is, of course, reformatory in its action; it is somewhat similar to that endured by other Egos, who are linked to bodies human in form, but without normal brains—those we call idiots, lunatics, &c. Idiocy and lunacy are the results of vices different in kind from those that bring about the animal servitude above explained, but the Ego in these cases also is attached to a form through which he cannot express himself."

"True reason," says Proclus,[111] "affirms that the human soul may at times find lodgment in brutes, but that it is possible for it to live its own life and rise above the lower nature whilst bound to it by the similarity of its tendencies and desires. We have never meant anything else, as has often been proved by the reasoning in our commentaries on *Phædrus*."

There is a note in the *Vâhan*[112] on a passage from *Phædrus* which sheds all the light that can be shed on the question of metempsychosis; in the space of a few lines everything is said that may be publicly revealed, without trespassing on forbidden ground.

After stating that, on returning from the internal regions, the soul passes into the "life" of a beast, and that if it were human previously, it afterwards goes into another human body, the note continues:

"We must not understand by this that the soul of a man becomes the soul of a brute, but that by way of punishment it is bound to the soul of a brute, or carried in it, just as dæmons used to reside in our souls. Hence all the energies of the rational soul are absolutely impeded, and its intellectual eye beholds nothing but the dark and tumultuous phantasms of a brutal life."[113]

This passage contains the explanation of what might be called the metempsychosis of certain human souls at the present time; we once heard a great Teacher fully reveal this mystery to a chosen group of Hindus, but it must for some time to come remain a mystery to the western world. All that can be said on the matter is that it has nothing to do with the incarnation of a human soul in the body of an animal, but rather with a certain temporary karmic bond, in the life Hereafter, between a human soul and an animal one, a bond intended to teach many a hard lesson to the one who has brought upon himself so unpleasant an experience.

Metempsychosis included many other facts in human evolution, facts that were plainly taught to the disciples in the "inner circles" of the ancient Schools and passed out to the confused medley of public teaching.

The astral body, for instance, of a man of an exceedingly passionate nature, when the soul leaves the physical body, sometimes assumes forms resembling those of the animals which represent these passions on the physical plane, and so the disincarnate soul of an assassin has been said to pass into the body of a wild beast.

Metempsychosis, properly so-called, that is to say, the passing of a human soul into the body of a brute, did however exist during the infancy of the human race, when highly developed animal souls were becoming fit to enter the human kingdom. The bodies of these newly-born human souls were coarse and rudimentary in their nature, showing scarcely any difference in form and organic function from the bodies of the higher animals of that period, for these instruments were very similar to one another. The improvements subsequently effected by human bodies did not then exist; the difference, or distinction, which has now widened into a gulf, was scarcely perceptible, and in the early incarnations of these rudimentary human souls back-slidings and falls were so frequent that some of them, thus enfeebled, might find it to their advantage[114] to become incarnate, at times, in highly-developed animal bodies. But that was always an exception, and the exception has long ago become an impossibility.

We think these explanations, along with those given in other portions of this work, will throw as much light as is permitted publicly on the subject of metempsychosis—a subject frequently discussed and one that has hitherto been so obscure. Such illumination as is here given is due to the teachings of theosophy.

The Early Christian Church.

The documents to which we have access, dealing with the philosophical and religious history of Christianity in the first few centuries of our era, are so questionable, that we can place but faint reliance upon them, if we would really become acquainted with the thought of that period. We have already seen that the number of spurious or counterfeit productions was so great that a strange kind of sorting out, or selection, took place at the first Council of Nicæa, resulting in the choice of four so-called canonical Gospels. It is evident, too, that the copyists, compilers, and translators of the period were anxious, above all else, to make facts and opinions agree with their preconceived ideas and personal sympathies or likings. Each author worked *pro domo sua*, emphasising whatever fitted in with his personal views and carefully concealing what was calculated to weaken them; so that at the present time the only clues we have to guide us out of the labyrinth consist of the brief opinions expressed by a few historians, here and there, on whose honesty reliance may be placed.

In the present chapter, for instance, it is no easy matter to unravel the Truth from out of these tangled threads of personal opinions. Some believe that the early Christians and the Fathers of the Church were reincarnationists; others say they were not; the texts, we are in possession of, contradict one another. Thus, whereas Saint Jerome brings against Origen the reproach of having in his book *De Principiis* taught that, in certain cases, the transmigration of human souls into the bodies of animals, was possible —as, indeed, seems to be the case—certain writers deny that he ever said anything on the subject. These contradictory affirmations are easy to explain, once we know that Ruffinus, when translating into Latin the Greek text of *De Principiis*, omitted all that referred to this question, that the conspiracy of silence might be preserved on the matter of Origenian transmigration.

At the close of his article "*Origen on Reincarnation,*" in the *Theosophical*

Review, February, 1906, G. R. S. Mead says:

"It therefore follows that those who have claimed Origen as a believer in reincarnation—and many have done so, confounding reincarnation with pre-existence—have been mistaken. Origen himself answers in no uncertain tones, and stigmatises the belief as a false doctrine, utterly opposed to Scripture and the teaching of the Church."

Others affirm that Saint Justin Martyr believed in rebirths and even in the transmigration of human souls into animal bodies. In his book *Against Heresies*, volume 2, chapter 33, the *Absurdity of the Doctrine of the Transmigration of Souls* is dealt with; and in the following chapter, the pre-existence of the soul is denied! Is this another instance, like the one just mentioned, of tampering with the writings of this Father of the Church?[115]

At times an author gives two contradictory opinions on the same subject. In Tertullian's *Apology for the Christians*, for instance, we find the following:

"If you can find it reasonable to believe the transmigration of human souls from body to body, why should you think it incredible for the soul to return to the substance it first inhabited?[116] For this is our notion of a resurrection, to be that again after death which we were before, for according to the Pythagorean doctrine these souls now are not the same they were, because they cannot be what they were not without ceasing to be what they were.... I think it of more consequence to establish this doctrine of the resurrection; and we propose it as more consonant with reason and the dignity of human nature to believe that man will be remade man, each person the person he was, a human being a human being; in other words, that the soul shall be habited with the same qualities it was invested with in its former union, though the man may receive some alteration in his form.... The light which daily departs rises again with its original splendour, and darkness succeeds by equal turns; the stars which leave the world, revive; the seasons, when they have finished their course, renew it again; the fruits are consumed and bloom afresh; and that which we sow is not quickened except it die, and by that dissolution rises more fruitful. Thus you see how all things are renewed by corruption and reformed by dying.... How, then, could you imagine that man, the lord of all these dying and reviving things, should himself die for ever?"

After such a clear and noble profession of faith, we may well wonder if it were the same man who, in *De Anima*, could have both refuted and pitilessly ridiculed the idea of rebirth, and denied the separation of the soul from the body as well as the influence of the former upon the latter. We prefer to believe that we are dealing with two writers, or else that some literary forger, anxious to create a diversion, deliberately made Tertullian responsible for this strange contradiction.

Another reason for the difficulty in unravelling the tangled skein of the religious and philosophical teachings prevalent in the early centuries of Christianity is the lack of precision in the language of the writers, the loss of the key to the special vocabulary they used, and the veils which writers who possessed some degree of initiation, deliberately threw over teachings which could only be given to the masses in general terms.

There is one very important point to consider; and this is that in the earlier centuries, outside the circles of initiation, there was not that precision which the present-day teaching of theosophy has given to the doctrine of Reincarnation; this latter, in the mind of the people, became confused with the doctrine of Pre-existence, which affirms that the soul exists before coming into the present body, and will exist in other bodies after leaving this one. This confusion has continued up to the present time, and we find schools of spiritualism in England and America, as well as in other countries, teaching that existence on earth has been preceded and will be followed by a great number of existences on the invisible planes.

In reality, this is the doctrine of Rebirths, though there is nothing precise about the teaching. Whether the soul has a single physical body, or takes several in succession, it is none the less continually evolving as it passes into material vehicles, however subtle the matter be; the difference is, therefore, insignificant, unless we wish to enter into details of the process involved, as was the case in the West in the early centuries of Christianity.

Did the Fathers of the Church teach Pre-existence? There can be no doubt on this point. In a letter to St. Anastasius, Rufinus said that "this belief was common amongst the early Christian fathers." Arnobius[117] shows his sympathy with this teaching, and adds that St. Clement, of Alexandria, "wrote wonderful accounts of metempsychosis"; and afterwards, in other passages of the same book, he appears to criticise the idea of the plurality of lives. St. Jerome affirms that "the doctrine of transmigration has been secretly taught from ancient times to small numbers of people, as a traditional truth which was not to be divulged."[118] A. Franck quotes this passage on page 184 of his *Kabbale*; Huet, too, gives it in *Origeniana*.[119] The same Father proves himself to be a believer in Pre-existence, in his 94th *Letter to Avitus*, where he agrees with Origen on the subject of the interpretation of a passage from St. Paul,[120] and says that this means "that a divine abode and true repose are to be found in Heaven," and "that there dwell creatures endowed with reason in a state of bliss, before coming down to our visible world, before they fall into the grosser bodies of earth...."

Lactantius, whom St. Jerome called the Christian Cicero, though he opposed pagan doctrines, maintained that the soul was capable of immortality and of bodily survival only on the hypothesis that it existed before the body.[121]

Nemesius, Bishop of Emissa in Syria, stoutly affirmed the doctrine of Pre-existence, declaring that every Greek who believed in immortality believed also in the pre-existence of the soul. St. Augustine said: "Did I not live in another body, or somewhere else, before entering my mother's womb?"[122]

In his *Treatise, on Dreams*, Synesius states that "philosophy assures us that our past lives are a direct preparation for future lives...." When invited by the citizens of Ptolemais to become their bishop, he at once refused, saying that "he cherished certain opinions of which they might not approve, as, after mature reflection, they had struck deep root in his mind. Foremost among these, he mentioned the doctrine of Pre-existence."

Dr. Henry More, the famous Platonist of the seventeenth century, quotes Synesius as one of the masters who taught this doctrine[123], and Beausobre reports a typical phrase of his[124], "Father, grant that my soul may merge into Light and be no more thrust back into the illusion of earth."

St. Gregory of Nysa says it is absolutely necessary that the soul should be healed and purified, and if this does not take place during its life on earth, it must be accomplished in future lives.

St. Clement of Alexandria says that, although man was created after other beings, "the human species is more ancient than all these things."[125] In his *Exhortations to the Pagans*, he adds:

"We were in being long before the foundation of the world; we existed in the eye of God, for it is our destiny to live in him. We are the reasonable creatures of the divine Word; therefore, we have existed from the beginning, for in the beginning was the Word.... Not for the first time does He show pity on us in out wanderings. He pitied us from the very beginning."

He also adds : "Philolaus, the Pythagorean, taught that the soul was flung into the body as a punishment for the misdeeds it had committed, and his opinion was confirmed by the most ancient of the prophets."

As regards Reincarnation, *i.e.*, the descent of the human soul into successive physical bodies, and even its temporary association with the physical bodies of animals, more than one Christian writer advocated this teaching.

Chalcidius, quoted by Beausobre in the book just mentioned, says:

"The souls, that are not able to unite with God, are destined to return to life until they repent of their misdeeds."

In the *Pistis Sophia*, a Christian treatise on the mysteries of the divine Hierarchies and the evolution of souls in the three worlds, we find the doctrine of Rebirth frequently mentioned:

"If he is a man who (after passing out of his body)[126] shall have come to the end of his cycles of transmigrations, without repenting, ... he is cast into outer darkness."

A few pages earlier, in the same work, we find:

"The disincarnate soul which has not solved the mystery of the breaking of the bonds and of the seals is brought before the virgin of light, who, after judging it, hands it over to her agents (*receivers*), who carry it into a new body."

Let us now see what Origen says on the matter[127]:

"Celsus, then, is altogether ignorant of the purpose of our writings, and it is therefore upon his own acceptation of them that he casts discredit and not upon their real meaning; whereas if he had reflected on what is appropriate[128] to a soul which is to enjoy an everlasting life, and on the idea which we are to form of its essence and principles, he would not so have ridiculed the entrance of the immortal into a mortal body, which took place, not according to the metempsychosis of Plato, but agreeably to another and higher order of things."

The teaching of Origen is not easy to set forth clearly, for he is very reticent about many things, and employs a language to which present-day philosophy cannot always find the key; still, the teaching seems full and complete. It comprises pre-existence and even those special associations of certain human souls with animal souls, which we have just spoken of and which form one of the chief mysteries of metempsychosis.

In the following words he explains the existence of souls in previous worlds:

"The soul has neither beginning nor end....

"Rational creatures existed undoubtedly from the very beginning in those (ages) which are invisible and eternal. And if this is so, then there has been a descent from a higher to a lower condition on the part not only of those souls who have deserved the change, by the variety of their movements, but also on that of those who, in order to serve the whole world, were brought down from those higher and invisible spheres to these lower and visible ones, although against their will. 'For the creature was made subject to vanity, not willingly, but by reason of him who hath subjected the same in hope' (*Rom.*, chap. 8, v. 20); so that both sun and moon and stars and angels might discharge their duly to the world, and to those souls who, on account of their excessive mental defects, stood in need of bodies of a grosser and more solid nature; and for the sake of those for whom this arrangement was necessary, this visible world was also called into being.

"This arrangement of things, then, which God afterwards appointed not being understood by some, who failed to perceive that it was owing to preceding causes originating in free will, that this variety of arrangement had been instituted by God, they have concluded that all things in this world are directed either by fortuitous movements or by a necessary fate, and that nothing is in the power of our own will."[129]

"Is it not rational that souls should be introduced into bodies, in accordance with their merits and previous deeds, and that those who have used their bodies in doing the utmost possible good should have a right to bodies endowed with qualities superior to the bodies of others?"[130]

All souls will arrive at the same goal[131]; it is the will of souls that makes of them angels, men or demons, and their fall can be of such a nature that they may be chained down to the bodies of animals.[132] Certain souls, on attaining to perfect peace, return to new worlds; some remain faithful, others degenerate to such a degree that they become demons.[133] Concerning bodies, he says:

"The soul, which is immaterial and invisible in its nature, exists in no material place, without having a body suited to the nature of that place; accordingly, it at one time puts off one body which was necessary before, but which is no longer adequate in its changed state, and it exchanges it for a second."[134]

Although *metensomatosis* (re-embodiment of the soul), *i.e.*, the true teaching of Origen, was not clearly expounded, it considerably influenced the early Christian philosophers, and was favourably received up to the time of its condemnation by the Synod of Constantinople. It appeared in most of the sects of that time and in those of the following centuries: Simonians, Basilidians, Valentinians, Marcionites, Gnostics, Manichæans, Priscillianites, Cathari, Patarins, Albigenses, Bogomiles, &c....

Chivalry, too, in these ages of darkness and persecution, was an instrument for the dissemination of esoteric doctrines, including Reincarnation. The heart of this noble institution consisted of students of divine Wisdom, pure devoted souls who communicated with one another by means of passwords.

The Troubadours were their messengers of the sacred Teaching, which they skilfully concealed in their songs, carrying it from group to group, from sect to sect, in their wanderings. "Sons of the teachings of the Albigenses and of the Manichæan-Marcion tradition"[135] they kept alive belief in the rebirths of the soul, "Izarn the Monk," in his book *Historie d' un Hérétique*[136], apostrophised an Albigensian bishop in the following terms:

"Tell me what school it was in which you learnt that the spirit of man, after losing his body, passes into an ox, an ass, a sheep, or a fowl, and transmigrates from one animal to another, until a new human body is born for it?"

Izarn was acquainted with only so much of the teachings of the Troubadours as had got abroad and been distorted and misrepresented by ignorant or evil-minded persons; still, his criticism plainly shows traces of the teachings of palingenesis in the darkest and most blood-stained periods of the Middle Ages.

The Inquisition put an end to the Troubadours, though certain of them,

Dante and St. Francis of Assisi, for instance, by reason of their popularity or the special circumstances of the case, were left in peace. In Europe the secret teaching was continued by the Rosicrucians; the *Roman de la Rose* is pure Hermetic esotericism. The struggle of official Christianity—that of the letter—against those who represented the spirit of the Scriptures, raged ever more bitterly, and the idea of Rebirth disappeared more and more from the Church; its sole representatives during the Middle Ages were St. Francis of Assisi, the learned Irish monk, Johannes Scotus Erigena, and St. Bonaventura, "the Seraphic Doctor." At the present time there remains nothing more than a disfigured and misunderstood fragment of this idea: the dogma of the *Resurrection of the Body*.

ISLAMISM.[137]

It has been said that the Arabs believed in Reincarnation before Mohammed forbade it. Some, however, think that the Koran was written only after the death of the Prophet, and that the latter committed nothing to writing, but taught by word of mouth. Besides, it is clear that Mohammedanism is an offshoot of Zoroastrianism and Christianity. Like these, it teaches the Unity of the Whole, the divine Presence in all creatures and things (*Ubiquity*), Predestination, which is only one form of *Karma*, and Resurrection, which expresses one phase of Palingenesis.

Mohammed, like all great mystics, had discovered or learnt many of the truths of esotericism. The verses of the Koran that refer to the "Companions of the Cave"[138] indicate that he knew more than he taught in public, and that there may be some ground for certain Asiatic nations holding the exaggerated belief that he was an *Avâtâr*[139], the tenth incarnation of the *Aum*—the Amed, the Nations' Desire.[140] He was a Disciple.

Had there not been in the heart of Islamism a strong germ of esoteric teaching, Sufism could never have sprung from it. The Sufis are the saints of Mohammedanism, they are those who aspire after the union of the individual "I" with the cosmic "I," of man with God; they are frequently endowed with wonderful powers, and their chiefs have almost always been thaumaturgists.

The *New Koran*, a modern exposition of part of the secret doctrine of Islam, shows the correctness of this view. In it we find the following passages on the subject of Palingenesis:

"And when his body falleth off altogether, as an old fish-shell, his soul doeth welt by the releasing, and formeth a new one instead.

"The disembodied spirits of man and beast return as the clouds to renew the young streamlets of infancy....

"When a man dieth or leaveth his body, he wendeth through the gate of oblivion and goeth to God, and when he is born again he cometh from God and in a new body maketh his dwelling; hence is this saying:

"The body to the tomb and the spirit to the womb....

"This doctrine is none other than what God hath taught openly from the very beginning....

"For truly the soul of a man goeth not to the body of a beast, as some say....

"But the soul of the lower beast goeth to the body of the higher, and the soul of the higher beast to the body of the savage, and the soul of the savage to the man....

"And so a man shall be immortal in one body and one garment that neither can fade nor decay.

"Ye who now lament to go out of this body, wept also when ye were born into it...."[141]

"The person of man is only a mask which the soul putteth on for a season; it weareth its proper time and then is cast off, and another is worn in its stead....

"I tell you, of a truth, that the spirits which now have affinity shall be kindred together, although they all meet in new persons and names."[142]

In *Asiatic Researches*, Colebrooke states that the present Mohammedan sect of the *Bohrahs* believes in metempsychosis, as do the Hindus, and, like the latter, abstains from flesh, for the same reason.

Thus we find the doctrine of Reincarnation at the heart of all the great religions of antiquity. The reason it has remained in a germinal state in recent religions—Christianity and Islamism—is that in the latter Mohammed did not attain to the degree of a Hierophant, and in all likelihood the race to which he brought light did not greatly need to become acquainted with the law relating to the return to earth life; whereas in the former the real teachings of the Christ were lost when the Gnostics were exterminated, and Eusebius and Irenæus, the founders of exoteric Christianity, unable to grasp the *spirit*, imposed the *letter* throughout the religion.

THE DOCTRINE OF REBIRTH IN MODERN PHILOSOPHY.

In antiquity, science and philosophy were scarcely anything else than parts of religion[143]; the most eminent scientists and the greatest philosophers alike were all supporters of the established form of religion, whenever they did not happen to be its priests, for the temples were the common cradle of science and philosophy. No wonder, then, that we find these three great aspects of Truth always hand in hand, never opposed to or in conflict with one another through the whole of antiquity. Science was for the body, philosophy for the intellect, and religion for that divine spark which is destined to flash forth and finally become a "god" in the bosom of the World Soul. Every intelligent man knew that on this tripod lay the life of the individual, the life of society, and the life of the world. Divorce between these took place only at a later date, when the divine Teachers had disappeared, and mutilated traditions handed down to the nations nothing but disfigured and incomplete teachings buried beneath the ruins of temples that had been crumbling away ever since spiritual Life had left them.

Then followed the era of separation; science and philosophy became debased and went their own ways, whilst a degenerate religion reflected nothing higher than the narrow mentality of fallen ministers. As this degradation continued, there sprang into being religious wars, monstrosities that were unknown in those times when Divinity shed illumination and guidance on the nations by means of those mighty souls, the Adept-Kings: gods, demi-gods, and heroes.

Nevertheless, Truth never remained without her guardians, and when apostleship had been destroyed by persecutions the sacred treasure which was to be handed down from age to age was secretly entrusted by the sages to faithful disciples. Thus did Esoterism pass through fire and bloodshed, and one of its greatest teachings, the doctrine of Palingenesis, has left a stream of light in its wake. Now we will give a rapid sketch of it in modern times, examining the philosophical teachings of the greatest of recent thinkers. We will borrow mainly from Walker's work on this subject, quoting only the writers most deserving of mention, and making only short extracts, for all that is needed is to plant a few sign-posts to guide the student along the path.

In the 128th verse of *Lalla Rookh*, Thomas Moore speaks of rebirths:

> *"Stranger, though new the frame*
> *Thy soul inhabits now, I've traced its flame*
> *For many an age, in every chance and change*
> *Of that Existence, through whose varied range,—*
> *As through a torch-race, where, from hand to hand*
> *The flying youths transmit their shining brand,—*
> *From frame to frame the unextinguished soul*
> *Rapidly passes, till it reach the goal!"*

Paracelsus, like every Initiate, was acquainted with it, and Jacob Böhme, the "nursling of the Nirmânakâyas,"[144] knew that it was a law of Nature.

Giordano Bruno—also a great Soul—quotes from Ovid's *Metamorphoses*, Book 15, Line 156, &c., as follows:

> "O mortals! chilled by dreams of icy death,
> Whom air-blown bubbles of a poet's breath,
> Darkness and Styx in error's gulph have hurl'd,
> With fabled terrors of a fabled world;
> Think not, whene'er material forms expire,
> Consumed by wasting age or funeral fire,
> Aught else can die: souls, spurning death's decay,
> Freed from their old, new tenements of clay
> Forthwith assume, and wake to life again.
> . . . All is change,
> Nought perishes" . . .[145]

Campanella, the Dominican monk, was sent into exile on account of his belief in the successive returns of the soul to earth.

The Younger Helmont, in his turn, was attacked by the inquisition for leaching this doctrine in his *De Revolutione Animarum*, in which he brings forward, in two hundred problems, all the arguments; that make reincarnation necessary.

Cudworth and Dr. Henry More, the Platonists of Cambridge, were faithful believers in Palingenesis; whilst Joseph Glanvill, in *Lux Orientalis*, finds that there are "Seven Pillars" on which Pre-existence rests.

Dr. Edward Beecher, in *The Conflict of Ages* and *The Concord of Ages*, as well as Julius Muller, the well-known German theologian, in *The Christian Doctrine of Sin*, warmly uphold it.

Schelling acknowledges it in his *Dissertation on Metempsychosis*.

Leibnitz, in his *Monadology*, and more especially his *Theodicy*, witnessed to his belief in this doctrine. Had he dared to speak out his thoughts openly, he would more effectively have advocated his "Optimism," by the teachings of evolution and rebirths, than by all the other arguments he advanced.

Chevalier Ramsey, in *The Philosophical Principles of Natural and Revealed Religion*, writes:

"The holy oracles always represent Paradise as our native country, and our present life as an exile. How can we be said to have been banished from a place in which we never were? This argument alone would suffice to convince us of pre-existence, if the prejudice of infancy inspired by the schoolmen had not accustomed us to look upon these expressions as metaphorical, and to believe, contrary to Scripture and reason, that we were exiled from a happy state, only for the fault and personal disobedience of our first parents....

"Our Saviour seems to approve the doctrine of pre-existence in his answer to the disciples, when they interrogate him thus about the man born blind,[146] 'Master, who did sin, this man or his parents, that he was born blind?' It is clear that this question would have been ridiculous and impertinent if the disciples had not believed that the man born blind had sinned before his corporal birth, and consequently that he had existed in another state long ere he was born on earth. Our Saviour's answer is remarkable, 'Neither hath this man sinned nor his parents, but that the works of God might be manifested in him.' Jesus Christ could not mean that neither this man nor his parents had ever committed any sin, for this can be said of no mortal; but the meaning is that it was neither for the sins committed by this man in a state of pre-existence, nor for those of his parents, that he was born blind; but that he was deprived of sight from his birth, by a particular dispensation of Providence, in order to manifest, one day, the power of God in our Saviour. Our Lord, therefore, far from blaming and redressing this error in his disciples, as he did those concerning his temporal kingdom, answers in a way that seems to suppose with them, and confirm them in the doctrine of pre-existence. If he had looked upon this opinion as a capital error, would it have been consonant or compatible with his eternal wisdom to have passed it over so lightly and thus tacitly authorised it by such silence? On the contrary, does not his silence manifestly indicate that he looked upon this doctrine, which was a received maxim of the Jewish Church, as the true explanation of original sin?

"Since God says that he loved Jacob and detested Esau ere they were born, and before they had done good or evil in this mortal life, since God's love and hatred depend upon the moral dispositions of the creature, ... it follows clearly that if God hated Esau, type of the reprobate, and loved Jacob, type of the elect, before their natural birth, they must have pre-existed in another state.

"If it be said that all these texts are obscure, that pre-existence is largely drawn from them by induction, and that this belief is not revealed in Scripture by express words, I answer that the doctrines of the immortality of the soul are nowhere revealed, least of all in the oracles of the *Old* and *New Testament*. We may say the same of pre-existence. This doctrine is nowhere expressly revealed as an article of faith, but it is evidently implied in the *Wisdom of Solomon*, by the author of *Ecclesiasticus*, by our Saviour's silence, by St. Paul's comparisons, and by the sacred doctrine of original sin, which becomes not only inexplicable, but absurd, repugnant, and impossible, if that of pre-existence be not true.... The Fifth General Council held at Constantinople pronounces anathema against all those who maintain the fabulous doctrine of pre-existence in the Origenian sense. It was not then the simple doctrine of pre-existence that was condemned by the council, but the fictitious mixtures and erroneous disguises by which this ancient tradition had been adulterated by the Origenites."

Soame Jenyns writes:

"That mankind had existed in some state previous to the present was the opinion of the wisest sages of the most remote antiquity. It was held by the Gymnosophists of Egypt, the Brâhmans of India, the Magi of Persia, and the greatest philosophers of Greece and Rome; it was likewise adopted by the *Fathers of the Christian Church, and frequently enforced by her early writers*; why it has been so little noticed, so much overlooked rather than rejected, by the divines and metaphysicians of latter ages, I am at a loss to account for, as it is undoubtedly confirmed by reason, by all the appearances of nature and the doctrines of revelation.

"In the first place, then, it is confirmed by reason, which teaches us that it is impossible that the conjunction of a male and female can create an immortal soul; they may prepare a material habitation for it; but there cannot be an immortal, pre-existent inhabitant ready to take possession. Reason assures us that an immortal soul, which will exist eternally after the dissolution of the body, must have eternally existed before the formation of it; *for whatever has no end can never have had any beginning*....

"Reason likewise tells us that an omnipotent and benevolent Creator would never have formed such a world as this, and filled it with such inhabitants if the present was the only, or even the first, state of their existence; for this state which, if unconnected with the past and the future, would seem calculated for no purpose intelligible to our understanding, neither of good or evil, of happiness or misery, of virtue or vice, of reward or punishment; but a confused jumble of them all together, proceeding from no visible cause and tending to no end....

"Pre-existence, although perhaps it is nowhere in the *New Testament* explicitly enforced, yet throughout the whole tenour of these writings is everywhere implied; in them, mankind is constantly represented as coming into the world under a load of guilt; as condemned criminals, the children of wrath and objects of divine indignation; placed in it for a time by the mercies of God to give them an opportunity of expiating this guilt by sufferings, and regaining, by a pious and virtuous conduct, their lost state of happiness and innocence....

"Now if by all this a pre-existent state is not constantly supposed, that is, that mankind has existed in some state previous to the present, in which this guilt was incurred, and this depravity contracted, there can be no meaning at all or such a meaning as contradicts every principle of common sense, that guilt can be contracted without acting, or that we can act without existing...."

The following is a quotation from Hume, the great positivist philosopher:

"Reasoning from the common course of nature, what is incorruptible must also be ingenerable. The soul, therefore, if immortal, existed before our birth, and if the former existence in noway concerned us, neither will the latter.... Metempsychosis is, therefore, the only system of this kind that philosophy can hearken to." (*The Immortality of the Soul*.)

Young, in his *Night Thoughts* (Night the Sixth), has the following lines:

> "Look nature through, 'tis revolution all;
> All change, no death. Day follows night; and night
> The dying day; stars rise, and set, and rise;
> Earth takes th' example ...
> ... All, to reflourish, fades;
> As in a wheel, all sinks, to re-ascend.
> Emblems of man, who passes, not expires."

"It is not more surprising to be born twice than once; everything in Nature is resurrection," said Voltaire.

Delormel, Descartes, and Lavater were struck with the tremendous importance of the doctrine of Palingenesis.

The Philosophy of the Universe, of Dupont de Nemours, is full of the idea of successive lives, as a necessary corollary of the law of progress; whilst Fontenelle strongly advocates it in his *Entretiens sur la Pluralité des Mondes*.

It is needless to state that these ideas formed part of the esoteric teachings of Martinez Pasqualis, Claude Saint-Martin, and their followers.

Saint-Martin lived in times that were too troubled for him to speak freely. In his works, however, not a few passages are found in which there can be no doubt that reincarnation is hinted at, to anyone able to read between the lines. (*Tableau nat.*, vol. i, p. 136; *L'homme de Désir*, p. 312.)

In his *Œuvres Posthumes* (vol. i, p. 286) appears this remarkable passage:

"Death ought to be looked upon only as one stage in our journey. We reach this stage with tired, worn-out horses, and we start again with horses that are fresh and able to take us farther on our road; all the same, we must pay what we owe for the portion of the journey that has been traversed, and until the account is settled, we are not allowed to continue our way."

Goethe writes as follows to his friend Madame von Stein:

"Tell me what destiny has in store for us? Wherefore has it bound us so closely to each other? Ah! in bygone times, thou must have been my sister or my wife ... and there remains, from the whole of those past ages, only one memory, hovering like a doubt above my heart, a memory of that truth of old that is ever present in me."

Ballanche, an orthodox Christian mystic, says:

"Each one of us is a reincarnating being, ignorant both of his present and of his former transformations." (*Pal. Sociale*, book III., p. 154.)

"Man is brought to perfection only by becoming a more perfect order of things, and even then he does nothing more than bring back, as Plato said, a confused memory of the state that preceded his fall." (*Essai sur les Instit. Sociales*, vol. ii., p. 170.)

"This life we spend on earth, shut in between an apparent birth and an equally apparent death, is, in reality, only a portion of our existence, one manifestation of man in time." (*Orphée*, vol. iv., p. 424.)

"Our former lives belong to astronomical cycles lost in the mighty bosom of previous ages; not yet has it been given to us to know them." (*Orphée*, vol. iv., p. 432.)

Balzac's *Seraphita* abounds with references to the idea of successive lives:

"All human beings spend their first life in the sphere of instincts, in which they endeavour to discover how useless are the treasures of earth."

".... How often we live in this first world...."

"Then we have other existences to wear out before we reach the path on which the light shines. Death is one stage on this journey."

Constant Savy[147] describes as follows the conditions of immortality and a succession of lives by means of reincarnation:

"In proportion as its soul is developed by successive lives, the body to which it is to be united will necessarily be superior to those it has worn out; otherwise there would be no harmony between these two elements of human existence; the means given to the soul would bear no relation to the development of its power. This body, gifted with more perfect and numerous senses, could not have an equal value for all....

"Besides, these natural inequalities are also advantageous for individual progress in another way; the errors resulting therefrom cause truths to be discovered; vices laid bare almost form a reason for the practice of virtue by all men, or at all events they protect one from vice by reason of the horror they inspire; the ignorance of some arouses the love of science in others; the very idleness which dishonours some men inspires others with a love for work.

"So that these inequalities, inevitable because they are necessary, are present in the successive lives we pass through. There is nothing in them contrary to universal harmony; rather, they are a means for effecting this harmony, and are the inevitable result of the difference in value that bodies possess. Besides, no man remains stationary; all advance at a more or less rapid rate of progress....

"When faith is born, it is an illumination. Since man's immortality is one progressive advance, and, to effect this, he prepares the life he enters by the life he is leaving; since, in short, there are necessarily two worlds, one material, the other intellectual, these two worlds, which make up the life to come, must be in harmonious relationship with our own.

"Man's work will, therefore, be a continuation of his past work....

"I would never believe that our intelligence, which begins to develop in this life, comes to a halt after such an imperfect growth, and is not exercised or perfected after death....

"... Nature always advances, always labours, because God is life and he is eternal, and life is the progressive movement in the direction of the supreme good, which is God himself. Could man alone in the whole of nature, man so imperfect and full of faults, stop in his onward course, either to be annihilated, or suddenly, without participating in it, though he was created free, find that he was as perfect as he could possibly be? This is more than I can understand.

"No, when the time comes, man will not find that his life has been useless, a thing for mere contemplation; he will not find that he is improved without personal participation therein, without effort and toil on his part; above all, he will not be reduced to a state of nothingness. He will again have a life of toil; he will participate, to the extent God has permitted him, in the endless creations produced by divine omnipotence; he will again love, he will never cease to love; he will continue his eternal progress, because the distance between himself and God is infinite."

Pierre Leroux says:

"If God, after creating the world and all creation, were then to abandon them, instead of guiding them from life to life, from one state of progress to another, to a goal of real happiness, he would be an unjust God. It is unnecessary for St. Paul to say; 'Shall the thing formed say to him that formed it. Why hast thou made me thus?' (*Romans*, chap, 9, v. 20.) There is an inner voice, doubtless coming to us from God himself, which tells us that God cannot bring about evil, or create in order to cause suffering. Now this is what would certainly happen were God to abandon his creatures after an imperfect, a truly unhappy life.

"On the other hand, if we regard the world as a series of successive lives for each creature, we see very well how it comes about that God, to whom there is neither time nor space, and who perceives the final goal of all things, permits evil and suffering as being necessary phases through which creatures must pass, in order to reach a state of happiness which the creature does not see, and, consequently, cannot enjoy in so far as it is a creature, but which God sees, and which, therefore, the creature virtually enjoys in him, for the time will come when it will partake of that happiness."[148]

In Fourier we find the following lines[149]:

"Where is there an old man who would not like to feel certain that he would be born again and bring back into another life the experience he has gained in the present one? To affirm that this desire cannot be realised is to confess that God is capable of deceiving us. We must, therefore, recognise that we have already lived before being what we now are, and that many another life awaits us, some in this world, and the rest in a higher sphere, with a finer body and more delicate senses...."

Alphonse Esquiros expresses himself as follows[150]:

"The question may well be asked whether the talents, the good and the evil tendencies man brings with him at birth may not be the fruit of acquired intelligence, of qualities and vices gained in one or many former existences. Is there a previous life the elements of which have prepared the conditions of the life now being lived by each of us? People in ancient times thought so. Inborn dispositions, so different in children, caused them to believe in impressions left by previous existences in the imperishable germ of man. From the time when intelligence begins to show itself in children we faintly discern a general attitude towards things, which is very like a memory thereof. It would appear that, according to this system, no one is unconnected with the elements he introduces into life at each birth.

"All the same, rebirth in humanity constitutes no more than an initial circle of tests. When, after one or several incarnations, man has attained to the degree of perfection necessary to cause a change, he passes to another life, and, in another sphere, begins an existence of which we know nothing, though it is possible for us to regard it as linked to the present life by the closest of bonds....

"The limit to the progress man must have attained to, before entering upon another circle of tests in another sphere, is at present unknown to us; science and philosophy will doubtless succeed in determining this limit later on.

"They alone are reborn to earthly flesh who have in no way raised the immortal principle of their nature to a degree of perfection that will enable them to be reborn in glory....

"I affirm the perpetual union of the soul to organic bodies; these bodies succeed each other, being born from one another, and fitting themselves for the constitutive forms of the worlds traversed by the immortal ego in its successive existences. The principle of life, extended to divers evolutions of rebirth, is ever for the Creator nothing more than a continuation of one and the same state. God does not regard the duration of a being as limited to the interval between birth and death; he includes all possible segments of existence, the succession of which, after many interruptions and renewals, forms the real unity of life. Must souls, when they leave our globe, put on, from sphere to sphere, an existence hidden from us, whose organic elements would continually be fitting themselves for the characters and natures of the different worlds? Reason can come to no decision on this point. Only let us not forget that the soul always carries off a material germ from one existence to the next, making itself anew, so to speak, several times, in that endless ascent of lives through the worlds, wherein it attains, heaven after heaven, a degree of perfection increasingly linked with the eternal elements of our growing personality.

"It may be seen, from what is here stated, how vain is the hypothesis of perfect bliss following on the death of the righteous.

"It is useless for the Christian to soar beyond time, beyond some limit that separates him from infinite good; he cannot do this by a single effort. God proportions his intervention and aid to the totality of the states man must pass through in the course of an indefinitely long series of existences...."

M. d'Orient, an orthodox Catholic, writes as follows[151]:

"In this doctrine, so evidently based on reason, everything is linked and held together: the foreknowledge of God and the agreement thereof with man's free-will. This problem, hitherto impossible to solve, no longer offers any difficulty, if by it is meant that God, knowing before birth, by reason of his previous deeds, what there is in the heart of man, brings man to life and removes him from it in circumstances that best fit in with the accomplishment of his purposes....

"We see in this way how it is that God is the controller of all the main events that take place in the world, for the knowledge he has of souls in former lives, and his power to dispose of each and all in the way he pleases, enable him to foresee events in his infinite knowledge and arrange the whole sequence of things in conformity with his plans, somewhat as an ingenious, skilful workman, by the aid of various colours, conceives of and arranges the life-like reproduction of a mosaic, a picture, or a piece of inlaid work. We understand all his forecasts of the future, how it was that Daniel foretold so exactly the greatness of Alexander and his conquests; how Isaiah called Cyrus by name many centuries before these mighty conquerors appeared to spread confusion and terror over the world; how God, in order to show forth his might before the nations and spread abroad the glory of his name, is said to have hardened Pharaoh's heart and roused his obstinate will; for all that was needed in order to bring to pass these various results was for God to call back into existence certain souls he knew to be naturally suited to his purpose. This is distinctly pointed out in the passage from the apostle St. Jude, which, if we accept the meaning that first offers itself to the mind, would seem positively to imply that certain souls had undergone a sentence of eternal reprobation: 'For there are certain men crept in unawares, who were before of old ordained to this condemnation, turning the grace of our God into lasciviousness....'

"And so there falls away and disappears the greatest difficulty in the doctrine of grace, which consisted in explaining how it came about that God made some men pitiful and others hard-hearted, without there being in him either justice or acceptance of persons; showing pity, says St. Augustine, only by grace that was unmerited, and hardening hearts only by judgment that was always just; since evidently according to this theory it is not (as Origen has already said) apart from previous merit that some are formed for vessels of honour, and others for vessels of shame and wrath. That harsh sentence pronounced upon Judas by the Bishop of Hippon, which so grievously scandalised most of the Catholic theologians, although only the confirmation of the quotation from St. Jude, viz., that the wretched man had been predestined to shed the Saviour's blood, will seem to be a very just one in the sense that God causes that already lost soul to be born again, that demon, as Jesus Christ called him, for the very purpose of perpetrating the hateful crime.

"Consequently the most sublime mysteries of religion, the most wonderful facts regarding the destiny of the soul, find their natural explanation in a clear understanding of this doctrine of metempsychosis, however strange and extraordinary it may at first appear. What more striking proof can be asked for, what stronger and more convincing reason than such agreement, concerning matter wherein all positive proof will always, humanly speaking, be impossible? A doctrine which meets all the facts of the case so accurately, which explains, without difficulty, all the phenomena of our existence in this world, can, of necessity, be nothing else than true."

Jean Reynaud expresses himself in these terms in *Terre el Ciel*:

"How glorious the light that would be cast on the present order of things on earth by a knowledge of our former existences! And yet, not only is our memory helpless regarding the times that preceded birth, it is not even conscious of the whole of the intervening period, often playing us false in the course of a lifetime. It retains absolutely nothing of the period immediately preceding birth, and scarcely any trace of our education as children; we might even be altogether ignorant of the fact that we were children once, were there not around us witnesses of that time. On every hand we are wrapped in a veil of ignorance, as with a pall of darkness, we no more distinguish the light beyond the cradle than that beyond the tomb. So far as memory is concerned, it would seem that we might be compared with a rocket such as we sometimes see flashing through the sky in the night-time, leaving behind it a line of light, this light never shows anything more than a limited portion of the way. Of like nature is memory, a trail of light left behind on our journey; we die, and everything is dark around us; we are born again, and the light begins to appear, like a star through the mist; we live, and it develops and grows, suddenly disappears again and reappears once more; from one eclipse to another we continue our way, and this way, interrupted by periods of darkness, is a continuous one, whose elements, only apparently separated, are linked to each other by the closest of bonds; we always bear within ourselves the principle of what we shall be later on, we are always rising higher. Question us on our past, and, like the rocket, we reply that we are going forward, but that our path is illumined only in our immediate neighbourhood, and that the rest of the road is lost in the blackness of night; we no more know from where we came than we know our destination, but we do know that we came from below and are rising higher, and that is all that is necessary to interest us in ourselves and make us conscious of what we are. And who knows but what our soul, in the unknown secret of its essence, has power some day to throw light on its successive journeyings, like those streaks of flame to which we are comparing it? There are strong reasons for thinking that such is the case, since the entire restoration of memory appears, with good reason, to be one of the main conditions of our future happiness....

"In like manner the soul, passing from one abode to another, and leaving its first body for a new one, ever changing its appearance and its dwelling, guided by the Creator's beams, from transmigration to transmigration, from metamorphosis to metamorphosis, pursues the palingenesic course of its eternal destiny....

"... Let us, then, add the teachings of metempsychosis to those of the Gospel, and place Pythagoras by the side of Jesus...."

André Pezzani concludes in the following words his remarkable book on *The Plurality of the Soul's Lives*:

"Apart from the belief in previous lives, nothing can be explained, neither the coming of a new soul into this evil world, the often incurable bodily infirmities, the disproportionate division of wealth, nor the inequality in intelligence and morality. The justice of God lies behind the monstrous phantom of chance. We understand neither what man is, whence he comes, nor whither he goes; original sin does not account for the particular fate of individuals, as it is the same for all. Roughly speaking, it clears up no difficulties, but rather adds to them the most revolting injustice. Once accept the theory of pre-existence, and a glorious light is thrown on the dogma of sin, for it becomes the result of personal faults from which the guilty soul must be purified.

"Pre-existence, once admitted as regards the past, logically implies a succession of future existences for all souls that have not yet attained to the goal and that have imperfections and defilements from which to be cleansed. In order to enter *the circle of happiness* and leave *the circle of wanderings*, one must be pure.

"We have opposed error, and proclaimed truth, and we firmly believe that the dogmas of pre-existence and the plurality of lives are true."

Thomas Browne, in *Religio Medici*, section 6, hints at Reincarnation:

"Heresies perish not with their authors, but, like the river Arethusa, though they lose their currents in one place, they rise up again in another ... revolution of time will restore it, when it will flourish till it be condemned again. For as though there were a Metempsychosis, and the soul of one man passed into another, opinions do find, after certain Revolutions, men and minds like those that first begat them.... Each man is not only himself, there hath been many Diogenes and as many Timons, though but few of that name; men are lived over again, the world is now as it was in ages past; there was none then but there hath been someone since that parallels him, and is, as it were, his revived self."

Lessing, in *The Divine Education of the Human Race*, vigorously opposes a Lutheran divine who rejects reincarnation: "The very same way by which the race reaches its perfection must every individual man—one sooner, another later—have travelled over. Have travelled over in one and the same life? Can he have been in one and the self-same life a sensual Jew and a spiritual Christian?

"Surely not that! But why should not every individual man have existed more than once in this world?

"Is this hypothesis so laughable merely because it is the oldest? Because the human understanding, before the sophistries of the schools had disciplined and debilitated it, lighted upon it at once? Why may not even I have already performed those steps of my perfecting which bring to men only temporal punishments and rewards? And once more, why not another time all those steps, to perform which the views of Eternal Rewards so powerfully assist us? Why should I not come back as often as I am capable of acquiring fresh knowledge, fresh expertness? Do I bring away so much from once that there is nothing to repay the trouble of coming back?

"Is this a reason against it? Or because I forget that I have been here already? Happy is it for me that I do forget. The recollection of my former condition would permit me to make only a bad use of the present. And that which even I must forget *now*, is that necessarily forgotten for ever?"

Schlosser gives expression to similar thoughts in a fine work of his: *Über die Seelenwanderung*.

Lichtemberg says in his *Seibstcharacteristik*:

"I cannot get rid of the thought that I died before I was born, and that by this death I was led to this rebirth. I feel so many things that, were I to write them down, the world would regard me as a madman. Consequently, I prefer to hold my peace."

Charles Bonnet is the author of a splendid work, full of noble and lofty thoughts, on this subject. It is entitled *Philosophic Palingenesis*.

Emmanuel Kant believes that our souls start imperfect from the sun, and travel through planetary stages farther and farther away to a paradise in the coldest and remotest star in our system. (*General History of Nature*.)

In *The Destiny of Man*, J. G. Fichte says:

"These two systems, the purely spiritual and the sensuous—which last may consist of an immeasurable series of particular lives—exist in me from the moment when my active reason is developed and pursue their parallel course....

"All death in nature is birth.... There is no death-bringing principle in nature, for nature is only life throughout.... Even because Nature puts me to death, she must quicken me anew...."

Herder, in his *Dialogues on Metempsychosis*, deals with this subject more fully:

"Do you not know great and rare men who cannot have been what they are in a single human existence; who must have often existed before in order to have attained that purity of feeling, that instinctive impulse for all that is true, beautiful, and good?... Have you never had remembrances of a former state?... Pythagoras, Iarchas, Apollonius, and others remembered distinctly what and how many times they had been in the world before. If we are blind or can see but two steps before our noses, ought we, therefore, to deny that others may see a hundred or a thousand degrees farther, even to the bottom of time ...?"

"He who has not become ripe in one form of humanity is put into the experience again, and, some time or other, must be perfected."

"I am not ashamed of my half-brothers the brutes; on the contrary, so far as I am concerned, I am a great advocate of metempsychosis. I believe for a certainty that they will ascend to a higher grade of being, and am unable to understand how anyone can object to this hypothesis, which seems to have the analogy of the whole creation in its favour." Sir Walter Scott had such vivid memories of his past lives that they compelled a belief in pre-existence. Instances of this belief may be found in *The Life of Scott*, by Lockhart (vol. 7, p. 114, first edition).

According to Schlegel:

"Nature is nothing less than the ladder of resurrection, which, step by step, leads upward, or rather is carried from the abyss of eternal death up to the apex of life." (*Æsthetic and Miscellaneous Works*; and, *The Philosophy of History*.)

Shelley held a firm belief in Reincarnation:

"It is not the less certain, notwithstanding the cunning attempts to conceal the truth, that all knowledge is reminiscence. The doctrine is far more ancient than the times of Plato," (Dowden's *Life of Shelley*, vol. 1, p. 82.)

Schopenhauer adopted the idea of Reincarnation which he had found in the *Upanishads*; regarding this portion of his teaching, his contemporaries and followers set up a kind of conspiracy of silence. In *Parerga and Paralipomena*, vol. 2, chap. 15, *Essay on Religions*, he says:

"I have said that the combination of the *Old Testament* with the *New* gives rise to absurdities. As an example, I may cite the Christian doctrine of Predestination and Grace as formulated by Augustine and adopted from him by Luther, according to which one man is endowed with grace and another is not. Grace thus comes to be a privilege received at birth and brought ready into the world.... What is obnoxious and absurd in this doctrine may be traced to the idea contained in the *Old Testament*, that man is the creation of an external will which called him into existence out of nothing. It is quite true that genuine moral excellence is really innate; but the meaning of the Christian doctrine is expressed in another and more rational way by the theory of Metempsychosis, common to Brâhmans and Buddhists. According to this theory, the qualities which distinguish one man from another are received at birth, *i.e.*, are brought from another world and a former life; these qualities are not an external gift of grace, but are the fruits of the acts committed in that other world....

"What is absurd and revolting in this dogma is, in the main, as I said, the simple outcome of Jewish theism with its 'creation out of nothing,' and the really foolish and paradoxical denial of the doctrine of metempsychosis which is involved in that idea, a doctrine which is natural to a certain extent, self-evident, and, with the exception of the Jews, accepted by nearly the whole human race at all times.... Were an Asiatic to ask me for a definition of Europe, I should be forced to answer him: It is that part of the world which is haunted by the incredible delusion that man was created out of nothing, and that his present birth is his first entrance into life."

In *The World as Will and Idea,* he also says:

"What sleep is for the individual, death is for the Will (character).

"It flings off memory and individuality, and this is Lethe; and through this sleep of death it reappears refreshed and fitted out with another intellect, as a new being."

In *Parerga and Paralipomena*, vol. 2, chap. 10, he adds:

"Did we clearly understand the real nature of our inmost being, we should see how absurd it is to desire that individuality should exist eternally. This wish implies that we confuse real Being with one of its innumerable manifestations. The individuality disappears at death, but we lose nothing thereby, for it is only the manifestation of quite a different Being— a Being ignorant of time, and, consequently, knowing neither life nor death. The loss of intellect is the Lethe, but for which the Will would remember the various manifestations it has caused. When we die, we throw off our individuality, like a worn-out garment, and rejoice because we are about to receive a new and a better one."

Edgar Allen Poe, speaking of the dim memories of bygone lives, says:

"We walk about, amid the destinies of our world-existence, encompassed by divine but ever present Memories of a Destiny more vast—very distant in the bygone time and infinitely awful.

"We live out a Youth peculiarly haunted by such dreams, yet never mistaking them for dreams. As Memories we *know* them. During our *Youth* the distinction is too clear to deceive us even for a moment.

"But now comes the period at which a conventional World-Reason awakens us from the truth of our dream ... a mis-shapen day or a misfortune that could not be traced back to our own doings in this or in another life...." (*Eureka.*)

Georges Sand, in *Consuelo*, sets forth the logic of Reincarnation; and G. Flammarion expounds this doctrine in most of his works: *Uranie; Les Mondes Imaginaires et les Mondes Réels; La Pluralité des Mondes Habités*, etc.

Professor William Knight wrote in the *Fortnightly Review* for September, 1878:

"It seems surprising that in the discussions of contemporary philosophy on the origin and destiny of the soul there has been no explicit revival of the doctrines of Pre-existence and Metempsychosis.

... They offer quite a remarkable solution of the mystery of Creation, Translation, and Extinction....

"Stripped of all extravagances and expressed in the modest terms of probability, the theory has immense speculative interest and great ethical value. It is much to have the puzzle of the origin of evil thrown back for an indefinite number of cycles of lives and to have a workable explanation of Nemesis...."

Professor W. A. Butler, in his *Lectures on the History of Ancient Philosophy*, says:

"There is internally no greater improbability that the present may be the result of a former state now almost wholly forgotten than that the present should be followed by a future form of existence in which, perhaps, or in some departments of which, the oblivion may be as complete."

The Rev. William R. Alger, a Unitarian minister, adds:

"Our present lack of recollection of past lives is no disproof of their actuality.... The most striking fact about the doctrine of the repeated incarnations of the soul ... is the constant reappearance of that faith in all parts of the world and its permanent hold on certain great nations....

"The advocates of the resurrection should not confine their attention to the repellent or ludicrous aspects of metempsychosis, ... but do justice to its claim and charm." (*A Critical History of the Doctrine of a Future Life.*)

Professor Francis Bowen, of Harvard University, writes in the *Princetown Review* for May, 1881, when dealing with the subject of *Christian Metempsychosis*:

"Our life upon earth is rightly held to be a discipline and a preparation for a higher and eternal life hereafter. But if limited to the duration of a single mortal body, it is so brief as to seem hardly sufficient for so great a purpose.... Why may not the probation of the soul be continued or repeated through a long series of successive generations, the same personality animating, one after another, an indefinite number of tenements of flesh, and carrying forward into each the training it has received, the character it has formed, the temper and dispositions it has indulged, in the stage of existence immediately preceding?...

"Every human being thus dwells successively in many bodies, even during one short life.[152] If every birth were an act of absolute creation, the introduction to life of an entirely new creature, we might reasonably ask why different souls are so variously constituted at the outset.... One child seems a perverse goblin, while another has the early promise of a Cowley or a Pascal.... The birthplace of one is in Central Africa, and of another in the heart of civilised and Christian Europe. Where lingers eternal justice then? How can such frightful inequalities be made to appear consistent with the infinite wisdom and goodness of God?...

"If metempsychosis is included in the scheme of the divine government of the world, this difficulty disappears altogether. Considered from this point of view, everyone is born into the state which he has fairly earned by his own previous history.... We submit with enforced resignation to the stern decree; ... that the iniquities of the fathers shall be visited upon the children even to the third and fourth generation. But no one can complain of the dispositions and endowments which he has inherited, so to speak, from himself, that is, from his former self in a previous stage of existence.

"And it matters not, so far as the justice of the sentence is concerned, whether the former self from whom we receive this heritage bore the same name with our present self, or bore a different name...."

Professor F. H. Hedge, in *Ways of the Spirit, and other Essays*, p. 359, maintains that:

"Whatever had a beginning in time, it should seem, must end in time. The eternal destination which faith ascribes to the soul presupposes an eternal origin.... An obvious objection, and one often urged against this hypothesis, is the absence of any recollection of a previous life.... The new organisation with its new entries must necessarily efface the record of the old. For memory depends on continuity of association. When the thread of that continuity is broken, the knowledge of the past is gone....

"And a happy thing, if the soul pre-existed, it is for us that we remember nothing of its former life.... Of all the theories respecting the origin of the soul this seems to me the most plausible, and therefore the one most likely to throw light on the question of a life to come."

The Spiritualists of Europe—those belonging to the school of Allan Kardec, at all events—place reincarnation in the very forefront of their teaching. We may add that those of America do not acknowledge that the soul has more than one existence on earth, driven, however, by the logic of things, which insists on progress, they state that there are a series of lives passed in subtler bodies on invisible planets and worlds.

All true philosophers have been attracted by the mystery of palingenesis, and have found that its acceptance has thrown a flood of light on the questions that perplexed them.

In Asia there are 400 millions of believers in reincarnation, including the Chinese, Tartars, Thibetans, Hindus, Siamese, Mongolians, Burmese, Cambodians, Koreans, and the people of Japan.

Tradition has handed down this teaching even to the most savage tribes. In Madagascar, when a man is on the point of death, a hole is made in the roof of his straw hut, through which his soul may pass out and enter the body of a woman in labour. This may be looked upon as a stupid superstition, still it is one which, in spite of its degenerate form, sets forth the doctrine of the return of souls back to evolution through earthly experiences. The Sontals, Somalis, and Zulus, the Dyaks of Borneo and Sumatra, and the Powhatans of Mexico have similar traditions. In Central Africa, slaves who are hunchbacked or maimed forestall the hour of death by voluntary self-immolation, in the hope of being reborn in the bodies of men who will be free and perfectly formed.

To sum up: all tradition, whether popular, philosophical, or religious, is instinct with the teaching of Rebirth.

Objection.
Reincarnation and Forgetfulness of the Past.

Sceptics are ever bringing forward against reincarnation the absence of all memory of past lives, convinced that there can be no answer to this argument.

They do not reflect that human ignorance is a bottomless abyss, whilst the possibilities of Life are endless. The schools of the future will smile at the claims made by those of the present, just as the latter doubtless regard with pitying indulgence that school which, only a few years ago, in the person of one of its most famous members, Dr. Bouillaud, mercilessly condemned the exponent of Edison's invention, because the *savant*, listening to a phonograph for the first time, could not believe that it was anything else than ventriloquism! Instances of this kind are sufficiently numerous and recent not to be forgotten, in spite of the shortness of human memory.

In the present instance, there are many men of science who have not yet been made sufficiently wise by experience to see that the very mystery of memory itself might furnish an explanation of that general absence of all power of recollection, which now seems to them altogether incompatible with the doctrine of Rebirth.

So as not to appear to be running away from this objection, by dealing with it only on the surface, we will endeavour to develop the question somewhat, for we shall have to set forth to readers unacquainted with theosophical teachings—which alone, up to the present, have thrown light on these difficult subjects—certain doctrines which will be well understood by none but theosophists, since they are incapable of proof by a simple statement thereof, but form part, of a long chain of teachings. We will offer them simply as theories—though they are facts to us—theories that contain many an error, it may be, and are imperfectly stated, though capable of widening the horizon of thought and shedding a brilliant light upon many an obscure question. Earnest seekers after truth, it is hoped, will not be disheartened by the difficulties of the subject, but will endeavour to grasp the meaning of the following pages, by reading them over again, if need be.

First, a few words must be said on memory in general, next we will give a rapid sketch of what constitutes memory in atoms and molecules, in the varied forms of the many kingdoms of nature and in human forms; finally, we will speak of cosmic Memory, that veritable *Judgment Book* which takes account of all the vibrations of the Universe.

Amongst beings capable of memory, a distinction must be made between those which have not reached the stage of self-consciousness, and those which have done so, for memory, properly so-called, takes for granted an "I." That which has not an "I" can only have a memory of which it is not conscious[153]; the atom, for instance, of whose memory we shall speak later on; that which has only a rudimentary "I" possesses only a rudimentary memory from the point of view of its bearing on the individual—such is that possessed by the souls of the lower kingdoms, that which constitutes instinct; to the perfect "I" alone belongs an individual memory—the human memory, and that of beings who have attained to the superhuman stage. This memory may be defined as the faculty possessed by an individualised "centre of consciousness" voluntarily to reproduce the vibrations it has received or generated.

A "centre of consciousness" is a form that serves, for the time being, as the instrument of an individualised ray of that indefinable principle called the soul. But for the presence of this individual soul in a form, this latter would remain inactive as a centre of consciousness—although active in its constituent parts[154]—and could it not then, consciously, either generate or receive vibrations on the plane from which the soul is momentarily absent—it could only transmit them; for instance, when a man is in a brown study, he is not conscious in his brain, of what is taking place on the physical plane.[155]

The vehicles of consciousness are often numerous in a being, and the more numerous in proportion to the degree this latter has attained in the scale of evolution. The present day man possesses four bodies: the visible, the astral, the mental, and the causal. They are not all equally developed, and therefore not equally conscious, for the clearness and intensity of consciousness depend on the decree of perfection of its vehicles, just as the beauty of electric light depends on the perfection of the apparatus producing it.

The Ego—the man—is the consciousness that is called forth by the soul in the causal body. This consciousness varies in power with the development of the body that gives birth to it. At first it is dim and uncertain,[156] and acquires some degree of intensity only when it receives, through the mental and astral vehicles, the simple and intense vibrations of the physical body.[157] In savage races, for instance, man possesses a definite consciousness only in his waking condition; as soon as the soul is attached to the astral body, externalised by sleep, it experiences only a dim consciousness in this undeveloped vehicle. In advanced races, the astral body, being far more developed, brings about distinct consciousness during sleep. As man evolves, consciousness begins to function in the mental and the astral bodies, without the assistance of the vibrations of the lower vehicles, and when all the grades[158] of matter which compose the human constitution are thus vitalised, man has become perfect; he knows the Universe because he feels it within himself—he echoes it, so to speak, and possesses all its powers.[159]

In ordinary man, the memory of events that have taken place in his waking state can be brought back by that special effort of will which sets in motion the cerebral molecules that have previously been put into vibration by these events.

Sometimes the will, of itself, is powerless to recall this vibration, either because the brain is tired or in some unfavourable condition or other; it is then aided by bringing its automatism into play, by endeavouring, for instance, to call back one constituent element of the fact desired, a place, sound, scent, person, &c., and often in this way is brought about the vibration of the molecules that constituted the rest of the circuit, and the fact sought for presents itself; association of ideas is a phenomenon based on this mechanical process.

A third method—a far more difficult one—is also used; the bringing of every mental effort, to a standstill. The suppression of thought, when sufficiently complete, brings the brain into a state of calm, allows of the soul concentrating on the astral body whose memory is keen and only slightly subject to obstruction, and then it often happens that the vibration of the astral memory repercusses on to the physical apparatus which suddenly remembers the thing desired.

On the death of the physical, the soul acts in the astral body; there it retains a complete memory of life on earth, but the vibrations of the physical plane no longer reach it,[160] these memories soon cease to occupy its attention, and it gives itself up wholly to the impressions received from the new world into which it has entered. In this first stage of the after-life, then, there is a kind of darkening of the memory of the past earth life—darkening, not oblivion.

When the purgatorial life is at an end and the astral body disintegrates in its turn, the soul functions in the mental body, in the mental world.[161] On this new plane, the memory of the worlds left behind continues, though far less clearly than the memory of the physical existed in the astral world; this is owing to the fact that, in ordinary man, the mental body is not sufficiently developed to constitute a complete vehicle of consciousness, capable of registering all the vibrations that come to it; everything in the past that has been *purely* the work of the astral or the physical plane then disappears from his memory; there remain only memories that have been caused either by the mental qualities or qualities superior to these, all the highest elements concerned with affection, intelligence, or art. The mental world, generally speaking, is seen only to a small extent or not at all, because of the incomplete development of the mental body. Besides, recollections assume a new character[162]; every thought takes a concrete form—that of a friend, for instance, appears as the friend himself, speaking and thinking, more vivid than on the earth plane[163]; everything is dramatised in marvellous fashion, and life is intense throughout the realms of paradise.

The mental body, after exhausting the forces that make it up, also dies, and the soul is "centred" in the only vehicle it has left, the causal body, a body that is immortal, one may say, up to a certain point, since the soul retains it until the time comes when it can function in a still higher and more lasting vehicle[164], and this happens only after millions of years.[165] Here, another diminution of memory takes place, because the soul loses a large portion of its consciousness when it comes into contact with none but the vibrations of this body, which is even more incompletely developed than the former ones, though holding within itself all the germs of these latter. The Ego then remains apparently sunk in sleep for a varying period, though never for very long; then the germs in the causal body become active, build up a new series of bodies in succession—the mental, the astral, and finally the physical—and the soul returns once more to incarnation.

It will now be understood how it comes about that a soul of average development—on entering a new cycle, with the memory of the last cycle considerably obliterated by the loss of the physical, astral, and mental bodies, sheathed in new bodies on these planes, bodies that have nothing in common with the life of the past—is unable to impress its dim memories on to the brain; but it will also be seen that, with the progress of evolution, the soul acquires ever clearer consciousness in the causal body, in which it finally preserves the memory of the various life-cycles. Since, at this stage, it has become capable of projecting its vibrations, voluntarily, through the lower bodies, it is able to transmit this memory first to the mental body, then to the astral, and lastly to the physical body; when this is possible, man, in waking consciousness, remembers his former lives.

This transmission requires a purificatory process in the vehicles and a special training of the will. The matter of all the bodies—that of the brain in particular—must be refined, its constituent elements must be subtler, and its atoms must be fully awakened to activity[166]; whereupon the cerebral cell becomes capable of responding to the thought of the Ego, *i.e.*, of vibrating in harmony with the higher matter.

The second condition of the brain's receptivity is that this organ be brought into a state of complete rest. So long as the waking consciousness is active, the brain vibrates powerfully, and if, at this time, the soul sends the brain its thought, this latter can no more make an impression on the existing cerebral activity than a faint note could be heard amid the clash of an orchestra. Consequently, man, by the training of his will, must have acquired the power to stop the thinking activity in the waking state, and to "centre" his attention on the causal body, the only vehicle in which he can know the facts of his past incarnations; this done he is able, at will, to project on to his brain the scenes of his former lives and to imprint them thereon with greater distinctness, in proportion to his development and training.

In order to avoid continued explanations, we will deal with another side of the question, however incomprehensible it be to such as have not studied theosophy.

A vehicle of consciousness is both a registering apparatus[167] and a conductor of vibrations.[168] The kinds of matter of which forms are made up are perfectly graduated; the finest atom of the physical body is built up of the densest atoms of the astral plane, the finest atom of the astral body is made of the densest atoms of the mental plane, and so on. Each atom is linked to the one that precedes and to the one that follows it in that immense chain which stretches from the densest to the subtlest plane of the Cosmos. Every vibration follows this path, passes in all directions—in the seven[169] dimensions of space-and terminates in the very Centre of consciousness, the Logos, God incarnate in the world.

It is then comprehensible, even logical, that God should be both conscious, on his receptive side, of everything that takes place in the world (*omniscient*), and should produce, on his active side, all the forces of the world (*omnipotent*). It is likewise admissible that the human soul, when fully developed, should find in the causal body the memory of the facts that have echoed therein, from the time when it could function consciously in it. But, it will be asked, how could it find, in the causal body, memories of existences it has not been able to register individually, of which it has not been conscious, those, for instance, that form the early stages of its evolution at a time when it was conscious only in the lower vehicles?

Memory possesses many store-houses. The vibrations of which it is composed affect the whole Universe, there is not a single local shock that is not felt throughout all the worlds. The eternal registering of things takes place in the great centre of consciousness, God, or rather, it exists in him, for to him there is neither future nor past, only one eternal present; evolution is unceasingly accomplished[170]; but if we look upon ourselves as finite beings, living in the illusion of time and space, we find that vibrating matter preserves for a longer or a shorter period the movement imparted to it. The denser the substance, which forms the medium in which vibration takes place, the feebler the vibration; that is why it speedily ceases on the physical plane; it continues long, however, in the higher conditions of matter, and it is there we must look for it,[171] if we would recall certain events at which we have not been present. When anything exciting, a murder, a battle, for instance, has happened anywhere, the subtler atoms of the surrounding objects receive a powerful shock and continue to vibrate for centuries. Those who have developed their inner senses can thus witness the scene which is continually repeating itself, or rather, is happening all the time.[172] Thus, psychometrists[173], in presence of a portion of a fossil, are enabled to bring back scenes that this fragment has witnessed millions of years ago.[174]

In these cases, the memory of the facts is connected with that of the atoms which register it; this memory can only be recalled by coming into contact with these atoms.[175]

There is also another memory, midway between the unconscious memory of atoms and the conscious memory of the human soul; that of the forms of the various sub-human kingdoms. It is only slightly conscious, for it is not individualised; all the same, it is precise in its nature. It dwells in the vital essence of the form, an essence taken from a collective "block" which supplies a portion of its substance to the individuals of the same species; this incarnate portion of essence, when the form disintegrates at death, returns to the parent "block," to which it communicates the result of its experiences, and when the latter sends out a portion of itself, into a new form, this tentacle, which is, so to speak, the soul of the form, is in possession of the whole of the experiences of the "block."[176] This explains how it is that the individual members of certain hostile species know one another from birth—the chicken, for instance, which, immediately it has left the egg, trembles before the hawk hovering above in the air; such is also the reason why a duckling plunges into water as soon as it comes to a pond, and the same instinct impels a bird to leave its nest and trust itself to the air when fully fledged.

In these collective souls, belonging to the mineral, vegetable, and animal kingdoms, there can be recovered the past to which they bore witness, when the atoms of their bodies have been dispersed and entered into new combinations.

When the elemental Essence[177] has definitely split up, and the "blocks" have become separate, individualised, human fragments[178], each of these fragments is a causal body, a definite, immortal *centre* in the total Centre. Consequently there are in man three kinds of memory: atomic memory, that of the atoms of his bodies; instinctive memory of the special elemental essences which are the collective souls of his various vehicles; and finally, the individual memory of the centre[179], which is one with the total Centre from which it comes.

This element of unity, this human "I" in the divine "I," when sufficiently developed, is able to evoke the memory of all the events in which it has participated in the causal body, and also the memory of those it has witnessed as a collective soul (elemental "block") in bygone ages when active in various mineral, vegetable, and animal species. As a centre in the great Centre, it can also call forth the memory of everything in the Universe that its consciousness can grasp.[180] And when, in this long pilgrimage, it has developed to the farthest limits of the Universe it knows all that has been, is now, and is to be in this Universe, consequently it knows both what it has and what it has not participated in, for everything in the Universe has then become part of itself.

Thus it is seen that the memory of the past is everywhere registered, and that the difficulty a man has in bringing it back is caused by nothing more than his imperfect development. Once he has entered the "Strait Gate,"[181] and his consciousness is awake on the first plane of Unity[182], he becomes able to read the Great Book of Nature, in which all vibrations are kept in potentiality; he can revive them by an effort of will, similar to that he makes in a waking state, when he wishes to bring back past impressions to his brain. The difference lies in the fact that, in the latter case, being in the physical body, he calls up the memory retained in the astral body; whilst in the former case, being in the causal body, he brings memory within the influence of the buddhic body, or even at times of higher bodies still. The more the Being grows, and becomes able to fix his consciousness on the higher planes, the wider extends his sphere of influence, approaching that of divine Consciousness.

It is ignorance that brings forward this objection regarding loss of memory, ignorance of life and of death, ignorance of the phenomena that follow the last breath of a dying man, as well as of those preceding the first faint cry of a new-born child. Sceptics, however, might have shown a little more indulgence, for, as they are well aware, ordinary memory *is* even now so unreliable that a man has great difficulty in recalling the whole of the thoughts that have entered his brain during the last few minutes; he has forgotten the details of the various events of the week; the facts of the past year have mostly vanished from his mind, and when he comes to the end of the journey, mere fragments of the story of his life are all that is left. For all that, he has all the time retained the notion of the identity of his "I"; he has the same body, the same senses, and the same brain; his environment is the same; everything is there to bring about association of ideas, to awaken memory. On the other hand, centuries have elapsed before Rebirth takes place; the human being has undergone the most radical changes and modifications; everything in him that was perishable has disappeared, and is preserved only in a germinal state. The visible bodily sheath has had its atoms scattered to the four elements; the etheric body[183] has become separated from the physical molecules whose vital support it formed; the body of passions and desires (*astral body*) has lived for a few years in what Catholics call *Purgatory*, Greeks, *Hades*, and Hindus, *Kâmaloka*; after which, only germs have been left behind; then the intelligence (*mental body*) has been dispersed in turn and endures only in a germinal state. Almost everything that made up the man of bygone times has disappeared, and is now concentrated in a complex germ hidden away in the causal body and destined to develop a new personality later on[184], heir to the former one, though it will not be capable of remembering events in which it took no part.

This is the explanation of the myth of Lethe.

The soul, in the causal body, drinks of the river of Life, and from its sleep-giving draught forms the sheaths of the new incarnation, the new bodies that altogether blot out the memory of the past; it is, in very truth, a new-born babe who appears on earth.

The Root-Being[185], however, survives the successive wrecks of fleeting personalities, remaining in the new man as a guide, as the "Voice of Conscience." He is the Watcher who strings, as on a thread, the numberless pearls (*personalities*) which form the inevitable cycle of human evolution, and is able, when fully developed, to summon up the distant panorama of past lives. For him, nothing is lost.

The pioneers of the race have obtained direct proof of successive incarnations, but apart from these rare and special instances, ordinary individuals frequently have reminiscences and distinct memories which are not investigated, either because they are fragmentary in their nature or are related by children. In India, where the natives believe in Reincarnation, such cases are regarded without astonishment, and efforts are made to prove their truth by serious investigation, whenever possible. And such proof is often possible. When a child dies in infancy, before he is able to use his body intelligently and of his own free will—before being able to generate karma—the higher sheaths (*the astral and mental bodies*) are not separated into their component parts. Return to earth quickly takes place, the memory of the past life exists in the astral body—which has not changed—and, more especially during the first few years of life, can be impressed on the new brain with tolerable ease, if this latter is at all delicately constituted. Then if reincarnation takes place in the same country and in the neighbourhood of the past incarnation, it can be proved to be true. Such instances do exist; the reason they are not mentioned here is that they would add nothing to the general proofs on which stress has been laid in this work. These proofs form part of universal Law; they cannot be separated therefrom.

---

1. The fifth, or Aryan race, in theosophic nomenclature; the fourth was that of Atlantis; the third lived on the great southern continent, Lemuria; the two preceding ones were, so to speak, only the embryologic preparation for the following races.
2. The "life-atoms," infinitesimal particles which by aggregation form the human body. Certain of these atoms are preserved, on the death of the body, as germs which will facilitate the reconstruction of the physical body at the next rebirth.
3. The divine Essence which animates animals, and so, in another sense the astral bodies of men and animals, bodies whose particles *transmigrate* as do the physical atoms.
4. H. P. Blavatsky, *Secret Doctrine*.
5. These words are relative; they express differences in the evolution of souls.
6. The atmosphere of subtle physical elements radiating round the human body and acting in a defensive *rôle* by preventing the penetration of unhealthy elements from the immediate surroundings.
7. The "material sin" of Manu.
8. One, here means the "life atoms" of a man's body.
9. The word is here used in a generic sense; in the present work, it would be more precise to replace it by the word Resurrection.
10. This "triad" comprises the visible matter of the body, the etheric substance, and the life (Prâna) which the human ether absorbs and specialises for the vitalising of the body. See *Man and his Bodies*, by A. Besant.
11. H. P. Blavatsky, *The Theosophist*, Vol. 4, pages 287, 288.
12. The finer elements invisible to physical eye. Their function is sensation, and by their association with the human mental body incarnated in them, they give birth to the emotions and passions, in a word, to the animal in man.
13. The *Umbra* of the Latin races.
14. The *Kâma Rûpa* of the Hindus.
15. The purgatory of Christians, the astral plane of theosophists, and the *Kâmaloka* of Hindus.
16. By the *fire* of purgatory, says the Catholic metaphor.
17. See A. Besant's masterly work on *Reincarnation*.
18. Dharma is a wide word, primarily meaning the essential nature of a thing; hence the laws of its being, its duty; and it includes religious rites, appropriate to those laws. This definition, as also the extracts quoted, are taken from A. Besant's translation of the *Bhagavad Gîtâ*.
19. Human souls, not all of them, but only the pious ones, are daimonic and divine. Once separated from the body, and after the struggle to acquire piety, which consists in knowing God and injuring none, such a soul becomes all intelligence. The impious soul, however, remains in its own essence and punishes itself by seeking a human body to enter into, for no other body can receive a human soul, it cannot enter the body of an animal

devoid of reason: divine law preserves the human soul from such infamy. Hermes Trismegistus, Book I, *Laclé*: Hermes to his son Tat.
20. Bodies.
21. The physical body with its etheric "double," and life (*Prâna*).
22. The kâmic body.
23. The causal body.
24. *History*. Book 2, chap. 123.
25. The causal body.
26. The buddhic body, which, in ordinary man, is only in an embryonic stage.
27. Generally called *Prâna*, in man. *Jiva* is the solar life which, on being transmuted by the physical body, becomes *Prâna*, the human physical life. Both *Jiva* and *Prâna* differ from each other in nature and in vibration.
28. The mental body.
29. The causal body. In annihilation—what has been called the loss of the soul—the kâmic principle (astral body) in the course of a rather long succession of lives, does not allow the mental body to become separated from it in purgatory; it keeps it imprisoned up to the time of its disintegration; the causal body reaps nothing from the incarnations, at each rebirth it loses the forces it is putting forth in order to form the new mental body. It gradually atrophies until the time comes when it is no longer fit to make use of the ordinary bodies of the race to which it belongs. Then it remains at rest, whilst the mental body gradually disintegrates; afterwards it takes up once again its series of incarnations in the imperfectly evolved bodies of primitive races. This will be understood only by those who have studied theosophy.
30. In this passage, H. P. Blavatsky alludes to the few etheric, astral, and mental atoms which, at each disincarnation, are incorporated in the causal body and form the nuclei of the future bodies corresponding to them.
31. *History*. Vol. 2, book 2, chap. 123 (already quoted).
32. Of the elements of the personality—of the astral body, in all probability.
33. The Ego (soul) also lives in the air (the symbol of heaven) and on the earth (whose symbol is water, dense matter)—in heaven, after disincarnation; on earth, during incarnation.
34. The soul is immortal and needs no food.
35. Its name, Khopiroo, comes from the root Koproo, to become, to be born again (H. P. Blavatsky).
Hartley says: "At the centre of the solar disk appears the Scarabeus as the symbol of the soul re-uniting itself with the body. The Scarabeus is called by Pierret the synthesis of the Egyptian religion—type of resurrection—of self-existence—of self-engendering like the Gods. As Tori, or Chepi, the Sun is the Scarabeus, or self-engenderer, and the mystery of God."
36. Also called kâmic body, astral body, body of desire, etc.
37. Reincarnation.
38. Vol. 3, p. 124.
39. The causal body illumined by the divine Essence, which theosophy names Âtmâ-Buddhi.
40. He calls him "the prince of lying fathers and dishonest writers." (*Egypt*, vol. 1, p. 200).
41. Eusebius even confesses this himself: "I have set forth whatever is calculated to enhance the glory of our religion, and kept back everything likely to cast a stain upon it." (*Præparatio Evangelica*. Book 12, chap. 31).
42. *Namae-Sat Vakhshûr-i-Mahabad*, also in the fourth "Journey" in chap. 4 of *Jam-i-Kaikhoshru* (see *The Theosophist*, p. 333, vol. 21).
43. See *Bardic Triads*, by E. Williams. Translated from the original Welsh.
44. "'Abred' is the circle of the migrations through which every animated being proceeds from death: man has passed through it." *Triad* 13.
"Transmigration is in 'Abred.'" *Triad* 14.
"There are three primitive calamities in 'Abred': the necessity of evolution (of rebirths), the absence of memory (of past incarnations) and death (followed by rebirth)." *Triad* 18 (the words in parentheses are our own).
"By reason of three things man is subjected to 'Abred' (or transmigration): by the absence of the effort to attain knowledge, by non-attachment to good, and by attachment to evil. As the result of these, he descends into 'Abred,' to the stage corresponding to his development, and begins his transmigrations anew." *Triad* 25.
"The three foundations of science are: complete transmigration through every state of

being, the memory of the details of each transmigration, the power to pass again at will through any state, to acquire experience and judgment, (a) This comes to pass in the circle of Gwynvyd." *Triad* 36.

(a) The liberated being has power to call up the past, to tune his consciousness with that of every being, to feel everything that being feels, to be that being.

45. In the poem *Cad-Godden*, quoted by Pezzani in *La Pluralité des Existences de l'Âme*, p. 93. Taliesin is a generic name indicating a function rather than the name of an individual.
46. *Gallic War* (Book 2, chap. 6). Valerius Maximus relates that these nations lent one another money which was to be paid back in the other world, and that at Marseilles a sweet-tasted poison was given to anyone who, wishing to commit suicide, offered the judges satisfactory reasons for leaving his body.
47. *The Mystery of the Ages*, by the Duchesse de Pomar.
48. In *Theologia* or the *Seven Adyta*.
49. The "Cycle of Necessity" extends from the time when the soul begins to evolve to the moment when it attains to liberation.
50. *Life of Pythagoras*. Book 8, chap. 14.
51. Ovid's *Metamorphoses*. Book 15.
52. All that remained of the shield was the carved ivory ornamentation, the iron had been eaten away by rust.
53. Philostratus, *Life of Apollonius of Tyana*.
54. Philostratus, *Life of Apollonius of Tyana*.
55. Marinas, *Vita Procli*.
56. The Ego, the human soul properly so-called, what Egypt named the liberated intelligence which resumes its sheath of light, and again becomes a "daimon" (*Maspero*). In antiquity the name of daimon was given to the human soul or to higher intelligences.
57. *Hades*; the Purgatory of Catholics; the *Kâmalôka* of Hindus.
58. Allusion to the struggle which separates the mental from the astral body in Purgatory.
59. *Kâmalôka*; Purgatory.
60. The subterranean hell, the lowest world in Purgatory.
61. Plato's *Laws*, Book 10.
62. Plato's *Republic*, Book 10.
63. They are in the causal body.
64. *Phædo*.
65. These considerations are taken from the writings of H. P. Blavatsky, and are also confirmed by modern criticism of biblical texts.
66. Maimonides. Quoted in *The Perfect Way*, by A. Kingsford and E. Maitland.
67. *Galatians*, chap. 4, verses 24, 25.
68. *Starli*, part 4, p. 5.
69. *Deuteronomy*, chap. 24, verses 1 to 4.
70. *Deuteronomy*, chap. 17, verse 17.
71. *Exodus*, chap. 21, verses 2 to 11.
72. *Exodus*, chap. 21, verses 23, 24, 25.
73. *Genesis*, chap. 9, verses 5, 6; also *Leviticus*, chap. 7.
74. *Exodus*, chapters 6, 12, 14, 22, 32.
75. *Ecclesiastes*, chap. 3, verses 18, 19, 20, 22.
76. The souls of a race in its maturity are of a more advanced type than those of its infancy or old age.
77. The Kabala is the secret teaching of the Jews; in it lie hidden doctrines that are too profound to be taught in public.
78. *Zohar*, 2, 99, quoted in Myer's *Qabbalah*, p. 198.
79. Evolution develops the soul, enabling it to reach its goal: the divine state.
80. The force of evolution comes from God and ceases only when the soul is fully developed, and has reached the "promised land" at the end of its pilgrimage: the divine state.
81. Franck, *La Kabbale*, p. 244, etc.
82. *The Hidden Wisdom of Christ*, 1864, vol. 1, p. 39.
83. *De Bell. jud.* 2, 11.
84. One of the lowest sub-planes of *Kâmaloka* (Purgatory).
85. The Christian Heaven (*Devachan* of theosophy).

86. The earth, which is above when compared with Tartarus, but not so in relation to the Elysian Fields; versification imposes such strict limits on expression, that it must have the benefit of poetic licence.
87. Fréret, *Examen crit. des apologistes de la relig. chrét.*, pages 12 and 13, Paris, 1823.
88. Faustus.
89. And yet the *Gospel of Saint John* denies this (chap. 1, v. 21). The contradictions in the gospels are so numerous that they alone have created thousands of infidels.
90. Stolberg expresses himself as follows on this matter: "This question was evidently based on the opinion that the disciples of Jesus had formed, that this man, whose punishment dated from his very birth, had sinned in a previous life." (*Histoire de N. S. Jésus-Christ et de son siècle*, Book 3, chap. 43).
91. *Revelation*, chap. 3, v. 12.
92. *Revelation*, chap. 2, v. 28.
93. *Revelation*, chap. 22, v. 16.
94. *Revelation*, chap. 2, v. 17.
95. H. P. Blavatsky.
96. "Taken literally, the Book of the Creation gives us the most absurd and extravagant ideas of Divinity."
97. First *Ennead*, chap. I.
98. The Universe, which can exist only through *multiplicity*.
99. Second *Ennead*, chap. 3.
100. Second *Ennead*, chap. 8.
101. Third *Ennead*, chap. 4.
102. *Concerning Abstinence*; Book 2.
103. *Egyptian Mysteries*, Book 4, chap. 4.
104. Here, *reincarnation* is meant.
105. This philosopher was surnamed *Peisithanatos* (the death-persuader).
106. *Vie de Pythagore*, vol. I, p. 28.
107. *Hist. de l'Ec. a'Alex.*, vol. I, p 588.
108. In this work, he says:
    "The winged tribe, that has feathers instead of hair, is formed of innocent but superficial human beings, pompous and frivolous in speech, who, in their simplicity, imagine that the sense of vision is the best judge of the existence of things. Those who take no interest whatever in philosophy become four-footed animals and wild beasts...."
109. *Commentaries on the Golden Verses of Pythagoras.*
110. Hermes, *Commentaries of Chalcidius on the Timæus.*
111. *Procli Diadochi in Platonis Timæum Commentaria.*
112. September, 1898, p. 3.
113. The life of the animal to which it is bound.
114. The instrument must be suited to the development of the artist; too highly developed a body would be bad for a man very low down in the scale of humanity. This will, in some measure, explain the paradoxical word here used; the *advantage* there may sometimes be in putting on a rudimentary body.
115. G. R. S. Mead tells us that Justin believed in Reincarnation only whilst he was a Platonist; he opposed this teaching after his conversion to Christianity (See *Theosophical Review*, April, 1906).
116. Does this obscure passage refer to the resurrection of the body?
117. *Adversus Gentes.* "We die many times, and as often do we rise again from the dead."
118. Hyeronim., *Epistola ad Demetr....*
119. Book 2, quest. 6, No. 17.
120. *Ephesians*, ch. 1, v. 4 ... he hath chosen us in him before the foundation of the world.
121. *Instit. divin.*, 3, 18.
122. *Confessions*, I, ch. 6.
123. *On the Immortality of the Soul*, chap. 12.
124. *Hist. de Manichée et du Manichéisme*, vol. 2, p. 492.
125. *Stromata.*, vol. 3, p. 433. Edition des Bénédictins.
126. The words in parenthesis are by the author.
127. *Cont. Cels.* Book 4, chap. 17.
128. [Greek: ti akolouthei].
129. *De Principiis*, Book 3, chap. 5.

130. *Contra Celsum*, Book 1.
131. *Contra Celsum*, Book 1, chap. 6.
132. *De Principiis*, Book 3, chap. 5.
133. *De Principiis*, Book 4, chap. 5.
134. *Contra Celsum*, Book 7, chap. 32.
135. E. Aroux. *Les Mystères de la Chevalerie.*
136. Quoted by I. Cooper Oakley in *Traces of a Hidden Tradition in Masonry and Mediæval Mysticism*, a very interesting work on the sects which connect the early centuries with modern times.
137. See *L'Islamisme et son Enseignement Ésotérique*, by Ed. Bailly. *Publications théosophiques*, Paris, 1903.
138. Chapter 18.
139. Islam is now awaiting the coming of the Mahdi, its last prophet; prophecy says that he will be the reincarnation of Mohammed (*Borderland*, April, 1907).
140. This is the reason Afghans still undertake pilgrimages to Mecca.
141. Chap. 22, verses 5, 14, 15, 17, 18, 19, 20, 41. Quoted by Lady Caithness in *Old Truths in a New Light.*
142. Chap. 23, verses 17, 26, 27, etc.
143. By religion is here understood the devotional aspect and the scientific side of the teaching of Truth, *i.e.*, the science of the divine Soul.
144. *Nirmânakâyas* are beings who have become perfect, and who, instead of entering the Nirvâna their efforts have won, renounce peace and bliss in order to help forward their human brothers in their evolution.
145. O! genus attonitum gelidæ formidine mortis,
    Quid Styga, quid tenebras, quid nomina vana timetis,
    Materiam vatum, falsique piacula mundi?
    Corpora sive rogus flammâ, seu tabe vetustas
    Abstulerit, mala posse pati non ulla putetis
    Morte carent animæ: semperque priore relictâ
    Sede, novis domibus habitant vivuntque receptæ
    . . . .
    Omnia mutantur, nihil interit ...
    Orger's translation
146. *S. John's Gospel*, chap. 9, verse 2.
147. The following passages are taken from three of C. Savy's works: *Comment. du Sermon sur la Montagne* (1818); *Pensées et Méditations* (1829); *Dieu et l'Homme en cette Vie et Audelà* (1838).
148. *De l'Humanité*, vol. 1., p. 233.
149. *Théorie de l'Unité Universelle*, vol. 2, p. 304-348.
150. *Vie Future au Point de Vue Socialiste*, and *Confession d'un Curé de Village.*
151. *Destinées de l'Âme.*
152. Alluding to the complete renewing of the material molecules of the body, every seven years.
153. Whose consciousness, however (along with memory), is at the summit of the hierarchy which is its origin.
154. Molecules and atoms have a particular consciousness of their own which does not cease to function when, on the departure of the individual soul, the body, as such, ceases to function.
155. If sufficiently developed, however, he can be made conscious of this in a higher vehicle.
156. When man has barely entered the human stage—in primitive man.
157. Consciousness begins in the physical body, its simplest instrument.
158. There are other vehicles above the causal body.
159. All the powers of the Universe are in the divine germ, as the tree is in its seed.
160. Because it no longer has a dense physical body. There are exceptions to this rule, but there is no necessity to mention them here.
161. The Christian Heaven, the *Devachan* of Theosophy.
162. This character has already appeared on the astral plane, though not in so striking a fashion.

163. Unity exists on the plane of the Ego, and the latter sends his thought into the forms made out of his vehicles; this will be understood only by the few, but an explanation cannot be given at this point, without writing a volume on the whole of theosophy.
164. We are still dealing with the ordinary man.
165. When liberation is attained. This can be effected rapidly by those who *will* to attain it.
166. Only four of the seven atomic *spirillæ* are active in this our fourth planetary Round (one for each Round). They can be rapidly vitalised by the will.
167. When the soul is "centred" in it.
168. The vibrations, whether registered as they pass or not registered, continue their course through the substance of the Universe.
169. Science even now recognises four of these dimensions.
170. This is said in order to satisfy such as are of a metaphysical turn of mind, and frequently prone to criticism.
171. When the inner senses are developed.
172. A question will doubtless at once rise to the minds of many readers; how can the same atoms produce, at once and almost eternally, millions of different facts? We will reply briefly. Science has been able to conceive of an explanation of a fact apparently quite as absurd—the phenomenon of the balls of Russian platinum mentioned by Zöllner (*Transcendental Physics*, ch. 9) which pass through hermetically sealed glass tubes, and that of the German copper coins dropping through the bottom of a sealed box on to a slate—by accepting a fourth dimension of space. Who would affirm that the dimensions of space are limited to four? Or that the science of the immediate future will not be brought face to face with facts, and find, in a fifth or sixth dimension of space, a possible explanation of the phenomenon here mentioned, one which initiated seers can test whenever they please, because it is a real fact?

Still, as these seers say, the coarsest atoms generally register only one image, others register fresh images, so that in many cases there is quite a superposition of images which must be carefully examined to avoid errors.
173. A psychometrist is a person endowed with a very fine nervous system, capable of repeating the delicate vibrations which act upon the inmost atoms of a body. In this way, by placing himself in presence of an object that has been in contact with some individual, he can clearly describe the latter's physical, moral, and mental characteristics. Hitherto, Buchanan and Professor Denton have been the most remarkable psychometrists; the experiments related in their works have been made before witnesses and permit of no doubt whatever as to the reality of this strange faculty.
174. Instances of this are numerous in Professor Denton's *The Soul of Things*.
175. This memory is preserved in the first "life-wave."
176. This is *instinct, i.e.*, a semi-conscious memory, located in the "life-wave" of the second Logos.
177. The divine Essence incarnated in the matter of the lower planes of the Universe.
178. When the "essence," after the destruction of the form to which it gives life, no more returns to the parent-block from which it came, it has become individualised, ready to enter into the *human kingdom*.
179. The memory of the third life-wave, of the first Logos.
180. Everything, for instance, that concerns the planes of the planetary system, on which it has finished its evolution.
181. The passing of consciousness from the causal body to the nascent buddhic body.
182. The buddhic plane (the one immediately above the mental) is one in which the forms are so subtle that they no longer *limit* the Life (*the Soul of the World*) animating them. This Life comes directly into contact with the Life which causes all forms to live; it then sees Unity: it sees itself everywhere and in everything, the joys and sorrows of forms other than its own are its joys and sorrows, for it is universal Life.
183. This body is composed of physical matter, and therefore belongs to the physical plane. It has been given a special name, not only because it is made of ether, but because it can be separated from the physical body.
184. The whole of the bodies: mental, astral, and physical.
185. The Ego (soul) in the causal body.

CONCLUSION.

We have now come to the end of our study: a task to which we have certainly not been equal, so far is it beyond our powers. As, however, we have drawn inspiration from our predecessors, so have we also, in our turn, endeavoured to shed a few more rays of light on certain points of this important subject, and indicate fresh paths that may be followed by such as enter upon this line of investigation in the future.

It is our most ardent desire to see this fertile soil well tilled, for it will yield an abundant harvest. Mankind is dying in strife and despair; the torrent of human activity is everywhere seething and foaming. Here ignorance buries its victims in a noisome den of slime and filth; there, the strong and ruthless, veritable vampires, batten on the labour and drain away the very life of the weak and helpless; farther away, science stumbles against the wall of the Unknown; philosophy takes up its stand on the cold barren glacier of intellectualism; religions are stifled and struggle for existence beneath the age-long accumulations of the "letter that killeth." More now than ever before do we need to find a reason for morality, a guide for science, an Ariadne's thread for philosophy, a torch to throw light on religion, and Love over all, for if mankind continues to devote the whole of its strength to the pursuit of material benefits, if its most glorious conquests become instruments to advance selfishness, if its progress merely increases physical wretchedness and makes moral decadence more terrible than before, if the head continues to silence the appeals of the heart, then divine Compassion will have no alternative but to destroy beneath the waters of another flood this cruel, implacable civilisation, which has transformed earth into an inferno.

Amongst the most pressing and urgent truths, the most fruitful teachings, the most illuminating doctrines, the most comforting promises, we have no hesitation in placing the Law of Rebirths in the very front. It is supported by ethics, by reason, and by science; it offers an explanation of the enigma of life, it alone solves almost all the problems that have harassed the mind of man throughout the ages; and so we hope that, in spite of its many imperfections, this work of ours will induce many a reader to say: *Reincarnation must be true, if could not be otherwise!*

Copyright © 2021 by FV Éditions
Cover design: Canva.com
All rights reserved.

www.ingramcontent.com/pod-product-compliance
Lightning Source LLC
LaVergne TN
LVHW091619070526
838199LV00044B/855